Frontiers in African Business Research

Series editor

Almas Heshmati, Jönköping International Business School,
Jönköping, Sweden

This book series publishes monographs and edited volumes devoted to studies on entrepreneurship, innovation, as well as business development and management-related issues in Africa. Volumes cover in-depth analyses of individual countries, regions, cases, and comparative studies. They include both a specific and a general focus on the latest advances of the various aspects of entrepreneurship, innovation, business development, management and the policies that set the business environment. It provides a platform for researchers globally to carry out rigorous analyses, to promote, share, and discuss issues, findings and perspectives in various areas of business development, management, finance, human resources, technology, and the implementation of policies and strategies of the African continent. Frontiers in African Business Research allows for a deeper appreciation of the various issues around African business development with high quality and peer reviewed contributions. Volumes published in the series are important reading for academicians, consultants, business professionals, entrepreneurs, managers, as well as policy makers, interested in the private sector development of the African continent.

More information about this series at http://www.springer.com/series/13889

Almas Heshmati
Editor

Studies on Economic Development and Growth in Selected African Countries

Springer

Editor
Almas Heshmati
Jönköping International Business School
Jönköping University
Jönköping
Sweden

and

Department of Economics
Sogang University
Seoul
South Korea

ISSN 2367-1033 ISSN 2367-1041 (electronic)
Frontiers in African Business Research
ISBN 978-981-10-4450-2 ISBN 978-981-10-4451-9 (eBook)
DOI 10.1007/978-981-10-4451-9

Library of Congress Control Number: 2017936352

Printed on acid-free paper

This Springer imprint is published by Springer Nature
The registered company is Springer Nature Singapore Pte Ltd.
The registered company address is: 152 Beach Road, #21-01/04 Gateway East, Singapore 189721, Singapore

Contents

Contributors

Olaide Rufai Akande Department of Agricultural Economics, University of AgricultureMakurdiNigeria

Melesse Asfaw School of Graduate Studies, Ethiopian Civil Service University, Addis Ababa, Ethiopia

Hassen Azime Institute of Tax and Customs Administration, Department of Public Finance Ethiopian Civil Service University, Addis Ababa, Ethiopia

Fentahun Baylie Department of Economics, Addis Ababa University, Addis Ababa, Ethiopia

Daniel Beshir Libya Oil Ethiopia Ltd, Addis Ababa, Ethiopia

Johannes O. Bockmann Department of Economics and Logistics, International School of Management Hamburg, Hamburg, Germany

Thomas Bwire Bank of Uganda, Kampala, Uganda

Djomo-Raoul Fani Department of Agricultural Economics, University of Agriculture, Makurdi, Nigeria

Atnafu Gebremeskel Department of Economics, Addis Ababa University, Addis Ababa, Ethiopia

Kokeb G. Giorgis Department of Economics, Addis Ababa University, Addis Ababa, Ethiopia

Almas Heshmati Jönköping International Business School (JIBS), Jönköping University, Jönköping, Sweden; Department of Economics, Sogang University, Seoul, South Korea

Urbanus Mutuku Kioko University of Nairobi, Nairobi, Kenya

Pascal Munyankindi National Bank of Rwanda, Kigali, Rwanda

Edouard Musabanganji Economy and Rural Development Unit, Gembloux Agro-Bio Tech, University of Liège, Liège, Belgium

Emmanuel Mushimiyimana Department of Political Science and International Relations, College of Arts and Social Sciences, University of Rwanda, Butare, Rwanda

Abdou Musonera MIFOTRA-SPIU, Kigali, Rwanda

Joseph Ndagijimana College of Business and Economics, University of Rwanda, Butare, Rwanda

Ferdinand Nkikabahizi College of Business and Economics, University of Rwanda, Butare, Rwanda

Hephzibah Onyeje Obekpa Department of Agricultural Economics, University of Agriculture, Makurdi, Nigeria

Gollagari Ramakrishna School of Graduate Studies, Ethiopian Civil Service University, Addis Ababa, Ethiopia

Masoomeh Rashidghalam Department of Agricultural Economics, University of Tabriz, Tabriz, Iran

Charles Mulindabigwi Ruhara University of Rwanda, Butare, Rwanda

Yitbarek Takele College of Business and Economics, Addis Ababa University, Addis Ababa, Ethiopia

Caleb Tamwesigire University of Kigali, Kigali, Rwanda

Eric Uwitonze Ministry of Gender and Family Promotion (MIGEPROF), MIGEPROF, Single Project Implementation Unit, Kigali, Rwanda

Addis Yimer Department of Economics, Addis Ababa University, Addis Ababa, Ethiopia

Abbreviations

AD	Aggregate demand
ADF	Augmented Dickey-Fuller
AfDB	African Development Bank
AIC	Akaike information criteria
ANOVA	Analysis of variance
AR	Autoregressive
ARDL	Autoregressive distributed lag
AS	Aggregate supply
ATM	Automatic teller machines
AVC	Agriculture value chains
CBHIS	Community-based health insurance schemes
CD	Cobb–Douglas function
CEO	Chief executive officer
CLRM	Classical linear regression models
COPIMAR	Mining Cooperative of Artisan Miners
CORR	Control of corruption
CPI	Consumer Price Index
CS	Capital structure
CUSUM	Cumulative sum
CUSUMQ	Cumulative sum of squares
DC	Developing countries
DHS	Demographic and Heath Survey
EAC	East African Countries
ECM	Error correction model
EDPRS	Economic Development and Poverty Reduction Strategy
EIA	Ethiopian Investment Authority
EICV	Integrated Household Living Conditions Survey
ELH	Ethno-linguistic heterogeneity

EP	Export performance
EPRDF	Ethiopian People Revolutionarily Democratic Front
EU	European Union
FAO	Food and Agricultural Organization
FDI	Foreign direct investment
GDP	Gross domestic product
GLR	Great Lakes region
GMM	Generalized methods of moment
GOVEFFE	Government effectiveness
HAC	Heteroskedasticity and auto-correlation consistent covariance
ICMM	International Council on Mining and Metals
ICT	Information and communication technologies
IMF	International Monetary Fund
KES	Kenyan shilling
KEU	Kenya Economic Update
LDE	Logistic diffusion equation
LDEFO	Logistic differential equation of first order
LIC	Low-income countries
LM	Lagrangian multiplier
LSDV	Least square dummy variable
MDG	Millennium development goals
MIC	Middle-income countries
MLE	Maximum likelihood estimation
MNC	Multinational corporation
MOFED	Ministry of Finance and Economic Development
NBE	National Bank of Ethiopia
NGO	Non-Governmental Organization
NISR	National Institute of Statistics for Rwanda
NRG	New Resolutions Geophysics
OECD	Organization for Economic Development and Cooperation
OLS	Ordinary least squares
OOPE	Out-of-pocket healthcare expenditures
PMG	Pooled mean group
POLS	Pooled OLS
POLSTAB	Political stability
PPP	Purchasing power parity
PTA	Prospective target areas
PWT	Penn World Tables
R&D	Research and Development
RA	Representative Agent
RoL	Rule of Law
RQ	Regulatory Quality
SAP	Structural adjustment programs
SIDA	Swedish International Development Cooperation Agency
SME	Small- and medium-sized enterprises

SSA	Sub-Saharan African
TFP	Total factor productivity
UK	United Kingdom
UN	United Nation
UNCTAD	United Nations
UNDP	United Nations Development Program
UNECA	United Nations Economic Commission for Africa
USD	United States Dollar
VAR	Vector Auto-Regression
VAT	Value-added tax
VECM	Vector error correction model
VOIACC	Voice and accountability
WB	World Bank
WDI	World development indicators
WGI	World governance indicators

Chapter 1
Introduction to Studies on Economic Development and Growth in Selected African Countries

Almas Heshmati

Abstract A major policy challenge facing Africa is how to sustain a high rate of economic growth that is both socially inclusive and environmentally sustainable. Growth and its sustainability influence many other challenges facing the continent. This volume is a collection of selected empirical studies on economic development and growth in Africa. The papers were presented at the second conference on Recent Trends in Economic Development, Finance and Management Research in Eastern Africa, Kigali, Rwanda, June 20-22, 2016. The studies are grouped into domains influencing economic development and growth in Africa.

Keywords Economic Development · Economic Growth · Sustainable Growth · Determinants of Growth · Governance and Institutions · African Countries

1.1 Background

The major policy challenges facing Africa are how to sustain a high rate of economic growth that is both socially inclusive and environmentally sustainable. Population aging, population growth, rapid urbanization, infrastructure for providing services, facilitating production expansion, the need to reverse declined economic growth after the 2008 global financial crisis, corruption, inefficiency, and responding to climate change are among the other challenges facing Africa. In this background, Jönköping International Business School and the University of Rwanda organize a conference on economic development in the region every year. This volume is a collection of selected empirical studies on economic development and growth in Africa. The papers were selected from a set of more than 90 papers presented at the second conference on *Recent Trends in Economic Development, Finance and Management Research in Eastern Africa*, Kigali, Rwanda, June

A. Heshmati (✉)
Jönköping International Business School, Jönköping University, Jönköping, Sweden
e-mail: almas.heshmati@gmail.com

A. Heshmati
Department of Economics, Sogang University, Seoul, South Korea

A. Heshmati (ed.), *Studies on Economic Development and Growth in Selected African Countries*, Frontiers in African Business Research,
DOI 10.1007/978-981-10-4451-9_1

20–22, 2016. Following a process of review and revisions, 15 papers were accepted for publication in this edited volume on economic development and growth.

The studies are grouped into domains influencing economic development and growth in Africa. The core argument for using a multiple approach perspective is the need to account for different approaches for enhancing growth and development. The aim is not to identify specific determinants of growth and development and to apply them to a set of countries assuming that every country is affected in the same way and by the same factors. This volume realizes that the countries have different initial and factor endowment conditions, and as such, they respond differently to development and growth policies. Together, the chapters included in the volume provide a comprehensive picture of the state of development and growth and their country-specific determinants and policies. Heterogeneity of countries and efficient policies and practices in growth and their distribution on selected parts of the African continent as a whole and also in selected countries mainly in Eastern Africa are considered. Development and growth represent a major challenge for governments and organizations whose aim is development and alleviating poverty.

This volume contains a collection of empirical studies on the level of development and growth, and their variations and determinants in Africa. The first chapter is an introduction/summary written by the volume's Editor. The remaining 15 chapters are inter-related studies that are grouped into five domains which influence the level, variations, and developments on the African continent as a whole and also in individual countries. The results can have strong implications for the development and policies in Africa.

1.2 Summary of Individual Studies

This edited volume is a collection of studies on economic development and growth in selected African countries. The volume consists of 16 chapters including an introduction/summary and 15 inter-related empirical studies. The studies are largely grouped into five research areas: women's empowerment and demand for health care; the impact of institutions, aid, inflation, and FDI on economic growth; capital structure and bank loan growth effects; trade, mineral exports, and exchange rate; and growth, productivity, and efficiency in various industries. The studies provide a comprehensive picture of the state of economic development and growth in most parts of the African continent. Though several studies cover major parts of the continent, the main focus of the edited volume is on economic development and growth in Ethiopia and Rwanda—two countries on the path of rapid economic and social development.

Africa is developing rapidly. Among the aspects of development in the region are region-wise formations of groups of countries cooperating to establish economic integration, a currency union, trade zones, and sustainability of growth. The chapters investigate in single and comparative cases factors such as gender equality, health care, the quality of the institutions, and their effectiveness along with the effect of institutions on growth and development in the nations on the continent. The chapters also investigate other factors of importance for the industry, service, and agricultural sectors. Among the factors that are explored are those that influence production and flows of factors including inflation rate, foreign direct investment, sources of finance, and trade and exchange rate. These issues have not been well researched so far. With contributions from African professionals in the field, this book attempts to shed light on the importance and effects of various determinants of economic development and growth. Hence, it will help fill existing gaps in the region-specific literature and also provide necessary policy tools for decision makers.

Part A. Women's Empowerment and Demand for Health care

Part A covers two important development areas—women's empowerment and demand for health care—in Rwanda.

The first study (Chap. 2), *Measuring Women's Empowerment in Rwanda*, by Abdou MUSONERA and Almas HESHMATI, examines the determinants of women's empowerment in Rwanda using demographic and health survey data. It uses a regression analysis to investigate the association between women's empowerment and its covariates. The study also uses a multinomial logistic regression to assess what determines households' decision making and attitudes toward physical abuse of spouses. It finds that education and media exposure are positively associated, while residence and the age at first marriage are negatively associated with women's empowerment. Strengthening regulations and public support improves women's empowerment.

The second study (Chap. 3), *Determinants of Demand for Outpatient Health care in Rwanda*, by Charles M. RUHARA and Urbanus M. KIOKO, examines the factors that influence the demand for outpatient care in Rwanda using the household living conditions survey. It estimates a structural model of demand for health care to measure the healthcare demand effects of covariates. The findings indicate that health insurance is a significant determinant of outpatient medical care. In addition, the price of health care and household income are among the main drivers of the utilization of health care. The study recommends that the government should reduce out-of-pocket health care expenditure through subsidies and reduce the premium for community-based health insurance schemes to increase coverage rates.

Part B. The Impact of Institutions, Aid, Inflation, and FDI on Economic Growth

This part analyses the impact of institutional quality, provision of aid, inflation, and foreign direct investment on economic growth in a large number of African countries.

The first study (Chap. 4), *Economic Growth and the Impact of Institutions*, by Kokeb G. GIORGIS, discusses the effect that institutional variables have on economic growth. It empirically investigates the impact of institutional quality proxied by control of corruption, government effectiveness, and protection of property rights on economic growth in 21 sub-Saharan African countries during the sample period 1996–2012. The results indicate that improving institutional quality and specifically protecting property rights will contribute positively to growth in output per capita.

The second study (Chap. 5), *Fiscal Effects of Aid in Rwanda*, by Thomas BWIRE, Caleb TAMWESIGIRE and Pascal MUNYANKINDI, analyses the dynamic relationship between foreign aid and domestic fiscal variables in Rwanda. The hypothesis of aid exogeneity is not statistically supported. The anticipated aid appears to have been taken into account in budget planning. Aid is associated with increased tax efforts and public spending and lower domestic borrowings. In terms of policy, continued efforts by donors to coordinate aid delivery systems, making aid more transparent, and supporting improvements in government fiscal statistics are contributing to improving fiscal planning in Rwanda. Estimation results show that aid has contributed to Rwanda's improved fiscal performance.

The third study (Chap. 6), *Exploring the Relationship between Inflation and Real Economic Growth in Rwanda*, by Ferdinand NKIKABAHIZI, Joseph NDAGIJIMANA and Edouard MUSABANGANJI, examines the impact that economic stability measures of inflation and unemployment rates have had on real GDP in Rwanda. The study concludes that inflation and unemployment have a long-run negative and significant relationship with real GDP. Real GDP increases when inflation and unemployment decrease. The effect of the shock reduces by 19.32% in each of the four quarters, ending after a five-year period. The study also finds a weak relationship between real GDP and inflation and unemployment rates.

The fourth research (Chap. 7), *Macroeconomic, Political and Institutional Determinants of FDI Inflows to Ethiopia: An ARDL Approach*, by Addis YIMER, investigates the various determinants of FDI inflows to Ethiopia. Using the time series methodology, it finds that political and institutional factors are crucial both in the long and in the short run for FDI inflows to the country. On the one hand, market size, availability of natural resources, and openness to trade and exchange rate depreciation affect FDI inflows positively. On the other hand, macroeconomic instability affects FDI inflows negatively. In addition, political stability, the absence of violence, and the effectiveness of the government in formulating and implementing sound development policies are found to affect FDI inflows positively.

Part C. Capital Structure and Bank Loan Growth Effects

Part C discusses the insurance companies' capital structure and manufacturing firms' bank loans income distribution and growth effects in Ethiopia.

Using the panel data methodology, the first study (Chap. 8), *Firm-specific Determinants of Insurance Companies' Capital Structures in Ethiopia*, by Yitbarek TAKELE and Daniel BESHIR, examines the impact that a firm's characteristics have on decisions about the capital structure in the Ethiopian insurance industry. A number of tests are conducted to validate the results. It finds that pecking order, static trade-off, and agency cost theories are the most important in explaining decisions on the capital structure of insurance companies, though pecking order appears to be dominant. Profitability, asset tangibility, growth, and liquidity play a significant role in shaping the insurance industry's financing decisions, while business risk and size of the firm do not.

The second study (Chap. 9), *Income Distribution and Economic Growth*, by Atnafu GEBREMESKEL, links access to bank loans and income distribution to productivity growth of firms. Using Ethiopian manufacturing firm-level data, the study examines how functional income distribution can influence the evolution of productivity, thereby promoting economic growth. It employs an evolutionary economic framework and econometric approach for the analysis. The results show lack of strong evidence of intra-industry selection for fostering productivity growth and structural change. The key policy lesson is that access to bank loans is of great importance to firms for their structural transformation.

Part D. Trade, Mineral Exports, and Exchange Rate

Part D covers German SMEs' trade with sub-Saharan Africa, contributions of mineral exports to Rwanda's trade, and the relationship between economic growth and real exchange rate in low- and middle-income countries.

The first paper (Chap. 10), *SME Trade with sub-Saharan Africa: The secret of German companies*' success, by Johannes O. BOCKMANN, evaluates the degree to which internal, micro- and macro-environmental variables explain how some SMEs based in Germany export more successfully to sub-Saharan Africa than others in the same category. The econometric methodology is used for identifying the determinants of export performance. Estimation results indicate that sub-Saharan Africa has specific requirements for successful exports. Knowledge about these particular characteristics of the market enables managers and policy-makers to improve trade relations. By focusing on the export performance of German SMEs in SSA, this study fills a research gap since no previous study has dealt with this specific aspect.

The second study (Chap. 11), *An Assessment of the Contribution of Mineral Exports to Rwanda's Total Exports*, by Emmanuel MUSHIMIYIMANA, is an assessment of the mineral industry's contribution to Rwanda's growing mineral exports. Mineral exports can be a means of increasing exports for agrarian and low- and middle-income countries. The results, based on the econometric methodology, show that mineral exports are the main contributor in increasing Rwanda's total exports. This implies that the Government of Rwanda needs to introduce significant reforms in the mining sector and take Botswana and Namibia as its role models in developing its mineral industry which can play a role in the industrialization of the country.

The third study (Chap. 12), *Testing the External Balassa Hypothesis in Low- and Middle-Income Countries*, by Fentahun BAYLIE, analyzes the long-run relationship between economic growth and the real exchange rate for 15 low- and middle-income countries. It establishes a co-integration relationship between growth and exchange rate by controlling for heterogeneity and cross-sectional dependence. It implies that the productivity effect is estimated consistently and without any bias. Moreover, the results indicate that the effect of the Balassa term depends more on income levels than on the rate of economic growth. In general, the power of the effect is stronger for higher income countries in the long run. However, in the short run, fiscal policy and exchange rate volatility clearly explain the variations in the real exchange rate.

Part E. Growth, Productivity, and Efficiency in Various Industries

Part E deals with tax-growth responsiveness, productivity, and efficiency in agriculture, manufacturing, and services in select African countries.

The first study (Chap. 13), *Agricultural Tax Responsiveness and Economic Growth in Ethiopia*, by Hassen AZIME, Gollagari RAMAKRISHNA, and Melesse ASFAW, looks at the pattern of tax revenues and its nexus with economic growth in developing countries. Since tax revenue is one of the important sources of government revenue, tax policy assumes significance as a viable and long-term source of revenue and economic growth. Similarly, economic growth has augmenting effects on tax revenues. The relationship between the two is essential for formulating fiscal policy. The study suggests policy interventions for improving tax revenue structures.

The second study (Chap. 14), *Improving Agricultural Productivity in sub-Saharan Africa*, by Olaide R. AKANDE, Hephzibah O. OBEKPA and Djomo-Raoul FANI, looks at improved agricultural productivity which is central to achieving inclusive development, reducing poverty, and enhancing the living standards of most people in sub-Saharan Africa. The study seeks answers to questions of whether agro-processing activities and export of raw agricultural materials have a backward linkages' effect on agricultural production activities. The estimation results indicate that while agro-processing activities have a positive effect on agricultural productivity, increased exports of agricultural raw materials negatively influence productivity growth in agriculture.

The third study (Chap. 15), *Determinants of Service Sector Firms' Growth in Rwanda*, by Eric UWITONZE and Almas HESHMATI, views the service sector as an avenue for economic transformation. It discusses the role that services can play in the economic growth of African economies leading to their transformation into service-based economies. Services are considered as an alternative to manufacturing-led development. This research attempts to study the development of the service sector and investigates the factors behind the development of this sector in Rwanda. It specifies and estimates models to assess the factors contributing to sales growth, innovation, and turnover of service firms in speeding up the shift from a low-income to a middle-income development state.

The last study (Chap. 16), *Labor-use Efficiency in Kenyan Manufacturing and Service Industries*, by Masoomeh RASHIDGHALAM, estimates the efficiency in the use of labor in Kenyan manufacturing and service industries at the firm level. The study provides evidence of efficiency in the use of labor in the country. It identifies the determinants of labor-use efficiency and estimates their effects. Labor-use efficiency is important for firms' competitiveness in both the domestic and international labor and goods markets. It makes a number of recommendations for promoting higher labor-use efficiency at the firm level and also through public labor market and industrial policies.

1.3 Final Words

The primary market for this edited book includes undergraduate and graduate students, lecturers, researchers, public and private institutions, NGOs, international aid agencies, and decision makers. This book can serve as complementary reading to texts on economic growth, development, welfare, inequality, and poverty analyses in Africa. The organizers of the annual conference on economic development in East Africa will market the book at their annual East Africa conferences. There are many books on growth and development in Africa, but they rarely cover such diversity in approaches and their country specificity character and policy recommendations.

This edited book is authored by African experts in the field who employ diverse up-to-date methods to provide robust empirical results based on representative disaggregate data at the household and firm levels and aggregate data covering individual or multiple countries on the continent. It contains a wealth of empirical evidence, deep analyses, and sound recommendations for policymakers and researchers for designing and implementing effective economic policies and strategies to achieve rapid and higher levels of development. As such, the book is a useful resource for policymakers and researchers involved in development- and growth-related tasks. It will also appeal to a broader audience interested in economic development, resources, policies, economic welfare, and inclusive growth.

The Editor is grateful to a host of dedicated authors and rigorous referees who helped in assessing the submitted papers. Many were presenters at the 2016 conference at the University of Rwanda. Special thanks go to Bideri Ishuheri Nyamulinda, Rama Rao, and Lars Hartvigson and the remaining members of the Organization Committee for their efforts in organizing the conference. The Editor would also like to thank William Achauer at Springer Singapore for guidance and for assessing this manuscript for publication by Springer. Financial support by the Swedish International Development Cooperation Agency (SIDA) to organize the conference is gratefully acknowledged.

Part I
Women's Empowerment and Demand for Healthcare

Chapter 2
Measuring Women's Empowerment in Rwanda

Abdou Musonera and Almas Heshmati

Abstract This study examines the determinants of women's empowerment in Rwanda using the data obtained from the Demographic and Heath Survey (DHS) (2010). It uses a regression analysis to investigate the association between women's empowerment and its covariates. The study also uses a multinomial logistic regression to assess what determines households' decision-making and attitudes toward physical abuse of spouses. It finds variables of sources of empowerment such as education and media exposure to have a net positive association with women's empowerment, while other variables such as residence and the age at first marriage to be negatively associated with women's empowerment. A further analysis shows that the effects of education, age of the respondent, wealth and the number of children ever born remain strong conditions which effect households' decision-making and attitudes about physical abuse. In general, it seems that for women to fully realize their potential and rights, specific emphasis should be put on variables that increase their access to resources and knowledge such as education, employment for cash, and media exposure, but variables that are negatively associated with their empowerment such as higher age at first marriage should also be taken into account.

Keywords Women's empowerment · Physical abuses · Household decision-making · Rwanda

JEL Classification Codes D63 · D91 · I15 · I25 · J12

A. Musonera
MIFOTRA-SPIU, Kigali, Rwanda
e-mail: abdoumusonera@gmail.com

A. Heshmati (✉)
Jönköping International Business School (JIBS),
Jönköping University, Jönköping, Sweden
e-mail: almas.heshmati@gmail.com

A. Heshmati
Department of Economics, Sogang University, Seoul, South Korea

A. Heshmati (ed.), *Studies on Economic Development and Growth in Selected African Countries*, Frontiers in African Business Research,
DOI 10.1007/978-981-10-4451-9_2

2.1 Introduction

In recent years, a range of organizations have increasingly shown commitment to women's empowerment; they have also realized that empowering women is a win-win situation that benefits both women and society. Golla et al. (2011) claim that women's economic empowerment is fast becoming a key instrument in promoting their abilities to achieve their rights and well-being which subsequently reduces household poverty and increases economic growth, productivity, and efficiency.

There is a growing body of literature which recognizes the social and economic importance of involving women in the development process. Some literature focuses on spillover benefits resulting from allowing women to have greater control over resources and the impact that this has on the health and education of their children and on better well-being prospects for future generations (The World Bank Poverty, Inequality and Gender Group 2012). Other literature pays particular attention to the relationship between women's empowerment and health outcomes (see, for example, Abadian 1996; Bloom et al. 2001; Fotso et al. 2009; Larsen and Hollos 2003; Lee-Rife 2010; Patrikar et al. 2014; Sado et al. 2014; Schuler et al. 1996, 1997; Upadhyay and Karasek 2012; Upadhyay et al. 2014; Bloom et al. 2001).

A great deal of previous literature on women's empowerment focused on two indicators of their empowerment—household decision-making and self-esteem (El-Halawany 2009; Ghuman et al. 2004; Kishor and Subaiya 2008; Mahmud and Tasmeen 2014; Mahmud et al. 2012; Malhotra and Mather 1997; Sado et al. 2014). However, other studies have described the role of women's access to finance and labor force participation in the empowerment process (Ali et al. 2014; Allendorf 2007; Allsopp and Tallontire 2014; Faridi et al. 2009; Ganle et al. 2015; Naqvi and Shahnaz 2002). Together, these studies provide evidence that measurement issues still exist in the process of translating 'evidence of empowerment' and 'access to sources of empowerment' into agency especially using cross-sectional survey data (Kishor and Subaiya 2008) and thus highlight the need for going beyond structural and merely simplistic factors (family, social, and economic) to be able to measure women's empowerment in a comprehensive way (Malhotra and Mather 1997). In the same vein, Ghuman et al. (2004) argue that difficulties in measuring women's empowerment call for an in-depth understanding of gender relations by spending enough time in the community and doing pre-testing.

There is evidence also of positive effects of women's empowerment from around the world. There is also internationally recognized knowledge about channels of empowerment and effects. For example, the World Bank Poverty and Gender Group Report (2012) shows that women's control over resources creates spillover benefits that have a significant positive impact on the health and education of children, thus leading to better well-being prospects for future generations.

Similarly, Golla et al. (2011) highlight women's empowerment as one of the key drivers in promoting their abilities, rights, and well-being which subsequently reduce poverty and increase economic growth, productivity, and efficiency. However, very few empirical studies use Rwandan data, for example Ali et al. (2014) in their study on the environmental and gender impact of land tenure regularization in Africa and Mukashimana, and Sapsford (2013) in their study on marital conflicts in Rwanda.

In this study, we investigate the determinants of women's empowerment in Rwanda, especially what determines household decision-making and self-esteem. We address two questions: Whether variables of sources of empowerment (education, employment for cash, regular media exposure, and wealth) have a significant positive association with women's empowerment. Some variables of 'setting' (age of the respondent and children ever born) are positively related to women's empowerment, while others such as residence and the age at first marriage are negatively associated with women's empowerment.

Data used in the current study are from the Demographic and Health Survey (DHS) conducted in 2010 by the National Institute of Statistics for Rwanda (NISR 2010a, 2013). Respondents were married women aged between 15 and 49. A multiple regression analysis was used to empirically analyze the determinants of women's empowerment in Rwanda. A multinomial logistic regression was also used to examine the relationship between household decision-making, justifications about wife beating, and women's empowerment covariates.

We found evidence that women's empowerment can be achieved through providing education, media exposure, labor force participation, shifting negative traditional cultural norms (such as giving respect to women with more children, marrying girls at an earlier age), and by focusing on integrated development.

The rest of this paper is organized as follows: The next section reviews literature on the relationship between women's empowerment and health outcomes, labor force participation, access to finance and cultural norms. Section 2.3 describes the empirical strategy. After an overview of the findings in Sect. 2.4, these are discussed in Sect. 2.5. The last section gives a conclusion.

2.2 Literature Review

We review literature from three perspectives: The first is concerned with the definitions of women's empowerment. The second pertains to the determinants of women's empowerment and the association between their empowerment and different health outcomes, cultural norms and the influence of labor force participation and women's access to finance on their empowerment. The third strand relates to the conceptual framework.

2.2.1 Definitions of Women's Empowerment

Several attempts have been made by authors to improve upon definitions of women's empowerment. Empowerment is a continuous, phased, and relational process that occurs across scales and pathways (Goldman and Little 2014). Allsopp and Tallontire (2014) define empowerment as a dynamic process that follows a series of sequential steps in which ownership of one type of power increases the likelihood and the ability to exercise other forms of power thus creating a positive 'power spiral.'

Kabeer (2005) views the empowerment concept as revolving around the idea of power to make a choice and conceptualizes disempowerment as the denial of the possibility of making a choice by people who deserve to make the choice. Put differently, empowerment can be conceptualized as a dynamic process by which people who were previously deprived of the ability to make a choice gain such an ability. For this to happen and the choice to be successful, there should be the capacity or possibility to choose otherwise.

Empowerment is a person's potential to make functional choices, that is, the ability to translate choices into desired outcomes and actions (Alsop and Heinsohn 2005). Kishor and Subaiya (2008) define empowerment as a process that enables powerless people to have control over the circumstances of their lives. The idea behind this is not power to dominate over others but power to achieve goals and ends, and this process appears to be affected by different social, cultural and economic factors (Upadhyay et al. 2014).

Empowerment is a process which results from two milestones—agency and opportunity structure. Agency is defined as the potential to make effective choices, and opportunity structure is conceptualized as the environment/context in which individuals exercise agency or pursue their interests including institutional, political and social contexts, and societal informal rules and norms (Samman and Santos 2009).

However, three main concepts should be analyzed cautiously while defining and measuring empowerment—the existence of choice (whether a choice exists), use of choice (whether individuals use a chance to choose), and the achievement of choice (whether the choice generates desired outcomes/results) (Samman and Santos 2009).

Choice can either be the first choice or a 'strategic life choice' (choice of livelihood, choice of residence, choice of a partner, whether to have children or not and the number of children to have, who has rights over the children, freedom of movement, and the choice of friends). Second-order choices are choices that are not strategic to life (Kabeer 1999a, b). The potential to make strategic life choices can be conceptualized in the form of three dimensions or 'moments'—resources (pre-conditions to empowerment), agency (process), and achievements (outcomes). According to Kabeer (2005), agency can be either passive (action taken when the choice is limited), active (meaningful and purposeful choice), greater effectiveness of agency (carrying out their roles and responsibilities), and transformative (capacity to act on the restrictive aspects of roles and responsibilities and being able to challenge them).

2.2.2 Some Major Theories on Women's Empowerment

In the new global economy, women's empowerment has become a central issue for countries to achieve development goals such as economic growth, poverty reduction, health, education, and welfare (Golla et al. 2011). Of late there is a renewed interest in the relationship between women's empowerment and health outcomes. Some of these theories focus on women's empowerment and health care use (Bloom et al. 2001; Fotso et al. 2009; Lee-Rife 2010; Sado et al. 2014). Women's empowerment has been identified as a driving force in ensuring improved maternal health care (Sado et al. 2014). The place of delivery is mainly influenced by wealth, education, and demographic and health covariates, while autonomy, decision-making and freedom of movement are found to have little influence on the place of delivery (Fotso et al. 2009).

Women's involvement in decision-making and their attitudes toward negative cultural norms such as domestic violence have been highlighted as the main determinants in the use of maternal healthcare services (Sado et al. 2014).

Overall, these studies highlight the need for policy actions that focus not only on education but also on other factors that are likely to enhance health status with the aim of improving health outcomes for women and their families.

However, a majority of these maternal health studies mainly focus on women's individual-level variables such as age, education, and income or community-level factors while little attention is paid to the effect of bargaining powers within households. Thus, without an unbiased and accurate measurement of power, decision-making processes and different paths through which they affect reproductive health outcomes, our understanding of the covariates of maternal health and child health are incomplete.

A large and growing body of literature has investigated the association between women's empowerment and fertility preferences (Abadian 1996; Al Riyami et al. 2004; Larsen and Hollos 2003; Patrikar et al. 2014; Schuler et al. 1996; Upadhyay and Karasek 2012; Upadhyay et al. 2014). Fertility preferences are mainly influenced by women's resource control, freedom of movement, and freedom from household domination. The most striking result to emerge from the data is that all three variables exert little influence on contraceptive use (Schuler et al. 1996). The results are not consistent with regard to the number of children because some of the studies show a negative relationship between women's empowerment and the number of children, while others show that there is a positive connection between women's empowerment and fertility preferences (having children or not). A few studies also show that there is no connection between empowerment and fertility preferences (Upadhyay et al. 2014).

Women's access to fundamental freedoms and increased access to and control over resources improves not only their welfare but also contributes to a reduction in fertility (Abadian 1996). Women's autonomy, as measured by the level of education, age at first marriage, and spousal age difference, is inversely associated with fertility (Abadian 1996). Wealth is likely to increase not only access to health care and reducing child mortality rates but also in increasing access to education and reducing child labor through increased chances for children to attend school (Abadian 1996). Larsen and Hollos (2003) postulate that the progression from having one child to the next declines owing to the status of women, especially free partner choice, women's education, and household wealth. Attitudes toward wife beating have a negative relationship with a small ideal number of children while household decision-making and positive attitudes toward violence are strongly associated with a larger ideal number of children (Upadhyay and Karasek 2012). However, these findings suggest the need for further research to determine the most appropriate empowerment measures that are context-specific. These findings also highlight the need to emphasize on not only factors enhancing health outcomes but also on other factors that are driving forces for an improved quality of life.

A lot of previous research on women's empowerment has mainly focused on the determinants of women's empowerment indicators, including household decision-making and self-esteem (El-Halawany 2009; Ghuman et al. 2004; Kishor and Subaiya 2008; Mahmud and Tasmeen 2014; Mahmud et al. 2012; Malhotra and Mather 1997; Sado et al. 2014; Trommlerova et al. 2015). Measuring a dynamic process like women's empowerment necessitates indicators that measure the end result, that is, indicators that measure evidence of empowerment, the various sources of empowerment, and the setting of empowerment. Potential sources of empowerment are defined as those factors which provide a basis for empowerment, including knowledge, media exposure, and access to and control over resources (as explained by being employed for cash). Indicators of the setting for empowerment are those conditions that reflect both the past and current environments of the respondents, and these factors appear to condition the views and the chances available for women (Kishor and Subaiya 2008).

Empowerment is largely determined by education, age, economic activity, country of residence, and being a polygamous married male (see Trommlerova et al. 2015). Kishor and Subaiya (2008) argue that social development indicators such as education are positively associated both with taking decisions alone and jointly. They further show that women's empowerment is largely determined by access to and control over resources, indicators of sources of empowerment (educational attainment, employment for cash and media exposure) and a setting of empowerment including indicators such as a higher age at first marriage and smaller spousal age difference.

A positive association has been found between household decision-making and other factors related to women's economic empowerment (Sado et al. 2014). Household wealth is a strong determinant of resource control but it has a significant negative association with women's overall household decision-making, and the association between covariates and different empowerment indicators is not consistent (Mahmud et al. 2012). Factors associated with sources of empowerment (employment, education, and wealth status) have higher explanatory powers than factors related to the setting of empowerment (age and family structure) (see Sado et al. 2014).

Mahmud et al. (2012) show that there is no association between women's freedom of mobility and household wealth. This is not surprising because freedom of mobility is high for the poorest women who are always obliged to travel outside their homes to participate in the labor force. They further state that women from wealthier households are less likely to have a say in household decision-making; instead, they tend to have the view that their voice is not relatively worthwhile but there is a high likelihood of their having access to cash for spending. Conversely and surprisingly, residing in an extended family increases the likelihood of a woman having high decision-making powers and self-esteem (Sado et al. 2014).

However, there are variations and differences in the nature and determination of financial, social, and organizational dimensions which imply that women's control over one of the family aspects does not necessarily imply control over other aspects. For example, while education and employment are the main determinants of a woman's input in financial decision-making, these variables exert no influence on social and organizational related household decision-making.

Three important themes emerge from studies on the determinants of women's empowerment discussed so far: (i) measurement issues still exist while translating 'evidence of empowerment' and 'access to sources of empowerment' into agency especially using cross-sectional survey data; (ii) it is very important to go beyond structural and merely simplistic factors (family, social, and economic) to measure women's empowerment in a comprehensive way; and (iii) these difficulties in measuring women's empowerment call for an in-depth understanding of gender relations by spending enough time in the community and doing pre-testing.

2.2.3 Conceptual Framework

Women get empowered through two pathways (different ways of being and experience sharing) that operate individually. However, it is also found that a woman's potential to attain positive outcomes is accelerated when she possesses more than one pathway (Allsopp and Tallontire 2014). The level of empowerment in a village depends on different pathways (personal, economic, and political) and linkages across scale ranging from personal bodies and household relations to the community (Goldman and Little 2014). Kabeer (1999a, b) points out that women's empowerment is conceptualized as a three-dimensional process that encompasses resources or pre-conditions of empowerment, agency, or process and achievements that measure outcomes. Kabeer further argues that women's potential to exercise strategic life choices is conceptualized in terms of three dimensions or moments for the social change process to be completed:

Resources (pre-conditions) > agency (process) > achievements (outcomes)

Kabeer (2001) conceptualize empowerment in terms of agency, resources, and achievements. Kishor and Subaiya (2008) conceptualize the empowerment process in terms of evidence and sources of empowerment but acknowledge that the extent of translating evidence on empowerment and access to sources into agency and the capacity to make a choice and act upon it is not yet measured. Samman and Santos (2009) claim the importance of three indicators of empowerment: source, evidence, and setting.

Measuring the empowerment process is conceptualized at different levels, in different domains, and at different levels of an actor's life (Alsop and Heinsohn 2005). These domains include the state in which people are civic actors, the market in which persons are economic actors, and society in which they are social actors. These domains also contain sub-domains which in turn comprise of different levels. For example, the market domain is composed of the sub-domains of credit, labor, and production and consumption of goods. Society comprises of family and community. There also exist three levels at which empowerment is exercised: the local level which is contiguous with people's residence, the intermediate level which is between the residential and national levels, and finally, the national level which is thought to be the furthest from an individual.

Kabeer (2005) claims that the empowerment concept can be measured through three interlinked dimensions—agency, resources, and achievements. Agency is central to the concept of empowerment and is defined as the process by which a choice is made and transformed into effect. Resources are conceptualized as a medium through which agency is exercised and achievements are conceptualized as outcomes of agency. Similarly, Rowlands (1997) and Samman and Santos (2009) highlight that agency and empowerment are interrelated concepts, that is, empowerment does not happen in a vacuum. In the categorization of power, Rowlands classifies empowerment as a process by which people gain power over (resistance to manipulation), power to (ability to create new possibilities), power with (ability to be an actor in a group), and power from within (enhancing self-respect and self-acceptance).

Alsop and Heinsohn (2005) postulate that the level of empowerment for a given person is associated with his/her personal capacity to make meaningful and purposive choices (agency) and the institutional environment in which the choices are made (opportunity structure). Similarly, Samman and Santos (2009) argue that empowerment occurs along different dimensions including economic, social-cultural, legal, political, and psychological. They further find that agency is exercised at different levels—the micro-level (household), meso-level (community), and macro-level (state and the country). The empowerment model consists of five stages: motivation for action, empowerment support, initial individual action, empowerment program, and institutionalization and replication (Kar et al. 1999).

2.3 Empirical Strategy

Our study set out to assess what determines women's empowerment in Rwanda using household decision-making and self-esteem indicators. The results will extend our knowledge of variables which are a source and setting of empowerment. The data used are from the 2010 Demographic and Health Survey (DHS) by the National Institute of Statistics for Rwanda (NISR 2010b, 2013). The respondents were married women aged between 15 and 49. A multiple regression analysis was used to empirically analyze the determinants of women's empowerment in Rwanda. A multinomial logistic regression was used to examine the relationship between household decision-making, justifications for wife beating and, women's empowerment covariates.

2.3.1 Model Specification

2.3.1.1 Women's Empowerment and Its Covariates

In order to provide a proper specification of the model and to conduct a sensitivity analysis of the results, the baseline model was specified in three ways:

- CEI = f(Age, Educ Wealth, PaidWork, Resid, Media, Children, AgeFM).
- DEC.IND = f(Age, Educ, Wealth, PaidWork, Resid, Media, Children, AgeFM)
- EST.IND = f(Age, Educ, Wealth, EmpCash, Resid, Media, Children, AgeFM)

where CEI is the cumulative empowerment index which is obtained by combining the decision-making and self-esteem indices. DEC.IND is the decision-making index. EST.IND is the self-esteem index. Age in age cohorts represents the age of the respondents classified into four categories (15–19, 20–29, 30–39, and 40–49). Educ is a respondent's education level (no education, primary education, secondary education, and higher education). Wealth is a respondent's wealth that falls in five categories (poorest, poorer, middle, richer, and richest). EmpCash is defined as a respondent's employment status where the respondent can either be employed for cash or not. Resid is the residence of a respondent (either in an urban area or a rural area). Media is media exposure that is defined as either regular media exposure or no-media exposure. The variable Children indicates number of children ever born (none, 1 or 2, 3 or 4, and 5 and above). AgeFM represents the age of a respondent at first marriage. This is classified into three groups (less than 18, 18–24, and 25 years and above).

2.3.1.2 Household Decision-Making and Attitudes Toward Physical Abuse

Questions on who had the final say on what to do with a respondent's earnings, respondent's health care, large household purchases, and visits to family or relatives were asked during the survey. Different responses for each question were labeled as: others (0), joint decision (1), and decision alone (2). Then, each decision was used as a dependent variable to determine the likelihood of that decision being taken given different covariates of women's empowerment using a multinomial logistic regression.

Moreover, attitude toward physical abuse (in the survey labeled as wife beating) was investigated using five questions that were asked to know the circumstances under which wife beating was justified: going outside without permission, neglecting children, arguing with husband, burning food and refusing to have sex with her husband. Responses to the questions were labeled: Yes (1), No (2) and others (0). Then, a multinomial logistic regression was used to regress each decision on different covariates of women's empowerment to determine the odds in their ratios. The covariates used were the same as those used in the previous model with women's empowerment, that is, age group, children ever born, education, media exposure, employment for cash, residence, wealth and age at first marriage.

This baseline model is associated with models used by Kabeer and Subaiya (2008), Sado et al. (2014), Mahmud et al. (2012), and Mahmud and Tasmeen (2014). Kabeer and Subaiya (2008) point out that women's empowerment is largely determined by access and control over resources, indicators of sources of empowerment (educational attainment, employment for cash and media exposure) and a setting of empowerment including indicators such as a higher age at first marriage and smaller spousal age difference.

The main weakness of Kabeer and Subaiya's (2008) study is the paucity of data on all indicators of women's empowerment (only data on household decision-making and attitudes toward wife beating was available) and some of the covariates that were used in previous studies. Another weakness of their study is that the results might have been affected by measuring women's empowerment using data which contained missing values.

2.3.1.3 Data and Variables

Data used in our study were obtained from the Demographic and Health Survey (DHS 2010a). The respondents were married women aged between 15 and 49. Women's empowerment was investigated using two indicators—household decision-making and attitudes toward gender roles.

A. Dependent variables

The dependent variables used in our study were the cumulative empowerment index (the main component) and its constituents, that is, the decision-making index, the self-esteem index, decision-making (alone and jointly) and agreeing with justifications for wife beating (yes or no).

The decision-making index

Respondents were asked different questions regarding who had the final say on different household decisions such as respondent's health care, visits to family and relatives, large household purchases and decision on what to do with the money that the husband earned. The responses were coded 1 if the decision was taken by the respondent alone, 2 if the decision was jointly taken by the respondent and her husband, 3 if the decision was taken by the respondent and another person, 4 if the decision was taken by the husband/partner alone, 5 if the decision was taken by someone else, and 6 for others.

The decision-making index was computed by assigning scores to different responses. A (2) was assigned to every response where the decision was taken alone by the respondent, (1) was assigned to every response where the decision was jointly taken and (0) otherwise. Then, individual scores for the different decisions were added to get total scores out of 10 (10 is the maximum score), that is, 2 (marks maximum/decision) * 5 questions.

The self-esteem index

Respondents were asked questions about their attitudes toward gender roles and norms. They were also asked whether wife beating was justified under one of the following circumstances:

- When she goes out without telling her husband.
- If she neglects the children.
- If she argues with her husband.
- If she refuses to have sex with her husband.
- If she burns the food.

Responses were coded (1) if the respondent said yes and (0) if the respondent said no.

In our study, the scores assigned to different responses were: (1) for every response where the respondent said no and (0) for every response where the respondent answered yes. Finally, individual scores were added to get the total scores out of five (maximum 1 mark *5 questions).

The value of either the decision-making index or the self-esteem index should fall in the interval 0–1 or alternatively between 0 and 100%.

The cumulative empowerment index

While conducting DHS, the respondents were not asked to assign weights to different indicators of women's empowerment. Therefore, we assumed that all the indicators had the same weight and then computed the cumulative empowerment index using a nonparametric method as indicated by:

$$\text{CEI} = (\text{W1} * \text{Dec.Index} + \text{W2} * \text{S.Est.Index})/2$$

where W1 and W2 are weights assigned to each woman's empowerment indices which reflect weights attached to each indicator in the aggregation.

Dec.Index is the decision-making index which was obtained by adding the scores obtained from responses to different questions about household decision-making.

S.Est.Index is the self-esteem index which was obtained by adding scores of different responses about respondents' attitudes toward justifications for wife beating.

The same approach for computing women's empowerment has been followed by authors in previous studies such as by Lee-Rife (2010), Mahmud and Tasneem (2014), Mahmud et al. (2012), Patrikar et al. (2014), Sado et al. (2014), Sultana and Hossen (2013), Upadhyay and Karasek (2012).

Decision-making (alone or jointly)

Different decisions were labeled according to who took the decision. Any decision that was taken by the respondent herself was labeled (2). A decision that was jointly taken by the respondent and her husband or by the respondent and another person was labeled (1). Finally, other possible options mentioned earlier were labeled (0).

Agreeing with justifications for wife beating

Agreement with any of five reasons was coded (1) while rejection of wife beating for any of the five reasons was coded (2). Others were coded (0).

This type of computation is consistent with that used by Kishor and Gupta (2004) and Kishor and Subaiya (2008).

B. **Independent variables**

Women's empowerment covariates include variables at household and community levels. These variables include age in years, children ever born, regular exposure to media, employment for cash, age at first marriage, residence in urban area, spousal age difference, and household wealth. Some of these variables are considered the potential sources of empowerment, specifically age, media exposure, educational level, and employment for cash. Other variables are conceptualized as aspects of a setting for empowerment (nuclear family and urban residence, wealth, age at first marriage and spousal age difference) (Kishor and Subaiya 2008).

Age: women's age is positively associated with her level of empowerment as believed by a majority of religions around the world especially when women's empowerment is measured using indicators that measure household decision-making. Nonetheless, when empowerment is measured using indicators of attitudes toward gender equality, it is not clear whether empowerment is positively associated with age.

Number of children ever born: More respect is accorded to women who have children. Nonetheless, it is hard to predict the direction of causality between the number of children ever born and attitudes to gender roles.

Education and media exposure: Education and media exposure equip women with information and means that can allow them to effectively adapt to the changing modern world thus increasing their level of empowerment. People with higher education are exposed to new ideas and alternative behaviors and gender norms and roles. Thus, education is a critical source of empowerment. For example, women with higher education are less likely to accept wife beating for any reason and are more likely to believe that it is a woman's right to refuse sex with her husband.

Employment for cash: Earning cash is more likely to increase women's bargaining powers within households. It gives women a sense of personal achievement, and it also helps in creating awareness about the fact that they are like men and can provide financial support for their families. In addition, off-farm professional occupations potentially empower women through financial autonomy and alternative sources of identity and social exposure to new structures of power free of kin networks (Kishor and Subaiya 2008).

Media exposure: Access to media (watching television on a regular basis, reading newspapers, and frequency of listening to the radio) have the same direction of causality as education as they too expose women to new ideas and gender roles and norms. This postulates that women with frequent exposure to media have a low likelihood of accepting that their being beaten is justified for any reason and they are more likely to accept that it is a woman's right to refuse sex with her husband when necessary.

Age at first marriage: A younger age at first marriage is negatively associated with women's empowerment as it puts to an end a woman's chances to have access to sources of empowerment like education (Kishor and Subaiya 2008). In addition, a younger age at first marriage is associated with a high probability of a woman agreeing that wife beating is justified for any reason.

Urban residence: In cities, there are people from different backgrounds doing a variety of off-farm jobs with a variety of services, including easy access to education and regular media exposure. Hence, as compared to rural women, urban women are more likely to reject wife beating for any reason. These women are of the view that they have the right to refuse sex with their husbands.

Wealth: Wealth and gender equality do not go hand in hand easily. On the one hand, household wealth is a source of empowerment as it brings education, exposure to media and exposure to networks of intellectuals, but on the other hand, wealthier households are more likely to be strongly attached to patriarchal gender norms.

Husband's education: A husband's education level, especially secondary education and above, is likely to have a positive association with women's empowerment.

2.4 Empirical Results

The results of a linear regression analysis between women's empowerment (cumulative empowerment index, decision-making index and self-esteem index) and its covariates are presented in Table 2.1. The results of a multinomial logistic regression analysis between women's empowerment indicators (taking decisions alone or jointly), attitudes toward justifications for wife beating), and women's empowerment covariates are summarized in Tables 2.2, 2.3, and 2.4.

2.4.1 Relationship Between Women's Empowerment and Its Covariates

Table 2.1 depicts the relationship between women's empowerment and its covariates. In column 1, it gives the association between the cumulative empowerment index and its covariates. It is apparent from this column that there is a significant positive correlation between women's empowerment and some of its covariates such as age, number of children ever born, education, employment for cash, exposure to media and wealth. Younger women in their twenties are less likely to be empowered (0.0274) as compared to older women (0.0339). The results show that women with more children (five and above) are more likely to be empowered (0.160) than women with less children (one or two) whose coefficient is only 0.114. The results also indicate that women with higher education are more empowered (0.171) than those with primary education (0.030). Similarly, employment for cash and media exposure is positively associated with the cumulative empowerment index (see Table 2.1, column 1). Women in wealthier families are more likely to be empowered (0.0525) as compared to those from poor families (0.0190).

In the same way, the same direction of causality is observed with the decision-making index (see Table 2.1, column 2). These results match those observed in previous studies. Women's empowerment was found to be positively associated with education levels, age, household wealth (income), and employment status (such as in Sultana and Hossen 2013). Likewise, Khan and Noreen (2012) found that women's empowerment was mainly determined by age, husband's education, assets inherited from the father, number of children alive, and the amount of microfinance.

On the contrary, living in a rural area and getting married at a younger age were found to be negatively associated with both the cumulative empowerment and decision-making indices. Moreover, the results reveal a significant positive association between self-esteem and variables such as education, wealth, and age of the respondent (see Table 2.1, column 3). Women with higher education had higher levels of self-esteem (0.268) than those with primary education (0.0527). Women from wealthier families had higher self-esteem (0.080) than those from poor

Table 2.1 Women's empowerment and its covariates

	Cumulative empowerment index	Decision-making index	Self-esteem index
Age groups			
15–19 (Ref.)			
20–29	0.0274***	0.0525***	0.00225
	(5.22)	(9.62)	(0.26)
30–39	0.0455***	0.0591***	0.0320**
	(6.45)	(8.04)	(2.77)
40–49	0.0339***	0.0230*	0.0448**
	(3.58)	(2.33)	(2.89)
Children categories			
None (Ref.)			
1 or 2	0.114***	0.223***	0.00424
	(22.15)	(41.77)	(0.50)
3 or 4	0.134***	0.276***	−0.00743
	(21.43)	(42.32)	(−0.72)
5 and above	0.160***	0.332***	−0.0116
	(21.72)	(43.25)	(−0.96)
Education			
None (Ref.)			
Primary	0.0365***	0.0203***	0.0527***
	(7.34)	(3.92)	(6.47)
Secondary	0.104***	0.0193**	0.188***
	(15.18)	(2.71)	(16.83)
Higher	0.171***	0.0730***	0.268***
	(12.19)	(5.01)	(11.71)
Employment for cash			
No paid work (Ref.)			
Paid work	0.0202***	0.0332***	0.00734
	(5.26)	(8.28)	(1.17)
Media exposure			
No regular media exposure (Ref.)			
Regular media exposure	0.0159***	0.0237***	0.00820
	(4.54)	(6.47)	(1.43)
Residence			
Urban (Ref.)			
Rural	−0.0230***	−0.00642	−0.0396***
	(−4.36)	(−1.17)	(−4.59)

(continued)

Table 2.1 (continued)

	Cumulative empowerment index	Decision-making index	Self-esteem index
Age at first marriage			
Less than 18 years (Ref.)			
18–24 years	−0.0238**	−0.0473***	−0.000
	(−3.10)	(−5.91)	(−0.02)
25 years and above	−0.0281**	−0.0578***	0.0014
	(−2.79)	(−5.49)	(0.09)
Wealth index			
Poorest (Ref.)			
Poorer	0.0190***	0.0103	0.0278**
	(3.52)	(1.82)	(3.14)
Middle	0.0295***	0.0102	0.0488***
	(5.37)	(1.78)	(5.43)
Richer	0.0381***	0.0194***	0.0568***
	(6.77)	(3.31)	(6.17)
Richest	0.0525***	0.0250***	0.0800***
	(8.44)	(3.86)	(7.86)
Cons	0.265***	−0.0639***	0.593***
	(31.02)	(−7.20)	(42.48)
N	13,671	13,671	13,671

Note *t*-statistics in parenthesis
$^*p < 0.05$, $^{**}p < 0.01$, $^{***}p < 0.001$

families (0.020). However, residence (rural) and age at first marriage were found to be negatively associated with self-esteem (see Table 2.1, column 3).

These results are in agreement with those obtained by Kishor and Subaiya (2008) who found that women in urban areas were more likely to reject wife beating as compared to women in rural areas and younger age at first marriage was associated with a high likelihood of accepting justifications for wife beating.

2.4.2 *Determinants of Household Decision-Making*

Tables 2.2 and 2.3 present odds ratios (using a multinomial logistic regression) for respondents' decision-making (jointly and alone) on five household decisions—what to do with a respondent's earnings, respondent's health care, large household purchases, visits to family or relatives, and what to do with the money that the husband earns. Women in their twenties had high odds in favor of taking decisions alone on all the five aspects as compared to older women. Table 2.2 shows that women with more children (five and above) were more likely to take the five

Table 2.2 Odds ratios (using a multinomial logistic regression) for household decision-making (alone)

	What to do with respondent's earnings	Respondent's health care	Large household purchases	Visits to family and relatives	What to do with husband's earnings
Age groups					
15–19					
20–29	1.902***	1.919***	2.039***	2.117***	1.985***
	(9.81)	(12.42)	(13.56)	(14.20)	(13.58)
30–39	1.741***	1.805***	2.020***	2.039***	1.850***
	(8.60)	(10.94)	(12.65)	(12.79)	(11.87)
40–49	1.304***	1.480***	1.678***	1.482***	1.376***
	(5.96)	(8.08)	(9.53)	(8.33)	(7.98)
Children categories					
None					
1 or 2	2.318***	2.405***	2.354***	2.524***	2.412***
	(23.88)	(28.28)	(29.94)	(32.17)	(30.50)
3 or 4	2.588***	2.822***	2.556***	2.839***	2.628***
	(24.24)	(29.22)	(28.69)	(31.30)	(29.30)
5 and above	2.806***	3.305***	2.979***	3.494***	3.101***
	(23.68)	(30.22)	(29.49)	(33.28)	(30.47)
Education					
No education					
Primary	0.0980	0.208***	0.133*	0.151*	0.158**
	(1.51)	(3.33)	(2.25)	(2.45)	(2.70)
Secondary	0.149	0.0228	0.0248	0.0289	0.0267
	(1.45)	(0.23)	(0.27)	(0.30)	(0.29)
Higher	0.904***	0.516**	0.733***	0.707***	0.613***
	(4.56)	(2.60)	(4.00)	(3.73)	(3.38)
Employment for cash					
No paid work					
Paid work	1.186***	−0.0383	0.127*	0.190***	0.0558
Exposure to media					
No media exposure					
Low media exposure	0.359***	0.365***	0.430***	0.463***	0.471***
	(6.33)	(6.75)	(8.41)	(8.71)	(9.26)
High media exposure	0.344*	0.442**	0.273	0.362*	0.464**
	(2.20)	(2.89)	(1.89)	(2.43)	(3.25)

(continued)

Table 2.2 (continued)

	What to do with respondent's earnings	Respondent's health care	Large household purchases	Visits to family and relatives	What to do with husband's earnings
Residence					
Rural	0.138	0.0805	0.0677	0.0465	0.192**
	(1.73)	(1.06)	(0.95)	(0.63)	(2.71)
Age at first marriage					
Less than 18					
18–24 years	−0.246**	−0.454***	−0.369***	−0.502***	−0.439***
	(−2.61)	(−4.92)	(−4.25)	(−5.43)	(−5.10)
25 and above	−0.311*	−0.693***	−0.509***	−0.607***	−0.575***
	(−2.45)	(−5.65)	(−4.44)	(−5.03)	(−5.05)
Wealth index					
Poorest					
Poorer	0.250**	0.289***	0.140*	0.259***	0.193**
	(3.21)	(3.89)	(1.99)	(3.54)	(2.77)
Middle	0.311***	0.291***	0.224**	0.324***	0.244***
	(3.90)	(3.80)	(3.11)	(4.31)	(3.41)
Richer	0.404***	0.560***	0.379***	0.527***	0.440***
	(4.97)	(7.13)	(5.13)	(6.81)	(5.98)
Richest	0.473***	0.542***	0.442***	0.500***	0.493***
	(5.09)	(6.07)	(5.26)	(5.71)	(5.90)
Cons	−6.478***	−5.230***	−5.141***	−5.317***	−5.242***
	(−29.19)	(−28.86)	(−29.33)	(−29.88)	(−30.49)
N	13,671	13,671	13,671	13,671	13,671

Note *t*-statistics in parenthesis
$^{*}p < 0.05$, $^{**}p < 0.01$, $^{***}p < 0.001$

household decisions alone as compared to women with less children. The results also show that women with higher education had higher chances of taking decisions alone compared to those with primary education. Media exposure was found to increase a respondent's likelihood of taking decisions alone for all the five questions. Likewise, women from wealthier families had higher odds when it comes to taking decisions alone as compared to those from poor families. Surprisingly, women with low age at first marriage (18–24) were found to be more likely to take decisions alone compared to those with a higher age at first marriage. However, employment for cash influenced taking decisions alone for some decisions, while residence had no influence on decision-making alone.

As shown in Table 2.3, the odds of joint decision-making for four of the five questions were high among younger women as compared to older women.

Table 2.3 Odds ratios (using a multinomial logistic regression) for household decision-making (jointly)

	What to do with respondent earnings	Respondent's health care	Large household purchases	Visits to family or relatives	What to do with husband's earnings
Age groups					
15–19					
20–29	2.402***	2.399***	2.019***	2.090***	2.193**
	(4.03)	(5.66)	(3.31)	(5.25)	(2.95)
30–39	2.613***	2.585***	2.576***	2.184***	2.461**
	(4.33)	(6.01)	(4.16)	(5.36)	(3.24)
40–49	2.296***	2.623***	2.568***	2.059***	2.217**
	(3.74)	(5.95)	(4.05)	(4.88)	(2.84)
Children categories					
None					
1 or 2	2.460***	2.706***	2.162***	2.659***	2.269***
	(10.94)	(15.54)	(7.82)	(13.56)	(6.91)
3 or 4	2.845***	3.280***	2.610***	3.253***	2.535***
	(12.13)	(17.92)	(9.11)	(15.83)	(7.28)
5 and above	3.171***	3.588***	2.949***	3.824***	3.113***
	(12.92)	(18.44)	(9.87)	(17.52)	(8.54)
Education					
No education					
Primary	0.0189	0.175*	0.177	0.0860	0.0294
	(0.19)	(2.06)	(1.47)	(0.94)	(0.19)
Secondary	0.0915	0.465***	0.368	0.189	-0.005
	(0.57)	(3.49)	(1.79)	(1.21)	(-0.02)
Higher	0.611*	1.155***	0.799	0.710*	0.137
	(2.04)	(4.59)	(1.93)	(2.13)	(0.27)
Employment for cash					
No paid work					
Paid work	1.298***	0.553***	0.531***	0.513***	−0.000
	(10.54)	(6.11)	(3.86)	(5.20)	(−0.00)
Exposure to media					
No media exposure					
Low media exposure	−0.0250	0.241**	−0.0912	0.277***	0.093
	(−0.28)	(3.21)	(−0.85)	(3.38)	(0.66)
High media exposure	−0.0962	0.209	−0.00921	0.0677	0.477
	(−0.38)	(0.99)	(−0.03)	(0.26)	(1.28)

(continued)

Table 2.3 (continued)

	What to do with respondent earnings	Respondent's health care	Large household purchases	Visits to family or relatives	What to do with husband's earnings
Residence					
Urban					
Rural	−0.612***	−0.140	−0.528***	−0.223	−0.234
	(−5.39)	(−1.36)	(−3.55)	(−1.87)	(−1.28)
Age at first marriage					
Less than 18					
18–24 years	−0.00261	−0.484***	−0.162	−0.447***	−0.219
	(−0.02)	(−4.06)	(−0.99)	(−3.40)	(−1.03)
25 and above	0.0264	−0.556***	−0.0500	−0.482**	−0.253
	(0.15)	(−3.65)	(−0.24)	(−2.89)	(−0.91)
Wealth index					
Poorest					
Poorer	−0.0432	−0.106	−0.238	0.0791	−0.291
	(−0.36)	(−1.05)	(−1.74)	(0.75)	(−1.58)
Middle	−0.117	−0.128	−0.514***	−0.0800	−0.745***
	(−0.92)	(−1.23)	(−3.32)	(−0.70)	(−3.38)
Richer	−0.236	−0.0575	−0.677***	−0.215	−0.371
	(−1.76)	(−0.53)	(−4.02)	(−1.75)	(−1.78)
Richest	0.245	0.0635	−0.536**	−0.287*	0.022
	(1.77)	(0.52)	(−2.95)	(−2.04)	(0.11)
Cons	−7.697***	−7.235***	−6.827***	−6.784***	−7.265***
	(−12.60)	(−16.40)	(−11.02)	(−16.11)	(−9.58)
N	13,671	13,671	13,671	13,671	13,671

Note *t*-statistics in parenthesis
*$p < 0.05$, **$p < 0.01$, ***$p < 0.001$

Surprisingly, older women were more likely to take a decision jointly on their health care as compared to younger women. Joint decision-making was found to be an increasing function of the number of children that a woman had. Employment for cash increased the odds of joint decision-making on all five household decisions. However, variables such as education, wealth, media exposure, and residence influenced only a few of the decisions. For example, residence (rural areas) reduced a respondent's likelihood to jointly decide about what to do with her earnings and about large household purchases.

Table 2.4 Odds ratios (using a multinomial logistic regression): justifications for physically abusing a wife

	Beating justified if she goes without telling her husband	Beating justified if she neglects children	Beating justified if wife argues with her husband	Beating justified if wife refuses to have sex with her husband	Beating justified if wife burns the food
Age group					
15–19					
20–29	0.130*	−0.056	0.003	−0.026	0.007
	(2.18)	(−0.98)	(0.05)	(−0.44)	(0.10)
30–39	−0.0866	−0.276***	−0.185*	−0.0731	−0.159
	(−1.09)	(−3.59)	(−2.25)	(−0.91)	(−1.61)
40–49	−0.229*	−0.320**	−0.299**	−0.115	−0.310*
	(−2.14)	(−3.10)	(−2.72)	(−1.07)	(−2.34)
Children categories					
None					
1 or 2	−0.040	−0.053	0.092	0.037	0.051
	(−0.70)	(−0.96)	(1.54)	(0.64)	(0.71)
3 or 4	0.0267	0.0606	0.178*	0.0465	0.124
	(0.38)	(0.89)	(2.48)	(0.66)	(1.44)
5 and above	0.0799	0.0889	0.203*	0.0501	0.127
	(0.97)	(1.11)	(2.41)	(0.61)	(1.25)
Education					
No education					
Primary	−0.225***	−0.230***	−0.315***	−0.320***	−0.367***
	(−4.24)	(−4.39)	(−5.88)	(−6.02)	(−6.00)
Secondary	−1.090***	−1.021***	−1.215***	−1.257***	−1.295***
	(−13.35)	(−13.34)	(−14.32)	(−15.23)	(−12.03)
Higher	−2.814***	−2.566***	−2.695***	−2.384***	−3.006***
	(−7.62)	(−8.64)	(−7.28)	(−7.99)	(−5.09)
Employment for cash					
No paid work					
Paid work	0.0412	−0.0121	−0.115**	−0.0948*	−0.178***
	(0.95)	(−0.29)	(−2.59)	(−2.17)	(−3.39)
Exposure to media					
No media exposure					
Low media exposure	−0.111**	−0.068	0.024	−0.0946*	0.018
	(−2.61)	(−1.66)	(0.57)	(−2.20)	(0.36)
High media exposure	−0.0934	0.106	0.0754	0.0459	0.206
	(−0.73)	(0.90)	(0.57)	(0.36)	(1.29)

(continued)

Table 2.4 (continued)

	Beating justified if she goes without telling her husband	Beating justified if she neglects children	Beating justified if wife argues with her husband	Beating justified if wife refuses to have sex with her husband	Beating justified if wife burns the food
Residence					
Urban					
Rural	0.148*	0.331***	0.194**	0.299***	0.209*
	(2.37)	(5.56)	(2.99)	(4.71)	(2.57)
Age at first marriage					
Less than 18					
18–25 years	0.007	−0.005	0.009	0.0331	0.128
	(0.09)	(−0.07)	(0.11)	(0.39)	(1.24)
25 and above	0.0850	0.054	−0.0337	−0.084	−0.001
	(0.75)	(0.50)	(−0.29)	(−0.76)	(−0.01)
Wealth index					
Poorest					
Poorer	−0.178**	−0.0917	−0.157**	−0.137*	−0.180**
	(−3.08)	(−1.61)	(−2.67)	(−2.35)	(−2.65)
Middle	−0.262***	−0.137*	−0.284***	−0.310***	−0.272***
	(−4.40)	(−2.35)	(−4.68)	(−5.17)	(−3.85)
Richer	−0.328***	−0.218***	−0.302***	−0.288***	−0.344***
	(−5.33)	(−3.62)	(−4.82)	(−4.67)	(−4.63)
Richest	−0.433***	−0.361***	−0.486***	−0.474***	−0.516***
	(−6.20)	(−5.36)	(−6.75)	(−6.71)	(−5.88)
Cons	−0.124	0.111	−0.202*	0.0142	−0.875***
	(−1.29)	(1.19)	(−2.06)	(0.15)	(−7.46)
N	13,671	13,671	13,671	13,671	13,671

Note t-statistics in parenthesis
$^{*}p < 0.05$, $^{**}p < 0.01$, $^{***}p < 0.001$

2.4.3 Determinants of Respondents' Attitudes Toward Justifications for Wife Beating

Table 2.4 illustrates the odds ratios about respondents' attitudes on justifications for wife beating. Women with higher education were less likely to agree with wife beating (for all the five reasons) than those with primary education. Women from wealthier families were less likely to agree with wife beating for all five reasons than those from poor families. Residing in rural areas was found to increase the odds for agreeing with wife beating for all five reasons. However, variables such as age, children ever born, media exposure, and paid work influenced some of the reasons. Unlike our expectations, age at first marriage had no influence on attitudes toward wife beating.

2.5 Discussion of the Results

Our study was designed to measure women's empowerment in Rwanda using indicators of household decision-making and self-esteem. Kabeer (2001) and Kishor (2008) conceptualize empowerment in terms of agency, resources, and achievements.

It was hypothesized that variables of sources of empowerment (education, employment for cash, media exposure, and wealth) had a positive association with women's empowerment while variables of the setting for empowerment (residence, age, children, age at first marriage) had either a positive or a negative influence on women's empowerment. For example, younger age at first marriage was expected to be negatively associated with women's empowerment while a higher age at first marriage tended to be positively associated with women's empowerment.

The results from our study show that older women were more likely to be empowered (0.074) than younger women (0.039). Household decision-making was found to be high among older women as compared to young women (see Table 2.1). Similarly, the results show that old respondents had higher self-esteem (0.0448) as compared to younger women (0.0225). A possible explanation for these results is that marriage and child bearing are highly valued by a majority of the societies and this allows women to gain respect, rights, and freedom. These results are consistent with those obtained by Kishor and Subaiya (2008) in a cross-country women's empowerment comparison using DHS data.

Women with more children (five and above) were found to be more empowered than women with less children (one or two). Likewise, household decision-making was higher among women with more children than among those with lesser children. Surprisingly, no relationship was found between self-esteem and the number of children ever born. A possible explanation for this positive relationship between women's empowerment, decision-making, and child bearing is that more empowerment and status are accorded to women with children and this goes hand in hand with a woman's age.

The findings also reveal that women's educational levels were positively associated with their levels of empowerment. Women with higher education were more empowered than those with primary education. Similarly, women with higher education had higher decision-making abilities than those with primary education; this is consistent with the findings of Sado et al. (2014). Women with higher education had higher self-esteem than those with primary education (see Table 2.1), and a possible explanation for this is that higher education exposes women to new ideas and alternative gender norms and behaviors thus having a gender-egalitarian view of the world. These results are in agreement with those obtained by Mahmud et al. (2012). Employment for cash had a positive association with both the cumulative empowerment index (0.0202) and the decision-making index (0.0332). However, employment for cash had no association with the self-esteem index.

Regular media exposure was positively associated with both the cumulative empowerment and decision-making indices. This can be attributed to the fact that the media exposes women to a world outside their homes, including new ideas and non-traditional roles for them. These results are consistent with Mahmud et al.'s (2012) findings. Unlike our expectations, no relationship was found between media exposure and women's empowerment and self-esteem. Residence (rural area) was negatively associated with the cumulative empowerment and self-esteem indices, but it was unrelated to the household decision-making index (see Table 2.1).

Age at first marriage had a significant negative relationship with the cumulative empowerment and decision-making indices (see Table 2.1). One possible explanation for this is that an early age at first marriage limits the access that a woman has to education. She also has less time for her development and maturity without the interference of marriage and the responsibilities of raising children. Moreover, being young she is less likely to be accorded much power and independence in her parents' home. These findings are similar to those by Kishor and Subaiya (2008). However, unlike them, our study did not find any association between self-esteem and age at first marriage.

Wealth was found to be positively associated with the cumulative empowerment and self-esteem indices. Women from wealthier families were more empowered and had higher self-esteem than those from poor families. However, wealth was positively associated with household decision-making for only the rich but was unrelated to the poorest, poorer, and middle-income families (see Table 2.1).

Younger women (20–29) were less likely to take decisions alone and jointly as compared to those in the 30–39 years age bracket, but women in the 40–49 years age group were less likely to take four or five decisions alone and jointly as compared to women in their twenties (see Table 2.1). Surprisingly, older women were more likely to take decisions jointly about their health care than younger women (see Tables 2.2 and 2.3). These results are in line with those of previous studies such as those by Mahmud et al. (2012), whose findings revealed that young and older women had lower decision-making powers while women in their mid-twenties had high decision-making powers. This phenomenon can be explained by the fact that there are chances that young women live in extended families and old women are no longer involved in decision-making as most of them rely on their adult sons.

Decision-making alone and jointly increased with the number of children for all five decisions (see Tables 2.2 and 2.3). These results further support Kishor and Subaiya's (2008) findings who state that the proportion of women who take decisions alone or jointly increases with the number children.

As a potential source of empowerment, education was positively associated with household decision-making, notably with decision-making alone. The odds of women's participation in decision-making increased with the level of education but with variations in terms of type of participation and decisions. The results show that compared to primary education, higher education was positively associated with decision-making alone for all five decisions (see Tables 2.2 and 2.3). However, the proportion of women with higher education who took decisions jointly was higher for only three decisions (what to do with respondent's earnings, respondent's health care and large household purchases). These results are in agreement with El-Halawany's (2009) findings which show that education was strongly associated with women's autonomy, empowerment, and gender equality through their participation in household decision-making.

Employment for cash-affected decision-making alone (positive association) for only three decisions (what to do with respondent's earnings, large household purchases, and visits to family or relatives) (see Table 2.2). Unlike our expectations, employment for cash-affected decision-making jointly for four decisions (what to do with respondent's earnings, respondent's health care, large household purchases, and visits to family or relatives) (Table 2.3). These results match those observed in earlier studies such as those by Mahmud and Tasmeen (2014) who argue that the likelihood of spending one's own income on clothes, health care, investments in major assets, and having a bank account were higher among women with formal employment outside the family than in other categories. Similarly, Malhotra et al. (2009) found that innovations promoted women's empowerment through increased freedom, having a say in household decision-making, control over household resources, and confidence to challenge gender inequalities.

The odds in favor of taking a decision alone increased with the level of media exposure for all five decisions. However, exposure to media affected joint decision-making for only two decisions (respondent's health care and visits to family or relatives). These findings further support Kishor and Subaiya's (2008) findings that women with regular exposure to the media tend to have positive attitudes toward gender equality than those who are not exposed to the media. They further argue that women who live in communities that favor women's exposure to the media or allow them to benefit from social development levels have a higher likelihood of taking decisions alone and a low likelihood of taking decisions jointly.

Age at first marriage had a significant negative association with decision-making alone for all five questions (see Table 2.2), while it had significant negative association with decision-making jointly for only two decisions (what to do with respondent's earnings and large household purchases) (see Table 2.3). Contrary to our expectations, residence (rural area) increased the odds in favor of taking decisions alone on what to do with husband's earnings (see Table 2.2), while residence (rural area) reduced the likelihood of taking a decision jointly for only two decisions (what to do with respondent's earnings and large household purchases) (see Table 2.3).

Wealth had a significant positive relationship with taking decisions alone for all five questions with women from wealthier families having higher chances of taking decisions alone compared to those from poor families (see Table 2.2). Wealth had a statistically negative association with decision-making jointly for only two decisions (large household purchases and visits to family or relatives). These results are in accordance with recent studies which indicate that women from wealthier households were less likely to have a say in household decision-making and that they tended to have the view that their voices were relatively not worthwhile but there was a high likelihood of their having access to cash to spend (Mahmud et al. 2012).

Older women were found to be less likely to agree with four of the five justifications for wife beating. Education was negatively associated with agreeing with justifications for wife beating for all five reasons (see Table 2.4). Women with higher education were less likely to agree with wife beating for any of the five reasons as compared to those with lower education levels (primary education). These findings are in agreement with Kishor and Subaiya's (2008) findings which show that the higher the education level, the lower the likelihood of a woman agreeing that wife beating was justified for any reason, and the higher the likelihood of her agreeing with the fact that it was a woman's right to refuse sex with her husband.

Women with paid work were less likely to agree with justifications for wife beating for three of the five reasons (see Table 2.4). Women with regular exposure to the media were less likely to agree with wife beating for two of the five reasons. Women residing in rural areas were more likely to agree with justifications for wife beating for all the five reasons. Wealth reduced the odds in favor of saying yes to justifications for wife beating for all the five reasons. Women from wealthier families were less likely to agree with justifications for wife beating for all five reasons as compared to women from poor families.

Table 2.4 illustrates the odds ratios about respondents' attitudes toward justifications for wife beating. Women with higher education were less likely to agree with wife beating (for all five reasons) than those with primary education. Women from wealthier families were also less likely to agree with wife beating for all five reasons than those from poor families. Residing in rural areas increased the odds in favor of justifications for wife beating for all five reasons. However, variables such as age, children ever born, media exposure, and paid work influenced some of the reasons. Unlike our expectations, age at first marriage had no influence on attitudes toward wife beating.

2.6 Conclusions

The most obvious finding of this study is that education, age of the respondent, media exposure, and employment for cash and wealth had a positive relationship with women's empowerment. Our study also found that education, wealth, age, and the number of children had high explanatory powers for women's empowerment as compared to the other variables. Taken together, the findings suggest that women's empowerment can be achieved by providing them education, labor force participation, media exposure, shifting negative traditional cultural norms, and by focusing on integrated development.

The main weakness of this study is the paucity of data on all indicators of women's empowerment (only data on household decision-making and attitudes toward wife beating was available) and some of the covariates that were used in previous studies. Another weakness is that the results might have been affected by missing values on the data on measuring women's empowerment. As society is evolving fast through education, technology, urbanization, and globalization, continuous improvement in survey structures is required; there is also a need to collect data on women's empowerment indicators that have not been taken into account in previous surveys.

More studies need be carried out on the uncovered aspects of women's empowerment, especially the relationship between women's empowerment and variables such as fertility, health care, contraceptive use, and microfinance. Women's autonomy and their determination to participate in the labor force, as well as their contribution to economic growth and well-being also need to be considered.

References

Abadian S (1996) Women's autonomy and its impact on fertility. World Dev 24(12):1793–1809

Al Riyami A, Afifi M, Mabry RM (2004) Women's autonomy, education and employment in Oman and their influence on contraceptive use. Reprod Health Matters 12(23):144–154

Ali DA, Deininger K, Goldstein M (2014) Environmental and gender impacts of land tenure regularisation in Africa: pilot evidence from Rwanda. J Dev Econ 110:262–275

Allendorf K (2007) Do women's land rights promote empowerment and child health in Nepal? World Dev 35(11):1975–1988

Allsopp MS, Tallontire A (2014) Pathways to empowerment? Dynamics of women's participation in global value chains. J Cleaner Prod 107:114–121

Alsop R, Heinsohn N (2005) Measuring empowerment in practice: structuring, analysing and framing indicators. World Bank Policy Research Working Paper 3510

Bloom SS, Wypij D, Gupta MD (2001) Dimensions of women's autonomy and the influence of maternal health care utilization in a north Indian city. Demography 38(1):67–78

El-Halawany HS (2009) Higher education and some upper Egyptian women's negotiation of self-autonomy at work and home. Res Comp Int Educ 4(4):423–436

Faridi MZ, Chaudhry IS, Anwar M (2009) The social-economic and demographic determinants of women's work participation in Pakistan: evidence from Bahawalpur district. MPRA Paper 22831

Fotso JC, Ezeh AC, Essendi H (2009) Maternal health in resource-poor urban settings: How does women's autonomy influence the utilization of obstetric care services? Reprod Health, 16 June 2009

Ganle JK, Afriyie K, Segbefia AO (2015) Microcredit: empowerment and disempowerment of rural women in Ghana. World Dev 66:335–345

Ghuman SJ, Lee HJ, Smith HL (2004) Measurement of women's autonomy according to women and their husbands: results from five Asian countries. Soc Sci Res 35:1–28

Goldman MJ, Little JS (2014) Innovative grassroots NGOs and the complex processes of women's empowerment: an empirical investigation from northern Tanzania. World Dev 66:762–777

Golla AM, Malhotra A, Nanda P, Mehra R (2011) Understanding and measuring women's economic empowerment: definitions, framework and indicators. International Center for Research on Women (ICRW)

Kabeer N (1999a) Resources, agency, achievements: reflections on the measurement of women's empowerment. Dev Change 30:435–464
Kabeer N (1999b) The conditions and consequences of choice: reflections on the measurement of women's empowerment. UNRISD discussion paper 108
Kabeer N (2001) Conflicts over credit: re-evaluating the empowerment potential of loans to women in rural Bangladesh. World Dev 29(1):63–84
Kabeer N (2005) Gender equality and women's empowerment: a critical analysis of the third millennium development goal 1. Gender Dev 13(1):13–24
Kar SB, Pascual CA, Chickering KL (1999) Empowerment of women for health promotion: a meta-analysis. Soc Sci Med 49:1431–1460
Khan A, Noreen S (2012) Microfinance and women's empowerment: a case study of Bahawalpur district (Pakistan). Afr J Bus Manage 6(12):4514–4521
Kishor S, Gupta K (2004) Women's empowerment in India and its states: evidence from the NFHS. Econ Polit Wkly 39(7):694–712
Kishor S, Subaiya L (2008) Understanding women's empowerment: a comparative analysis of Demographic and Health Survey (DHS) data. USAID
Larsen U, Hollos M (2003) Women's empowerment and fertility decline among the pare of Kilimanjaro region, northern Tanzania. Soc Sci Med 57:1099–1115
Lee-Rife SM (2010) Women's empowerment and reproductive experiences over the life course. Soc Sci Med 71:634–642
Mahmud S, Tasneem S (2014) Measuring 'empowerment' using quantitative household survey data. Women's Stud Int Forum 45:90–97
Mahmud S, Shah NM, Becker S (2012) Measuring women's empowerment in rural Bangladesh. World Dev 40(3):610–619
Malhotra A, Mather M (1997) Do schooling and work empower women in developing countries? Gender and domestic decisions in Sri Lanka. Sociol Forum 12(4):559–630
Malhotra A, Schulte J, Patel P, Petesch P (2009) Innovations for Women's empowerment and gender equality. International Center for Research on Women (ICRW)
Mukashema I, Sapsford R (2013) Marital conflicts in Rwanda: points of view of Rwandan psycho-socio-medical professionals. Procedia-Soc Behav Sci 82:149–168
Naqvi ZF, Shahnaz L (2002) How do women decide to work in Pakistan? Pak Dev Rev 41 (4):495–513
NISR (2010a) Demographic and Health Survey (DHS). National Institute of Statistics for Rwanda, Kigali
NISR (2010b) Integrated Household Living Conditions (EICV3): Gender thematic report. National Institute of Statistics for Rwanda
NISR (2013) Statistical year book. National Institute of Statistics for Rwanda, Kigali
Patrikar SR, Basannar DR, Sharma MS (2014) Women empowerment and use of contraception. Med J Armed Forces INDIA 70:253–256
Rowlands J (1997) Questioning empowerment. Oxfam, Oxford
Sado L, Spaho A, Hotchkiss DR (2014) The influence of women's empowerment on maternal health care utilization: evidence from Albania. Soc Sci Med 114:169–177
Samman E, Santos ME (2009) Agency and empowerment: a review of concepts, indicators and empirical evidence. Oxford Poverty and Human Development Initiative
Schuler SR, Hashemi SM, Riley AP, Akther S (1996) Credit programs, patriarchy and men's violence against women in rural Bangladesh. Soc Sci Med 43(12):1729–1742
Schuler SR, Hashemi SM, Riley AP (1997) The influence of women's changing roles and status in Bangladesh's fertility transition: evidence from a study on credit programs and contraceptive use. World Dev 25(4):563–575
Sultana A, Hossen S (2013) Role of employment in women empowerment: evidence from Khulna city of Bangladesh. Int J Soc Sci Interdisc Res 2(7):117–125
The World Bank (2012) Gender inequality and development. World Development Report 2012. The World Bank

Trommlerova SK, Klasen S, Lebmann O (2015) Determinants of empowerment in capability-based poverty approach: evidence from the Gambia. World Dev 66:1–15

Upadhyay UD, Karasek D (2012) Women's empowerment and the ideal family size: an examination of DHS empowerment measures in sub-Saharan Africa. Int Perspect Sexual Reprod Health 38(2):78–89

Upadhyay UD, Gipson JD, Withers M, Lewis S, Ciaraldi EJ, Fraser A, Huchko MJ, Prata N (2014) Women empowerment and fertility: a review of literature. Soc Sci Med 115:110–120

[illegible]

[illegible]

Chapter 3
Determinants of Demand for Outpatient Health Care in Rwanda

Charles Mulindabigwi Ruhara and Urbanus Mutuku Kioko

Abstract In the 2000s, the Government of Rwanda initiated health sector reforms aimed at increasing access to health care. Despite these reforms, there has not been a corresponding increase in demand for health services, as only about 30% of the sick use modern care (NISR in Preliminary results of interim demographic and health survey 2010. NISR, Kigali, 2011). The objective of this paper was to examine the factors influencing the demand for outpatient care in Rwanda and suggesting appropriate measures to improve utilization of health services. The data are from the Integrated Household Living Conditions Survey (EICV2) conducted in 2005 by the National Institute of Statistics Rwanda (NISR). A structural model of demand for health care is estimated to measure the demand effects of covariates. The findings indicate that health insurance is a significant determinant of outpatient medical care. In addition, the price of health care and household income are among the main drivers of utilization of health care. Women are more likely to seek outpatient health care as compared to men. Two main policy recommendations emerge from these findings. First, the government should reduce out-of-pocket healthcare expenditures (OOPE) through subsidies for public health facilities. Second, the government should reduce the premiums for community-based health insurance schemes (CBHIs) to increase coverage rates.

Keywords Outpatient · Health insurance · Endogeneity · User fees · Logit model

JEL Classification Codes I10 · I11 · I12 · I13 · D12

C.M. Ruhara (✉)
University of Rwanda, Butare, Rwanda
e-mail: ruharamch@yahoo.fr

U.M. Kioko
University of Nairobi, Nairobi, Kenya
e-mail: urbanusmutukukioko@gmail.com

A. Heshmati (ed.), *Studies on Economic Development and Growth in Selected African Countries*, Frontiers in African Business Research,
DOI 10.1007/978-981-10-4451-9_3

3.1 Introduction

The theoretical model for analyzing human capital and health and its effect on productivity, earnings, and labor supply was first developed by Grossman (1972). The premise of his theory was that an increase in a person's stock of health raises his or her productivity in both market and non-market activities. There exist large productivity and wage payments benefits of a better health. There is evidence to show that sickness can have adverse effects on learning, and that these impacts can later influence economic outcomes (Bhargava et al. 2001). Better health can make workers more productive either through fewer days off or through increased productivity while working. Improved nutrition and reduced diseases, particularly in early childhood, lead to improved cognitive development, enhancing the ability to learn. Healthy children also gain more from school because they are absent for fewer days due to ill health.

While health is determined by many factors including medical care, food, housing conditions, and exercising, it is accepted that medical care is one of the key determinants in the health production function (McKeown 1976). Santerre and Neun (2010) argue that as a firm uses various inputs such as capital and labor to manufacture a product, an individual uses healthcare inputs to produce health. When other factors are held constant, an individual's health status indicates the maximum amount of health that can be generated from the quantity of medical care consumed.

Considering the importance of medical care, both policymakers and researchers have directed much attention to the question of how broad access to health services can be ensured (Lindelow 2002). Early policy and research initiatives focused on the need to improve physical access through an expansion of the network of health facilities. This consisted of improving healthcare delivery including healthcare professionals, equipment, and buildings. A growing literature on health care, however, points out that supply is not sufficient and this means that providing maximum access to health care remains a challenge for governments in many low-income countries.

In Rwanda, access to health care was identified as an important objective for formulating public policies since good health is recognized as a necessary condition for enjoying economic and social opportunities. The country has developed a healthcare setting open to all Rwandans that is accessible to everyone regardless of socioeconomic status. For instance, in the Rwanda Economic Development and Poverty Reduction Strategy (EDPRS, 2008), access to health care is one of the strategies for eradicating poverty. The strategy's objective is promoting health care among the entire population, increasing geographical accessibility, increasing the availability and affordability of drugs, and improving the quality of services. Increased accessibility to health care has several benefits particularly among the poor segments of the population (The World Bank 2001). The millennium development goals (MDGs) also recognize health as an essential ingredient in the social and economic progress of any country. However, despite improvements in access to health care through community-based health insurance schemes (CBHIs) and other insurance providers, it is not known why healthcare utilization has remained low in Rwanda.

To increase access to health services, the Government of Rwanda initiated a number of health policies and other economic stimulus efforts, some of them targeting the supply side of the market while other policies are aimed at increasing service utilization. The policies include Vision 2020, the Economic Development and Poverty Reduction Strategy (EDPRS) 2008–2012, One-Cow-One-Family, the Social Security Policy 2009, and the Health Policy 2004 (Ministry of Health 2009). These policies are meant to increase access to health services and hence improve the health status of the population. The reforms are also meant to strengthen the healthcare system and make it more accessible. Despite these reforms, less than two out of five sick people sought formal health care in Rwanda (NISR 2011). The ineffectiveness of previous policies aimed at increasing healthcare utilization is due to their implementation without adequate evidence about the factors influencing health service utilization in Rwanda. The aim of this study is to examine the factors that influence demand for outpatient healthcare services in Rwanda.

Although economic theory offers potential factors that influence demand for health care, there is lack of a quantitative assessment of their effects in Rwanda. Evidence on these factors is needed for implementing policies designed to improve health service utilization in the country. To my knowledge, no studies have been done in Rwanda in recent years to determine the factors influencing healthcare demand. The only available evidence on this is from studies by Jayaraman et al. (2008) and Shimeles (2010), which focus on maternal health care and on effects of CBHIs at the district level. In countries in which estimates of demand for health care exist, research results provide conflicting evidence of the demand effects of price, income, and insurance suggesting that more studies are needed.

Most studies on demand for health care do not address the problems of endogeneity (reverse causality) and heterogeneity (variations in the estimated effect size due to unobservables). Failure to address these problems leads to biased estimates (Kabubo-Mariara et al. 2009; Lawson 2004; Rosenzweig and Schultz 1982). McCool et al. (1994) point out that differences in data, model specifications, and/or empirical methods can contribute to diversity in demand estimates and hinder clarity in healthcare financing policies. Our paper addresses these estimation problems by providing rigorous evidence on outpatient healthcare demand determinants in Rwanda that policymakers can use for improving health service utilization across all the regions.

3.2 Literature Review

Healthcare services are demanded as an input into the production of health that is part of an individual's utility function together with other goods. Empirically, an analysis of health services examines their determinants based on the microeconomic theory of consumer behavior. These determinants include factors related to individuals, households, and the community. Numerous studies have attempted to quantify how much healthcare people consume, the type of health care that they use, and the factors underlying the utilization of health care.

Several studies have documented the impact of insurance on demand for health care and found that the effect of insurance on utilization varies across the population and the level and type of coverage (see Barros and Machado 2008; Buchmueller et al. 2005). Hahn's (1994) study found that uninsured households had lower average rates of utilization compared to persons with private or Medicaid coverage. Those with Medicaid for the full year were found to have the highest rate of healthcare utilization while uninsured persons were found to have the lowest mean utilization for all types of services. In a similar study, Barros and Machado (2008) estimated the effect of private health insurance coverage beyond a National Health System on the demand for several health services in Portugal. Their study estimated the impact of having additional coverage on demand for three different health services: the number of visits, number of blood and urine tests, and the probability of visiting a dentist. The results showed large positive effects of the coverage on the number of visits and tests.

Similar findings were also reported by Jones et al. (2006), who found private insurance to be positively associated with the probability of health visits in Ireland, Italy, Portugal, Spain, and the UK. Another study by Shimeles (2010) examined the effects of CBHIs on healthcare utilization at the district level in Rwanda. The study used the matching estimator to address the endogeneity problem. As in Hahn (1994), higher utilization of healthcare services was reported among insured as compared to uninsured households. The results indicate that CBHIs had a strong positive impact on access to health care. These results are consistent with the findings of Saksena et al. (2010), Rashad and Markowitz (2009), and Jutting (2003), who found that insurance was an important factor in explaining health seeking behavior.

However, other studies have found that insurance may have little effect on demand for health care depending on geographical locations (Buchmueller et al. 2005). Cunningham and Kemper (1998) document that in areas where a well-functioning healthcare system exists, the lack or reduction of insurance coverage may not imply a significant lack of access to care. The expansion of coverage would then result in smaller changes in utilization than in locations where the uninsured have fewer. Mwabu et al. (2003) reported a negative effect of insurance suggesting that insured people made fewer visits to health facilities relative to uninsured people. The reason for this unlikely result was that people with insurance may have better health endowments and thus demand lesser health care relative to uninsured people. However, none of the studies controlled for heterogeneity of insurance. Since the effect of insurance on utilization may vary across the population, geographical location, and the level and type of insurance coverage, research on healthcare demand needs to handle the problem of heterogeneities to produce reliable estimates.

There is extensive literature on health economics that seeks to estimate the elasticity of income on demand for health services. Most of the literature shows that demand for medical care is income inelastic indicating that medical care is a necessity (Mocan et al. 2004). The positive sign of the elasticity indicates that as income increases, demand for health services also increases. However, literature is inconclusive but notes that income effects vary widely across studies, countries, and regions. Ringel et al. (2002) report that income elasticity of demand using cross-sectional data ranged between 0 and 0.2. This kind of magnitude suggests that the effect of income on demand is relatively small. The difference in estimates across time frames relies on the inclusion of the effects of changes in medical technology that use long time series data (Ringel et al. 2002). Income elasticities based on cross-sectional data or on time series data covering a relatively short period assume that the level of available medical technology is constant. As real incomes in the population increase, the aggregate demand for new medical technologies and new treatment approaches increases as well. Thus, from previous studies on the effect of income, no consensus has emerged and the debate on whether health care is a luxury or necessity continues (Blomqvist and Carter 1997).

To account for the price effect at different levels of visits rather than the average effect obtained using ordinary least squares (OLS), Mwabu et al. (2003) used the quintile regression method to analyze the effects of price on demand for health services in Kenya. The fees were found to have a negative effect on demand for health care but it differed across the quintiles. Their findings established that an increase of 10 shillings reduced visits by 0.2%. The price elasticity of demand for medical care was found to be small in magnitude and consistent with Akin et al. (1986) and Sauerborn et al. (1994). The study did not, however, address the endogeneity and heterogeneity problems to produce unbiased estimates. Given that demand for treatment is not determined by an individual alone, several studies have investigated household and community factors. Controlling for the unobserved effects at the household and community levels that affect health seeking behavior Lépine and Nestour (2008) shows that household economic status and quality of health care are important determinants of the probability of seeking treatment from a qualified provider. In addition, transportation costs were found to be an important determinant of the likelihood of seeking care as an increase in the average transport cost decreased the likelihood of seeking curative care by 25%.

Evidence from empirical studies on the relationship between demand for health care and its main determinants differs in several ways. In addition, most of the previous studies have assumed an exogenous insurance and do not consider the reverse causality that is more likely to exist between demand for medical care and health insurance. Our study provides new evidence on the factors, which affect demand for health care using data from Rwanda, and handles the endogeneity and heterogeneity problems to ensure that the estimates are unbiased and consistent.

3.3 Methodology

Following Grossman (1972), individuals maximize their utility over health and other goods subject to market and non-market factors. Health is one of the several commodities over which individuals have well-defined preferences. Market factors include availability of health inputs and their prices, insurance, and household incomes. Non-market factors include household characteristics, location or distance, and individual characteristics such as age, education, health status, and the perceptions that they have about the quality of health services (Ajakaiye and Mwabu 2007; Appleton and Song 1999; Bategeka et al. 2009). Assuming that health care is a consumption good, a consumer's problem can be expressed as

$$\text{Max } U = U(H, Z, X, Y) \tag{3.1}$$

where U is the utility derived from consumption of different goods; Y represents health-related goods that yield utility to the sick person and improve health status; H is the health production function; Z stands for health inputs such as health care while X represents all other goods and services.

The utility function is maximized subject to the following constraints:

$$B = XP_x + YP_y + ZP_z \tag{3.2}$$

$$H = H(Z, I, S, C, A, h_s, P_h, N_O) \tag{3.3}$$

where Z is defined as in Eq. 3.1 and I is household characteristics including insurance; S represents socio-demographic variables including age, sex, and education; C is community characteristics including distance to health facility; A is the household asset; h_s is the size of the household; P_h is the price of health while N_O are household non-observable characteristics. In the first constraint, B is the exogenous income and P_x, P_y, and P_z are, respectively, the price of health neutral goods (such as clothing), health-related consumer goods Z (such as health care), and health investment goods Y such as exercising.

The maximization problem is then expressed as

$$\text{Max } U = U(H, Z, X, Y) \tag{3.4}$$

Given $H = H(Z, I, S, C, A, h_s, P_h, N_O)$

$$\text{s.t. } B = XP_x + YP_y + ZP_z$$

Solving the maximization problem yields a demand function for health care specified as

$$D_{\mathrm{h}} = f(I, B, A, S, C, h_{\mathrm{s}}, P_{\mathrm{h}}, N_{\mathrm{O}}) \tag{3.5}$$

where D_{h} refers to the demand for outpatient; I is health insurance; B is the budget or income; A is household asset; and S represents socio-demographic variables; C represents community characteristics including distance to health facility; h_{s} is the household composition; P_{h} is the price of health care; and N_{O} are household non-observable characteristics.

Equation 3.5 is a structural outpatient healthcare demand equation that includes an endogenous variable among the independent variables. The endogenous variable is health insurance because of reverse causality between demand for health care and insurance while exogenous variables include the monetary price for health care, income, age, gender, educational attainment of the individual, household size, location, and region. In our study, the demand for outpatient care is discrete rather than continuous because patients seek or do not seek health care. In Eqs. 3.1 and 3.2, a health investment good is purchased only for the purpose of improving health so that it enters an individual's utility function only through H.

In the demand for outpatient model, insurance is assumed to improve access to health services. In addition, the heterogeneity of health insurance due to a nonlinear interaction of demand for health services with unobservable and omitted variables could bias the estimates. Our study assumes that demand for health services has only one endogenous variable and demand for outpatient refers to any curative outpatient service provided by a physician or any other medical staff. Given the dichotomous nature of outpatient care, the estimation adopts a binary discrete model, where health care is either sought or not. Assuming that the errors are distributed logistically, we adopt a logit regression method to estimate both outpatient and inpatient healthcare demands. The dependent variable takes any two values: 1 if an individual uses outpatient health care and zero representing individuals who do not use any health services. The logit regression is also preferred because most of the studies on demand for health services use a logit regression (see Hahn 1994; Lépine and Nestour 2008). This relationship can be expressed as

$$Y_i = \begin{cases} 1 & \text{if the event takes place (the individual seeks outpatient service)} \\ 0 & \text{if the event has not taken place (the individual has not sought treatment)} \end{cases}$$

Equation 3.5 expressing the demand for health care can be rewritten as

$$y_i^* = x_i'\beta + \varepsilon_i \tag{3.6}$$

where y_i^* is a latent variable showing the probability that medical care is sought or not sought, x_i' is a vector of characteristics related to the individual, household, and community, and ε_i is the error term.

$$\begin{aligned} &\text{Y} = 1 \text{ if } y_i^* > 0, \quad \text{that is, } (x_i'\beta + \varepsilon_i) > 0 \\ &\text{and } \text{Y} = 0 \text{ if } y_i^* < 0, \quad \text{that is, } (x_i'\beta + \varepsilon_i) < 0 \end{aligned}$$

The values zero and 1 are used because they allow the definition of probability of occurrence of an event as the mathematical expectation of the variable Y. This can be expressed as

$$E[Y_i] = \Pr(Y_i = 1) * 1 + \Pr(Y_i) * 0 = \Pr(Y_i = 1) = \pi_i \tag{3.7}$$

Equation 3.7 shows that we need to compute the probability of occurrence ($Y = 1$) over the probability of no occurrence ($Y = 0$). Assuming that the error term has an extreme value distribution, this can be done using the logit relation as shown by

$$\Pr(Y_i = 1) = \frac{\exp(\beta_0 + \beta_1 X_{1i} + \beta_2 X_{2i} + \cdots + \beta_k X_{ki})}{1 + \exp(\beta_0 + \beta_1 X_{1i} + \beta_2 X_{2i} + \cdots + \beta_k X_{ki})} \tag{3.8}$$

In terms of log odds, Eq. 3.8 can be reformulated as

$$\begin{aligned} \left(\ln \frac{\Pr(Y_i = 1)}{1 - \Pr(Y_i = 1)}\right) = \left(\ln \frac{\Pr(Y_i = 1)}{\Pr(Y_i = 0)}\right) = \ln\left(\frac{\pi_i}{1 - \pi_i}\right) = \beta_0 + \sum_{j=1}^{k} \beta_j X_{ji} \\ = \log it(\pi_i) \end{aligned} \tag{3.9}$$

which can be expressed as

$$\log it(\pi_i) = \beta_0 + \sum_{j=1}^{3} \beta_j X_{ji} = \beta_0 + \beta_1 X_{1i} + \beta_2 X_{2i} + \beta_3 X_{3i} + \varepsilon_i \tag{3.10}$$

where

- Y_i is an indicator of the choice of modern health care (outpatient) by the ith household member,
- X_{1i} Vector of characteristics related to an individual such as age, education, and sex,
- X_{2i} Vector of characteristics related to a household such as income and insurance, and
- X_{3i} Vector of characteristics related to community-level characteristics such as a medical specialist and the distance from the household to the health facility.

If in Eq. 3.10, $\beta_j > 0$, then an increase in X_{ji} (for instance, household income), while all other exogenous variables remain unchanged will increase the log-odds ratio of individual i seeking health services. If $\beta_j < 0$, then an increase in X_{ji} (for example, user fee) will reduce the log-odds ratio. If $\beta_j = 0$, then the variable has no effect.

However, in the case of Eq. 3.10, βs indicates changes in the logistic index with the sign of β indicating the direction of the eventual change in the probability of seeking care from a given health facility. Equation 3.10 is the structural form of the probabilistic healthcare demand function. In this equation, as in recent literature, one of the independent variables—health insurance—is endogenous and the estimation has to address this problem. Endogeneity is due to reverse causality between health insurance and demand for health care. So, in order to obtain unbiased and consistent estimates, instrumentation of the endogenous variable is required. The instrumental variable should be correlated with the endogenous regressor but unrelated directly to the dependent variable (Ajakaiye and Mwabu 2007).

Health insurance in Eq. 3.10 is endogenous to the dependent variable. Thus, estimating the equation without taking into account this problem might encounter the problem of simultaneity which is due to the possibility of reverse causality between demand functions and health insurance. Endogeneity of health insurance arises because the decision to purchase health insurance and the utilization of health services are intertwined. First, since insurance reduces the effective price of medical care, insured people tend to consume more health services (Rashad and Markowitz 2009). Second, even if individuals cannot perfectly predict their future health needs, they are likely to have information about their health status which could lead them to anticipate higher use of health services and then decide to buy health insurance. Thus, healthcare utilization not only depends on an individual's health insurance coverage, but the level of coverage may also be influenced by the anticipated utilization of health services (Jutting 2004). Manning et al. (1987) argue that treating insurance as exogenous in demand for healthcare models produces biased results because people who anticipate consuming more health services have an obvious incentive to obtain insurance cover either by selecting a more generous option at the place of employment by working for an employer with a generous insurance plan, or by purchasing a generous coverage privately.

Existing literature suggests useful methods for dealing with the endogeneity problem. Among the common approaches to this problem is the use of the two-stage residuals inclusion (2SRI) regression method which is appropriate for nonlinear models. The procedure is used to address problems relating to measurement error, simultaneity, and omitted variables. This method requires identifying an observable variable or instrument that is correlated with the endogenous variable but uncorrelated with the error term (Ajakaiye and Mwabu 2007; Kioko 2008; Rosenzweig and Schultz 1982; Strauss and Thomas 1995; Wooldridge 2002). The problem, however, is identifying an observable variable, z_i, that satisfies two conditions. First, the selected variable is uncorrelated with the error term. This means that $\text{cov}(z_i, \varepsilon) = 0$, that is, z_i is exogenous in the estimation of the endogenous equation (see Wooldridge 2002; Behrman and Deolalikar 1988; Griliches and Mairesse 1998; Ackerberg and Caves 2003). The second requirement involves the relationship between the identified instrument, z_i, and demand for health services. This means that the identified variable should not have an impact on health insurance, that is, z_i must be relevant. This requires regressing health insurance against all the exogenous variables, including the instrument (Greene 2007; Jowett et al. 2004; Wooldridge 2002). In the first regression, the variables should have significant coefficients when the choice variable is regressed on the identifying variable together with all other exogenous variables (Ackerberg and Caves 2003).

In the first stage, we estimated the reduced form of health insurance on all exogenous variables including instrumental variables. In the second stage, we regressed demand for health care on all independent variables plus insurance and insurance residuals obtained from the first-stage regression (Palmer et al. 2008; Terza et al. 2008).

Following Ajakaiye and Mwabu (2007) and Kabubo-Mariara et al. (2009), we can re-formulate the demand for health services in the form of simultaneous equations as

$$D = \delta_d Z_1 + \beta_j I_j + \varepsilon_{ij}, \quad j = 1\ldots2 \tag{3.11}$$

$$I = \delta_j Z + \varepsilon_2 \tag{3.12}$$

where D and I are demand for health care and health insurance, respectively. Z is a vector of independent variables consisting of Z_1 covariates that belong to the demand for health services function and a vector of instrumental variables that affect insurance but have no direct impact on demand for health services. δ and β are parameters to be estimated and ε is a disturbance term. Equation 3.11 is the structural equation to be estimated while Eq. 3.12 is the linear projection of the potentially endogenous variable I on all the exogenous variables. The system of equations assumes that there is only one endogenous regressor in the demand equation.

A major challenge of the instrumental variable approach is obtaining a valid instrument for identifying the effect of endogenous variables in a structural model. Once the potential instrument is identified, it is important to test for its suitability by assessing whether it has three properties: relevance, strength, and exogeneity of instruments (Kabubo-Mariara et al. 2009; Stock 2010). An instrument satisfying all three properties is said to be a strong and valid instrument. As used in Meer and Harvey (2004), after testing for validity and strength, the variables' employment status and community health association membership were used as an instrument for insurance.

We tested for the endogeneity of insurance and the validity of instruments. First, we carried out the test for endogeneity of health insurance. If insurance was exogenous, there would be no justification to estimate the structural model of demand for health care because the logit models will yield unbiased estimates. We used the Durbin–Wu–Hausman test. The results showed that the Durbin–Wu–Hausman statistic values were significant at the 10% level.

We also conducted the Wald test of exogeneity of the insurance variable which showed that the values were significant at the 1% level. We then rejected the null hypothesis of exogenous insurance. Second, the coefficients of insurance residuals' variable were also significant at the 1% level to the demand for medical care services. Third, we tested the impact of the instruments on the dependent variable.

These were found to be insignificant. Fourth, the strength of the instruments was tested by considering the impact of the instruments on the endogenous variable. As the coefficients of instruments were large and significant at the 1% level, the instruments were strong. In addition, we conducted the F-test to check the role of the instruments on the endogenous variable. While an F-statistic of at least 10 is recommended (Kioko 2008; Staiger and Stock 1997), the minimum eigenvalue statistic for the F-test was 133.04 suggesting that the null hypothesis of weak instrument had to be rejected.

A second estimation issue is the heterogeneity bias which arises from unobserved factors interacting with the variable of interest and thus biasing the results. These are some unobservable preferences and health endowments of individuals that influence their demand for health care (Kabubo-Mariara et al. 2009; Schultz 2008). Even with valid instruments, in practice, it is not easy to separate the impact of endogenous variables from the effect of unobservables on a structural model. Failure to take into account heterogeneity could lead to unreliable estimates.

In our study, heterogeneity may arise from at least three sources. First, a risk reduction effect where the preferred level of utilization is greater because of the financial certainty created by insurance than utilization under uncertainty (Meza 1983). Second, an access effect where the insurance may extend an individual's opportunity set by giving access to health care that would otherwise not be available. Nyman (2005) has argued that the pooling effect of insurance provides access to expensive medical technologies that would otherwise not be affordable. Third, an income transfer effect where insurance creates an ex-post transfer of income from the healthy to the ill and this may increase utilization through an income effect on the demand for medical care (Nyman 2005). The three sources relate to reasons known by an individual but not by a researcher because of which health insurance may affect demand for health services.

To handle the problem of heterogeneity, we used the control function approach (CFA) (Florens et al. 2008). This involved estimating a reduced form of insurance residual (I^*), where the inclusion of the residuals was identical to the one obtained by 2SRI using an instrument for insurance. Assuming that the unobserved component was linear in the insurance residual (I^*), we introduced an interaction term [of the insurance and its residual (II^*)] as a second control variable to eliminate an endogeneity bias even in a case where the reduced-form insurance was heteroscedastic (Card 2001).

Introducing the control function variables (insurance residual and interaction) gives

$$D = \beta_0 + \delta_d Z_1 + \tau I^* + \gamma II^* + \varepsilon_1 \tag{3.13}$$

where I^* are the fitted residuals from the reduced form of the insurance variable, which is explained by Z_1; all other variables are as defined earlier. τI^* captures the nonlinear indirect effects of insurance (I) on demand for health services (D), because the fitted residuals serve as a control for unobservable variables which are correlated with insurance. Inclusion of both I^* and the interaction term II^* controls for the effects of unobservable factors and therefore purges the coefficients of the effects of the unobservables (Ajakaiye and Mwabu 2007; Card 2001). If any unobservable variable is linear in I^*, it is only the intercept in Eq. 3.13 that is affected by inclusion of the unobservable variable, and therefore, the 2SRI estimates are efficient without the interaction term (II^*). The 2SRI estimates will be unbiased and consistent if at least one of two conditions holds: First, the expected value of the interaction between insurance and its fitted residuals is zero. Second, the expectation of the interaction between insurance and the fitted residuals is linear.

The data used in this paper are drawn from the Integrated Household Living Conditions Survey (EICV2) conducted in 2005 by the National Institute of Statistics of Rwanda (NISR). This nationally representative survey collected data from 7620 households and 34,819 individuals. Data were collected at the household and individual levels. EICV2 aimed at enabling the government to assess the impact of its different policies and programs which had been implemented for improving the living conditions of the population in general.

The survey covered all the 30 districts in Rwanda and collected data on a wide spectrum of socioeconomic indicators—labor, housing, health, agriculture, debt, livestock and expenditure and consumption in different areas, regions, and locations in the country. Household level information included consumption expenditures on health and OOPE (consultation, laboratory tests, hospitalization, and medication costs). Individual level information included socioeconomic indicators and insurance status. There were also a number of community variables such as distance to the nearest health facility. To improve the reliability of the data, the recall period for the use of health services was two weeks prior to the survey. In this paper, demand for healthcare services was estimated for a single visit because the survey did not capture multi-visits to health facilities. Hence, the demand for outpatient care was limited to the last consultation or admission.

3.4 Results and Discussion

In Table 3.1, Wald chi2 tests measuring the goodness of fit indicate that the estimated models give an adequate description of the data because it is highly significant implying that all the model's parameters are jointly different from zero. The 2SRI results are reported in columns 4–5 of Table 3.1 while the first-stage regression estimates are given in Table 3.3 in the Annexure 1. Columns 6–7 in Table 3.1 present the results of demand for outpatient care after correcting for heterogeneity of insurance. Due to the inclusion of insurance residuals and interaction between insurance residuals and insurance, the results remain close to the 2SRI results in terms of signs of coefficients although they are different in magnitude. The significance of the coefficient on insurance residuals suggests that insurance is endogenous to outpatient medical care. The coefficient on the

Table 3.1 Logistic demand estimates for outpatient care: Dependent variable is probability of an outpatient visit

Explanatory variables	Baseline estimates	*z*-statistics	2SRI estimates	*z*-statistics	Control function estimates	*z*-statistics
Household income	0.00030	3.50***	0.0004	3.60***	0.003	3.40***
User fees	−1.108	−26.74***	−0.980	−15.40**	−1.43	−18.9***
Quality of health care (=1)	−0.011	−0.27	−0.010	−0.41	−0.004	−0.11
Health insurance (=1)	0.492	13.26***	0.921	1.87*	4.106	29.29***
Distance to the health facility	−0.434	−8.00***	−0.072	−5.2***	−0.239	−4.29***
Household size	−0.019	−2.52**	0.004	1.79*	−0.017	−2.31**
Age	0.013	2.57**	0.056	1.91*	−0.0008	−0.74
Square age	−0.001	−2.90**	−0.0051	−2.79**	−0.0002	−1.80*
Primary (=1)	0.006	1.89*	0.021	3.2**	0.018	2.4**
Secondary (=1)	0.030	2.90*	0.040	1.95*	0.028	1.99*
Tertiary (=1)	0.002	5.8***	0.008	4.12***	0.067	2.02**
Male (=1)	−0.163	−4.44***	−0.023	−3.66***	−0.148	−3.85***
Urban (=1)	−0.311	−4.19***	−0.340	−5.15***	−0.164	−2.14**
Kigali region (=1)	−0.035	−0.45	−0.070	−1.43	−0.024	−0.26
Southern region (=1)	−0.066	1.23	−0.204	−2.67**	−0.063	−1.18
Western region (=1)	0.027	0.53	0.024	2.40**	0.035	0.68
Northern region (=1)	0.195	3.25***	0.17	3.54***	0.164	2.73**
Insurance residuals	–	–	−1.3	−4.7***	−2.869	19.05***
Interaction of insurance and insurance residuals	–	–	–	–	−1.269	−6.88***
Constant	−2.644	−24.56	−1.789	−5.67	−2.411	−25.62
Number of observations=	5040		5040		5040	
Durbin–Wu–Hausman chi-sq			0.054*			
F(1, 5040)=			133.88			
LR chi2(19)	5880.20***		5889.70***		5897.44***	
Log likelihood	−3020.4388		−3016.3138		−3006.2254	

Source Researcher's construction
Note ***, **, and * = significant at the 1, 5, and 10% levels, respectively

interaction between the insurance residuals and insurance is significant at the 1% level indicating the presence of heterogeneity arising from an interaction of insurance with unobserved determinants of demand for outpatient care. For comparison purposes, the baseline model (logit) estimates are also presented in columns 2–3. They appear to be weaker than the 2SRI results since the coefficient on health insurance increases from 0.49 to 0.9 across model specifications (moving from logit to 2SRI) while the z-value remains statistically significant. This shows that treating insurance as exogenous highly understates its impact on demand for outpatient medical care.

On average, higher user fees reduce the probability of using outpatient health services. This finding is similar to the results reported by Diop et al. (1995), Litvack and Bodart (1993), Manji et al. (1992) and Ridde (2003) who report negative effects of user fees on health service uptake. In particular, Manji et al. (1992) show that uptake of treatment in Kenyan schools fell from 75 to 19% after fees were introduced. This suggests that the introduction of cost sharing was responsible for a major part of the reduction in uptake. Similarly, De Bethune et al. (1989) and Yoder (1989) found the price of health care to be a significant hindrance to demand for medical services in Swaziland. However, their studies confirmed the results of other cross-sectional studies that demand for health care are inelastic to price. Oxaal and Cook (1998) show that the relationship between price and health is inelastic because of failure to disaggregate its effect from the income one.

The coefficients on education indicate a positive association with demand for outpatient health services in Rwanda. This result is consistent with Katz et al. (2001), which shows that the more the individuals get educated, the more they come in contact with other educated individuals who have a high demand for health care. Social interaction which begins during schooling years continues to the workplace and leads to the adoption of health-improving behaviors, including health service utilization. The evidence from Rwanda is also in line with Elo (1992) and Blunch (2004) who observed a strong positive association between education and the use of health services.

Insurance was found to be an important determinant of demand for outpatient medical services in Rwanda. Insurance reduced the price of health care which made the service more affordable than it would be without insurance. The result on insurance finds support in findings from previous studies which addressed the endogeneity problem when estimating the demand effect of insurance (see, for example, Rashad and Markowitz 2009; Shimeles 2010; Meer and Harvey 2004). Similar results were reported by Phelps and Newhouse (1974) who used data on co-insurance plans in the USA, Canada, and the UK. The results were such that the level of sensitivity of demand depended on the co-insurance rate.

The evidence presented in our paper reveals that gender is an important factor affecting the use of outpatient health services in Rwanda where females are more likely to use outpatient services as compared to men. The results are in line with those reported by Miller (1994) who argued that females demanded more health care than males because of their role in childbearing. Miller (1994) adds that some illnesses such as cardiovascular diseases, osteoporosis, immunologic diseases, and

Alzheimer's disease are more prevalent in women than men. In line with this, Ahmad (2001) further adds that gender differences in healthcare utilization for women were related to specific diseases such as cardiovascular and chronic illnesses.

Some research has shown that women use less outpatient health care than men because of the time they spend taking care of the elderly and other people with disabilities. Caregivers, especially women elderly caregivers, were found to neglect their own health in order to fulfill this responsibility (Fredman et al. 2008). These responsibilities made it difficult for severely disadvantaged women to take steps to improve their living situations and health behaviors by consuming less health services than men. Similarly, Oxaal and Cook (1998) show that the constraints to access for poor women and girls made them less likely to have access to appropriate care and to seek adequate treatment. Their paper notes that the range of factors limiting access for women includes the socioeconomic status of the household, time constraints, composition of households, intra-household resource allocation and decision-making, less education and employment and legal or social constraints on access to care, heavy work burdens, and the opportunity costs of time in seeking care.

Given these results, a number of recommendations emerge. Since user fees are an impediment in using health care in Rwanda, the government should reduce user fees in health facilities through increased budget allocations for all health facilities, particularly in the public sector, where the poor go for medical care. From 2003, OOPE increased gradually to reach 32.2% of the total health expenditure in 2010. High OOPE has a variety of negative consequences, including household impoverishment. Subsidies on user fees should target vulnerable groups such as children and women or low-income households. The government should also consider subsidizing private health facilities to increase access to high-quality services by low-income households. The subsidies will help reduce the effect of income inequalities on healthcare utilization.

Health insurance is an important determinant of healthcare seeking behavior in Rwanda. Thus, policies that increase health insurance coverage will substantially increase health service utilization. The 2013 health insurance coverage rate in Rwanda was 73%, the highest in the East African Community, but the high premiums associated with this coverage are not sustainable. The government should subsidize health insurance to make it accessible to the most disadvantaged people. The current level of premium (of $4.5) for CBHIs per year, per person should be reduced. The premium rate more than doubled in 2011 from $1.7 to $4.5, and this reduced the coverage rate from 91 to 73%. In addition, while with the earlier premium level, healthcare expenditure represented 10% of the total household expenditure holding other factors constant, and with the new premium, the healthcare expenditure for households represents 26% of household expenditure. This will cause households to incur catastrophic expenditures and push them into poverty. Further, with an average household size of 6.6 persons, this level of premium per individual does not seem to be sustainable given that 44.9% of the population lives on less than $1 per day.

Annexure 1

See Tables 3.2 and 3.3.

Table 3.2 Marginal effects for the determinants of outpatient care

Explanatory variables	Baseline model marginal effects	*z*-statistics	2SRI marginal effects	*z*-statistics
Household income	0.0004	3.46***	0.00083	3.09***
User fees	−0.0810	−11.47***	−0.170	−21.46***
Quality of health care (=1)	−0.0002	−0.27	−0.008	−0.20
Health insurance (=1)	0.0130	10.20***	0.942	1.99*
Distance to the health facility	−0.0120	−6.13***	−0.535	−7.43***
Household size	−0.0004	−2.51**	0.011	0.77
Age	0.0003	2.56**	0.005	2.13**
Square age	−0.0002	−2.13**	−0.00004	−2.40*
Male (=1)	−0.0030	−4.38***	0.149	3.89***
Urban (=1)	−0.0060	−4.71***	−0.391	−4.65***
Kigali region (=1)	−0.0008	−0.46	−0.370	−1.25
Southern region (=1)	−0.0010	−1.27	−0.280	−2.67**
Western region (=1)	0.0006	0.52	0.140	2.01**
Northern region (=1)	0.0050	2.76**	0.317	3.94***
Primary (=1)	0.0001	1.96*	0.001	1.98*
Secondary (=1)	0.0004	2.50**	0.023	2.10*
Tertiary (=1)	0.0006	2.67*	0.006	0.90
Insurance residuals	–	–	0.0054	2.31**

Source Researcher's construction
Note ***, **, and * = significant at the 1, 5, and 10% levels, respectively

Table 3.3 Determinants of demand for health insurance, first-stage regression (demand for outpatient care model)

Explanatory variables	Estimates	Standard errors	*z*-statistics
Employment status (=1)	0.0510	0.0064	7.90***
Household income	0.0034	0.0004	8.50***
User fees	−0.0278	0.0231	−1.20
Quality of health care (=1)	0.0033	0.0069	0.47
Distance to the health facility	−0.0483	0.0108	−4.47***
Household size	−0.0132	0.0013	−10.58***
Age	0.0072	0.0008	9.20***
Age squared	−0.0001	0.00001	−6.00***
Primary (=1)	0.0023	0.0045	5.10***
Secondary (=1)	0.0052	0.0085	0.61
Tertiary (=1)	0.0023	0.0087	0.26
Male (=1)	0.0068	0.0058	1.17
Urban (=1)	0.0847	0.0138	6.13***
Kigali (=1)	−0.0385	0.0129	−2.98***
Southern (=1)	−0.0624	0.0088	−7.04***
Western (=1)	0.0555	0.0087	6.32***
Northern (=1)	0.0582	0.0099	5.87***
Constant	0.3250	0.0174	18.62***
Number of observations			5040
F(18, 27934) = 56.19***			

Source Researcher's construction
Note ***, **, and * = significant at the 1, 5, and 10% levels, respectively

References

Ackerberg DA, Caves K (2003) Structural identification of production functions: an application to the timing of input choice. UCLA, Department of Economics, Los Angeles, CA

Ahmad F (2001) Rural physicians perspectives on cervical and breast cancer screening: a Gender-based analysis. J Women's Health Gender-Based Med 5(2):201–208

Ajakaiye O, Mwabu G (2007) The demand for reproductive health services: an application of control function approach. AERC, Nairobi

Akin JS, Griffin DK, Popkin BM (1986) The demand for primary health services in the bicol region of the Philippines. Econ Dev Cult Change 34(4):755–782

Appleton S, Song L (1999) Income and human development at the household level, evidence from six countries. Oxford University, Mimeo

Barros P, Machado P (2008) Moral hazard and the demand for health services: a matching estimator approach. J Health Econ 27(4):1006–1025

Bategeka LO, Asekeny L, Musiime JA (2009) The determinants of birth weight in Uganda. AERC, Nairobi

Behrman JR, Deolalikar AB (1988) Health and nutrition. In: Chenery H, Srinivasan TN (eds) Handbook of development economics. Elsevier Science Publishers BV, North Holland

Bhargava A, Jamison D, Lau L, Murray C (2001) Modeling the effects of health on economic growth. J Health Econ 20:423–440

Blomqvist AG, Carter RAL (1997) Is healthcare really a luxury? J Health Econ 16(2):207–229

Blunch N (2004) Maternal literacy and numeracy skills and child health in Ghana. Paper presented at the Northeast Universities Development Consortium Conference, HEC Montreal

Buchmueller TC, Grumbach K, Kronick R, Kahn JG (2005) The effect of health insurance on medical care utilization and implications for insurance expansion: a review of the literature. Med Care Res Rev 62(1):3–10

Card D (2001) Estimating the return to schooling: progress on some persistent econometric problems. Econometrica 69(5):1127–1160

Cunningham P, Kemper P (1998) Ability to obtain medical care for the uninsured: How much does it vary across communities? JAMA 280(10):921–927

De Bethune X, Alfani S, Lahaye JP (1989) The influence of an abrupt price increase on health service utilization: evidence from Zaire. Health Policy Plan 4(1):76–81

Diop F, Yazbeck A, Bitrán R (1995) The impact of alternative cost recovery schemes on access and equity in Niger. Health Policy Plan 10:223–240

Elo I (1992) Utilization of maternal health-care services in Peru; the role of women's education. Population Studies Center, University of Pennsylvania

Florens JP, Heckman MC, Vytlacil E (2008) Identification of treatment effects using control functions in models with continuous, endogenous treatment and heterogeneous effects. Econometrica 76(5):1191–1206

Fredman L, Cauley JA, Satterfield S (2008) Caregiving, mortality, and mobility decline: the health, aging, and body composition (Health ABC) study. Arch Intern Med 168:2154–2162

Greene WL (2007) Econometric analysis. Macmillan Publishing Company, New York

Griliches Z, Mairesse J (1998) Production functions: the search for identification. National Bureau of Economic Research, Working paper no. 5067

Grossman M (1972) On the concept of health capital and the demand for health. J Polit Econ 80 (2):223–235

Hahn B (1994) Healthcare utilization: the effect of extending insurance to adults on medicaid or uninsured. Med Care 32(3):227–239

Jayaraman AS, Chandrasekhar T, Gebreselassie T (2008) Factors affecting maternal healthcare seeking in Rwanda. USAID, Working paper

Jones AM, Koolman X, Doorslaer EV (2006) The impact of having supplementary private health insurance on the use of specialists in European Countries. Anales d'Economie et de Statistique 83(84):251–275

Jowett M, Deolalikar A, Martinsson P (2004) Health insurance and treatment seeking behaviour: evidence from a low-income country. Health Econ 13:845–857

Jütting JP (2003) Do community-based health insurance schemes improve poor people's access to healthcare? Evidence from rural Senegal. World Dev 32:273–288

Katz L, Kling J, Liebman J (2001) Moving to opportunity in Boston: early results of a randomized mobility experiment. Q J Econ 116(2):607–654

Kioko MU (2008) The economic burden of malaria in Kenya: a household level investigation. PhD thesis, University of Nairobi

Lawson D (2004) A microeconomic analysis of health, healthcare and chronic poverty, The University of Nottingham (unpublished)

Lépine A, Nestour A (2008) Healthcare utilization in rural Senegal: the factors before the extension of health insurance to farmers. International Labor Office, Research paper no. 2

Lindelow M (2002) Healthcare demand in rural Mozambique: evidence from 1996/97 household survey. International Food Policy Research Institute (IFPRI), FCND discussion paper no. 126

Litvack JI, Bodart C (1993) User fees plus quality equals improved access to health care: results of a field experiment in Cameroon. Soc Sci Med 37:369–383
Manji JE, Moses SF, Bradley NJ, Nagelkerke MA, Plummer FA (1992) Impact of user fees on attendance at a referral centre for sexually transmitted diseases in Kenya. Lancet 340:463–466
Manning WG, Newhouse JP, Duan N, Keeler EB, Leibowitz A (1987) Health insurance and the demand for medical care: evidence from a randomized experiment. Am Econ Assoc Rev 77 (3):251–277
McCool JH, Kiker BF, Ng YC (1994) Estimates of the demand for medical care under different functional forms. J Appl Econometrics 9(2):201–218
McKeown T (1976) The role of medicine: dream, mirage or nemesis? Basil Blackwell, Oxford
Meer J, Harvey SR (2004) Insurance and the utilization of medical services. Soc Sci Med 58:1623–1632
Meza D (1983) Health insurance and the demand for healthcare. J Health Econ 2:47–54
Miller L (1994) Medical schools put women in curricula. Wall Street J B1
Ministry of Health (MoH), Republic of Rwanda (2009) Health sector strategic plan (unpublished)
Ministry of Health Rwanda (2009) Rwanda health financing policy review of Rwanda—options for universal coverage. World Health Organization
Mocan NH, Tekin E, Jeffrey SZ (2004) The demand for medical care in urban China. World Dev 32(2):289–304
Mwabu KMJD, Nd'enge GK (2009) The consequences of fertility for child health in Kenya: endogeneity, heterogeneity and the control function approach. AERC, Nairobi
Mwabu GJ, Wang'ombe B, Nganda B (2003) The demand for medical care in Kenya. African Development Bank, Oxford
National Institute of Statistics of Rwanda (NISR) (2011) Preliminary results of interim demographic and health survey 2010. NISR, Kigali
Nyman JA (2005) Health insurance theory: the case of the missing welfare gain, University of Minnesota (unpublished)
Oxaal Z, Cook S (1998) Health and poverty gender analysis. Swedish International Development Co-operation (unpublished)
Palmer T, Thompson J, Tobin M, Sheehan N, Burton P (2008) Adjusting for bias and unmeasured confounding in Mendelian randomization studies with binary responses. Int J Epidemiol 37(5):1161–1168
Phelps CE, Newhouse JP (1974) Coinsurance, the price of time, and the demand or medical service. Rev Econ Stat 56:334–342
Rashad IK, Markowitz S (2009) Incentives in obesity and health insurance. Inquiry 46:418–432
Ridde V (2003) Fees-for-services, cost recovery, and equity in a district of Burkina Faso operating the Bamako Initiative. Bull World Health Organ 81:532–538
Ringel JS, Hosek SD, Ben AV, Mahnovski S (2002) The elasticity of demand for healthcare. A review of the literature and its application to the military health system. National Defense Research Institute (unpublished)
Rosenzweig MR, Schultz TP (1982) The behavior of mothers as inputs to child health: the determinants of birth weight, gestation, and the rate of fetal growth. In: Fuchs VR (ed) Economic aspects of health. The University of Chicago Press, Chicago, pp 53–92
Saksena P, Xu K, Elovaino R, Perrot J (2010) Health services utilization and out-of-pocket expenditure at public and private facilities in low-income countries. World Health Organization, Background paper no. 20, Geneva
Santerre RE, Neun SP (2010) Health economics: theories, insights and industry studies, 5th ed. Cengage Learning
Sauerborn R, Nougtara A, Latimer E (1994) The elasticity of demand for healthcare in Burkina Faso: differences across age and income groups. Health Policy Plan 9(2):186–192
Schultz TP (2008) Population policies, fertility, women's human capital. In Schultz TP, Strauss J (eds) Handbook of development economics, vol 4, Chap. 52. Elsevier, Amsterdam
Shimeles A (2010) Community based health insurance schemes in Africa: the case of Rwanda. African Development Bank group, Working paper no. 120

Staiger D, Stock JH (1997) Instrumental variables regression with weak instruments. Econometrica 65(3):557–586

Stock JH (2010) The other transformation in econometric practice: tools for inference. J Econ Perspect 24(2):83–94

Strauss J, Thomas D (1995) Human resources: empirical modeling of household and family decisions. In: Behrman J, Srinivasan TN (eds) Handbook of development economics, vol 3A. Elsevier Science, Amsterdam, pp 1883–2023

Terza J, Basu A, Rathouz P (2008) Two-stage residual inclusion estimation: addressing endogeneity in health econometric modeling. J Health Econ 27(3):531–543

The World Bank (2001) World Bank Development Report 2000–2001: attacking poverty. Oxford University Press, Washington, DC

Wooldridge JM (2002) Econometric analysis of cross-section and panel data. MIT Press, Cambridge, MA

Yoder R (1989) Are people willing and able to pay for health services? Soc Sci Med 29(1):35–42

Part II
The Impact of Institutions, Aid, Inflation and FDI on Economic Growth

Chapter 4
The Impact of Institutions on Economic Growth in Sub-Saharan Africa: Evidence from a Panel Data Approach

Kokeb G. Giorgis

Abstract This study sheds light on the effect of institutional variables on economic growth in sub-Saharan African countries. It empirically analyzes the impact of institutional quality proxied by control for corruption, government effectiveness, and protection of the property right index among others on economic growth in sub-Saharan African countries during the sample period 1996–2012. The sample consisted of 21 sub-Saharan African countries. The methodology is based on first-differenced GMM estimator proposed by Arellano and Bond (Rev Econ Stud 58(2):277–297, 1991) for dynamic panel data, which is robust for taking care of individual fixed effects, heteroskedasticity, and auto-correlation in the presence of endogenous covariates. The results of this study indicate that improving institutional quality, specifically protecting property rights on average had a positive contribution to growth in output per capita in the sampled countries though its effect was small. However, institutional variables such as control for corruption and government effectiveness had a positive effect on growth though they were statistically insignificant. These findings agree with some of the studies conducted so far on the effect of institutions on growth.

Keywords Economic growth · Institutions · Panel data · GMM · Sub-Saharan Africa

4.1 Introduction

After the independence of many African countries in the 1950s and 1960s there was a widely held expectation that poor countries in Africa would 'catch up,' that is, converge in per capita income terms with developed countries. However, this was confirmed to be an unrealistic expectation as more than half a century after independence the continent is still the poorest in the world by any standard where more

K.G. Giorgis (✉)
Department of Economics, Addis Ababa University, Addis Ababa, Ethiopia
e-mail: kokebgg@gmail.com

A. Heshmati (ed.), *Studies on Economic Development and Growth in Selected African Countries*, Frontiers in African Business Research,
DOI 10.1007/978-981-10-4451-9_4

than a quarter of its population is estimated to be food-insecure. Achieving high and persistent economic growth is a prerequisite to decreasing widespread poverty yet for long years after independence most of the African countries have failed to achieve even moderate economic growth rates. It is only in the last eight years or so that African countries have started recording a moderate growth rate. So the puzzle is why unlike other countries in the world, the African continent and other poor countries in the world are still poor whereas some others are at the top of the per capita income ladder?

As there is a dearth and incompleteness of macroeconomic and institutional data for sub-Saharan Africa, it is motivating to investigate the determinants of Africa's poor economic growth record. Since the 1990s, with increasing data availability, cross-country regression analyses have indicated that the 'classical determinants of growth' such as level of technology, international trade, availability of natural resources or population have not fully explained the poor performance of growth in many poor countries. During the last 20 years or so, growth economists have increasingly referred to institutions as answers to the long-standing question concerning what determines economic growth.

There are two rationales for our study. First, studies which assess the effect of institutions on economic growth in developing countries and particularly in sub-Saharan Africa are limited and inadequate even though theoretically the importance of institutions affecting growth is getting more emphasis. A paper worth mentioning here is a study by Naude (2004) in sub-Saharan Africa which investigates the effect of policy, institutions, and geography on economic growth in the continent. It used panel data from 1970 to 1990 using data from 44 African countries. This study, among others, is justified by the fact that it used not one but three major indicators of institutions to achieve its objectives. Second, although few studies have been done so far on the effect of institutions on growth in developing and emerging countries, there is no consensus on which specific indicators of an institution matter the most for growth. Thus, our study also investigated institutions' indicators that are important in affecting growth in the context of Africa.

Based on literature there are two broader classifications of institutions to look to determine how institutions affect growth: an informal one represented by social capital or culture (such as work culture of the society) and formal ones such as laws or regulations. Our paper is based on the formal classification where according to North (1990) institutions are defined as follows:

> the rules of the game in a society, or more formally, the humanly devised constraints that shape human interaction … they structure incentives in human exchange, whether political, social, or economic.

By including proxy variables for institutional quality in traditional growth equations such as the Solow-Swan growth model (the neo-classical growth equation), the effect of institutions can be seen in economic growth.

As far as a proxy for institutional quality is concerned, our paper uses 'protection of property rights,' 'corruption and graft,' and 'government effectiveness.' Thus, our paper tries to investigate the determinants of Africa's poor economic growth record taking into account the effects of institutions using the Arellano-Bond GMM estimator. The regression is based on data from 21 sub-Saharan Africa countries employing panel data covering the period 1996–2012.

This paper is organized as follows: Section 4.2 provides a brief review of theoretical and empirical literature; Sect. 4.3 deals with descriptive statistics of the growth and institutional patterns in sub-Saharan Africa during the sample period; The empirical methodology is described in Sect. 4.4; and the results are presented in Sect. 4.5; Section 4.6 gives the conclusion.

4.2 Literature Review

4.2.1 Theoretical Review of Institutions Versus Growth

Growth literature uses three major theories to explain the difference in output per capita among nations. First, the neo-classical and endogenous growth theories which have long recognized that differences in output per capita in a society are intimately related to differences in the amount of human capital, physical capital, and technology that workers and firms in that country have access to. For instance, the Solow model emphasizes capital accumulation as a major driver of growth (Solow 1956) while Grossman and Helpman's (1991) theoretical model highlights the quality of capital stock to boost growth. Second, the geographic theory which explains how essential the geographic location of a country is in affecting its growth; this is linked to market access and climatic conditions. Theoretical and empirical research has so far found strong causality between geographic location and the level of income in a country. Third, the last and recent theory, deals with an institutional approach. It emphasizes the importance of institutions in affecting growth.

Institutions are often seen as providing the 'rules of the game' required to set up baseline situations for human interactions which consequently have an impact on social, economic, and political relationships in a society. Institutions include the moral, ethical, and behavioral norms of a society so as such they matter for growth and development (Nelson and Sampat 2001).

To empirically analyze the effect of institutions on economic growth, it is important to identify which types of institutions are more important in affecting economic growth. Different researchers and international organizations including the Heritage Foundation have different classifications of institutions depending on their respective objectives. According to literature, there are at least three types of institutions: political, economic, and financial. The quality of each of these types of institutions is measured through different variables. For example, the main variables of economic institutions are protection of property rights; regulation and the business freedom index; freedom in doing business; financial freedom; investment freedom; and the quality of the regulation system. The main variables for political institutions are the rule of law that contains the rule of law index, controlling corruption and corruption freedom, and other variables.

Our study used the main economic and political institutional indicators which are expected to have an impact on economic growth in the context of Africa. With this objective, the three indicators used are 'protection of property rights,' 'control of corruption,' and 'government effectiveness.'

When it comes to the extent to which institutional aspects such as property rights, incentive structures, and transaction costs affect economic growth, North (1981) was a pioneer who developed the contract and predatory theory by extending the neo-classical theory to include institutional variables. The contract theory states that if contracts are well enforced, then they contribute beneficially to the efficiency of business and society. If a state provides the legal framework that reduces transaction costs in the presence of some institutions, productivity and innovation increase. On the other side, the predatory theory treats the state as a vehicle for collecting monopolistic rents and transferring the resources among different groups in order to maximize incomes.

4.2.2 Empirical Review of Institutions Versus Growth

How important institutions are in promoting growth in developing and emerging economies has sparked renewed interest in recent years. As a result, a growing literature seeks to determine the extent to which institutions (economic or/and political institutions) affect growth. However, the dearth and limitations of both institutional and macroeconomic data for many developing countries including those in sub-Saharan Africa prevent robust policy interpretations on a country-by-country basis.

A study by Hall and Jones (1999) focused on explaining the enormous differences in per capita incomes among countries. Their empirical findings suggest that differences in capital accumulation, productivity, and ultimately in per capita income are due to differences in institutions and government policies. The authors also argue that controlling for endogeneity of institutions and government policies' long-run economic performance is primarily determined by social infrastructure, which depends on differences in capital accumulation and productivity.

Rodrik et al. (2004) empirically investigated the contribution of institutions, geography, and trade on differences in per capita incomes across countries. Their study found that the effect of institutions was higher compared to the effects of geography and trade in explaining differences in per capita incomes across countries.

Redek and Sušjan (2005) using panel data from 1995 to 2002 based on 24 transition economies in the then eastern socialist economies of Europe examined the effect of institutional quality proxied by private property protection, legal system, regulation, government intervention, and international relations drawn from the Heritage Foundation index. Their study confirmed that the better the protection and regulation of property rights, the lower the fiscal burden and the higher the growth. That is, as institutional quality increased by 1%, the government's fiscal burden decreased by 0.03%. Similarly, Naude (2004) sheds light on the same objective, but this time using data from 44 African countries and employing both single-year cross-section data and panel data covering the period 1970–90. For comparative purposes, the study used different econometric estimation methods including a dynamic Arellano-Bond GMM estimator. Moreover, the study used three proxies for institutional quality (ethno-linguistic heterogeneity (ELH), corruption and graft and the incidence of revolutions and coups) as proxies. Based on the GMM estimator, the author concluded that none of these had a significant impact on growth but supported Acemoglu et al.'s (2001) 'reversal of fortune' thesis, namely that settler mortality (instrumenting for the quality of institutions) is inversely related to economic growth.

Likewise, a study by Valeriani and Peluso (2011) analyzed the impact of institutions on economic growth and examined whether the eventual impact differed depending on the level of development in a country. They used panel data from 1950 to 2009 for 181 countries (both developing and developed) through a pooled regression model and a fixed effects model. They employed institutional indicators of civil liberties, number of veto players, and quality of government and found that institutional quality impacted economic growth in a positive way. This was true for all three institutional indicators that were examined. The only difference between how developing and developed countries were affected by institutional quality was the size of the impact and not in the direction of it. On a more specific level, out of the three institutional indicators, improved civil liberties had a greater effect on economic growth in developing countries, whereas the number of veto players assumed more importance for developed countries' economies.

With a similar objective, a study by Dushko et al. (2011) used cross-country data from 212 groups of countries and geographic regions and applied different econometric models (OLS, G2SLS, 2SLS). It used the rule of law, revolutions, and Freedom House ratings as well as war casualties as indicators of institutional quality. Their study found that in all the models used, institutional quality had a positive and significant effect in enhancing GDP per capita on average for the sampled countries during the study period.

Acemoglu and Robinson (2010) investigated whether political or economic institutions should be given primacy. Even though their study emphasized that differences in prosperity across countries were due to differences in economic institutions, it also underscored that without building strong political institutions it was not possible to build strong economic institutions which could facilitate growth because economic institutions are the outcome of a political process. Hence, the study deduced that solving the problem of development entailed understanding what instruments can be used to push a society from a bad to a good political equilibrium.

Unlike Acemoglu and Robinson's (2010) study, Glaeser et al.'s (2004) study had the objective of exploring the causal link between institutions and growth. It confirmed that rather than political institutions, human capital had a causal effect on economic growth. Importantly, in that framework, institutions did not directly affect growth.

In general, the empirical literature discussed here indicates positive relationships between the different indicators of institutional quality and cross-country income differences. This means that better institutions foster long-run economic growth, and countries with better institutions have higher per capita income levels. But it is also important to stress that all indicators of institutional variables are not equally important for countries at different levels of development. Moreover, it is also clear from the reviewed literature that there is a dearth of studies on the effect of institutions on growth in general and in sub-Saharan Africa in particular. There is also a lack of consensus on which economic or political indicators of institutions are important in affecting growth and hence per capita income differences among countries.

4.3 Descriptive Statistics of Economic Growth and Institutional Quality in Sub-Saharan Africa

Our sample consists of 21 sub-Saharan African countries. It excludes countries such as Somalia, Eritrea, and others due to missing or incomplete data on one or more of the variables of interest. Mainly data on institutional variables such as protection of property rights, controlling corruption, and government effectiveness were incomplete for a number of countries in the sample region. The sampled countries are Burkina Faso, Botswana, Cameron, Ethiopia, Ghana, Guinea, Kenya, Lesotho, Mozambique, Mauritania, Mauritius, Malawi, Namibia, Niger, Nigeria, Rwanda, Senegal, Chad, Togo, Uganda, and South Africa.

Period average growth in per capita was near 2.6% with substantial differences across countries; this difference was due to internal or external factors (Table 4.1). During 1996–2012 on average, the sampled countries experience a real GDP growth rate of 5.16%, where growth in these countries intensified in the last five years. Table 4.1 also shows that the gross capital formation as a percentage of GDP was around 21%.

Table 4.1 Summary of explanatory variables (1996–2012)

Variable	Mean	Std. dev.	Min.	Max.
GDP (million USD)	2938.85	5010.85	1062.11	307,313
GDP growth rate (%)	5.16	4.14	−9.52	33.74
GDP per capita	1291.57	1757.25	128.24	6683.66
GDP per capita growth rate (%)	2.55	3.95	−12.18	30.344
Gross capital formation as % of GDP	21.14	8.37	5.46	74.82
Government spending % GDP	15.22	6.90	3.86	39.50
FDI_GDP as % of GDP	0.23	0.20	0.004	1.31
Gross enrollment rate/schooling	36.0	25.0	2.22	101.89

Source Author's calculations based on World Bank data

Table 4.2 Descriptive statistics for measures of institutional quality

Variable		Mean	Std. dev	Min	Max
Control of corruption	Overall	38.91	22.34	1.46	85.85
	Between		21.48	10.03	78.48
	Within		7.65	13.98	68.39
Protection of property rights	Overall	40.57	14.91	10	75
	Between		13.09	23.52	70.29
	Within		7.66	19.40	65.2
Government effectiveness	Overall	37.36	20.71	2.42	79.02
	Between		19.78	7.82	72.1
	Within		7.42	15.98	62.9

Source Author's calculations based on World Bank data

Table 4.2 shows that the average measures of institutional quality for the study period were not greater than 40% implying that sub-Saharan African countries had poor quality institutions. One can also see that there was a huge difference between the sampled countries. For example, regarding controlling corruption the minimum figure is 10% while the maximum is around 78% which shows that there was a clear difference among countries in the region concerning controlling corruption; this was also true for the other two variables.

Figure 4.1 shows the index for control of corruption proposed by the World Governance Indicators (WGI) of the World Bank which could serve as a proxy for a country's level of institutional development. It indicates the degree of corruption within a given political system by taking into consideration financial corruption (import and export licenses, exchange controls, tax assessments, or police protection), as well as the following forms of corruption: patronage, nepotism, job reservations, 'favor-for-favors,' and secret party funding. On average, for the

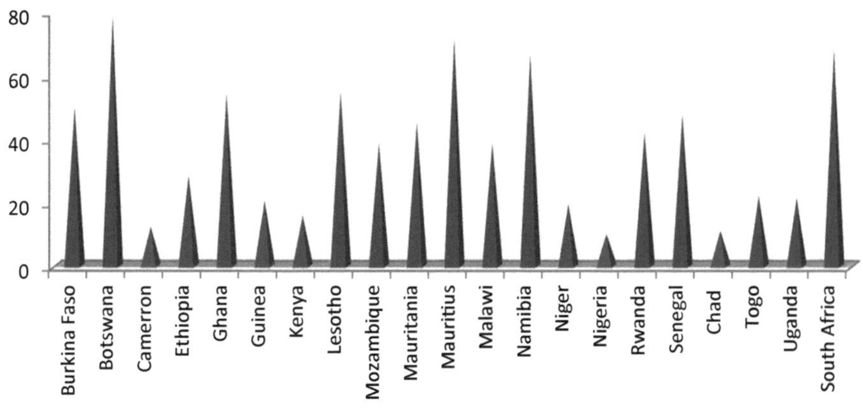

Fig. 4.1 Rank of sub-Saharan African countries by average control of corruption (1996–2012). *Source* Author's calculations based on WGI data, the World Bank

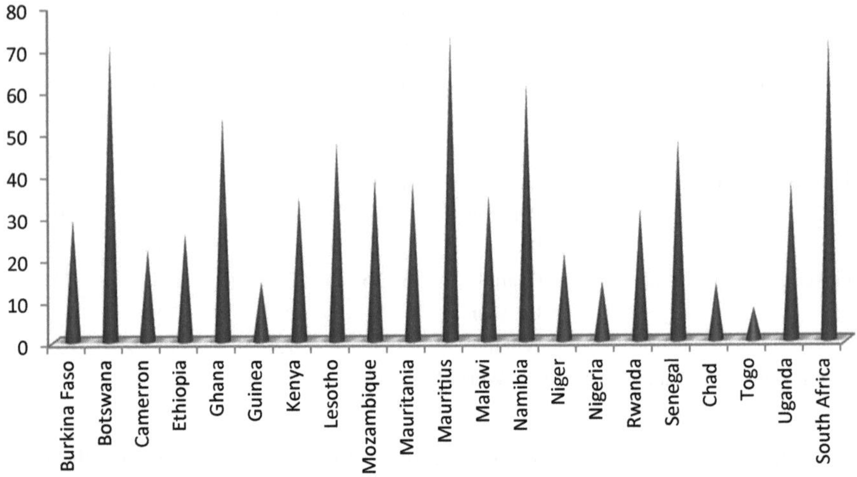

Fig. 4.2 Average rank of Sub-Saharan African countries by government effectiveness (1996–2012). *Source* Author's calculations based on WGI data, the World Bank

sample period, the worse corruption was in Nigeria, Niger, Chad, Cameroon, and Kenya while Botswana, South Africa, Mauritius, and Namibia had relative control over corruption.

Another proxy for institutional development is the quality of government policies which is analyzed through WGI's government effectiveness index. This is a multi-dimensional index which reflects both the quality of public services and of civil services. It accounts for the quality of policies formulated and implemented, for political pressures and also for the government's credibility. The country with the lowest level of government effectiveness was Togo, followed by Chad and Nigeria. South Africa and Botswana registered the highest average on the government effectiveness index during 1996–2012 (Fig. 4.2).

Figure 4.3 shows the average percentage of protection of property rights for the sampled countries in the study period. Botswana and Mauritius were relatively better in the protection of property rights. Rwanda, Chad, and Togo showed poor performance.

4.4 Data and Methodology

Following North (1981) our paper assesses the effect of institutions on economic growth. For this, one can incorporate a proxy for institutions in the neo-classical growth model. To do so we started with the aggregate production function which describes how inputs (labor, physical and human capital, and technology) are combined to produce the output:

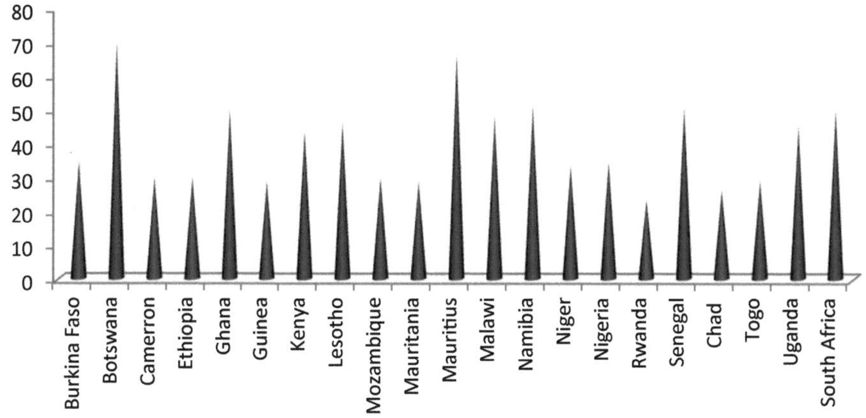

Fig. 4.3 Average rank of protection of property right for sub-Saharan African countries (1996–2012) (%). *Source* Author's calculations based on WGI data, the World Bank

$$Y_{it} = A_t K_t^{\theta} H_t^{\beta} L_t^{1-\theta-\beta} \tag{4.1}$$

where Y is output, H is human capital, L is labor and the parameter A represents the level of technology in the economy, and K is physical capital. Where human capital is the knowledge, skills, and abilities of people who are or who may be involved in the production process while the labor force is the number of people who are able to work. Rewriting Eq. 4.1 in per capita form yields:

$$y_{it} = A_t k_t^{\theta} h_t^{\beta} \tag{4.2}$$

Traditional macroeconomic growth models implicitly assumed an underlying set of good institutions. Hence, they did not take into account the influence of institutional quality as a factor of economic growth. However, the fact that institutions have an important role in the growth process makes economists try to implement institutional quality in growth models. Thus,

$$A_t = A_0 k_t^{\propto_1 (I-I^*)} h_t^{\propto_2 (I-I^*)} \tag{4.3}$$

where A_0 represents the basic level of technology, I^* and I denote the best-quality institutions and the country's current level of institutional quality, respectively. The traditional growth model considers that economies function close to best-quality institutions hence in these models $I = I^*$. This reduces the effect of institutional quality to zero. However, since North (1981) more recent growth theories recognize the importance of institutions. Accordingly, the mathematical statement, $I - I^*$, measures the degree to which a country's institutions fall short of the best conditions.

Therefore, substituting Eq. 4.3 in the equation on the production function per worker, and rewriting it, gives the following:

$$y_{it} = A_0 k_t^{\theta + \alpha_1 (I - I^*)} h_t^{\beta + \alpha_2 (I - I^*)} \tag{4.4}$$

To study the dynamic of output per capita, taking the log of Eq. 4.4 and a derivative with respect to time (t) and rearranging it gives the following:

$$\frac{\Delta y_t}{y_t} = \frac{\Delta A_0}{A_0} + [(\theta - \alpha_1 I^*) + \alpha_1 I]\frac{\Delta k_t}{k_t} + [(\beta - \alpha_2 I^*) + \alpha_2 I]\frac{\Delta h_t}{h_t}$$

$$\text{Let } \pi_0 = \frac{\Delta A_0}{A_0}, \quad \pi_1 = \theta - \alpha_1 I^*, \quad \pi_2 = \beta - \alpha_2 I^*, \quad \pi_3 = \alpha_1 \frac{\Delta k_t}{k_t} + \alpha_2 \frac{\Delta h_t}{h_t} \tag{4.5}$$

and adding an error term ε gives growth rate of output per capita as follows:

$$\frac{\Delta y_t}{y_t} = \pi_0 + \pi_1 \frac{\Delta k_t}{k_t} + \pi_2 \frac{\Delta h_t}{h_t} + \pi_3 \Delta I + \varepsilon \tag{4.6}$$

The coefficient estimates for π_1 and π_2 measure the return to physical and human capital investments, while coefficient π_3 measures an increasing return to physical and human capital investments as the country's institutional quality improves. Therefore, Eq. 4.6 is used to test the impact of institutions on growth where π_3 measures the effect of a change in institutional quality on growth through a change in the productivity of both human and physical capital.

To investigate the impact of institutions on economic growth, we used the first-differenced GMM estimator proposed by Arellano and Bond (1991) for dynamic panel data. Thus, Eq. 4.6 can further be rewritten in dynamic panel specification as follows:

$$\ln \mathrm{GDP}_{it} = \mu_0 + \mu_1 \ln \mathrm{GDP}_{i,t-1} + \mu_2 I_{i,t} + \mu_3 \ln X_{i.t} + \eta_i + \varepsilon_{i,t} \tag{4.7}$$

where, $\frac{1}{y_t} = w \ln \mathrm{GDP}_{it}$ represents the natural logarithm of real GDP per capita expressed in constant 2000 US$ for country i at time t and hence $\frac{\Delta y_t}{y_t}$ is the growth rate of GDP per capita as discussed earlier. $\boldsymbol{I}_{i,t}$ stands for the institutional variables for country i at time t (controlling of corruption, government effectiveness, and protection of property rights). $\boldsymbol{X}_{i.t}$ represents both physical and human capital variables as discussed earlier and other macroeconomic control variables. η_i signifies the individual fixed effects specific to each country, and it is constant in time. $\varepsilon_i \sim N(0,\sigma^2)$ is a random disturbance term.

Using the OLS method for estimating, Eq. 4.7 raises several concerns. First, the presence of the lagged dependent variable ln $\mathrm{GDP}_{i,t-1}$, which is correlated with the fixed effects η_i, gives rise to a dynamic panel bias (Nickell 1981). The coefficient estimate for lagged ln GDP is inflated by attributing a predictive power that actually belongs to the country's fixed effects. Moreover, it is clear that estimating a panel data model with a lagged dependent variable will lead to biased results at least in small samples with a small time period (Judson and Owen 1999).

Therefore, the alternative solution is to use the generalized method of moments (GMM) developed by Arellano and Bond (1991). It is an efficient estimator for dynamic panels. It is popular in the context of empirical growth research as it allows relaxing some of the OLS assumptions. The Arellano and Bond estimator corrects endogeneity in the lagged dependent variable and provides consistent estimates. Moreover, it allows auto-correlation and heteroskedasticity among others (Roodman 2006).

The first step of the GMM procedure is to differentiate Eq. 4.7 to remove individual effects, that is, η_i which gives the following:

$$\Delta \ln \mathrm{GDP}_{it} = \mu_1 \Delta \ln \mathrm{GDP}_{i,t-1} + \mu_2 \Delta I_{i,t} + \mu_3 \Delta \ln X_{i.t} + \Delta\varepsilon_{i,t} \tag{4.8}$$

In the differenced Eq. 4.8, we still have a correlation between $\Delta\varepsilon_{i,t}$ and $\Delta \ln \mathrm{GDP}_{i,t-1}$, which could be addressed by instrumenting $\Delta \ln \mathrm{GDP}_{i,t-1}$. Finding a valid external instrument is very difficult; hence, GMM draws instruments from within the dataset, that is, lagged values of the dependent and independent variables in case of endogeneity. Thus, the GMM procedure gains efficiency compared to OLS by exploiting additional moment restrictions.

The regression outputs from Eq. 4.7 are short-term estimates in the context of economic growth. Since the effect of different factors should be evaluated in the long run, it is also vital to compute the long-run coefficients. Hence, transforming Eq. 4.7 yields the following:

$$\Delta \ln \mathrm{GDP}_{it} = -\omega(\ln \mathrm{GDP}_{i,t-1} - \rho_2 I_{i,t} + \rho_3 \ln X_{i.t}) + \eta_i + \varepsilon_{i,t} \tag{4.9}$$

where $\omega = (1 - \mu_1)$ and $\rho_j = \left(\frac{\mu_j}{1-\omega}\right), j = 2, 3$.

According to Neuhaus (2006), in Eq. 4.9 the brackets show the long-term relationship among the variables and ρ_j are long-term coefficients of the model. ω is the speed of adjustment to the long-term value and $-\omega$ is the error correction coefficient denoting adjustment of the system of variables to the state of long-run equilibrium (Neuhaus 2006).

As a general estimation strategy, we first estimated a baseline equation containing the lagged GDP levels and the classical growth determinants: gross fixed capital formation (as a percentage of GDP) and trade openness (expressed in terms of exports as a percentage of GDP) which are expected to have a significant positive contribution to growth. In the second model institutional variables (protection of property rights, controlling of corruption and government effectiveness), and gross enrollment as a proxy for human capital, which is expected to have a positive contribution to growth are included. Finally, Model 3 is tested for robustness by introducing one control variable, the general government final consumption expenditure as a percentage of GDP.

Table 4.3 Variables used in the regression analysis

Variable	Description	Source
GDP	Real GDP per capita in constant 2000 US$	The World Bank
GFCF	Gross Fix Capital formation as % in GDP	The World Bank
Trade	Trade openness as % in GDP	The World Bank
Corrupt	Controlling of corruption	WGI
Govef	Government effectiveness	WGI
Pright	Protection of property rights	WGI
Schooling	Gross enrollment rate	World Bank
Gcons	General government final consumption expenditure (% of GDP)	World Bank

First, Eq. 4.8 is estimated using the Arellano-Bond first difference GMM estimator to get the short-run coefficients. Second, the long-run coefficients and the error correction term are computed and tested for its significance using the Wald test. The short-term equations correspond to Model 1 to Model 3 in Table 4.4, while the corresponding long-term equations (Model 1 to Model 3) are given in (Table 4.5).

Finally, to test the consistency of the GMM estimator, checking the validity of the moment conditions is required which can be done using two specification tests: the Hansen test which is a test for over-identifying restrictions and the joint null hypothesis (the instruments are valid) and the Arellano-Bond test for no second-order serial correlation in the error term. To ascertain the consistency of the estimator both the tests are applied.

Table 4.3 represents the various macroeconomic variables and national accounts data. To capture institutional quality, we used some of the vital indicators from the WGI database: controlling of corruption, government effectiveness, and protection of property rights. The dependent variable is represented by real GDP per capita in 21 sub-Saharan African countries. The analyzed period is 1996–2012, covering a series of financial and economic crises.

4.5 Empirical Results

As can be seen from short-run estimates in Table 4.4, Model 1 is the baseline equation where besides the lagged level of GDP, we also introduce classical growth determinants such as gross fixed capital formation and trade openness as a percentage of GDP (export to GDP ratio). Both the lagged levels of GDP and exports to the GDP ratio have the expected signs and are significant while gross fixed capital formation has an unexpected negative sign.

An increase in trade openness (exports as a percentage of GDP) by 1% will raise GDP per capita by 0.093%. The gross fixed capital formation (as a percentage of

Table 4.4 Institutions and economic growth—short-run estimations Dependent variable: Real per capita GDP (logarithm)

Regressors	Model 1	Model 2	Model 3
L.lngdpc	0.156*** (0.059)	0.132** (0.065)	0.106** (0.058)
lnGFCF	−0.067*** (0.018)	−0.07*** (0.018)	−0.063*** (0.023)
lnTrade	0.093** (0.027)	0.107*** (0.027)	0.113*** (0.027)
lnschooling		0.003 (0.016)	−0.003 (0.014)
Government effectiveness		0.001 (0.001)	0.0004 (0.002)
Controlling of corruption		−0.0001 (0.001)	−0.0002 (0.0008)
Property rights		0.003*** (0.001)	0.002*** (0.001)
lnGovernmentConsumption			−0.089** (0.051)
N	315	315	315
No. of instruments	75	79	80
Hansen *j* statistic (*p* value)	0.122	0.476	0.357
Serial correlation test AR2 (*p* value)	0.839	0.901	0.563

Note
Robust standard errors in brackets
*, ** and *** denote significance levels of 10, 5 and 1%
Dependent variable: Real per capita GDP (logarithm)
N represents the number of panel observations
Method used is Arellano and Bond's (1991) first difference GMM
Instruments, Arrelano-Bond type: the dependent variable from lags 2 to 5. Standard instruments: the level of all other regressors
The Hansen test reports the validity of the instrumental variables test. The null hypothesis is that the instruments are not correlated with the residuals (for robust estimations Stata reports the Hansen *j* statistic instead of the Sargan test)
For the Arellano-Bond test, the null hypothesis is that of no serial correlation between residuals

GDP) is negatively related to GDP per capita because of the crowding out effect—in this case, domestic investments are much more important than public investments. On a similar basis, if we look at the long-run estimates (Table 4.5 Model 1) an increase in trade openness by 1% will raise GDP per capita by 0.11%, moreover, a 1% increase in the gross fixed capital formation will reduce GDP per capita by 0.08%. Further, the catch-up term has the expected negative sign, and it is statistically significant.

In Table 4.4, Model 2, the proxy for institutional quality such as the index for controlling of the corruption, the government effectiveness index, and index for protection of property rights have been added to the classical growth determinants to see the effect of institutions on economic growth. The results show that the index

Table 4.5 Institutions and economic growth—long-run estimations Dependent variable: Real per capita GDP (logarithm)

Regressors	Model 1	Model 2	Model 3
L.lngdpc (Convergence.Coefficient)	−0.844*** (0.059)	−0.868*** (0.065)	−0.894*** (0.058)
lnGFCF	−0.079** (0.036)	−0.081** (0.041)	−0.071** (0.034)
lnTrade	0.110** (0.053)	0.123*** (0.027)	0.126*** (0.035)
lnschooling		0.004 (0.02)	−0.003 (0.014)
Government effectiveness		0.002 (0.01)	0.0004 (0.002)
Controlling of corruption		0.002 (0.001)	−0.0002 (0.001)
Property rights		0.004*** (0.001)	0.002*** (0.001)
lnGovernmentConsumption			−0.090** (0.056)

Note
Standard errors in brackets
*, ** and *** denote significance levels of 10, 5 and 1%

for protection of property rights has a positive though the negligible impact on growth in GDP per capita. However, government effectiveness and controlling of corruption indices are not statistically significant although they have the expected sign. Similarly, the gross enrollment rate (schooling) which is a proxy for human capital, even if it is insignificant has the expected positive sign in the presence of institutions. As expected, gross fixed capital formation and trade openness remain highly significant, and the impact of gross fixed capital formation on growth even increases slightly in the presence of institutions.

From Table 4.5, Model 2, the long-term effect of the institutional variable 'protection of property rights' is slightly higher as compared to its short-run estimate, that is, it increases from 0.003 to 0.004% for a 1% increase in the quality of protection of property rights indicating that even in the long run its effects are negligible. Besides, the introduction of institutional variables slightly raises the speed of convergence to the steady state from 0.84 to 0.86.

To test the robustness of the models, we introduced one control variable, the general government final consumption expenditure (as a percentage of GDP) in Model 3 (Tables 4.4 and 4.5). The impact of institutions on growth was still significant to the introduction of the macroeconomic policy variable. The impact of corruption and government effectiveness on economic growth remained insignificant.

Two major concerns in using GMM estimators is how valid the instruments are and controlling the serial correlations of residuals. The p values obtained (see

Table 4.4) using the Hansen test indicate exogeneity of the instruments used, that is, the instrument sets were orthogonal to the regressors and were therefore valid for estimation. Similarly, to tackle the problem of the serial correlation of residuals, we needed to test auto-correlation of second order or more in the errors. Therefore, as can be seen from Table 4.4, the Arellano and Bond test confirmed the null hypothesis of the absence of second-order auto-correlation.

4.6 Conclusion

Understanding the determinants of poor growth performance in poor countries like those in Africa is vital. To understand how important institutions are in determining the growth performance of sub-Saharan Africa countries, this paper empirically analyzed the impact of institutional quality proxied by controlling of corruption, government effectiveness, and the protection of property rights index among others on economic growth in sub-Saharan African countries during the sample period 1996–2012.

The study was based on 21 sub-Saharan African countries. The methodology was based on the first-differenced GMM estimator proposed by Arellano and Bond (1991) for dynamic panel data, which is robust to take into account individual fixed effects, auto-correlation, and heteroskedasticity in the presence of endogenous covariates.

Our study indicates that lagged GDP per capita and trade openness had a significantly positive effect on the growth of real per capita GDP, while gross fixed capital formation and government consumption had negative and significant effects both in the short and long run. While human capital represented by schooling had the expected sign it was not significant. Our study also shows that out of the three institutional variables protection of property rights had a positive and significant effect on growth both in the short and long term, that is, an increase in protection of property rights by 1% increased output per capita by 0.004% at the 99% level of significance in the long term. While institutional variables such as controlling of corruption and government effectiveness had a positive effect on growth, they were statistically insignificant.

Hence, this preliminary study indicates that improving institutional quality in terms of enhancing protection of property rights on average had a positive contribution to growth in output per capita in the sampled countries though its magnitude was very small. This result agrees with some of the studies conducted so far on the effect of institutions on growth. However, it must be considered that all the empirical researches have investigated the relationship between institutions and economic growth but we still face the difficulty of getting good institutional quality indicators which is also true for this study.

References

Acemoglu D, Robinson JA (2010) Why Africa is poor? Econ Hist Dev Reg 25:21–50

Acemoglu D, Johnson S, Robinson JA (2001) The colonial origins of comparative development. Am Econ Rev 91(5):1369–1401

Arellano M, Bond S (1991) Some tests of specification for panel data: Monte Carlo evidence and an application to employment equations. Rev Econ Stud 58(2):277–297

Dushko J, Darko L, Risto F, Cane K (2011) Inst and growth revisited: OLS, 2SLS, G2SLS, Random Effects IV regression and panel fixed (within) regression with cross Country data

Glaeser E, Porta RL, Lopez-de-Silanes F, Shleifer A (2004) Do inst cause growth? J Econ Growth 9:271–303

Grossman GM, Helpman E (1991) Comparative advantage and long-run growth. Am Econ Rev 80 (4):796–815

Hall RE, Jones CI (1999) Why do some countries produce so much more output per worker than others? Quart J Econ 114:83–116

Judson R, Owen A (1999) Estimating dynamic panel data models: a guide for macroeconomists. Econ Lett 65:9–15

Naude WA (2004) The effects of policy, inst and geography on economic growth in Africa: an econometric study based on cross-section and panel data. J Int Dev 16:821–849

Nelson RR, Sampat BN (2001) Making sense of institutions as a factor shaping economic performance. J Econ Behav Organ 44:31–54

Neuhaus M (2006) The impact of FDI on economic growth. Physica-Verlag, Wurzburg

Nickell S (1981) Biases in dynamic models using fixed effects. Econometrica 49:1417–1426

North DC (1981) Structure and change in economic history. Norton, New York

North DC (1990) Inst, inst change and economic performance. Cambridge University Press, New York

Redek T, Sušjan A (2005) The impact of inst on economic growth: the case of transition economies. J Econ Issues 39(4):995–1027

Rodrik D, Subramanian A, Trebbi F (2004) Institutions rule: the primacy of inst geography and integration in economic development. J Econ Growth 9:131–165

Roodman D (2006) How to do xtabond2: an introduction to difference and system GMM in STATA. Center for Global Development, Working paper no. 103

Solow RM (1956) A contribution to the theory of economic growth. Quart J Econ 70:65–94

Valeriani E, Pelso S (2011) The impact of inst quality on economic growth and development: an empirical investigation. J Knowl Manage 6:1–25

Chapter 5
Fiscal Effects of Aid in Rwanda

Thomas Bwire, Caleb Tamwesigire and Pascal Munyankindi

Abstract This paper analyzes the dynamic relationship between foreign aid and domestic fiscal variables in Rwanda using a co-integrated vector auto-regressive model for quarterly data over the period 1990Q1–2015Q4. The results show that aid and fiscal variables form a long-run stationary relationship and that aid is a significant element of long-run fiscal equilibrium and the hypothesis of aid exogeneity is not statistically supported; anticipated aid appears to have been taken into account in budget planning. Aid is associated with increased tax efforts, public spending, and lower domestic borrowings. Aid has contributed to improved fiscal performance in Rwanda, although the slow growth in tax revenue and regular aid shortfalls has prevented sustaining a balanced budget inclusive of aid. In terms of policy, continued efforts by donors to coordinate aid delivery systems, make aid more transparent, and support improvements in government fiscal statistics will all contribute to improving fiscal planning. Recipients need to know how much aid is available to finance spending and how this is delivered, that is, whether through donor projects or government budgets.

Keywords Domestic fiscal variables · Aid · CVAR · Rwanda

JEL Classification C32 · F35 · O23 · O55

The views expressed in this paper are those of the authors. They do not necessarily represent the views of the Bank of Uganda, University of Kigali and the National Bank of Rwanda or their affiliated organizations.

T. Bwire (✉)
Bank of Uganda, Kampala, Uganda
e-mail: tbwire@bou.or.ug

C. Tamwesigire
University of Kigali, Kigali, Rwanda
e-mail: ctamwesigire@yahoo.com

P. Munyankindi
National Bank of Rwanda, Kigali, Rwanda
e-mail: pmunyankindi@bnr.rw

A. Heshmati (ed.), *Studies on Economic Development and Growth in Selected African Countries*, Frontiers in African Business Research,
DOI 10.1007/978-981-10-4451-9_5

5.1 Introduction

The underlying economic rationale for foreign aid to developing countries can be traced back to Chenery and Strout's (1966) two-gap model. In their model, investments are the cornerstone of growth, but they require domestic savings and, at least initially, imported capital goods. Low-income countries are constrained by two gaps: insufficient domestic savings to provide the resources needed for financing the level of investments required to achieve their target growth rates and insufficient foreign exchange earnings (as they are unlikely to have sufficient export earnings) to finance capital imports. As these savings and foreign exchange gaps constrain growth, capital flows (of which foreign aid is one form) are an important source of development finance (Franco-Rodriguez et al. 1998; McGillivray and Morrissey 2000) as they relax savings and foreign exchange constraints.

Aid is premised on different development constraints. However, the fact that most of the aid that is spent in a country goes to (or through) the government or finances the provision of public goods and services that would otherwise place demands on the budget (Franco-Rodriguez et al. 1998; McGillivray 1994, 2001) makes understanding its effects on central government fiscal behavior a necessary condition for its effective and successful deployment.

Fiscal response models (hereafter FRM) offer important insights into how foreign aid donors expect their efforts to impact the fiscal behavior of a recipient government. This is because the new incentives and conditions created by the addition of foreign aid to the actions of the state definitely disrupt how the state disposes of the fiscal tools of tax revenues, expenditure, and public debt, but only in uncertain ways. Aid packages come with strong pressures to spend, so there is an expectation that aid will increase spending (O'Connell et al. 2008). Moreover, reforms linked to aid conditionalities are expected to increase tax revenues and tax rates either because of influences on tax efforts or because they affect tax rates or the tax base (Morrissey 2015). Perhaps because donors' conditionality often requires recipient governments to reduce budget deficits (Adam and O'Connell 1999; McGillivray and Morrissey 2000), aid is also expected to lower domestic borrowings. However, in reality, these are general expectations and may not always hold true.

In the 10 years before 2008, the total overseas development assistance (ODA) as a share of GDP averaged 29.7% (The World Bank 2008). Over the same time, a World Bank report puts foreign direct investments and domestic savings as shares of GDP at some dismal 0.23 and −1.4%, respectively, on average.

With the new G-8 initiative on debt forgiveness and donors' increased focus on the poorest countries, the level of support to Rwanda was scaled up until 2012 when the country suffered aid suspension. During FY 2013–14, Rwanda's budget and sector support as well as project financing, grants, and loans accounted for 11.6% of GDP and 40% of government spending. This is illuminating and clearly highlights the importance of ODA in sustaining Rwanda's broad growth prospects, making it an interesting case study for the effects of foreign aid.

Studies that have investigated the effect of aid on the fiscal behavior of recipient countries are reviewed and discussed in Morrissey (2015). As echoed in Riddell (2007), the debate suggests that country-based evidence provides the only reliable backdrop for exploring aid–fiscal behavior dynamics as experiences between countries vary due to their different institutional foundations. Our paper investigates the fiscal effects of foreign aid in Rwanda using a quarterly dataset for 1990Q1–2015Q4. The advantage of quarterly data is that aid is measured by the Ministry of Finance and Economic Planning and should be closer than the donors' measurement of aid as recorded in the budget. A potential disadvantage is that this may not correspond fully with an annual budget planning cycle. Nonetheless, as shown in Bwire et al. (2016), quarterly data give qualitative results similar to what are obtained from annual data and these in general are consistent with what is known about the fiscal effects of aid.

The rest of the paper is organized as follows. Section 5.2 provides a brief literature review, while the data, econometric methodology, and aid-related hypotheses of interest are presented in Sect. 5.3. Section 5.4 discusses the empirical results. Section 5.5 gives the conclusion and policy recommendations.

5.2 Literature Review of the Fiscal Effects of Aid

There is significant empirical literature on the impact of aid on the fiscal behavior of aid recipients. A detailed review of this literature is provided in McGillivray and Morrissey (2004) and Morrissey (2015). An important distinction is made between fungibility and fiscal response studies.

Fungibility studies analyze the effects of foreign aid on the composition of government spending. Aid is said to be fungible if the recipients fail to use it in the manner intended by the donor. As presented in World Bank (1998), the underlying assumption is that donors grant aid to finance public investments as increments to the capital stock which are the principle determinants of growth; fungibility arises when recipients divert the aid to finance government consumption spending. This is undesirable because such a diversion reduces the effectiveness of aid. However, to the extent that consumption spending is a necessary complement to investment spending (recurrent spending is required to operate investments such as nurses and medicines for a healthcare center), the assumption that fungibility diminishes the effectiveness of aid may be misleading.

Analogously, fungibility is said to occur if aid intended to finance a particular sector such as health or education services that would otherwise be funded by tax revenues, release domestic resources for spending in some other sectors of the economy. In this case, fungibility arises because donors and recipients have differing expenditure allocation preferences. Evidence as to whether aid has been fungible or not and whether fungibility limits aid effectiveness is imprecise largely due to data limitations. Morrissey (2015) details the practical difficulties of directly linking aid, donor intentions, and sector spending, given the need to distinguish between on-budget and off-budget aid and the problematic classification of spending. As this is not the focus of our study, readers are referred to a more detailed discussion on this in McGillivray and Morrissey (2004).

FRMs adopt a broader approach allowing for the dynamic effect of aid on expenditure (current and capital spending), tax revenue, and domestic borrowings. The traditional framework is based on the assumption that a government maximizes utility based on a quadratic loss function subject to targets for each revenue and expenditure category (Franco-Rodriguez et al. 1998: 1242–1243). However, empirical applications of FRMs are limiting on several grounds. For example, McGillivray and Morrissey (2004) show that they are notoriously difficult to estimate and highly sensitive to data, often yielding inconsistent estimates of core parameters. Moreover, the theoretical framework does not provide a thorough representation of government behavior (e.g., there is no explanation of how the targets are determined) and does not generate specific testable hypotheses of the effect of aid on fiscal behavior (Osei et al. 2005).

In an effort to overcome these difficulties, there is now a growing body of empirical literature estimating FRM within a co-integrated vector auto-regressive (CVAR) framework. The advantage of a CVAR estimation is that the tractable framework allows formulating and testing a number of different hypotheses on causal links between aid and domestic fiscal variables. The technique takes into account interactions between variables over time, allowing a distinction in estimating long-run (equilibrium) and short-run (adjustment to the equilibrium) relations. There is one equation for each and every variable, so all variables in the system are treated as potentially endogenous and each variable is explained by its own lags and lagged values of the other variables. Assumptions about exogeneity are tested directly, avoiding the need for strong a priori assumptions; by design, the econometric model allows the data to identify the statistical relationship between variables. And it is an atheoretical approach—that is, one does not have to maintain the existence of, estimate or test specific theoretical formulations of budgetary planning targets, nor is it necessary to estimate structural parameters. Rather, economic theory is invoked to choose the variables to include in the analysis, and select the appropriate normalizations and restrictions to identify particular effects and to interpret the results.

Surveys and discussions in the literature on country-specific fiscal effects of aid using a CVAR approach are provided in Morrissey (2015). These include the first CVAR studies: Osei et al. (2005) for Ghana; Morrissey et al. (2007) for Kenya; Martins (2010) and Mascagni and Timmis (2014) for Ethiopia; and very recently Bwire et al. (2013, 2016) for Uganda. It is clear that the impact of aid is country specific, but this should not be surprising as governments differ in their fiscal behavior. Osei et al. (2005) find that for Ghana, aid is weakly exogenous to domestic fiscal variables (i.e., donors do not respond to fiscal imbalances in determining how much aid to allocate), but aid has effects on spending, domestic borrowings, and domestic tax revenues. Specifically, aid was associated with reduced domestic borrowings and increased tax revenues. They also found that recurrent spending increased more than investment spending following an increase in aid and this was not because aid was fungible but because investment spending was linked to borrowing and declined as borrowing was reduced, whereas recurrent spending was linked to tax and this increased as revenues increased.

Morrissey et al. (2007) extended this approach with official Kenyan data for 1964–2004 and estimated two relationships: the fiscal effects of aid grants and loans, and the impact of aid on growth. They found that aid grants were associated with increased spending, while loans were a response to unanticipated deficits; that is, if spending exceeded revenues (tax and grants), the government sought loans to finance the deficit. Aid grants were positively associated with growth through financing government spending, and loans were negatively associated with growth perhaps because they were associated with deficits. There was no evidence that aid affected tax revenue or that tax had an effect on growth (except indirectly via financing spending).

Martins (2010) provides a comprehensive application of the CVAR method using quarterly data for Ethiopia over 1993–2008. He finds evidence of a long-run positive relationship between aid and development spending, but not between aid and recurrent spending (hence, no evidence that aid is fungible), domestic borrowings increased in response to shortfalls in revenue (tax and grants), and there was no evidence that aid reduced tax efforts. Further, aid grants adjusted to the level of development spending.

Bwire et al. (2013, 2016) formulated a set of testable hypotheses for the fiscal effects of aid (budgetary constraints, a balanced budget, aid additionality/illusion, tax revenue displacement, and aid-domestic borrowing substitution) in Uganda within the CVAR framework on both annual and quarterly fiscal data. They found that aid was a significant element in the long-run fiscal equilibrium and did not find evidence supporting the assumption that aid was exogenous in the fiscal equilibrium. Aid was associated with increased tax efforts, lower domestic borrowings, and increased public spending. Further investigation of the long-run relation among the fiscal variables revealed support for the existence of a budget constraint and a non-balanced budget excluding aid. Mascagni and Timmis (2014) applied a CVAR analysis to Ethiopian government data over 1960–2009: Aid (grants and loans) was positively related to tax revenue; tax did not adjust to aid but aid was an adjusting variable, implying that donors rewarded Ethiopia when tax revenues were increasing. Table 5.1 presents the results of selected country-specific studies on the dynamic effect of aid.

Our study used a CVAR model to evaluate hypotheses of interest relating to the interaction of aid with domestic fiscal aggregates in Rwanda based on quarterly time series data for the period 1990Q1–2015Q4. In particular, our study evaluated if there exists a fiscal equilibrium among the fiscal variables, including aid; if aid forms part of this fiscal equilibrium relation; if donor governments do not react to fiscal disequilibrium; if donors' aid allocation is not influenced by past fiscal conditions in Rwanda; if aid does not influence the fiscal conditions in Rwanda; and it also estimates the long-run impact of aid on domestic fiscal aggregates.

Table 5.1 Results of selected studies on the dynamic impact of aid

Study	Sample	Aid measure	Aid exogeneity	Current spending	Incremental impact of aid on			
					Capital spending	Total spending	Domestic revenue	Dom. borrowing
Bwire et al. (2016)	Uganda annual data (1972–2008) Quarterly data (1997–2014)	ODA from OECD ODA from MoFPED	Not supported Not supported	n.r	n.r	++ ++	++ ++	– –
Bwire et al. (2013)	Uganda	ODA from OECD	Not supported	n.r	n.r	++	++	–
Mascagni and Timmis (2014)	Ethiopia annual data (1960–2009)	Grants loans	Aid treated as an additional source of revenue		++	++ +	+ +	n.r n.r
Martins (2010)	Ethiopia (1993Q3–2008Q2)	Grants loans	Not supported	n.r n.r	++ n.r	n.r n.r	++ n.r	? n.r
Osei et al. (2005)	Ghana (1966–1998)	ODA	Not supported	++	+	++	++	–
Morrissey et al. (2007)	Kenya (1964–2004)	Grants loans	Aid treated as an additional source of revenue	n.r n.r	n.r n.r	+ +	n.r –	n.r n.r

Note
(i) ++ (strongly positive), + (moderately positive), – (strongly negative), - (moderately negative), (insignificant)? ambiguous), n.r (not reported or cannot be inferred)
(ii) Due to differences in the measurement of aid, results are not directly comparable across the table

5.3 Data and Econometric Methodology

5.3.1 Data

Our study used quarterly time series data (1990Q1–2015Q4) in Rwandan francs reported at constant 2011 prices. Fiscal data on foreign aid, tax revenue, domestic borrowings from the banking system, and recurrent and capital government spending are from Rwanda's Ministry of Finance and Economic Planning. The non-tax revenue component of domestic revenue and other forms of borrowing are omitted from the system as we are not estimating an identity. Aid data capture total net disbursements from all donors as recorded by the government and comprises capital and budgetary grants. As this data is from fiscal authorities, it is assumed to fairly measure the actual aid known to the fiscal authorities and should be capable of affecting budget planning. Nonetheless, while this is true for all on-budget or program support, caution should be taken as an appropriate treatment of capital grants is more complicated. Some of the these grants may be on-budget such as sector projects that are known to the government, especially if matching funds are required; some may be known and influence spending allocations such as health projects that permit the government to reduce its own health spending; and some may be genuinely off-budget such as technical assistance in an area that the government would not otherwise fund and this is spent either within the donor country or under the control of the donors or that the donors retain control over project aid.

Some previous applications (Martins 2010; Morrissey 2001) have disaggregated aid into grants and loans in principal, because they may have different effects (governments prefer grants because they do not have to be repaid; loans may encourage fiscal planning for future servicing and repayment costs), so that there could be an aid aggregation bias. However, as argued in McGillivray and Morrissey (2001) and Bwire et al. (2013), in practice, such a bias is likely to be minor. Aid loans are long term, and governments currently in power are unlikely to be around when repayments are due so they could be treated as grants. Indeed, the share of aid loans/GDP fell from 4.7% through the 1990s to 3.9% in the last 15 years. Over the same time, the share of aid grants/GDP rose sharply from an average of 1.6–6.3%. Thus, capital grants are similar to budgetary grants and are treated as grant or aid in this study.

Raw data are reported in Fig. 5.1. A visual inspection of the data reveals two important features. First, levels were low and relatively persistent until the start of the 2000s after which spending and revenue followed a clear upward trend but only a slight irregular upward trend for aid. Aid was generally low during the 1990s, hitting negatives in 1994 (perhaps reflecting the genocide) but increased dramatically between 2000 and 2010. It increased erratically until 2015, dropping sharply during 2012 when the country suffered aid suspension. In terms of spending, aid was equivalent to 28.1% through the 1990s, increased steadily through the 2000s to 43.7% and averaged 30.7% over the last five years. Within years, aid tended to be highest in the fourth quarter (or sometimes the second) and this was also the case,

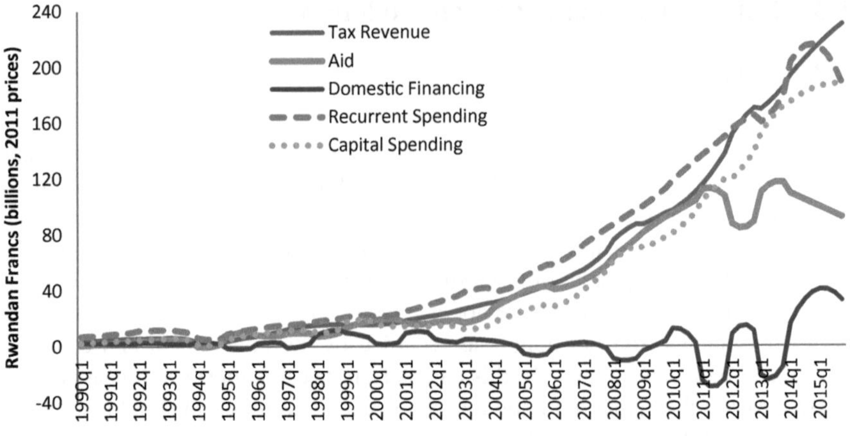

Fig. 5.1 Series in levels. *Source* Rwanda, Ministry of Finance and Economic Planning and Ministry of Finance and Economic Planning, Rwanda

but less pronounced, for tax revenue. Domestic borrowings were negative throughout most of the mid-1990s and late 2000s.

Second, all variables typically trended over time, suggesting a multiplicative rather than additive model specification which under log transformation is brought back into additive form. However, as argued in Bwire et al. (2013) and Juselius et al. (2011), such transformation is innocuous only and only if the series data points are strictly positive or are at least not too close to zero. In our study sample, log transformation of domestic borrowing series and some data points in the aid series are problematic with dire estimation consequences which perhaps make it even more undesirable. First, it obviously generates lost observations, shortening an already small sample. This alone weakens the power of the tests—making the CVAR analysis less reliable. Second, the omission of non-positive observations will be nonrandom, leading to a selection bias. And third, the trending in the data begins from the early 2000s—a shift that might be lost with log transformation.

Given this, all series are left in non-log specifications. However, while a trade-off in the choice between log and non-log specifications might matter, as we show our analysis gives results that are consistent with what is known about the fiscal impact of aid in some of the previous country-specific applications, particularly those that typically used log transformations due to trends in the variables. This in itself suggests that there is little to be gained from log over non-log specifications.

5.3.2 The Co-integrated VAR (CVAR) Model

Following Johansen's (1988) adoption of the estimation and testing of multivariate relationships among nonstationary data, vector auto-regressive (VAR) methods have become the "tool of choice" in much of time series macro-econometrics. As a reduced form representation of a large class of dynamic structural models (Hamilton 1994: 326–327), VAR offers both empirical tractability and a link between data and theory in economics.

The principal purpose of our econometric exercise is to investigate the role of aid to fiscal response in Rwanda. Therefore, the parallel between the economics and econometrics of fiscal response models is useful in assessing how aid is used in the budget. From an economic standpoint, aid can be used in the process of budget planning and/or in relaxing budget constraints. Where aid forms part of the process of budgetary planning, it may be viewed as having a long-run role, the recipient directly incorporating the level of aid in budgetary planning. In contrast, aid may simply relax budget constraints when it is received. This economic distinction corresponds to the econometric notions of the long and short run in that the process of budgetary planning defines an equilibrium relation among the fiscal variables (of which aid may be one element) and a transitory relaxation in fiscal constraints.

Accordingly, in our application where the fiscal aggregates are likely to be nonstationary and co-integrated, it is convenient to couch the empirical analysis in a CVAR framework. To facilitate interpretation of the potentially complex dynamic interactions among the fiscal variables, it is convenient to express CVAR in its error the variables adjust over time. This is given by:

$$\Delta \mathbf{x}_t = -\boldsymbol{\Pi}\mathbf{x}_{t-1} + \sum_{i=1}^{p-1} \boldsymbol{\Gamma}_i \Delta \mathbf{x}_{t-i} + \boldsymbol{\Psi}\mathbf{d}_t + \boldsymbol{\varepsilon}_t \tag{5.1}$$

where $\mathbf{x}_t$ is a $(n \times 1)$ vector of jointly determined variables at most integrated of order 1, $I(1)$, $\boldsymbol{\Gamma}_\mathbf{i}$ is a $(p \text{ x } p)$ matrix of short-run adjustment coefficients, $i = 1, \ldots,$ $(p - 1)$ is the number of lags included in the system, Δ is a first difference operator, $\mathbf{d}_t$ is a $(q \times 1)$ vector of deterministic terms (such as constants, linear trends, and dummies), and $\boldsymbol{\varepsilon}_t$ is a $(n \times 1)$ vector of errors with standard properties. Each of the $(n \times n)$ matrices $\boldsymbol{\Gamma}_i = (-\boldsymbol{\Pi}_{i+1})$ and $\boldsymbol{\Pi} = (\mathbf{I} - \boldsymbol{\Pi}_1 - \cdots - \boldsymbol{\Pi}_p)$ comprises coefficients estimated by Johansens's (1988) maximum likelihood procedure using a $(t = 1, \ldots T)$ sample of data.

Providing, as expected, some of the variables in $\mathbf{x}_t$ are nonstationary, $\boldsymbol{\Pi}$ has a reduced rank. This allows $\boldsymbol{\Pi}$ to be formulated as the hypothesis of co-integration:

$$\boldsymbol{\Pi} = \boldsymbol{\alpha}\boldsymbol{\beta}' \tag{5.2}$$

where $\boldsymbol{\alpha}$ and $\boldsymbol{\beta}$ are both $(n \times r)$, and r is the rank of $\boldsymbol{\Pi}$ corresponding to the number of linearly independent relationships among the variables in $\mathbf{x}_t$. The fiscal equilibrium thought of as the statistical analogue of the budgetary equilibrium in fiscal response models is defined by the parameters in $\boldsymbol{\beta}$. It follows then that $\boldsymbol{\beta}'\boldsymbol{x}_{t-1}$ measures the extent to which the budget is out of equilibrium and $\boldsymbol{\alpha}$ measures the long-run rate at which each of the variables adjusts to restore the equilibrium. Coefficients in the $\boldsymbol{\Gamma}_\mathbf{i}$ matrices allow short-run adjustment in each of the variables to differ from that given by their long-run rates (defined by the coefficients in $\boldsymbol{\alpha}$) and hence, potentially at least, accommodate a wide range of dynamic responses.

5.3.3 Model Specification and Hypothesis Testing

The VECM in Eq. (5.1) is particularly attractive in the current context, since it provides a natural framework in which parallels between the economics and econometrics of fiscal response models can be exploited. Specifically, the framework not only facilitates a statistical investigation of the role of aid in the budgets of recipient countries but also shows whether fiscal conditions in recipient countries affect aid-allocation behavior in donor countries. Because these economic hypotheses of interest represent parameter restrictions within VECM, they can be evaluated formally. In what follows, these economic issues of interest are set out as a number of key propositions.

As discussed earlier, insofar as aid represents an injection of foreign finance, it relaxes budget constraints. Aid allocated for financing debt or domestic consumption is unlikely to achieve longer term effects on the budget, in which case the impact of aid will be confined to the short run. In contrast, where aid is used as a source of investment for development projects such as health care or infrastructure, there may be more long-term effects on the budget as such investments spawn further spending (*aid illusion*) or increased tax revenues. Since development projects of this sort are likely to have come about as a result of aid's incorporation into the process of budgetary planning, it is convenient to think of the aid's long-run effects and its incorporation into budgetary planning synonymously. Clearly, whether aid is anticipated or not has a decisive bearing on the uses to which it is put and thus the (short and/or long run) effects that it has.

The economic distinction between short and long run ties in neatly with the VECM's econometric formulation which in turn offers insights into the role of aid in an empirical setting. The correspondence between the economics and econometrics of aid in fiscal response is central to our paper, since it provides the basis for the empirical testing of a range of economic hypotheses relating to the effects that aid has in developing countries.

5.3.3.1 Formulating Aid Hypotheses

As can be deduced from the discussion earlier, the co-integrating relation is the statistical analogue of the budgetary equilibrium in fiscal response models. Hence, the fiscal response theory predicts the presence of a single co-integrating relation (i.e., a stationary linear combination of the variables in $\mathbf{x}_t$) such that β is an $n \times 1$ vector, the coefficients of which quantify the budgetary equilibrium. Of course, this presupposes that all variables in $\mathbf{x}_t$ are integrated of order 1, [$I(1)$]. Where a variable is $I(0)$, it will form a stationary linear combination with itself, so that there can exist at most n of these stationary linear combinations; $n = r$ implies that all variables are $I(0)$. As Johansen (1992) demonstrates, each of the r columns of α corresponds to the r rows of β', so that inference on the number of co-integrating vectors (nonzero rows in β') can be evaluated by hypothesis testing on the adjustment coefficients (nonzero columns in α) using likelihood ratio methods. Specifically, standard tests for co-integration are equivalent to testing that the α_i's are insignificantly small for $r = 1, \ldots n$. This leads us to the first set of *co-integration hypothesis* tests, which amount to zero restrictions on each of the n columns of α in Eq. (5.2): $H_c(r)$: $\alpha_r = 0$, where $r = 1, \ldots n$.

To assist the exposition, consider a VAR (5.2) in VECM form with unrestricted constant partitioned conformably as mentioned earlier:

$$\begin{bmatrix} \Delta\mathbf{x}_{1t} \\ \Delta\mathbf{x}_{2t} \end{bmatrix} = \begin{bmatrix} \boldsymbol{\alpha}_{11} & \boldsymbol{\alpha}_{12} \\ \boldsymbol{\alpha}_{21} & \boldsymbol{\alpha}_{22} \end{bmatrix} \begin{bmatrix} \boldsymbol{\beta}'_{11} & \boldsymbol{\beta}'_{12} \\ \boldsymbol{\beta}'_{21} & \boldsymbol{\beta}'_{22} \end{bmatrix} \begin{bmatrix} \mathbf{x}_{1t-1} \\ \mathbf{x}_{2t-1} \end{bmatrix} + \begin{bmatrix} \boldsymbol{\Gamma}_{11} & \boldsymbol{\Gamma}_{12} \\ \boldsymbol{\Gamma}_{21} & \boldsymbol{\Gamma}_{22} \end{bmatrix} \begin{bmatrix} \Delta\mathbf{x}_{1t-1} \\ \Delta\mathbf{x}_{2t-1} \end{bmatrix} + \boldsymbol{\Psi}\mathbf{d}_t + \begin{bmatrix} \boldsymbol{\varepsilon}_{1t} \\ \boldsymbol{\varepsilon}_{2t} \end{bmatrix} \tag{5.3}$$

$\boldsymbol{\alpha}$ and $\boldsymbol{\beta}$ are partitioned by a co-integrating vector such that $\boldsymbol{\beta}'$ is divided by row into two subsets of co-integrating vectors $\boldsymbol{\beta}_1'$ and $\boldsymbol{\beta}_2'$ which are themselves partitioned by a variable in the same way as $\mathbf{x}_t$. Thus, $\boldsymbol{\alpha}_1$ and $\boldsymbol{\alpha}_2$ load each of the subsets of co-integrating vectors into each equation for correction. We assume that $\boldsymbol{\beta}_1'$ represents the budgetary equilibrium so that $\boldsymbol{\beta}_2'$ (and $\boldsymbol{\alpha}_2 = [\boldsymbol{\alpha}_{12}:\boldsymbol{\alpha}_{22}]$) will be a null matrix unless aid (or other variable(s)) is $I(0)$. Where aid is found to be $I(0)$, it cannot belong to the fiscal equilibrium relationship, and thus, its principal role is to relax budget constraints and may be indicative of countries where aid is too small to be included in the process of budget planning or the case that aid is diverted away from investment purposes for other reasons.

Proposition I (The existence of a fiscal equilibrium) *Evaluation of Proposition I is by $H_c(1)$ and is confirmed by $\boldsymbol{\alpha}_{11} = \boldsymbol{\alpha}_{21} \neq 0$ and $\boldsymbol{\alpha}_{12} = \boldsymbol{\alpha}_{22} = 0$ using co-integration tests. All variables in $\mathbf{x}_t$ are tested for the order of integration, but within a multivariate framework after estimation of Eq. (5.3). Where the result from testing $H_c(r)$ suggests two (or more) stationary linear combinations of the data, the stationarity of variables in $\mathbf{x}_t$ (such as aid) may account for it. As trivial stationary linear combinations, they are of no economic interest, and we confine them to $\boldsymbol{\beta}_2'$ before removing them from the model. This is achieved by transferring any stationary variables from $\mathbf{x}_t$ to $\mathbf{d}_t$, so that the former contains only those variables germane to the long run. Adjusting the dimensions of $\mathbf{x}_t$, $\Delta\mathbf{x}_t$, and $\mathbf{d}_t$ accordingly yields:*[1]

[1]Where variables are found to be $I(0)$ Rahbek and Mosconi (1999) suggest a tractable modification to ensure that the limiting distributions of the co-integration test statistics are invariant to the presence of the stationary regressors included in $\mathbf{d}_t$.

$$\begin{bmatrix} \Delta \mathbf{x}_{1t} \\ \Delta \mathbf{x}_{2t} \end{bmatrix} = \begin{bmatrix} \alpha_{11} \\ \alpha_{21} \end{bmatrix} \begin{bmatrix} \boldsymbol{\beta}'_{11} & \boldsymbol{\beta}'_{12} \end{bmatrix} \begin{bmatrix} \mathbf{x}_{1t-1} \\ \mathbf{x}_{2t-1} \end{bmatrix} + \begin{bmatrix} \boldsymbol{\Gamma}_{11} & \boldsymbol{\Gamma}_{12} \\ \boldsymbol{\Gamma}_{21} & \boldsymbol{\Gamma}_{22} \end{bmatrix} \begin{bmatrix} \Delta \mathbf{x}_{1t-1} \\ \Delta \mathbf{x}_{2t-1} \end{bmatrix} + \boldsymbol{\Psi}\mathbf{d}_t + \begin{bmatrix} \varepsilon_{1t} \\ \varepsilon_{2t} \end{bmatrix} \tag{5.4}$$

Having established the budgetary equilibrium within $\mathbf{x}_t$, *the next step is to establish the variables that each contains. We proceed on the assumption that* $r = 1$ *having dealt with the multiple co-integrating vector case earlier.*[2] *Testing the statistical significance of each variable in the co-integrating relation requires long-run exclusion tests, which amount to testing zero restrictions on each coefficient in* $\boldsymbol{\beta}'_1$, *namely* $H_e(j)\colon \boldsymbol{\beta}'_{1j} = 0, j = 1, \ldots n$.

As with the co-integration tests, long-run exclusion tests have economic and econometric implications. Since the limiting distributions of co-integration test statistics depend on the number of nonstationary variables in $\mathbf{x}_t$, *any that are redundant to the long-run relation can at most have a short-run impact and thus enter the model in differenced form via* $\mathbf{d}_t$ *as for the stationary variables discussed earlier. Of particular interest is the significance of the aid variable which gives rise to:*

Proposition II (Aid forms part of the fiscal equilibrium relation) *It is evaluated by* $H_e(f_t)\colon \boldsymbol{\beta}'_{11} = 0$ *in Eq. (5.4), while other* $\boldsymbol{\beta}$ *coefficients are unrestricted.*

Where aid is found to be I(1), but unimportant in the long run, it implies that it has not had any significant long-run impact on the fiscal variables in the country and could suggest that institutional factors prevented it from playing a role in the fiscal equilibrium (e.g., aid leakage where corrupt government officials diverted aid for private purposes).

*Further, in investigating the way in which aid impacts the budgets of recipient countries, attention naturally focuses on the causal mechanisms that exist between aid and the other components of the budget. Specifically, we want to establish whether aid is treated as given in the budget or whether its allocation actually reflects the state of the budget in some way. This can be accomplished econometrically by applying Johansen's (*1992*) long-run weak exogeneity test and leads to:*

Proposition III (Donor governments do not react to fiscal disequilibrium) *This is tested by* $H_{we}(\mathbf{x}_{1t})\colon \alpha_{11} = 0$ *in Eq. (5.4), while other* $\boldsymbol{\alpha}$ *coefficients are unrestricted. Where rejected, donors' aid allocations react to past fiscal imbalances in the recipient country. Conversely, a non-rejection implies that the aid is weakly exogenous to the long-run relation so that departures from the recipient's*

---

[2]In practice, long run exclusion tests are applied in conjunction with co-integration tests to determine whether multiple co-integrating vectors were indeed due to the presence of stationary variables in $\mathbf{x}_t$ or multiple co-integrating relations among $I(1)$ variables in $\mathbf{x}_t$. Since the latter case is implausible from an economic viewpoint it is ruled out in the following development.

budgetary equilibrium do not influence the donor's aid allocation. In effect, we establish whether aid in Rwanda's fiscal planning is treated as given or whether its allocation actually reflects the state of the budget in some way. Similar tests were applied to individual coefficients within $\boldsymbol{\alpha}_{21}$ *to establish which, if any, components were weakly exogenous.*

Moreover, as the VECM distinguishes the short-run relationships from long-run relationships among the data, we are able to evaluate whether variables such as aid are exogenous to both short- and long-run behaviors, which lead into Granger non-causality testing (Granger 1969*) and gives rise to:*

Proposition IV (Donors' aid allocation is not influenced by past fiscal conditions in the recipient country) *This can be expressed in terms of Eq. (5.4) as the null hypothesis that* $\mathbf{x}_{2t}$ *does not Granger-cause* $\mathbf{x}_{1t}$, $H_G(\mathbf{x}_2 \rightarrow \mathbf{x}_1)\colon (\boldsymbol{\alpha}_{11}\boldsymbol{\beta}'_{12}) = 0$ *and* $\boldsymbol{\Gamma}_{12} = 0$

Where they are upheld, these restrictions ensure that past values of the fiscal variables do not influence current values of aid, whether in terms of long- or short-run behaviors. Since the weak exogeneity of $\mathbf{x}_{1t}$ *(i.e.,* $\boldsymbol{\alpha}_{11} = 0$*) ensures that* $(\boldsymbol{\alpha}_{11}\boldsymbol{\beta}'_{12}) = 0$*, then* $\mathbf{x}_{2t}$ *does not Granger-cause* $\mathbf{x}_{1t}$ *provided lagged changes in* $\mathbf{x}_{2t}$ *do not influence* $\mathbf{x}_{1t}$*. Where this is so,* $\mathbf{x}_{1t}$ *is described as being strongly exogenous (Engle et al.* 1983*) and is evaluated using block exogenity Wald tests.*

It is also of interest to evaluate whether aid is Granger non-causal for the domestic budget (i.e., domestic fiscal variables). Where this hypothesis is upheld, aid is unlikely to be effective; however, in practice, it may result when aid is numerically small rather than statistically insignificant. This gives rise to the most fundamental of the economic hypotheses:

Proposition V (Aid does not influence fiscal conditions in Rwanda) *This proposition amounts to the null hypothesis that aid is Granger non-causal for the budget in the recipient country (i.e.,* $\mathbf{x}_{1t}$ *does not Granger-cause* $\mathbf{x}_{2t}$*) and is evaluated in Eq. (5.4) by:*

$H_G(\mathbf{x}_1 \rightarrow \mathbf{x}_2)\colon (/\boldsymbol{\alpha}_{21}\boldsymbol{\beta}'_{11}) = 0$ *and* $\boldsymbol{\Gamma}_{21} = 0$ *in an analogous manner to that given earlier.*

5.4 Empirical Results

5.4.1 Preliminaries

The unrestricted model was estimated with a restricted trend and an unrestricted constant—implying no quadratic growth in the data (Bwire et al. 2016; Juselius 2006). The lag-length was determined as the minimum number of lags that met the crucial assumption of time independence of the residuals based on a Lagrange multiplier (LM) test, starting with $k = 5$—this being quarterly frequency data.

Schwarz Bayesian Criterion (SC) suggests two lags, while both the Hannan-Quinn (HQ) criteria and the Akaike Information criteria favor five lags. With two lags, the LM test does not reject the null hypothesis of no serial correlation in the residuals, suggesting, inter alia, that the underlying CVAR model has to be estimated using two lags. In addition, this captures many more dynamics of the system. VAR model residuals are finally subjected to a battery of residual misspecification tests (Godfrey 1988), but as shown in Annexure 5.1, the histograms portray a reasonably normal distribution behavior.

5.4.2 *Evaluating the Behavior and the Long-Run Fiscal Impact of Foreign Aid in Rwanda*

5.4.2.1 The Existence of a Fiscal Equilibrium

Theoretical predictions suggest the existence of a budgetary equilibrium among the fiscal variables, especially allowing for a complete fiscal representation. On determining the appropriate specification of the data generating process, the co-integration rank was evaluated using Johansen's trace statistic—a top-to-bottom sequential procedure which is known to be asymptotically more correct than the bottom-to-top Max-Eigen statistic (Juselius 2006: 131–134). However, the test (trace) has been shown to have a finite sample bias with the implication that it often indicates too many co-integrating relations so that the test is oversized (Juselius 2006: 140–142). Thus, with a sample of 87 observations, though relatively large in the context of a developing country's time series, a small sample bias is corrected by using the Bartlett correction, which ensures a correct test size (Johansen 2002). Tests results in Table 5.2 support the presence of one equilibrium (stationary) relationship corrected for a small sample bias at the conventional 5% level of significance. Moreover, roots of the companion matrix (Annexure 5.1) and graphs of the potential co-integrating relations (available on request) both suggest that a rank of one (r = 1) is well supported by the data.

Following the confirmation of the co-integrating rank, the presence of unit roots is tested, but within the multivariate framework. Here, a stationarity test of a variable in $\boldsymbol{y}_i$ takes the following form:

$$H_o : \beta = (\beta_1^0, \beta_2), \tag{5.5}$$

where $\beta_1^0 = \varepsilon_i$ and β_2 is a (p x (r − 1)) dimensional matrix of unrestricted coefficients (Dennis 2006: 73).

In the test, the null hypothesis that a series is stationary against the alternative of a unit is conditional on the co-integrating rank, $r(\boldsymbol{\Pi})$ (Dennis 2006: 11–12), which here is 1 and is a $\chi^2(4)$ test. In Table 5.3, the stationarity of each variable by itself in the system is rejected in all cases, suggesting that the series are unit root nonstationary.

Table 5.2 Johansen's co-integration trace test results

$p-r$	r	Eig. value	Trace	Trace[a]	Frac 95
5	0	0.404	129.669	92.685	88.554
4	1	0.293	78.471	57.177	63.659
3	2	0.174	44.125	33.068	42.770
2	3	0.169	25.185	10.323	25.731
1	4	0.067	6.890	3.055	12.448

Note Trend assumption: linear deterministic trend restricted
[a]The small sample corrected test statistic (Dennis 2006: 159–160); Frac 95: the 5% critical value of the test of $H(r)$ against $H(p)$. The critical is approximated by the Gamma (Γ) distribution (Doornik 1998)

Table 5.3 Test of stationarity

Domfin	C_spending	K_spending	Aid	Tax_Rev
16.312 [0.003]	37.054 [0.000]	37.238 [0.000]	30.465 [0.000]	37.206 [0.000]

Note Restricted trend included in the co-integrating relation(s); 5% C.V = 9.488; *p*-values in brackets

Table 5.4 reports the long-run $\boldsymbol{\beta}$ parameters of the equilibrium relationship normalized on domestic borrowings (as this is a residual incorporated to identify the fiscal balance) and the associated adjustment coefficients ($\boldsymbol{\alpha}$). Estimates of the long-run coefficients are signed in accordance with fiscal equilibrium and suggest, ceteris paribus, that domestic borrowing is positively related to current and capital spending and negatively related to aid and tax revenue. The coefficients on tax revenue are larger, suggesting that in the long run, the budget is driven by tax revenue (or domestic revenue in general) more than aid. This implies that the fiscal variables are more strongly related to the known level of tax which reduces the risk of fiscal vulnerability associated with aid, which is both unpredictable and volatile (Bulir and Hamman 2003). Aid and tax revenue coefficients have the same sign, implying that in the long run, aid or associated reforms have increased tax revenues. Domestic borrowings are the main financing item in the system for a primary budget deficit net of aid. An increase in aid is associated with lower domestic borrowings (consistent with a lower deficit to finance or, when borrowings are negative, with enhanced ability to repay) and the net long-run effect of aid in Rwanda has, in part, been a reduction in domestic borrowings (aid may have been used to offset domestic borrowings).

The estimated coefficient for the effect of aid on capital spending (0.61) is higher than that on recurrent spendings (0.44). This suggests that in Rwanda, more aid has been used to finance public investments, but with a reasonable share of it diverted to consumption spending. While this resembles aid being fungible to the extent that consumption spending is a necessary complement to investment spending (recurrent spending is required to operate an investment such as teachers' salaries for schools and nurses, medicines and ambulances for a healthcare center), the assumption that fungibility diminishes the effectiveness of aid may be misleading.

Table 5.4 Estimates of long-run relationships for different normalizations of the fiscal equilibrium

Domfin	C_spending	K_spending	Aid	Tax_Rev
Coefficients of co-integrating relationship (β)				
−1.000 (.NA)	1.886 (7.029)	1.359 (4.826)	−0.835 (−5.946)	−2.533 (−6.473)
0.530 (7.506)	−1.000 (.NA)	−0.721 (−5.101)	0.443 (6.636)	1.343 (9.660)
0.736 (5.745)	−1.387 (−5.686)	−1.000 (.NA)	0.614 (4.411)	1.863 (10.739)
−1.198 (−8.314)	2.259 (8.690)	1.629 (5.182)	−1.000 (.NA)	−3.034 (−7.596)
−0.395 (−6.147)	0.745 (8.591)	0.537 (8.568)	−0.330 (−5.159)	−1.000 (.NA)
Adjustment coefficients (α)				
−0.378 (−5.467)	−0.079 (−2.768)	0.067 (3.417)	0.215 (6.146)	0.097 (6.695)

Note The rows of (β) represent different normalizations of the only uncovered co-integrating relationship (*t*-ratios in parentheses). The adjustment coefficients (α) are those obtained from normalizing the co-integrating vector on Domfin; *p*-values in brackets

Overall, more than three-fourth of the aid contributed to spending which is plausible and is consistent with aid being fully additional. Note that our measure of aid included project grants and not all of these are included directly as government spending, so there is no implication that aid has not been additional.

Relative to the coefficient on aid, the coefficient on tax revenue is larger: 1.34 for recurrent spending and 1.86 for capital spending, suggesting that spending over-responds to tax revenue. One interpretation is overoptimism regarding the sustainability of tax increases: The government commits to spending expected revenues, and if this is not realized, it resorts to some other deficit financing. This, however, is reflective of poor budget management. The α coefficients suggest that current spending and domestic financing adjust quite quickly to disequilibrium.

The results for the co-integrating relations in Table 5.4 imply that all variables are significant, so to provide an empirical content to the structural analysis underlying the causal link between aid and domestic fiscal variables, we now focus on two types of long-run parameter restrictions described in *Propositions II* and *III* earlier.

5.4.2.2 *Aid Forms Part of the Fiscal Equilibrium and Donor Governments Do Not React to Fiscal Disequilibrium*

Table 5.5 gives the results of the test for Proposition II, that is, long-run variable exclusion (zero restrictions on each β_i), and Proposition III, that is, weak exogeneity (zero restrictions on each α_i) for $r = 1$, based on the likelihood ratio

Table 5.5 Structural analysis

Test of	Domfin	C_spending	K_spending	Aid	Tax_Rev
Long-run exclusion	15.475 [0.000]	8.481 [0.004]	11.794 [0.001]	7.362 [0.007]	10.811 [0.001]
Weak erogeneity	10.612 [0.001]	3.078 [0.079]	7.426 [0.006]	14.846 [0.000]	16.789 [0.000]

Note Null hypotheses are that a variable can be excluded from the co-integrating relations (long-run exclusion) and that a variable is weakly exogenous (weak exogeneity); Obs: number of variables = 87; *p*-values in brackets

(LR) test distributed as $\chi^2(r)$. Consistent with the results in Table 5.4, the null hypothesis of the exclusion of the long-run variable is rejected for all variables (robust to small sample bias correction). Of particular interest is that aid is a significant element of a long-run fiscal equilibrium, so it supports spending, just like tax revenue and domestic borrowings.

Long-run weak exogeneity is also rejected for all variables in the system and importantly for aid at conventional levels. As in Franco-Rodriguez et al. (1998), this is consistent with fiscal planners having a target for aid revenue that is taken into account while forming the budget. Bwire et al. (2013) had a similar result for Uganda. It is the case that like in Uganda, donors incorporate government spending in deciding how much aid to allocate to Rwanda (Bwire et al. 2013; Foster and Killick 2006: 19). Fiscal planners in Rwanda have a forward-looking view and have achieved reasonable success in getting more aid allocated as budget support and released early in the budget year. In Rwanda, weak exogeneity of aid suggests that aid has been responsive to within the year budget planning.

In Rwanda, endogeneity of both current and capital spending as suggested by the results appears counterintuitive as spending is very difficult to reverse once implemented (especially if it involves increases in public payrolls or statutory expenditures). However, it implies that government spending is planned based on expected revenues, whereas the allocation is affected when the revenue outcome is realized; that is, spending allocations responds to revenue outturn. While it is surprising that weak exogeneity of domestic borrowings also cannot be rejected, both trend developments in Fig. 5.1 and estimates of the long-run relation in Table 5.4 suggest that it is determined by factors other than domestic fiscal variables—that is, it depends on aid outturn but not tax revenue.

5.4.2.3 Donors' Aid Allocation is Not Influenced by Past Fiscal Conditions and It Does Not Influence the Fiscal Conditions in Rwanda

Turning to the direction of causality, two issues are of interest: (1) whether past values of the fiscal variables do not influence current values of aid, whether in terms of long or short-run behaviors; and (2) whether aid is Granger non-causal for the

Table 5.6 Granger non-causality/block exogeneity Wald tests

Dependent variable→ Excluded↓	Aid	C_spending	Domfin	K_spending	Tax_rev
Aid: $\chi^2(2)$	–	2.662 (0.265)	5.041 (0.080)	4.515 (0.105)	1.756 (0.416)
All: $\chi^2(8)$	39.681 (0.000)	56.601 (0.000)	21.322 (0.006)	27.544 (0.001)	44.225 (0.000)

Note p-values in brackets

domestic budget. Results of block exogeneity, given in Table 5.6, suggest that domestic fiscal variables influence current values of aid, allowing for the possibility in particular, that government sets spending targets according to its development objectives and then tries to find aid resources to finance these ambitions, albeit with some level of unpredictability. This, however, should be interpreted with caution as it does not imply that the authorities have control over aid allocations by donors (aid commitments). Instead, as in Eifert and Gelb (2005), the disbursements could be a reaction to the government's ability to meet a donor's administrative requirements and/or other policy preconditions. As has been the case elsewhere, it may also reflect exercising incentive clauses by donors in response to events over which the Rwandan government has some direct control in the context of an ongoing aid relationship (O'Connell et al. 2008).

The hypothesis that aid is Granger non-causal for the domestic budget is rejected for domestic financing and for capital spending, although it is weakly significant. This is consistent with estimates of the long-run parameters and implies in part that the level of domestic debt is hugely influenced by the level of aid outturn such that the higher the level of aid outturn, the lower the fiscal deficit to finance or that aid enhances the authorities' ability to repay domestic debt. Elsewhere, the weak results are because overtime, aid as a share of the budget, has become numerically small as the country strives to become self-reliant.

5.5 Conclusion and Policy Implications

This paper assessed the dynamic relationship between foreign aid and domestic fiscal variables in Rwanda over 1990Q1 to 2015Q4 using a CVAR model. An investigation of the long-run relation between the fiscal variables provided interesting insights into the fiscal dynamics in Rwanda.

Aid and fiscal variables form a long-run stationary relationship. Aid is a significant element in the long-run fiscal equilibrium, and the hypothesis of aid exogeneity is not statistically supported; that is, anticipated aid appears to have been taken into account in budget planning. Rwandan budget planners may have had a target for aid revenue or the donors incorporated government spending in deciding how much aid to allocate to Rwanda or a combination of both. This implies that the government sets its spending targets according to its own development objectives and then tried to find resources to finance these ambitions in a priority order of domestic revenue, aid, and domestic borrowings. As improved public finance management and reduced domestic borrowings are common policy conditions attached to aid, the results suggest that aid was either associated with or caused beneficial policy responses in Rwanda.

Aid was associated with increased tax efforts, lower domestic borrowings, and increased public spending. Although the results suggest that spending was less than proportional to incremental aid, this was most probably because our measure of aid included project grants and not all of these are included directly as government spending, so this is consistent with aid being fully additional. It is evident that spending was higher than it could have been in the absence of aid. As tax revenue share of GDP relative to sub-Saharan African standards remained small over the period, the government was unable to maintain a budget balance including aid, so domestic borrowings remained frequent (with repayments in years of high aid).

These results suggest some policy implications. Corroborations from the trend analysis and estimates of the long-run coefficients suggest that domestic borrowings remain responsive to the uncertainties associated with aid inflows. Spending targets appear to have been formed according to anticipated aid and shortfalls in aid outturns induced domestic borrowings. If donors ensured that aid disbursements were more reliable and predictable, the Rwandan authorities could improve fiscal planning and reduce the instability associated with unanticipated deficits and the need to resort to costly domestic borrowings. Of course, some of the aid volatility arises because of absorption problems or failure to comply with conditionalities, so the Rwandan authorities also have a significant role to play in ensuring a stable aid relationship.

A comprehensive analysis of the relationship between aid and government spending requires reliable data on aid received by the government, and this is a deficiency in almost all government statistics, including in Rwanda which should be addressed. Project grants related to donor-operated projects cannot increase recorded spending as they do not go through the budget. If the government is aware of donor projects, this could reduce government spending in that area. Therefore, continued efforts by donors to coordinate aid delivery systems, make aid more transparent, and support improvement in government fiscal statistics will contribute to improving fiscal planning. Recipients need to know how much aid is available to finance spending and how this is delivered, that is, whether through donor projects or government budgets.

Acknowledgements The authors are grateful to an anonymous referee for constructive comments and participants of the EABEW 2016 conference held in Kigali on 20–22 June who heard evolving versions. The usual disclaimers apply. The data used in the analysis are available on request.

Annexure 1

1. Residual plots
   Figure 5.2 is a panel containing four plots for each error correction model equation: (a) actual and fitted values (top left); (b) standardized residuals (bottom left); (c) auto-correlations (top right); and (d) histogram (bottom right). Overlaid on the histogram is the estimated density function of the standardized residuals (appears as a dotted line in print) and the density of the standard normal distribution. It also contains some statistics: the univariate normality test by Doornik and Hansen (DH) (2008) and Kolmogorov–Smirnov (KS) (Lilliefors 1967) test for normality, and the Jarque-Bera test computed by the RATS' statistics instruction (Dennis 2006).
   The actual and fitted residuals show an outlying observation in about 2013 in virtually all residuals, except for tax revenue and domestic financing. This notwithstanding, the histograms portray reasonably normal distribution behavior.

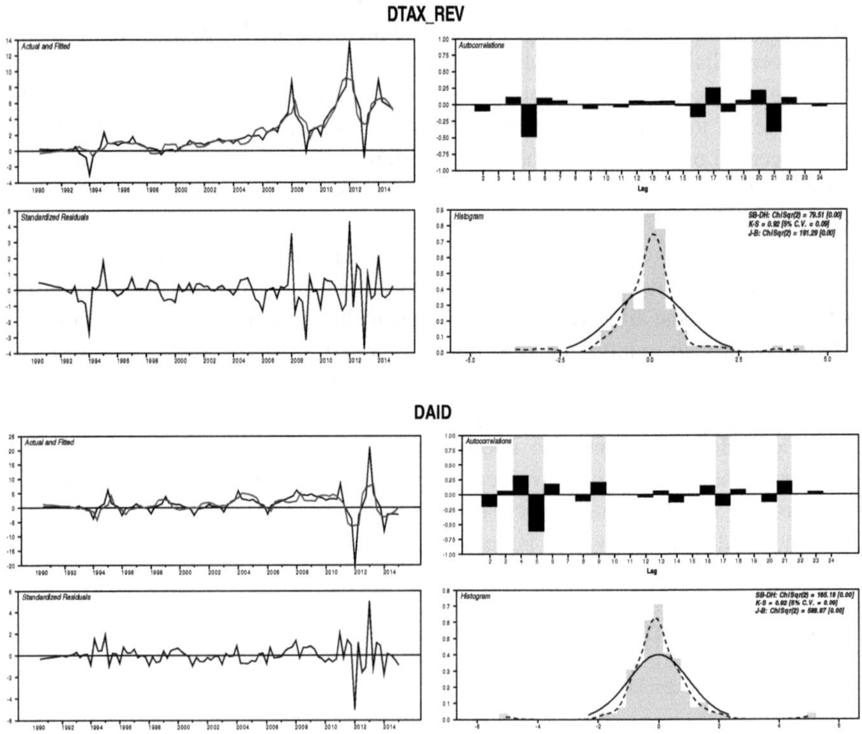

Fig. 5.2 Actual, fitted, and standardized residuals, auto-correlations, and histograms

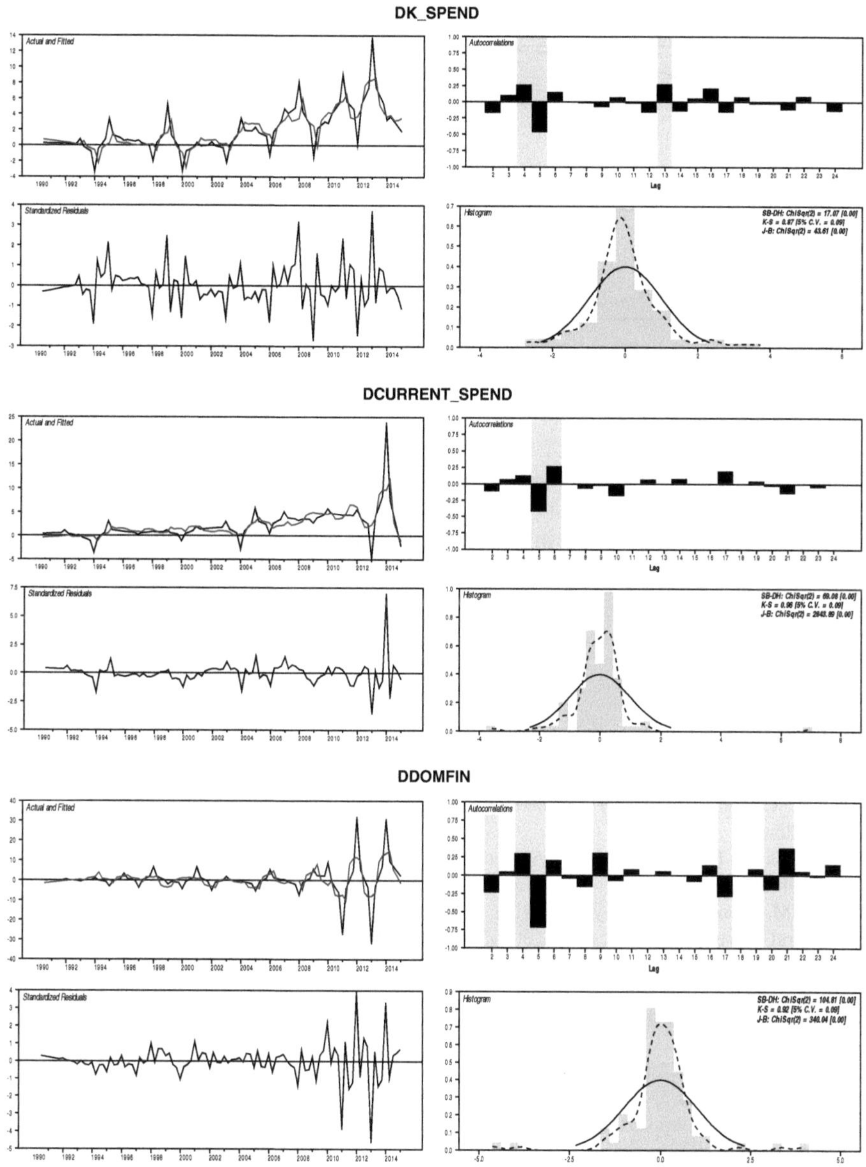

Fig. 5.2 (continued)

2. Roots of companion matrix
   The roots of the companion matrix are equal to the inverse of the roots of the characteristic equation (Juselius 2006). $y\{t\}$ is stationary when the roots of the characteristic equation are all outside the unit circle or equivalent when the roots of the companion matrix are all inside the unit circle. In practice, we need to

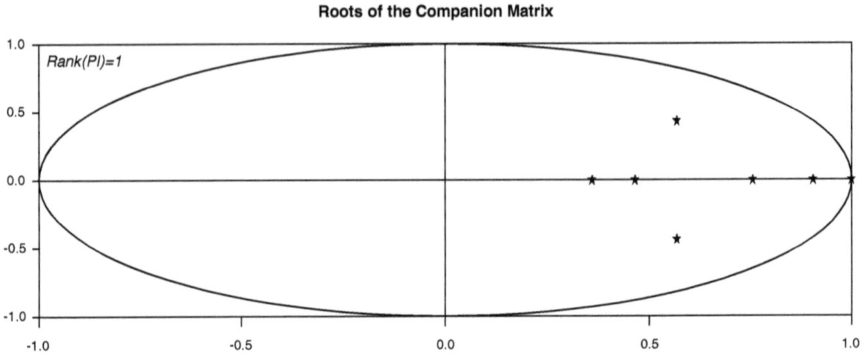

Fig. 5.3 Roots of the companion matrix

choose the rank so that the largest unrestricted root is far from a unit root; that is, it has modulus lower than 1. The model here is defined for $p = 5$, $k = 1$ implying $p \times k = 5$ roots in the characteristic polynomial (i.e., we assume full rank of the $\mathbf{\Pi}$ matrix). These are shown in Fig. 5.3, and as expected, all roots are inside the unit circle.

References

Adam C, O'Connell S (1999) Aid, taxation, and development in Sub-Saharan Africa. Econ Polit 11:225–253

Bulir A, Javier Hamman A (2003) Aid volatility: an empirical assessment. IMF Staff Papers 50 (1):64–89

Bwire TM, Morrissey O, Lloyd T (2013). A time series analysis of the impact of foreign aid on Central Government's fiscal budget in Uganda. WIDER Working Paper No. 2013/101

Bwire TM, Morrissey O, Lloyd T (2016) Fiscal reforms and the fiscal effects of aid in Uganda. J Dev Stud, forthcoming

Chenery H, Strout W (1966) Foreign assistance and economic development. Am Econ Rev 56:679–753

Dennis GJ (2006). CATS in RATS cointegration analysis of time series'. Version 2, Estima, Evanston, Illinois, USA

Doornik JA (1998) Approximations to the asymptotic distribution of cointegration tests. J Econ Surv 12:573–593

Doornik JA, Hansen H (2008) An omnibus test for univariate and multivariate normality. Oxford Bull Econ Stat 70:927–939

Eifert B, Gelb A (2005). Improving the dynamics of aid: towards more predictable budget support. The World Bank, Washington, DC, Policy Research Working Paper 3732

Engle RF, Hendry DF, Richard JF (1983) Exogeneity. Econometric 51:277–304

Foster M, Killick T (2006) What would doubling aid do for macroeconomic management in Africa? Overseas Development Institute, London, ODI Working Paper 264

Franco-Rodriguez S, McGillivray M, Morrissey O (1998) Aid and the public sector in Pakistan: evidence with endogenous Aid. World Dev 26:1241–1250

Godfrey LG (1988) Misspecification tests in econometrics. Cambridge University Press, Cambridge

Granger CWJ (1969) Investigating causal relations by econometric models and cross-spectral methods. Econometrica 37:424–438

Hamilton JD (1994) Time series analysis. Princeton University Press, Princeton

Johansen S (1988) Statistical analysis of cointegration vectors. J Econ Dyn Control 12(2–3):231–254

Johansen S (1992) Testing weak exogeneity and the order of integration in UK money demand. J Policy Model 14:313–334

Johansen S (2002) A small sample correction for tests of hypotheses on the cointegrating vectors. J Econ 111(2):195–221

Juselius K (2006) The cointegrated VAR model: methodology and application. Oxford University Press, Oxford

Juselius K, Møller FN, Tarp F (2011) The long-run impact of foreign aid in 36 African countries: insights from multivariate time series analysis. WIDER Working Paper 2011/51. UNU-WIDER, Helsinki

Lilliefors HW (1967) On the Kolmogorov-Smirnov test for normality with mean and variance unknown. Am Stat Assoc J 62:399–402

McGillivray M (1994) The impact of foreign aid on the fiscal behaviour of Asian LDC governments: a comment on Khan and Hoshino (1992). World Dev 22(12):2015–2017

McGillivray M, Morrissey O (2000) Aid fungibility in assessing aid: red herring or true concern? J Int Dev 12:413–428

McGillivray M, Morrissey O (2001) Aid illusion and public sector fiscal behaviour. J Dev Stud 37:188–236

McGillivray M, Morrissey O (2004) Fiscal effects of aid. In: Addison T, Roe A (eds) Fiscal policy for development. Palgrave for UNU-WIDER, Basingstoke, pp 72–96

Martins P (2010) Fiscal dynamics in Ethiopia: a cointegrated VAR model with quarterly data. University of Nottingham, School of Economics: CREDIT Research Paper 10/05

Mascagni G, Timmis E (2014) Fiscal effects of aid in Ethiopia: evidence from CVAR applications. University of Nottingham, School of Economics: CREDIT Research Paper 14/06

Morrissey O (2001) Does aid increase growth? Prog Dev Stud 1(1):37–50

Morrissey O (2015) Aid and government fiscal behaviour: what does the evidence say? World Dev 69:98–105

Morrissey O, M'Amanja D, Lloyd T (2007) Aid and growth in Kenya: a time series approach. In: Lahiri S (ed) Theory and practice of foreign aid. Elsevier, Amsterdam, pp 313–332

O'Connell S, Adam C, Buffie EF (2008) Aid and fiscal instability. Centre for the Study of African Economics, Oxford, CSAE WPS 18

Osei R, Morrissey O, Lloyd T (2005) The fiscal effects of aid in Ghana. J Int Dev 17:1–17

Rahbek A, Mosconi R (1999) Cointegration rank inference with stationary regressors in VAR models. Econ J 2:76–91

Riddell R (2007) Does foreign aid really work?. Oxford University Press, Oxford

The World Bank (1998) Assessing aid: what works, what doesn't and why. Oxford University Press for the World Bank, Washington, DC

The World Bank (2008) Rwanda—toward sustained growth and competitiveness. CEM 1

Chapter 6
Relationship Between Inflation and Real Economic Growth in Rwanda

Ferdinand Nkikabahizi, Joseph Ndagijimana and Edouard Musabanganji

Abstract This study examines the impact of economic stability measures (inflation and unemployment rates) on real gross domestic product (GDP) in Rwanda. It uses quarterly data for the period of $2000Q_1$–$2015Q_4$ collected from the Ministry of Finance and Economic Planning, Central Bank of Rwanda and the National Institute of Statistics of Rwanda (NISR). This study concludes that inflation and unemployment have a long-run negative and significant relationship on real gross domestic product. In the long run, the coefficients are not significant at the 5% level; it is only the inflation coefficient and error which are significant. Real gross domestic product increases when inflation reduces with a *p*-value of 0.00266; real gross domestic product increases when unemployment reduces with a *p*-value of 0.09882. The coefficient from the error correction model means that the effect of the shock will reduce by 0.0483% each quarter, meaning that the effect of the shock will reduce by 19.32% in each 4th quarter. This further means that it will end at 20 quarters, that is, after a five-year period. It has to be highlighted that there is a weak relationship between real gross domestic product and both inflation and unemployment rates.

Keywords Real gross domestic products · Inflation · Unemployment · Co-integration · Vector error correction model

JEL Classification E4 · E5 · E6

F. Nkikabahizi (✉) · J. Ndagijimana
College of Business and Economics, University of Rwanda, Butare, Rwanda
e-mail: fnkikabahizi@gmail.com

E. Musabanganji
Economy and Rural Development Unit, Gembloux Agro-Bio Tech,
University of Liège, Liège, Belgium

A. Heshmati (ed.), *Studies on Economic Development and Growth in Selected African Countries*, Frontiers in African Business Research,
DOI 10.1007/978-981-10-4451-9_6

6.1 Introduction

For all countries, both developed and developing, one of the fundamental objectives of macroeconomic policy is economic stability. Economic stability refers to an economy that experiences constant growth and low inflation. Advantages of having a stable economy include increased productivity, improved efficiencies, and low unemployment. The common signs of instability are extended time in a recession or crisis, rising inflation, and volatility in currency exchange rates. An unstable economy leads to a decline in consumer confidence, stunted economic growth, and reduced international investments. The main goals of any government usually include economic growth, price stability, and low unemployment. The most important means of moving toward these goals are detailed tax policies, spending, regulation, and government management. However, the macroeconomic levers of the fiscal stance and monetary policy also play a part. Attaining sustainable economic growth coupled with price stability continues to be the central objective of macroeconomic policies for most countries in the world today. Among others, the emphasis on price stability in conducting monetary policy is with a view to promoting sustainable economic growth as well as strengthening the purchasing power of the domestic currency (Umaru and Zubairu 2012).

The question on whether or not inflation is harmful to economic growth has recently been a subject of intense debate among policymakers and macroeconomists. Several studies have estimated a negative relationship between inflation and economic growth. It is imperative for studies which base their arguments on real business cycle theories to also base them on countries (Pradana and Rathnayaka 2013).

Luppu (2009) has established a positive relationship between inflation and GDP growth in Romania in the short run. This implies that as inflation increases, GDP must also increase in the short run. However, when inflation decreases, GDP should also decrease. Drukker et al. (2005) have noticed that if the inflation rate is below 19.16%, increases in inflation do not have a statistically significant effect on growth, but when inflation is above 19.16%, a further increase in inflation will decrease the long-run growth.

Mallik and Chowdury (2001) indicate a long-run positive relationship between the GDP growth rate and inflation among four South Asian countries. Specifically, the bone of contention is whether inflation is necessary for economic growth or is it detrimental to growth.

World economic growth and inflation rates have been fluctuating. Likewise, inflation rates have been dominating when compared to growth rates over many years; hence, the relationship between inflation and economic growth has continued to be one of the most significant macroeconomic problems (Madhukar and Nagarjuna 2011). Similarly, Ahmed (2010) maintains that this relationship has been argued in economic literature, and these arguments show differences in relation to the condition of the world economic order. In accordance with these policies, increases in total demand have led to increases in production and inflation too.

In the 1970s, countries with high inflation, especially Latin American countries, started experiencing a decrease in growth rates which led to the emergence of views which stated that inflation had negative effects and not positive effects on economic growth. Evidence showing a relationship between inflation and economic growth from some of the Asian countries such as India showed that its growth in GDP increased from 3.5% in the 1970s to 5.5% in the 1980s, while the inflation rate accelerated steadily from an annual average of 1.7% during the 1950s to 6.4% in the 1960s and further to 9.0% in the 1970s before easing marginally to 8.0% in the 1980s (Prasanna and Gopakumar 2010). Similarly, Xiao (2009) shows that from 1961 to 1977, China's real GDP growth and real GDP per capita growth averaged at 4.84 and 2.68%, respectively. Since 1978, China's economy has grown steadily, although the growth rate fluctuated among the years, and from 1978 to 2007, the growth rate of China's real GDP and real GDP per capita were recorded at 9.992 and 8.69%, respectively.

A study by Stein (2010) shows that in East African countries, Kenya had five years of very positive economic development with four consecutive years of above 4% growth. The same study shows that Uganda was one of the fastest growing economies in Africa with sustained growth averaging 7.8% since 2000 with the annual inflation rate decreasing from 5.1% in 2006 to 3.5% in 2009. The average annual real GDP growth rate for Rwanda in 1990–99 was −0.1 but from 2006 to 2009, the country had an annual average growth rate of 7.3%.

Since the late 1970s, the Tanzanian economy has experienced many internal and external shocks. Kilindo (1997) documents the issues and maintains that all sectors of the economy were affected by shocks, whose manifestations included large budget deficits and an imbalance between productive and non-productive activities. He also argues that the signs closely associated with these were high rates of inflation, large balance of payment (BOP) deficits, declining domestic savings, growing government expenditure, falling agricultural produce, and decreased utilization of industrial capacity which in turn hindered economic growth.

Macroeconomists, central bankers, and policymakers have often emphasized the costs associated with high and variable inflation. Inflation imposes negative externalities on the economy when it interferes with its efficiency. Examples of these inefficiencies are not hard to find, at least at the theoretical level. Inflation can lead to uncertainty about future profitability of investment projects (especially when high inflation is also associated with increased price variability). This leads to more conservative investment strategies than would otherwise be the case, ultimately leading to lower levels of investments and economic growth. Inflation may also reduce a country's international competitiveness by making its exports relatively more expensive, thus impacting its balance of payments (Gokal and Hanif 2004).

The conventional view in macroeconomics holds that permanent and predictable changes in inflation rates are neutral, and they do not affect real activity in the long run. However, a substantial body of evidence suggests that sustained high inflation rates can have adverse consequences for real economic growth even in the long run. Nowadays, a consensus among economists seems to be that high rates of inflation cause 'problems' not just for some individuals but for aggregate economic performance. However, there is much less agreement about the precise relationship between inflation and economic performance and the mechanism by which inflation affects economic activity. The effects of permanent increases in the inflation rate for long-run activity seem to be quite complicated.

The consensus about the adverse effects of inflation on real economic growth reveals only a small part of the whole picture. Recently, intensive research has focused on the nonlinear relationship between these two variables. That is, at lower rates of inflation, the relationship is not significant or even positive, but at higher rates, inflation has a significantly negative effect on growth. Bruno and Easterly (1998) demonstrate that a number of economies have experienced sustained inflation of 20–30% without suffering any apparently major adverse consequences. However, once the rate of inflation exceeds some critical level (estimated at 40%), significant declines occur in the level of real activity. The relationship between inflation and economic growth is one of the most important economic controversies among economists, policymakers, and monetary authorities. In particular, the core of the argument is whether inflation is necessary for economic growth or is it harmful for economic growth. Although the relationship between inflation and economic growth has been widely examined and investigated, it has also been debated in economic literature.

6.2 Literature Review

This section discusses different empirical studies which show the relationship between inflation and economic growth. Previous studies' concern was not only finding a simple relationship between inflation and economic growth, but also finding whether the relationship held in the long run or it was just a short-run phenomenon, finding the causal direction of the relationship and whether the relationship was linear or nonlinear and the like.

6.2.1 Theoretical Literature

Adam Smith founded the classical theory. He recognized three factors of production —land, labor, and capital. His production function can be expressed as: $Y = f(L, K, T)$, where Y is output, L is labor, K is capital, and T is land. Smith considered saving as the most important factor affecting the growth rate. In classical theories, there is no direct explanation of inflation and its tax effect on profit levels and output. But the relationship between the two variables is implicitly negative by a reduction in firms' profit levels and savings through higher wage costs (Gokal and Hanif 2004).

In 1936, John Maynard Keynes wrote *The General Theory of Employment, Interest and Money,* which established the foundation of Keynesianism. Keynesians believe that the government has to intervene to reach full production. They believe that intervention by the government in the economy through expansionary economic policies will boost investment and promote demand to reach full production. The Keynesian model is based on aggregate demand (AD) and aggregate supply (AS) curves. In this model, the AS curve is upward sloping in the short run, so that a change in the demand side of the economy affects both price and output (Dornbusch et al. 1996).

Dornbusch et al. (1996) have also argued that AD and AS yield an adjustment path which shows an initial positive relationship between inflation and economic growth but eventually which turns negative toward the latter part of the adjustment path. The initial positive relationship between inflation and economic growth is due to the time inconsistency problem. Producers feel that only the prices of their products have increased, while the other producers are operating at the same price level. However, in reality, overall prices have increased. Therefore, the producers continue with more and more output. Moreover, according to Blanchard and Kiyotaki (1987), inflation and economic growth are positively related because of firms' agreement to supply on an agreed price. So a firm has to produce even at increased prices. Later on, the relationship becomes negative. This describes the phenomenon of stagflation, that is, output decreases or remains the same when prices increase (Gokal and Hanif 2004).

'Stagflation' is a phenomenon that incorporates high inflation and low growth or high unemployment; this dominated almost all developed countries in the middle of the 1970s. Monetarism was proposed by Milton Friedman. For this school of thought, money supply is the only factor that determines price levels in an economy. They argue that government intervention manages the growth rate of money supply to harmonize it with the growth rate of output in the long run. Monetarists also argue that inflation will occur when money supply increases faster than the rate of growth of national income. But the effect of money supply is different in the long run and short run. In the short run, money supply has the dominant influence on real variables (real GDP and employment) and price levels. But in the long run, the influence of the variations in the money supply is primarily on price levels and on other nominal variables but not on real variables such as real output and employment (Richard 1998).

Monetarism looks at the concept of anticipation in two parts—the Phillips curve and the divide Phillips curve in the short run and long run (Gokal and Hanif 2004). For this theory, the Phillips curve holds in the short run but not in the long run. In the long run, anticipated inflation will be consistent with actual inflation. So inflation will not influence unemployment, output, and other real economic variables. This concept is called neutrality of money. Gokal and Hanif (2004) explain the concept of neutrality and super-neutrality as neutrality holds if the equilibrium values of real variables, including the level of GDP, are independent of the level of the money supply in the long run and super-neutrality holds when real variables including the GDP rate of growth are independent of the rate of growth in the money supply in the long run. Inflation will be harmless in the case of neutrality and super-neutrality. But this may not be true in reality. Inflation is bad for the economy because it affects capital accumulation, investments, and exports and hence, affects output.

The neoclassical growth theory started an era in which economists tried to generate long-run equilibrium models to formulate economic growth and its determinants. Solow and Swan are two pioneers who put forward their growth models under the framework of the neoclassical economic theory. The Solow growth model assumes 'diminishing returns to labor and capital separately and constant returns to both factors jointly' (Gokal and Hanif 2004). One of the features of this model is that the saving rate, the population growth rate, and technological progress are defined to be exogenous. The capital level will move to and stabilize at the steady state on which output will keep constant at given exogenous variables. Once this balance is broken by change of exogenous variables, a new steady state will be achieved. Although the growth accounting method tells us the channels through which variables influence economic growth, there is still lack of a direct explanation about the relationship between inflation and economic growth. Mundell (1963) and Tobin (1965) have successfully explained the effect of inflation on economic growth based on the neoclassical growth theory. They believe that increased nominal interest caused by inflation will make people opt for investments instead of consumption. This will result in increasing capital accumulation which will stimulate economic growth. This is the Mundell–Tobin effect. Mundell (1963) and Tobin (1965) depict a positive relationship between inflation and economic growth. Sidrauski (1967) collaborates monetary factors with the neoclassical growth model with the assumption of neutrality of money. He tries to testify how the model will react to a change in the growth rate of money supply. In this model, although he does not give a distinct path on how the new steady state is achieved upon the change in the growth rate of money supply, his conclusion is that inflation will have no relation to output growth rate in the long run. This finding supports the super-neutrality of money.

Contrary to the conclusion of the Mundell–Tobin effect, Stockman (1981) developed a long-run equilibrium growth model with the assumption of a 'cash-in-advance constraint.' In Mundell (1963) and Tobin's (1965) models, real money balances and investments can be substituted. But in Stockman's (1981) model, the two variables' relationship is complementary as returns on investments are also gained by individuals in the form of money in the future. Inflation will reduce both real money balances and investments. And then inflation will negatively influence growth. Generally, a theoretical review of the neoclassical growth theory demonstrates mixed results regarding the relationship between inflation and economic growth.

The new growth theory is also termed as the endogenous growth theory as it assumes technological progress as endogenous, which is contrary to the neoclassical growth theory whose assumption is based on the exogenous saving rate, population growth, and technological progress. Also, the new growth theory assumes that the marginal product of capital is constant, but in the neoclassical growth theory the capital is assumed to be diminishing on return. If discussing the new growth model under the framework of the monetary economy, the relationship between inflation and return rate on capital will depend on the relationship between the real money balance and investment. As discussed in the part of neoclassical theory and as also discussed in Mundell (1963) and Tobin's (1965) models and in Haslag (1997) and Stockman (1981), if real money balances substitute investment, inflation will decrease the return on real money balances, but the return on investment will increase. But if real money balances complement investment, inflation will have a negative effect on growth.

6.2.2 *Empirical Literature—The Relationship Between Inflation and Economic Growth*

Like theoretical models, existing empirical studies too reflect different views on the relationship between inflation and output growth. Their findings differ depending on the data period and countries, suggesting that the association between inflation and growth is not stable. Still, economists now widely accept the existence of a nonlinear and concave relationship between these two variables; the traditional point of view does not consider inflation as an important factor in the growth equation. This is reflected in the studies of Dorrance (1963) and Johanson (1967) who did not find any significant impact of inflation on growth in the 1960s. Nevertheless, the traditional point of view changed when high and chronic inflation was present in many countries in the 1970s; as a result, different researchers showed that inflation had a negative impact on output growth.

Fischer (1993) and De Gregorio (1992, 1996) investigated the link between inflation and growth in time series, cross-sectional and panel datasets for a large number of countries. The main result of these works is that there is a negative impact of inflation on growth. Fischer (1993) argues that inflation hampers the efficient allocation of resources due to harmful changes in relative prices. At the same time, relative prices appear to be one of the most important channels in the process of efficient decision making.

Barro (1987) studied the relationship between inflation and economic growth. He used 30 years data in 100 countries from 1960 to 1990. He included other determinants of economic growth besides inflation. To analyze the data, he used the systems of regression equation. The regression results indicated that an increase in average inflation by 10% per year led to a reduction in the growth rate of real per capita GDP by 0.2–0.3% per year and a decrease in the ratio of investment to GDP by 0.4–0.6%. But the result is statistically significant only when high inflation experiences are included in the sample.

Investigations into the existence and nature of the link between inflation and growth have had a long history. Although economists now widely accept that inflation has a negative effect on economic growth, researchers did not detect this effect in data in the 1950s and the 1960s. A series of studies in the IMF Staff Papers around 1960 found no evidence of damage from inflation (Bhatia 1960; Dorrance

1963, 1966; Wai 1959). Johanson (1967) found no conclusive empirical evidence for either a positive or a negative association between the two variables. Therefore, a popular view in the 1960s was that the effect of inflation on growth was not particularly important.

Motley (1994) includes inflation in his model to examine the effect of inflation on the real GDP growth rate. He extended the model developed by Mankiw et al. (1992), which was based on the Solow growth model by allowing for the possibility that inflation tended to reduce the rate of technical change. The result indicates a negative relationship between inflation and the growth rate of real GDP. Khan and Senhadji (2001) analyzed the relationship between inflation and economic growth separately for industrial and developing countries. They used new econometric techniques initially developed by Chan and Tsay (1998) and Hansen (2000) to show the existence of threshold effects in the relationship between inflation and economic growth. The authors used an unbalanced panel data containing 140 countries for the period 1960–98. The estimated value of the threshold was 1–3% and 11–12% for developed and developing countries, respectively. The results indicated that the threshold for industrialized countries was lower than developing countries. It also indicated that inflation levels below the threshold level of inflation had no effect on growth. But inflation rates above the threshold level had a significant negative effect on growth.

Mubarik (2005) also estimated the threshold level of inflation for Pakistan. He found a 9% threshold level of inflation as inflation above this level affected the economic growth negatively. But inflation below the estimated level was conductive for economic growth.

Some other studies have shown that the link between inflation and growth is significant only for certain levels of inflation. For instance, Bruno and Easterly (1995) studied the inflation–growth relationship for 26 countries over 1961–92. They found a negative relationship between inflation and growth when the level of inflation exceeded some threshold. At the same time, they showed that the impact of low and moderate inflation on growth was quite ambiguous. They argue that in this case inflation and growth were influenced jointly by different demand and supply shocks, and thus no stable pattern existed.

Numerous empirical studies have found that the inflation–growth interaction is nonlinear and concave. Fischer (1993) was the first to investigate this nonlinear relationship. He used cross-sectional data covering 93 countries and used the growth accounting framework to detect the channels through which inflation impacted growth. As a result, he found that inflation influenced growth by decreasing productivity, growth, and investment. Moreover, he also showed that the effect of inflation was nonlinear with breaks at 15 and 40%. Sarel (1995) found evidence of a structural break in the interaction between inflation and growth. He used the fixed effect technique to deal with a panel data sample covering 87 countries over 21 years (1970–90). His main result is that the estimated threshold level equaled 8%, exceeding which led to a negative, powerful, and robust impact of inflation on growth.

6.2.3 Empirical Literature—Causality Between Inflation and Economic Growth

Mubarik (2005) analyzed the causal relationship between inflation and economic growth. His test results indicated that causality between the two variables was unidirectional, that is, inflation caused GDP growth but not vice versa. Chimobi (2010) studied inflation and economic growth in Nigeria and found unidirectional causality from inflation to growth. Erbaykal and Okuyan (2008) analyzed the causal relationship between inflation and economic growth in the framework of the causality test. Their results indicated no causal relationship between economic growth and inflation, whereas there was a causality relationship from inflation to economic growth.

In addition to unidirectional causality from inflation to economic growth and bilateral causality, there are also studies which indicate unidirectional causality from growth to inflation. Gokal and Hanif (2004) studied inflation and economic growth in Fiji. They concluded that Granger causality runs one way, from growth to inflation but not from inflation to growth. It means that it is unidirectional. Datta and Kumar (2011) examined the relationship between inflation and economic growth in Malaysia with data from 1971 to 2007. Their findings show that there exists short-run causality between the variables and that the direction of causality is from inflation to economic growth, and in the long run, Granger causes inflation in economic growth.

Finally, there are also studies which indicate no causality relationship between inflation and economic growth. Kigume (2011) studied inflation and economic growth in Kenya from 1963 to 2000. The Granger causality test of his study showed no causality relation between these two variables.

6.3 Critical Review and Identification of Gaps

Many authors such as Luppu (2009) and Mallik and Chowdury (2001) who carried out research on related subjects found that both inflation and real economic growth were positively related in the long run, while Pradana and Rathnayaka (2013) show the existence of a negative relationship between inflation and economic growth. Drukker et al. (2005) and Bruno and Easterly (1998) indicate that the relationship between inflation and economic growth depends on the inflation rate to have either a positive or a negative impact. Empirical and theoretical evidence suggests that the relationship between inflation and economic growth is positive, negative, and none, which leads to ambiguity about the exact relationship.

In Rwanda, the inflation rate is likely to be stable which does not stop its economy from improving as the inflation rate is low in the short run. Studies which prove a relationship between variables on economic growth, however, do not focus on the Rwandan economy as they all focus on the long-run relationship rather than the short-run relationship. Our study, which examines the relationship between inflation and economic growth in Rwanda, will enable other scholars and even macroeconomists and authorities to know the exact relationship between inflation and real economic growth in Rwanda, and help macroeconomic policymakers to set strategies leading to economic stability in Rwanda.

6.4 Rationale, Objectives, and Research Questions

Our paper examines the relationship between inflation and economic growth and analyzes the causality relationship between the two. The research findings are significant for monetary policy authorities, business owners, and investors. They are also important for policymakers as they can get to know the link between inflation and GDP which will help them decide and set strategies concerning variables by taking into account the fact that all these variables have an impact on a country's well-being. As for researchers, apart from their contribution to knowledge about Rwandan society and inflation and GDP, our study will also give them an opportunity to know about the correlation between inflation and economic growth in the world, particularly in Rwanda, and its effect on investment decisions and business performance in Rwanda.

The purpose of our study is to investigate the relationship between inflation and economic growth in Rwanda and determine whether there is a turning point or a threshold level of inflation at which the inflation effect on economic growth switches from positive or insignificant to negative. For the purpose of economic stability, unemployment rates are also taken into account in our study.

Our study seeks to answer the following questions: (i) Is there a significant relationship between inflation and unemployment and economic growth? If so, is the relationship positive or negative? (ii) Is the causality relationship between inflation and unemployment and economic growth bidirectional, unidirectional (either from inflation to economic growth or from economic growth to inflation), or a no causality relation? (iii) Is the Rwandan economy stable?

6.5 Formulation of the Empirical Model

We believe Granger's (1969) model is simple and is also accurate in supporting the specificity of the effect of inflation on economic growth in Rwanda. This leads us to formulate this model in detail so that it is consistent with the hypotheses of the study, assuming that an increase in inflation rate has a negative effect on economic growth as the dependent variable. For the economic stability measure, unemployment rate is added to the model. The empirical model used for testing the relationship between real GDP and inflation rate and unemployment rate can be specified by a simple model as

$$\text{RGDP}_t = f(\text{INFR}_t, \text{UNER}_t) \tag{6.1}$$

where RGDP_t is the Rwandan real gross domestic product, INFR_t is inflation rate, and UNER_t is unemployment rate.

Next, we estimate the following co-integration equations by VAR:

$$\text{RGDP}_t = \alpha_0 + \alpha_1\text{INFR}_t + \alpha_2\text{UNER}_t + \varepsilon_t \tag{6.2}$$

The coefficients $\alpha_i\,(i = 0, 1, 2)$ of Model 2 are parameters associated with inflation and unemployment rates, respectively, and are to be estimated. The transformation of the dependent variable in its logarithm leads us to scale reducing and allows us to interpret the results in terms of elasticity. This leads us to write Eq. (6.2) in a log-linear format for all variables, and we obtain the following long-run equation of Rwandan real GDP:

$$\text{LOGRGDP}_t = \alpha_0 + \alpha_1\text{INFR}_t + \alpha_2\text{UNER}_t + \varepsilon_t \tag{6.3}$$

Both long- and short-term relationships were tested using the Johansen co-integration test and ECM, respectively. VAR was used to estimate all the parameters.

6.6 Data and Methodology

The data used for this study is basically time series data covering the period 2000–15. The two macroeconomic variables included in this study are inflation rate and unemployment rate as independent variables and the real gross domestic product at market prices as an indicator to measure economic growth. Data was sourced from the Central Bank of Rwanda (BNR), the National Institute of Statistics in Rwanda (NISR), a World Bank report, and the Ministry of Finance and Economic Planning.

We used a methodology which is presented as follows: test of lags, an analysis of the stationarity of the series, the Johansen co-integration test, the Granger causality test and the Chow test for the structure break, and the short-run relationship model specification by ECM. We performed an economic interpretation of the co-integration relation between the variables. We used GRETL as the appropriate software for performing the econometric analysis better, and VAR was adopted for estimating the parameter. The unit root test was initially performed to find the stationary properties of each time series. An augmented Dickey–Fuller (ADF) unit root test was used for this purpose. In testing, if any variable did not show stationary at level, then the stationary property was tested on its first difference. If the variables were stationary at their first difference long run, the association of the variable was tested by using the co-integration technique. To achieve the objective, the stationarity check used the unit root test named the augmented Dickey–Fuller test, while the Johansen co-integration test was used to confirm the existence of long-run relationships (Bourbonnais 2007) if the series was not stationary. As detailed in Bourbonnais (2007), this methodology is applied in three steps: an analysis of the stationarity of the series under study to check for the presence of units roots in the series or their integration order; the co-integration test which has to reveal the number of co-integrating vectors for a long-run relationship; and lastly, the estimation of both long- and short-run relationships between the series to be studied through the mechanism of the vector error correction model (VECM). The following dynamic model relationship (short-term or error correction model)

$$\Delta Y_t = \beta_1 \Delta X_{1\,t-1} + \beta_2 \Delta X_{2\,t-2} + \cdots + \beta_p \Delta X_{p\,t-p} + \gamma_1 e_{t-1} + \varepsilon_t \tag{6.4}$$

was estimated following that of the long-run relationship

$$Y_t = \hat{e}_0 + \hat{e}_1 X_{1\,t-1} + \hat{e}_2 X_{2\,t-2} + \cdots + \hat{e}_k X_{k\,t-k} + \mu_t \tag{6.5}$$

using the ordinary least squares (OLS) method.

6.7 Theory and Prior Signs (Expected)

6.7.1 Inflation and Real GDP

Investigations into the existence and nature of the link between inflation and growth have experienced a long history. Although economists now widely accept that inflation has a negative effect on economic growth, researchers did not detect this effect in data in the 1950s and the 1960s. A series of studies in the IMF Staff Papers around the 1960s found no evidence of damage from inflation (Bhatia 1960; Dorrance 1963, 1966; Wai 1959). Johanson (1967) quoted in Ferdous and Shahid (2013) found no conclusive empirical evidence for either a positive or a negative association between the two variables. Therefore, a popular view in the 1960s was that the effect of inflation on growth was not particularly important. Most empirical findings have established an inverse relationship between inflation and the GDP growth rate. The persistent increase in general prices of goods and services over time impedes efficient resource allocation by obscuring the signaling role of relative price changes which is an important guide to effective decision making (Fischer 1993 quoted in Enu et al. 2013). Inflation makes an economy's exports relatively expensive, affecting BOPs negatively thereby reducing a country's international competitiveness.

6.7.2 Unemployment and Real GDP

In the short run, the relationship between economic growth and unemployment rate may be a loose one. It is not unusual for the unemployment rate to show a sustained

Table 6.1 Summary of expected signs

Variable	Definition	Expected sign
$RGDP_t$	The real gross domestic product (the value of final goods and services evaluated at base year prices) for each year. $RGDP_t = Q_t * P_t$	Dependent variable
$INFR_t$	'Too much money in circulation causes the money to lose value'—this is the true meaning of inflation. In economics, inflation is an increase in the general level of prices of goods and services in an economy over a period of time (Ferdous and Shahid 2013)	(−) (+)
$UNER_t$	Unemployment is a macroeconomic problem that affects individuals differently and severely. The loss of employment means a reduced standard of living and psychological stress. Levinsohn (2008) explains that unemployment is associated with social problems such as poverty, crime, violence, a loss of morale and degradation $UNER = \frac{\text{Unemployed people}}{\text{Labor force}} \times 100$	(−)

Source Authors' interpretation

decline sometime after other broad measures of economic activity have turned positive. Hence, it is commonly referred to as a lagging economic indicator. Over an extended period of time, there is a negative relationship between changes in the rates of real GDP growth and unemployment. This long-run relationship between the two economic variables was most famously pointed out in the early 1960s by economist Arthur Okun. 'Okun's law' has been included in a list of 'core ideas' that are widely accepted in the economics profession. Okun's law, which economists have expanded upon since it was first articulated, states that real GDP growth about equal to the rate of potential output growth is usually required to maintain a stable unemployment rate (Levine 2013). Ernst and Berg (2009) as cited in Mosikari (2013) explain that high growth is associated with a high degree of employment intensity which is a necessary condition for the reduction of poverty. See Table 6.1.

6.8 Results, Findings, and Economic Interpretations of the Results

6.8.1 Lag Selection and Unit Root Test

The unit root test was used to examine the stationarity of the datasets. This enabled us to avoid the problems of spurious results that are associated with non-stationary time series models. We used the specific unit root test to check the stationarity of variables, that is, augmented Dickey–Fuller (ADF). The ADF test is based on the following regression:

$$\Delta Y_t = \alpha + \delta Y_{t-1} + \mu_t \tag{6.6}$$

where α is constant, δ is slope coefficient, t is a linear time trend, and μ is the error term (Granger 1969 as cited in Iqbal et al. 2012).

In the case of the Dickey–Fuller test, they may create a problem of auto-correlation. To tackle the auto-correlation problem, Dickey–Fuller developed a test called the ADF test:

$$\Delta Y_t = \beta_1 + ZY_{t-1} + \epsilon_i \quad \text{(Model 1—Intercept only)} \tag{6.7}$$

$$\Delta Y_t = \beta_1 + \beta_{2t} + ZY_{t-1} + \epsilon_i \quad \text{(Model 2—Trend and Intercept)} \tag{6.8}$$

$$\Delta Y_t = ZY_{t-1} + \epsilon_i \quad \text{(Model 3—No trend and No Intercept)} \tag{6.9}$$

Hypothesis, null hypothesis (H_0): The variable has a unit root, not stationary. Alternative hypothesis (H_1): The variable does not have a unit root, stationary. To make the variable stationary, we go for *I*(1), 1st differencing, or for *I*(2), 2nd differencing if the series has two unit roots in order to induce stationarity. The series is stationary when the p-value < 5%, H_0 is rejected. Same rule applies when ADF is calculated in absolute value > ADF critical value.

Lag was selected according to vector auto-regression estimates, we chose the lowest AIC value for the whole model, the lowest the AIC value, the better the model. Therefore, the lag value selected was equal to 10. It had the lowest AIC value compared to the others.

6.8.2 Auto-correlation Analysis

Based on the Durbin-Watson statistic value (0.044), which is less than 1, this means that there is evidence of a positive auto-correlation. In a regression analysis using time series data, with multiple interrelated data series, auto-correlation in variables of interest is typically modeled with the vector auto-regression (VAR).

6.8.3 An Analysis of the Stationarity of the Series

The ADF test shows that LRGDP is transformed into its first difference, the null hypothesis is rejected, and the series becomes stationary. INFR and UNER are *I*(0). Therefore, they are said to maintain stationarity at an integration of order one, *I*(1) and *I*(0), respectively. All the results from the ADF test are given in Table 6.2.

Table 6.2 Stationarity tests—augmented Dickey–Fuller (ADF) unit root tests

Variable	Crit. val. (5%)	ADF stat.	*p*-value	Decision
LRGDP	−2.909	−8.71	0.0000	Stationarity at first difference. $I(1)$
INFR	−2.909	−4.432	0.0007	Stationarity at level. $I(0)$
UNER	−1.946	−2.874	0.0048	Stationarity at level. $I(0)$

Source Authors' interpretation

As the times series variables are stationary, there is no need of testing for co-integration using Engel and Granger and Johansen tests because the co-integration test is equivalent to examining whether the residuals of regression between two non-stationary series are stationary (Gujarati 2004).

6.8.4 Granger Causality Test Among Variables

The Granger (1969) approach to the question of whether x causes y is to see whether the current y can be explained by p-values of y and then to see whether adding lagged values of x can improve the explanation. Y is said to be Granger-caused by x if x helps in the prediction of y, or equivalently if the coefficients on the lagged x's are statistically significant. It is important to note that the statement 'x Granger causes y' does not imply that y is the effect or the result of x. Granger causality measures precedence and information content but does not by itself indicate the causality in the more common use of the term. The results for the first null hypothesis, 'INFR does not Granger cause LRGDP' indicates a p-value of 0.9909 which is greater than the 5% critical value, meaning that we accept the null hypothesis stating that INFR does not Granger cause LRGDP. On the other side, the second null hypothesis 'LRGDP does not Granger cause INFR' indicates a p-value of 0.1668 which is greater than the 5% critical value, meaning that we accept the null hypothesis, meaning that LRGDP does not Granger cause INFR. The third null hypothesis 'UNER does not Granger cause LRGDP' gives a p-value of 0.9717 which is greater than the 5% critical value, meaning that we accept the null hypothesis stating that UNER does not Granger cause LRGDP. The fourth hypothesis 'LRGDP does not Granger cause UNER' has a p-value of 0.5299 which is greater than the 5% critical value; as result, we accept the null hypothesis, meaning that LRGDP does not Granger cause UNER. The fifth hypothesis 'UNER does not Granger cause INFR' has a p-value of 0.0847 which is greater than the 5% critical value. As a conclusion, we accept the statement which means that UNER does not Granger cause INFR. The sixth hypothesis 'INFR does not Granger cause UNER' has a p-value of 0.5156 which is also greater than the 5% critical value, that gives the same results. We conclude that we accept the null hypothesis, and INFR does not cause UNER. The outcome of the whole Granger causality test indicates that there is no causality between series.

6.8.5 Empirical Estimation of the Long-Run Relationship—VAR Model

Having confirmed the existence of a co-integrating relationship, we estimated the long-run VAR (1) model, using the OLS method. The co-integrating equation relating GDP, unemployment, and inflation is estimated as

$$\begin{array}{l} \mathrm{LRGDP}_{t-1} = 14.97 - 0.67\mathrm{INFR}_{t-1} - 7.05\,\mathrm{UNER}_{t-1} + \varepsilon_t \\ \text{Standard errors} \quad (0.14065) \qquad (3.83228) \end{array} \tag{6.10}$$

The values in brackets represent the standard errors associated with the estimated coefficient of Eq. (6.10).

Economic interpretations

All variables in the co-integrating equation have expected signs. Inflation rate, which is a measure of macroeconomic instability, has a negative sign. This implies that as inflation increases by 1%, RGDP reduces by 0.67%, inflation discourages investments and therefore leads to a contraction in real economic activity. Similarly, the unemployment rate also has a negative sign which means that when the unemployment rate increases by 1%, real GDP declines by 7.05%. However, the direction of causality may not necessarily run from unemployment to RGDP, since unemployment tends to be high during recessions because firms often lay off some workers. The appropriate method of analysis is using the error correction model (ECM) that leads to the real impact of all independent variables on LRGDP.

6.8.6 Empirical Estimation of the Short-Run Relationship

Existence of a long-run equilibrium model means that there is also a short-run relationship, which explains the short-run disequilibrium and shows how this disequilibrium is corrected in order to converge to the long-run equilibrium. ECM is also estimated using the OLS method as shown in Eq. (6.11). The error correction term (e_{t-1}) has an expected negative sign and is statistically significant at 5%. Other variables are also significant at 5%.

$$\begin{array}{l} \Delta\mathrm{LRDGP}_t = -0.127763\Delta\mathrm{LRGDP}_{t-1} - 0.000719\Delta\mathrm{INFR}_{t-1} - 0.045020\Delta\mathrm{UNER}_{t-1} - 0.000483e_{t-1} + \varepsilon_t \\ \qquad (0.13183) \qquad\qquad (0.00266) \qquad\qquad (0.09882) \qquad\qquad (0.00259) \end{array} \tag{6.11}$$

Economic interpretations

Just like in the long-run model, the variables in ECM have expected signs. The probability of $\Delta\mathrm{INFR}_{t-1}$ (0.00266) is less than 5%, meaning that $\Delta\mathrm{INFR}_{t-1}$ is significantly negatively related to LRGDP, since an increase of 1% in INFR reduces

LRGDP by 0.000719%, keeping other factors constant. As expected, $\Delta UNER_{t-1}$ also has a negative sign and is statistically significant at 10%, meaning that the coefficient of $\Delta UNER_{t-1}$ is not significant, and its probability (0.09882) is greater than 5%. Thus, a 1% increase in unemployment leads to a 0.045020% reduction in real economic activities. RGDP (−1) has a negative sign and a standard error (0.13183) which means that its coefficient is insignificant at the 5% level of significance. The error correction term has a probability of 0.00259 which is less than 5%. Therefore, its coefficient is significantly different from zero. The coefficient (−0.000483) means that for each quarter, the short-run disequilibrium will reduce by 0.000483%, meaning that the effect of the shock will reduce by 19.32% for each 4 quarters. This further means that it will end in 20th quarter (fifth year). R^2 values are small for all co-integrating equations (0.022675), (0.498962), (0.373759) which means that actually none of the variables are significant in the short run. Also, the co-integrating equation explains dynamics in real GDP; in other words, it is a growth mode.

6.8.7 *Chow Test and an Analysis of the Structural Stability of the Reduced ECM and Link Between Findings and Prior Signs*

The AR roots graph helps test whether the inverse roots of the AR characteristics polynomial are inside the unit circle. As shown in Fig. 6.1, the AR roots graph confirms that the estimated VAR model was stable over the period of the study (also see Table 6.3). We note that the residuals are normally distributed, and (0.3539) is greater than 5%.

Fig. 6.1 Stability test

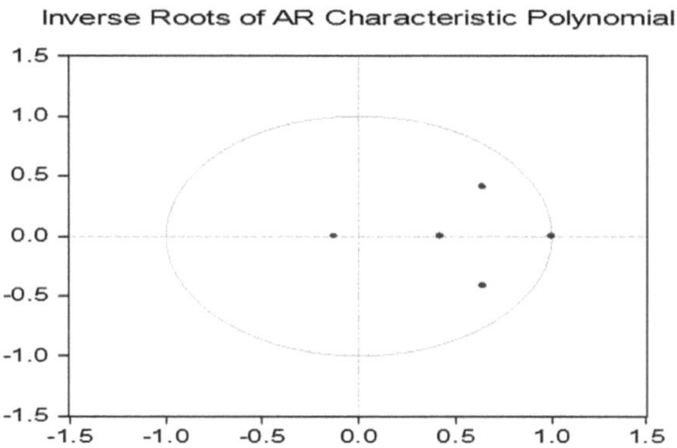

Table 6.3 Expected and obtained signs

Variables	Expected	Obtained	Decision
LRGDP			
INFR	Negative and positive	Negative	Confirmed
UNER	Negative	Negative	Confirmed

Source Authors' interpretation

6.9 Summary and Conclusion

Our research carried out a VAR model to trace the impact of economic stability measures (inflation rate and unemployment) on Rwandan real economic growth (RGDP). The conclusive outcome of the research shows that between inflation, unemployment and Rwandan real economic growth (RGDP) there is a long run negative and significant relationship. However, for Rwanda, a short-run negative relationship was found between real economic growth and both inflation and unemployment. In the long run, the related standard error for each coefficient was greater than 5%; thus, the coefficient was not significant. In the short run, only the coefficient of unemployment was not significant.

Countries like Rwanda which are characterized by relatively high economic growth and stability. Macroeconomic conditions do not suffer from an inflation impact, otherwise inflation and unemployment influence RGDP and thereby have a long term negative impact on economic growth. Therefore, policymaking bodies' attention has to aim at macroeconomic policies which provide cost efficiency and a route for steady and sustainable growth. Therefore, the Rwandan economy was stable over the period of study.

References

Ahmed S (2010) An empirical study on inflation and economic growth in Bangladesh. OIDA Int J Sustain Dev 2(3):41–48

Barro R (1987) Determinants of economic growth, a cross country empirical study. MIT Press, Cambridge, Mass

Bhatia RJ (1960) Inflation, deflation, and economic development. Int Monetary Fund 8(1): 101–114

Blanchard OJ, Kiyotaki N (1987) Monopolistic competition and the effects of aggregate demand. Am Econ Rev 77(4):647–666

Bourbonnais R (2007) Econométrie, 6ème édn. Dunod, Paris

Bruno M, Easterly W (1995) Inflation crises and long-run growth. NBER Working Papers No. 5209, National Bureau of Economic Research. Available at: http://ideas.repec.org/p/nbr/nberwo/5209.html

Bruno M, Easterly W (1998) Inflation crisis and long-run growth. J Monetary Econ 41:3–26

Chan KS, Tsay RS (1998) Limiting properties of the least square estimator of a continuous threshold autoregressive model. Biometrica 85:413–426

Chimobi OP (2010) Inflation and economic growth in Nigeria. J Sustain Dev 3(2):159–166

Datta K, Kumar C (2011) Relationship between inflation and economic growth in Malaysia. International conference on economics and finance research IPEDR Vol. 4, No. 2, pp 415–416
De Gregorio J (1992) The effect of inflation on economic growth. Eur Econ Rev 36(2–3):417–425
De Gregorio J (1996) Inflation, growth and Central Banks: theory and evidence. The World Bank, Policy Research Working Paper No. 1575
Dornbusch R, Fischer S, Kearney C (1996) Macroeconomics. The Mc-Graw-Hill Companies Inc., Sydney
Dorrance GS (1966) Inflation and growth. Int Monetary Fund 13(1):82–102
Dorrance S (1963) The effect of inflation on economic development. Int Monetary Fund 10(1): 1–47
Drukker D, Hernandez-Verme P, Gomis-Porgueras P (2005) Threshold effects in the relationship between Inflation and Growth: a new Panel-Data Approach. Working paper presented at the 11 th International conference on panel—data, Texas A&M University, College Station, Texas
Enu P, Attah-Obeng P, Hagan E (2013) The relationship between GDP growth rate and inflationary rate in Ghana: an elementary statistical approach. Acad Res Int 4(5):310–318
Erbaykal E, Okuyan H (2008) Does inflation depress economic growth? Evidence from Turkey. Int Res J Finance and Econ 13(17):40–48
Ernst C, Berg J (2009) The role of employment and labour markets in the fight against poverty. In: Promoting Pro-Poor Growth, Employment. OECD. http://www.oecd.org/dac/povertyreduction/43514554.pdf Accessed 15 Apr 2017
Ferdous M, Mahbuba Shahid E (2013) Study on nature of inflation and its relationship with GDP growth rate: a Case Study on Bangladesh. IOSR J Econ Finance 1(3):40–49
Fischer S (1993) The role of macroeconomic factors in growth. J Monetary Econ 32(3):485–511
Gokal V, Hanif S (2004) Relationship between Inflation and Economic Growth in Fiji. Reserve Bank of Fiji Suva, Fiji, Economics Department. Working Paper No. 4
Granger CWJ (1969) Investigating causal relationships by econometric models and cross-spectral methods. Econometrica 37(3):424–438
Gujarati DR (2004) Basic econometrics, 4th edn. Tata McGraw Hill
Hansen BE (2000) Sample splitting and threshold estimation. Econometrica 68:575–603
Haslag JH (1997) Output, growth, welfare, and inflation: a survey. Econ Rev Second Q, Int Monetary Fund 8(11–12):1011–1014
Iqbal N, Din M, Ghani E (2012) Fiscal decentralisation and economic growth: role of democratic institutions. Pak Develop Rev 52(3):176–196
Johanson HG (1967) Is inflation a retarding factor in economic growth? In fiscal and monetary problems in developing states. Proceedings of the third Rehoroth conference. Preager, New York, pp 121–130
Khan MS, Senhadji SA (2001) Threshold effects in the relationship between inflation and growth. Int Monetary Fund 48(1):1–21
Kigume RW (2011) The relationship between inflation and economic growth in Kenya. Int J Bus Soc Sci 3(10). Available at: http://ir-library.ku.ac.ke/handle/123456789/2124
Kilindo A (1997) Fiscal operations, money supply and inflation in Tanzania. Afr Econ Res Consortium 65(3):1–7
Levine L (2013) Economic growth and the unemployment rate. Congressional research service, 7-5700, R 42063, CRS report for congress, pp 1–10
Levinsohn J (2008) Two policies to alleviate unemployment in South Africa. Center for International Development, at Harvard University, CID Working Paper No. 166
Luppu DV (2009) The correlation between inflation and economic growth in Romania. Luccrari Stiintifice, p 53
Madhukar S, Nagarjuna B (2011) Inflation and growth rates in India and China: a perspective of transition economies. Int Conf Econ Finance Res 4(97):489–490
Mallik G, Chowdury A (2001) Inflation and economic growth: evidence from four South Asian countries. Asia-Pac Dev J 8(1):123–135
Mankiw NG, Romer D, Well DN (1992) A contribution to the empirics of economic growth. Quart J Econ 107(2):407–437

Mosikari TJ (2013) The effect of unemployment rate on gross domestic product: case of South Africa. Mediterr J Soc Sci 4(6):429–434

Motley B (1994) Growth and inflation: a cross-country study. Center for economic policy research, Stanford University, CEPR Publication No. 395, pp 15–28

Mubarik YA (2005) Inflation and growth: an estimate of the threshold level of INFLATION in Pakistan. SBP-Res Bull 1(1):35–43

Mundell R (1963) Inflation and real interest. J Polit Econ 71(3):280–283

Pradana MBJ, Rathnayaka MKTR (2013) Testing the link between inflation and economic growth: evidence from Asia. Mod Econ 4:87–92

Prasanna S, Gopakumar K (2010) An empirical analysis of inflation and economic growth in India. Int J Sustain Dev 15(2):4–5

Richard T (1998) Macroeconomics theories and policies, 6th edn. University of North Carolina at Chapel Hill

Sarel M (1995) Nonlinear effects of inflation on economic growth. Int Monetary Fund 43(1): 199–215

Sidrauski M (1967) Inflation and economic growth. J Polit Econ 75(6):796–810

Stein P (2010) The economics of Tanzania, Kenya, Uganda, Rwanda and Burundi. Report prepared for Swed Fund International AB, pp 12–32

Stockman AC (1981) Anticipated inflation and the capital stock in a cash-in-advance economy. J Monetary Econ 8:387–393

Tobin J (1965) Money and economic growth. Econometrica 33(4):671–684

Umaru A, Zubairu J (2012) The effect of inflation on the growth and development of the Nigerian economy: an empirical analysis. Int J Bus Soc Sci 3(10):187–188

Wai UT (1959) The relationship between inflation and economic development: a statistical inductive study. Int Monetary Fund 7(2):302–317

Xiao J (2009) The relationship between inflation and economic growth of China: empirical study from 1978–2007. Lund University, Sweden, pp 1–56

Chapter 7
Macroeconomic, Political, and Institutional Determinants of FDI Inflows to Ethiopia: An ARDL Approach

Addis Yimer

Abstract Based on the lines of the eclectic theoretical framework of Foreign direct investment (FDI) flows, this study investigates the macroeconomic, political, and institutional determinants of FDI inflows to Ethiopia for the period 1970–2013. Using the ARDL modeling approach, it finds that political and institutional factors are crucial both in the long run and the short run in FDI inflows to the country. On the macroeconomic side, the market size of the country, availability of natural resources, openness to trade, and deprecation in the nominal exchange rate are found to positively affect FDI inflows to the country. On the other hand, macroeconomic instability is found to effect FDI inflows negatively. In addition, better political stability, government effectiveness and regulatory quality, and better performance of the rule of law are found to positively affect FDI inflows to the country. A careful liberalization of the foreign exchange market and that of external trade, sustaining the current growth momentum of the economy, improving institutional quality, and strengthening the political stability of the country, among others, are fundamental areas that the government could work on to strengthen Ethiopia's position in FDI inflows on the continent.

Keywords ARDL · Determinants · Ethiopia · FDI · Macroeconomic stability · Political · Institutional

7.1 Introduction

Foreign direct investment (FDI) plays an important role in the growth process of poor nations (UNCTAD 2013). Not only does it provide the much needed capital for filling the saving-investment and foreign exchange gaps in these countries, but it is also important for generating employment opportunities and transferring technology and managerial know-how. In addition, by providing access to foreign

A. Yimer (✉)
Department of Economics, Addis Ababa University, Addis Ababa, Ethiopia
e-mail: addisyimer@gmail.com

A. Heshmati (ed.), *Studies on Economic Development and Growth in Selected African Countries*, Frontiers in African Business Research,
DOI 10.1007/978-981-10-4451-9_7

markets and building capacity through the transfer of technology, FDI improves the integration of the host country into the global economy thus fostering growth.

The Ethiopian economy has to grow at least at an annual growth rate of 11% for more than two decades so that it can attain the per capita income levels that have been achieved today by most sub-Saharan African (SSA) countries (UNDP 2011). However, the country's domestic sources of finance are limited and cannot help it achieve such a level of growth. In 2013, its gross domestic capital formation as a share of GDP was around 33%, with gross domestic savings lagging behind at around 6%. One alternative for filling this savings gap is through loans and development assistance from multilateral agencies such as the World Bank and IMF. However, as noted by Astatike and Assefa (2005) such a source of foreign finance is unstable in nature.

Acknowledging this fact, the current Ethiopian government has opened several economic sectors to foreign investors so that they fill the desired saving-investment gap. The government has issued several investment incentives, including tax holidays, duty-free imports of capital goods, and export tax exemptions to encourage FDI. Further, the Ethiopian Investment Authority (EIA) has been established to service investors and streamline investment procedures. In addition to liberalizing investments, other areas of the external sector have also been liberalized through unilateral, multilateral, and regional liberalization.

However, despite all these efforts, Ethiopia is not a major recipient of FDI inflows. The country's average share of global FDI inflows was only 0.01% in 2000–2013. In the same period, its annual average share in FDI inflows to the SSA region was only 2%. The central question, therefore, is Why does Ethiopia not attract much FDI?

There exists a very large body of literature on the determinants of FDI flows. While most of them are cross-country studies in the developing world in general, little has been done to investigate the determinants of FDI flows to Ethiopia specifically. While cross-country studies are able to identify the factors that drive FDI and examine its impact across countries, they fail to provide in-depth analyses and country specific factors that are crucial in attracting FDI. Even the few studies done on Ethiopia (which are by and large unpublished Masters' theses) deal with the economic determinants of FDI flows and ignore the role of political, governance, and institutional determinants of FDI flows to the host country. To the best of our knowledge, ours is among the first studies that try to capture the effects of a wide range of political and institutional quality indicators in the host country for attracting FDI inflows. Among other things, most studies also share the problem of a short series of data and omission of relevant macroeconomic variables in their models. They are not theoretically and empirically systematic either. Our study attempts to address these gaps.

The rest of the paper is organized as follows. Section 7.2 presents the trends in FDI inflows to Ethiopia. Section 7.3 gives a review of the theoretical and empirical literature on the determinants of FDI inflows to a host country. Our study's empirical methodology is discussed in Sect. 7.4 while Sect. 7.5 discusses the results of the empirical exercise. Finally, Sect. 7.6 gives a conclusion and some policy recommendations.

7.2 FDI Inflows to Ethiopia

Net FDI inflows to Ethiopia were at a mere US$3.9 million in 1970, representing a very negligible share in global investment flows. This figure increased substantially to US$953 million in 2013, although its share in global FDI flows was still a decimal. This increase in FDI inflows to the country may be explained by factors that characterized the economic and political landscape that prevailed over the period under study. This period mainly witnessed two distinct political regimes. The first period, 1974–1991 related to the Derg regime, where the socialist ideology of a centralized command economic system controlled the sphere of socioeconomic policy making in the country. As noted by Geda (2008), this regime was mainly characterized by a deliberate repression of market forces and socialization of the production and distribution process and adoption of a 'hard control' regime. In this period, the country's economic performance was highly irregular due to its dependence on the agricultural sector (which is vulnerable to the vagaries of nature) and the intense conflict that characterized the period (see Geda 2008). The second period, post-1991 to the present, started with the coming to power of the Ethiopian People Revolutionarily Democratic Front (EPRDF) in 1991, after the demise of Derg. In terms of socioeconomic policies, there was a significant move away from the doctrines of the command system in favor of a free market.

The regime has adopted structural adjustment policies of market liberalization with the support of the World Bank and IMF (see Geda 2008). Economic performance during this period has substantially improved not only by the Derg's standards but also by African standards. The improvements in economic performance in this period appear to be a combined result of the reforms, favorable weather conditions, and better political stability and relative peace that have prevailed (see Geda 2008). Likewise, FDI inflows to the country have also registered a significant increase in this period. They increased from a period's average of US$5.9 million during the Derg regime to around US$270 million in the EPRDF regime (UNCTAD 2013). Thanks to the ups and downs (due to the global financial crisis in 2008 and deteriorating peace as a result of the war with Eritrea in 1998–2000, among other things), net FDI inflows reached a level of nearly US$1 billion by 2013 (Fig. 7.1). As argued in a report of the Ethiopian Investment Commission (2014), this was mainly due to the various liberalization policies, better economic performance, and a stable political sphere that characterized the period.

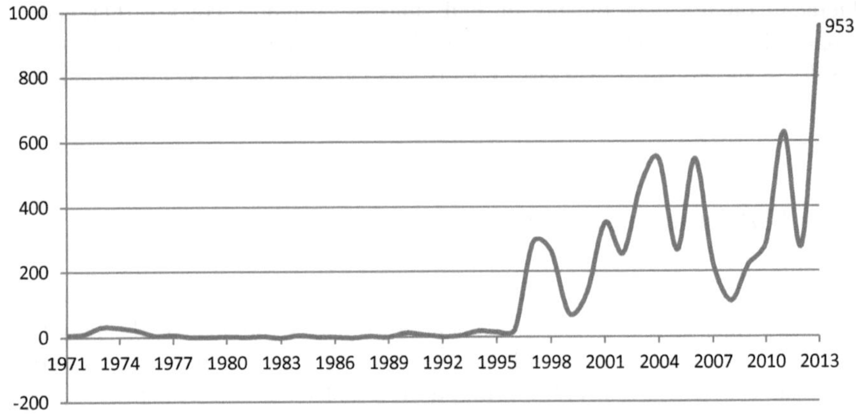

Fig. 7.1 FDI inflows to Ethiopia (1970–2013) (in million US$). *Source* Author's computation based on World Development Indicators (2015b) and UNCTAD (2013)

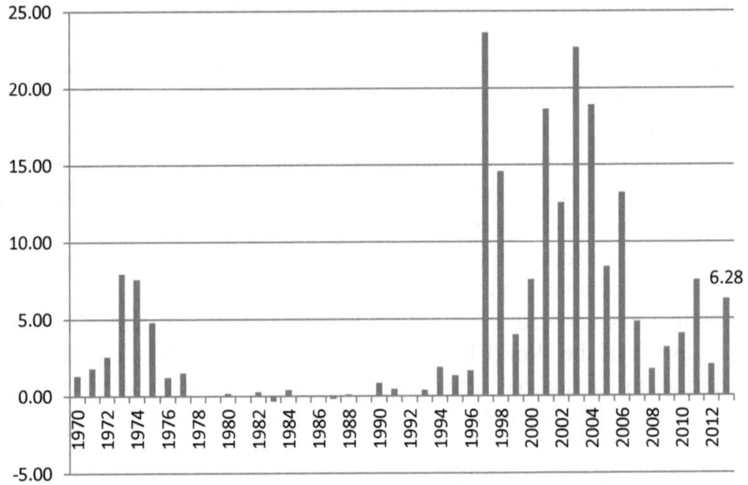

Fig. 7.2 Ethiopia's FDI inflows as percentage of gross fixed capital formation. *Source* Author's computation based on World Development Indicators (2015b) and UNCTAD (2013)

Total FDI inflows as a percentage of gross fixed capital formation in the country were around 0.7% in 1990. This reached a little over 6% in 2013, despite the ups and downs over the years. However, this is not a very big increase (see Fig. 7.2).

If we see the distribution of FDI inflows by sector, manufacturing led the list (with a 70.6% share of the total FDI inflows) followed by the service sector (10.7%) and agriculture (8.7%) (Ethiopian Investment Commission 2014).

7.3 Review of Related Literature

7.3.1 Theoretical Literature

The early neo-classical approach, summarized in MacDougall (1960), hypothesized that capital flows across countries were governed by differential rates of return. It argued that such capital inflows were welfare enhancing for both the parties engaged in the capital's movement. The MacDougall model assumes perfect competition, risk-free capital movement, mobility in factors of production, and no risk of default. The portfolio approach to FDI, presented in a reaction to the MacDougall model, emphasizes not only return differentials but also risk (Agarwal 1980). In line with this, Ohlin (1933) was one of the first to address the issue of determinants of FDI. According to Ohlin (1933), FDI was motivated mainly by the possibility of high profitability in growing markets, along with the possibility of financing these investments at relatively low rates of interest in the host country. Other determinants were the necessity to overcome trade barriers and to secure sources of raw materials. This is strengthened by a theory which emphasizes the positive relationship between FDI and output (sales in host country) along the lines of Jorgenson's (1963) model (see Agarwal 1980).

A major criticism of these theories relates to the question of perfection in markets. Hymer (1976) and Kindleberger (1969) argue that if foreign firms are to compete and succeed in the host country, then they must be in possession of a specific and transferable competitive advantage both over local firms and other potential entrants into the local market. Building on Hymer's (1960) analysis Kindleberger (1969) posited that instead of multinational firms' behavior determining the market structure, it is the market structure (monopolistic competition) that determines a firm's conduct by internalizing its production. Caves (1971) has supported such an analysis and has further argued that FDI is also related to trade barriers and could be taken as a way of avoiding uncertainties in supplies, or as a way of imposing barriers to new firms in the external market. This analysis also focuses on the micro-foundations of FDI by moving from a simple capital movement/ portfolio theory to a broader production and industrial organizational theory. This school of thought has formed the basis of a whole strand of literature. According to this line of thinking, some advantages of competitive foreign firms include cheaper sources of financing; the use of brand names and patent rights; technological, marketing, and managerial skills; economies of scale; and entry and exit barriers (Agarwal 1980; Kindleberger 1969).

A related micro-based theory of FDI has also emerged with the development of Vernon's product cycle theory (Vernon 1966). The product cycle theory is an advance over previous theories in that it incorporates an analysis of oligopoly and strategic market considerations. Based on Vernon's theory of 'product cycle,' and the existence of 'new' and 'old' goods, Krugman 1979) developed this theoretical avenue further for explaining FDI flows. Specifically, he extended the analysis to a North–South framework with innovation (in the 'North') and technology transfer (to the 'South') representing its crucial aspects. Krugman (1979) notes that technological progress raises the marginal product of capital and provides an incentive for FDI. On the other hand, this process may be reversed through technology transfer. Mainstream trade theories usually underlie this type of analysis. Recent theories of trade such as that of the 'economies of specialization' which emphasize the existence of intra-industry (as well as intra-firm) trade, also provide scope for an analysis of FDI (see, for instance, Ocampo's 1986 survey).

Notwithstanding Vernon's contribution, building on Hymer's original contribution a second wave of refinements to the neo-classical capital movement/portfolio theory of FDI has also come into being with the emergence of explanations based on the ideas of 'international firm' and 'industrial organization.' The fact that decision making about FDI takes place within the context of oligopolistic firm structures and that such an investment includes a package of other inputs such as intermediate imports and capital flows has led to the development of alternative explanations grounded in the theory of industrial organization (see Agarwal 1980; Dunning 1993; Helleiner 1989). In this approach as set out by Hymer, foreign firms are seen as having an advantage over local ones. The foreign firms' pursuit of FDI is explained by the theory of internalization. This is characterized by the desire to minimize transaction costs, *a la* Coase (1937) to tackle risks and uncertainties, increase control and market power, achieve economies of scale, and ensure advantageous transfer pricing (Buckley and Casson 1976; Hymer 1976). In this approach, oligopoly is seen as mitigating, rather than creating market imperfections (Helleiner 1989).

Dunning's (1993) work, which he terms the 'eclectic paradigm,' represents a culmination of this trend toward a refinement of FDI theories. Without departing much from the Heckscher–Ohlin–Samuelson theory of trade for explaining the spatial distribution of multinational firms, Dunning's paradigm summarizes this strand of theory under an 'ownership-specific, location and internalization' (OLI) framework (see Dunning 1993). Framed in a micro-macroeconomic framework, Dunning's (1981, 1988, 1993) approach provides a flexible and popular framework where he argues that FDI is determined by three sets of advantages which direct investments should have over the other institutional mechanisms available for a firm in satisfying the needs of its customers at home and abroad. The first of the advantages is an ownership (O)-specific one which includes the advantage that a firm has over its rivals in terms of its brand name, patent, or knowledge of technology and marketing. This allows the firm to compete with other firms in the markets that it serves regardless of the disadvantages of being foreign. The second is location (L)-specific advantages which relate to the importance for a firm operating and investing in the host country and these advantages that make the chosen foreign country a more attractive site for FDI than others. The third advantage is the internationalization (I) advantage which relates to the preference of a 'bundled' FDI approach over 'unbundled' product licensing, capital lending, or technical assistance (Wheeler and Mody 1992). These refer to the superior commercial benefits for firms resulting from the exploitation of ownership and location-specific advantages by investing in foreign affiliates that they control, rather than through transactions with unrelated firms located abroad. Helleiner (1989) notes that 'this "eclectic" theory of direct investment drawing on firm-specific attributes, location advantages and internalization advantages—is widely accepted.' There also exists an international trade version of FDI determination (termed the macro-approach) which is associated with Kojima (1973) work. The Kojima model argues that FDI may be explained by the 'comparative disadvantage' of industry in the investing countries. According to Kojima's theory, this may be mitigated by investing in a foreign industry, which may be able to achieve comparative advantages in the production of a particular product and potentially even export back to the home country. Naturally, this type of FDI will also have the effect of increasing trade volumes (Kojima 1973).

In sum, the determinants of the FDI theory cover a range of explanations: the pure capital movement, product cycle, industrial organization, the stagnation thesis, and other political considerations. In the African context, the pure capital theory does not work since the assumptions do not hold. Neither is Krugman's hypothesis workable since it is more relevant for countries with a good industrial base and infrastructure. On the other hand, the concentration of multinational corporations in the mining sectors in most African countries and, to a good degree, the importance of the colonial history in determining their spatial pattern (see Geda 2002) might be taken as lending support to the importance of the 'eclectic' approach. This theoretical insight is used in identifying FDI determinants in the empirical analysis and construction of our model.

7.3.2 Empirical Literature: Empirical Regularity in Africa

The empirical literature on the determinants of FDI in developing countries is voluminous and is based on both country case and cross-sectional analyses. However, in the discussion that follows, we focus on evidence found in African studies which offer some insights about the empirical analysis conducted in our study. In general, the findings of these studies reveal that labor costs, country size, economic openness, exchange rate regime, return on investment, human capital, and political factors are among the most important factors explaining FDI flows to the region.

Most studies on Africa report that FDI to Africa is largely motivated by natural resource endowments of the countries on the continent (Asiedu 2002, 2003; Asiedu and Gyimah-Brempong 2008; Basu and Srinivasan 2002; Morisset 2000; among others). Based on a survey conducted in 29 African countries using both panel and cross-sectional analysis, Morisset (2000) reported a high correlation between FDI inflows and total value of natural resources in each country. He further reported that economic growth and trade openness had a large impact on the level of FDI inflows that a given country received. Basu and Srinivasan (2002) found that almost 40% of the FDI in their African study found its way to the primary sector, particularly in the oil and mineral extraction business. Countries such as Angola, Botswana, Namibia, and Nigeria received foreign investments targeted at the oil and minerals sectors of their economies (Basu and Srinivasan 2002). Though natural resource abundance is a common factor which explains much of the FDI inflows, a few successful African countries have also managed to attract FDI by creating favorable economic, social, and political environments (Basu and Srinivasan 2002; UNCTAD 1998). For instance, countries such as Mauritius and Seychelles have managed to attract FDI by tailoring their FDI policies through liberalization, export orientation, tax, and other investment incentives. Moreover, some countries such as Lesotho and Swaziland have attracted FDI because they are near South Africa and investors wanting to serve the large market in South Africa have located their subsidiaries in these countries (Basu and Srinivasan 2002; UNCTAD 1998).

Asiedu (2002) analyzed 34 countries in sub-Saharan Africa over 1980–2000. Using a panel data analysis, she found that openness to trade, higher incomes and better growth prospects, and better institutional frameworks and infrastructure were 'rewarded' with more investments. Later studies by Asiedu (2003, 2006) show the significant role of a country's market size and natural resource endowment in enhancing FDI. Lower inflation, good infrastructure, an educated population, openness, less corruption, political stability, and a reliable legal system were also found to have similar positive effects on FDI flows into the continent in these studies. Asiedu and Gyimah-Brempong (2008) validated these finding to a large extent and noted that countries that were small or lacked natural resources could attract FDI by improving their institutions and policy environments.

Based on a co-integration analysis for 1970–2000 using data from 19 SSA countries, Bende-Nabende (2002) found market growth, export-oriented policies, and liberalization as the most dominant long-run determinants of FDI in Africa. In line with Bende-Nabende (2002), focusing on manufactured goods, primary commodities, and services, Kandiero and Chitiga (2003) analyzed the impact of openness on FDI flows to Africa in 51 African countries. Their findings indicate that FDI responds significantly to increased openness in the whole economy in general and in the service sector in particular.

Using fixed and random effects models on a panel dataset for 29 African countries over the period 1975–1999, Onyeiwu and Shrestha (2004) identified economic growth, inflation, openness of the economy, international reserves, and natural resource availability as important determinants of FDI to Africa. Contrary to conventional wisdom, political rights and infrastructure were found to be unimportant in their study. Krugell (2005) also empirically tested the significance of a number of hypothesized determinants of FDI in sub-Saharan Africa. The pooled cross-country and time-series estimation covered the period 1980–1999 in 17 countries. Krugell's results are in line with the findings mentioned earlier, particularly with respect to economic growth and openness.

Abdoul (2012) estimated a model of FDI determination using five-year panel data with the system-GMM technique over 1970–2009 for 53 African countries. He found that larger countries attracted more FDI. However, regardless of their size, more open and politically stable countries that offered higher returns to investments also attracted FDI. FDI inflows were also found to be persistent in the sense that countries that manage to attract FDI today are likely to attract more FDI in the future. Using cross-country data for 53 African countries for the period 1996–2008, Anyanwu (2012) found market size (whose proxy is urban population as percentage of total population and GDP per capita of the host country), openness to trade, the rule of law, foreign aid, natural resources, and past FDI inflows (increased agglomeration) to have a positive effect on FDI inflows. He also found domestic financial development to have a negative effect on FDI inflows. Further, he found that East and Southern African sub-regions appeared positively disposed to obtaining higher levels of inward FDI.

Among the most recent FDI studies on Africa, Geda and Yimer (2015) have estimated a model of FDI determination for Africa based on a new analytical country classification of African economies as ‘Fragile, Factor, and Investment driven’ economies. Using a panel co-integration approach over 1996–2012 they found market size, availability of natural resources, openness to international trade, a stable macroeconomic environment, better infrastructure, and an effective bureaucracy to have a strong positive impact on attracting FDI to the continent. On the other hand, they also found that political and macroeconomic instability and high financial and transfer risks had a negative effect on attracting FDI to the continent. However, the effect of these factors varied significantly across the analytical country classification that they developed (Geda and Yimer 2015). Among all determinants of FDI only government effectiveness and natural resource abundance were found to be important across all countries. They stress on the importance of emphasizing different policies in different countries or country groups.

Country case studies on Africa, which invariably use time series analyses, have reported results that are similar to those in recent cross section-based studies reviewed earlier. Among these, Astatike and Assefa (2005) examined determinants of FDI in Ethiopia over 1974–2001 using a time series analysis. Their empirical analysis shows that economic growth, export orientation (openness), and liberalization had a significant positive impact on FDI, while macroeconomic instability (measured by inflation) and a low level of physical infrastructure (measured by telephone lines per 1000 people) had a negative impact. Similarly, using a time series analysis for Cameroon, Sunday and Lydie (2006) show that the level of infrastructure development (increased electricity production and the ratio of paved roads) was the most significant determinant of FDI in the country. Market size (GDP per capita), openness, human capital development, and the rate of economic growth were also important but were found to be less significant. Exchange rate, political risk, the rate of inflation, debt burden, agglomeration effect, and the creation of an export-processing zone did not have any influence on FDI in Cameroon.

Seetanah and Rojid (2011) examined the determinants of FDI in Mauritius using reduced-form demand for the inward FDI function. In their study, openness, wages, and the quality of labor in the host country were important. Size of the market was reported to have a relatively lesser impact on FDI; this is probably related to the limited size of the population and the good export opportunities from Mauritius to other African countries especially in SADEC/COMESA regions. The significant coefficient of the lagged dependent variable in their model suggests the presence of dynamism in the system. Finally, Okpara (2012), using Granger causality and an error correction model investigated the determinants of FDI flows to Nigeria during 1970–2009. He found that natural resource abundance, fiscal incentives, favorable government policies, exchange rate, and infrastructural development had a positive and statistically significant effect on FDI flows to Nigeria. Though statistically insignificant, market size and trade openness were found to have a positive sign while political risk was found to have a negative sign. Further, the statistically significant error correction term revealed that past foreign investment flows could significantly stimulate current investment inflows.

In sum, both the theoretical discussion in the previous section and the brief review of empirical studies in this section show that market size, openness of the economy, natural resource endowments, and political and macroeconomic stability are important determinants of FDI flows to Africa. These are important factors that any model about determinants of FDI flows to Africa needs to consider. However, when examined in light of FDI theoretical literature, none of these African studies formulate their empirical models by explicitly following one or the other strand of literature. The variables used in their models, however, suggest the use of Dunning's eclectic paradigm without stating which variable is used as a proxy for which theoretical concept. This is partly a result of missing theoretical discussions and formulations in almost all these studies.

7.4 The Empirical Methodology

7.4.1 Auto-regressive Distributive Lag (ARDL) Approach to Co-integration

In economic literature, a number of co-integration techniques such as the Engle-Granger (1987), Johansen (1988), Johansen and Juselius (1990), Gregory and Hansen (1996), Saikkonen and Lütkepohl (2000), and Pesaran et al.'s (2001) ARDL approach have been used.

The ARDL approach developed by Pesaran et al. (1996, 2001) and Pesaran and Shin (1999) has become popular in recent years. This ARDL model has some advantages over other co-integration approaches. Firstly, this technique is comparatively more robust in small or finite samples consisting of 30–80 observations (Pattichis 1999). Secondly, it can be utilized irrespective of whether regressors are of $I(0)$ or $I(1)$ or mutually integrated though there still is a prerequisite that none of the explanatory variables is of $I(2)$ or higher order, that is, the ARDL procedure will be inefficient in the existence of $I(2)$ or higher order series. Thirdly, the ARDL model applies a general-to-specific modeling framework by taking a sufficient number of lags to capture the data-generating process.

Further, traditional co-integration methods may also experience the problems of endogeneity, whereas the ARDL method can distinguish between dependent and explanatory variables and remove the problems that may arise due to the presence of auto-correlation and endogeneity. The ARDL co-integration estimates short-run and long-run relationships simultaneously and provides unbiased and efficient estimates. The appropriateness of using the ARDL model is that it is based on a single equation framework. The ARDL model takes sufficient numbers of lags and directs the data-generating process in a general to specific modeling framework (Harvey 1981). Unlike other multivariate co-integration techniques such as Johansen and Juselius (1990), the ARDL model permits the co-integration relationship to be estimated by OLS once the lag order of the model is identified. The error correction model (ECM) can also be drawn by using the ARDL approach (Pesaran and Shin 1999). ECM allows drawing outcomes for long-run estimates while other traditional co-integration techniques do not provide such types of inferences. As noted by Pesaran and Shin (1999), ECM joins together short-run adjustments with long-run equilibrium without losing long-run information.

These advantages of the ARDL technique over other standard co-integration techniques justify the application of ARDL approach in our study to analyze the relationship among the FDI model's variables.

7.4.2 The Empirical Model in the ARDL Framework

In order to examine the long-run relationship and the dynamic interaction between FDI and institutions, our study employs an ARDL modeling approach. According to Pesaran et al. (2001) the ARDL approach requires three steps:

The first step is estimating the long-run relationship among the variables. This is done by testing the significance of the lagged levels of the variables in the error correction form of the underlying ARDL model. Following Pesaran et al. (2001), our ARDL model can be written as:

$$\begin{aligned}\Delta\mathrm{LFDI}_t = {} & \alpha_0 + \beta_1\mathrm{LFDI}_{t-1} + \beta_2\mathrm{LRGDP}_{t-1} + \beta_3\mathrm{LRES}_{t-1} \\ & + \beta_{41}\mathrm{LINF}_{t-1} + \beta_5\mathrm{LDEBGDP}_{t-1} + \beta_6\mathrm{LOPNES}_{t-1} \\ & + \beta_7\mathrm{LNER}_{t-1} + \beta_{86\mathrm{OLSTABDPountry}}\mathrm{Polinst}_{t-1} + \sum_{i=1}^{p}\delta_1\Delta\mathrm{LFDI}_{t-1} \\ & + \sum_{i=0}^{p}\delta_2\Delta\mathrm{RGDP}_{t-1} + \sum_{i=0}^{p}\delta_3\Delta\mathrm{LRES}_{t-1} + \sum_{i=0}^{p}\delta_4\Delta\mathrm{LINF}_{t-1} \\ & + \sum_{i=0}^{p}\delta_5\Delta\mathrm{LDEBGDP}_{t-1} + \sum_{i=0}^{p}\delta_6\Delta\mathrm{LOPNES}_{t-1} \\ & + \sum_{i=0}^{p}\delta_7\mathrm{LNER}_{t-1}\sum_{i=0}^{p}\delta_8\Delta\mathrm{Polinst}_{t-1} + \varepsilon_t\end{aligned}$$

where LFDI is log of FDI, LRGDP is log of real GDP, RES is log of natural resource abundance, INF is log of the domestic annual inflation rate, LDEBGDP is log of external debt to GDP ratio, LOPNES is log of openness, LNER is log of nominal exchange rate, Polinst is an indicator of political stability, and quality of institutions in the host country. As there is a high degree of multi-collinearity among the six political and institutional indicators, we used each of the political and institutional indicators separately. Hence, the variable Polinst indicates in all of the three steps a model that incorporates only a single political and institutional indicator among the macroeconomic variables. The selection of the optimum lagged orders of the ARDL models is based on the Schwarz Bayesian Criterion (SBC). In order to test co-integration among the variables, the Wald F-statistics for testing the joint hypotheses has to be compared with the critical values as tabulated by Pesaran et al. (2001).

The joint hypotheses to be tested are as follows:

$$H_0 : \beta_1 = \beta_2 = \beta_3 = \beta_4 = \beta_5 = \beta_6 = \beta_7 = \beta_8 = 0$$
$$H_1 : \beta_i \neq 0, i = 1, 2\ldots, 8$$

If the F-statistic is higher than the upper bound critical value, the null hypothesis (H_0) is rejected, indicating that there is a long-run relationship between the lagged level variables in the model. In contrast, if the F-statistic falls below the lower bound, then H_0 cannot be rejected and no long-run relationship exists. However, if the F-statistic falls in between the upper bound and lower bound critical values, the inference is inconclusive. At this condition, the order of integration of each variable should be determined before any inference can be made.

In the second step, once the co-integration is established, the conditional ARDL (p, q, r, s, t, u, v, w) long-run model of the determinants of LFDI_t can be estimated as follows:

$$\begin{aligned} \text{LFDI}_t = \alpha_0 &+ \sum_{i=1}^{p} \beta_1 \text{LFDI}_{t-1} + \sum_{i=0}^{q} \beta_2 \text{RGDP}_{t-1} + \sum_{i=0}^{r} \beta_3 \text{LRES}_{t-1} + \sum_{i=0}^{s} \beta_4 \text{LINF}_{t-1} \\ &+ \sum_{i=0}^{t} \beta_5 \text{LDEBGDP}_{t-1} + \sum_{i=0}^{u} \beta_6 \text{LOPNES}_{t-1} \\ &+ \sum_{i=0}^{v} \beta_7 \text{LNER}_{t-1} \sum_{i=0}^{w} \beta_8 \text{Polinst}_{t-1} + \varepsilon_t \end{aligned}$$

In the final step, we obtain the short-run dynamic parameters by estimating an error correction model (ECM) associated with the long-run estimates. This is specified as follows:

$$\Delta \text{LFDI}_t = \alpha_0 + \sum_{i=1}^{p} \delta_1 \Delta \text{LFDI}_{t-1} + \sum_{i=0}^{q} \delta_2 \Delta \text{LRGDP}_{t-1} + \sum_{i=0}^{r} \delta_3 \Delta \text{LRES}_{t-1} + \sum_{i=0}^{s} \delta_4 \Delta \text{LINF}_{t-1} + \sum_{i=0}^{t} \delta_5 \Delta \text{LDEBGDP}_{t-1} + \sum_{i=0}^{u} \delta_6 \Delta \text{LOPNESO}_{t-1} + \sum_{i=0}^{v} \delta_7 \text{LNER}_{t-1} + \sum_{i=0}^{w} \delta_8 \Delta \text{LPolins}_{t-1} + \theta \text{ECM}_{t-1} + \varepsilon_t$$

where, $\delta_1, \delta_2, \delta_3, \delta_4, \delta_5, \delta_6, \delta_7$ and δ_8 are the short-run dynamic coefficients of the model's convergence to equilibrium and θ is the speed of adjustment.

In specifying the equation of our FDI model, we used the theoretical lines of Dunning's (1981, 1988, 1993) 'eclectic theory' of OLI advantages as determinants of FDI flows to Africa. In addition to location advantages, Dunning's ownership and internalization (LI) advantages that may attract FDI to Ethiopia could be proxied by market size, natural endowments, and a stable macroeconomic and political environment as African empirical literature in the previous section shows. Thus, we used these variables which are now briefly described as part of our empirical model.

The FDI data (the dependent variable) series is taken from the African Development Indicators (2015) and the World Development Indicators (2015) of The World Bank (2015a, b).

7.4.3 Macroeconomic Variables

RGDP: Real GDP is a measure of the size of the host market, which also represents the host country's economic conditions and the potential demand for output. Following the literature, real GDP is used to proxy for market size. Since this variable is used as an indicator of the market potential for products of foreign investors, the expected sign is positive.

RES: Natural resource availability. The availability of natural resources might be a major determinant of FDI to the host country. FDI takes place when a country richly endowed with natural resources lacks the amount of capital or technical skills needed to extract or/and sell to the world market. Foreign firms embark on vertical FDI in the host country to produce raw materials or/and inputs for their production processes at home. This means that certain FDI may be less related to profitability or market size of the host country than natural resources which are unavailable to the domestic economy of foreign firms. As posited by the eclectic theory, all else being equal, countries that are endowed with natural resources receive more FDI. As noted by Asiedu (2002) very few studies on the determinants of FDI control for natural resource availability (except Morisset 2000; Geda and Yimer 2015). The omission of natural resources from estimations, especially for African countries may cause the estimates to be biased (Asiedu 2002). Given the absence of fuel and other petroleum related resources in the country, the share of mining and quarrying value added (current US$) is used to capture the availability of natural resource endowments. This variable is considered acknowledging the fact that a good share of FDI inflows to the country found its way to this sector.

OPNES: Trade openness as measured by total trade as a percentage of GDP. In literature, the degree of liberalization of the trade regime in the host country is regarded as a very important factor that promotes FDI inflows. This proxy is important for foreign direct investors who are motivated by the export market. More open economies usually follow 'appropriate' trade and exchange rate policies and espouse a relatively liberal investment regime (Geda and Yimer 2015).

DEBGDP: External debt as a percentage of GDP. External debt is considered a component of financial risk, influencing FDI inflows negatively (Nonnenberg and Mendonca 2004). In addition, heavily indebted countries represent higher transfer risks—the risk of potential restrictions on the ability to transfer funds across national boundaries. Transfer risks are an important component of country risks and a variable closely monitored by foreign investors. Higher transfer risks may cause foreign capital to move out of a country and new FDI flows to be re-routed to safer locations. The sign associated with *EXTDEBTGDP* is expected to be negative.

INF: Annual inflation rate. This is another important variable of macroeconomic stability indicators which may affect FDI. It represents changes in the general price level or inflationary conditions in the economy. In our study, the impact of inflation rates on FDI is expected to be negative.

NER: The nominal exchange rate. The effect of changes in exchange rates on FDI flows is ambiguous. Elbadawi and Mwega (1997), among others, used the real exchange rate as an indicator of a country's international competitiveness, hypothesizing that a real depreciation would attract larger FDI flows. However, it may be argued that unless the purpose of FDI flows to a country is to build an export platform overvalued exchange rates should not represent a considerable hurdle to foreign investors. On the contrary, depreciation increases the costs of imported inputs and reduces the foreign currency value of profit remittances, both of which have adverse effects on the profitability of FDI projects. This effect will dominate if FDI is undertaken primarily to serve the domestic market. Thus, if we assume that a prospective investor uses the previous year's change in the exchange rate as a guide to its evolution in the near future, we would expect a negative sign on the variable Δ ER (since an increase in the index represents a depreciation).

*7.4.4 Political and Institutional Variables (***Polinst***)*

As noted by Schneider and Frey (1985) political instability and the frequent occurrence of disorder 'create an unfavorable business climate which seriously erodes the risk-averse foreign investors' confidence in the local investment climate and thereby repels FDI away.' Political stability, as argued by Aseidu (2002), is a significant factor in location decisions of multinational corporations (MNCs), especially in their decisions to invest in African states.

Our study used the Worldwide Governance Indicators (WGI) research dataset of the Political Risk Services (2015) to capture the effect of political instability and quality of institutions in attracting FDI inflows to the host country. This dataset summarizes the views on the quality of governance provided by a large number of enterprises, citizens, and expert survey respondents in industrial and developing countries. This data was gathered from a number of survey institutes, think tanks, non-governmental organizations, international organizations, and private sector firms.

WGI projects constructs of aggregate indicators of six broad dimensions of governance: Voice and accountability; political stability and absence of violence/terrorism; government effectiveness; regulatory quality; the rule of law; and control of corruption. The six aggregate indicators are based on 31 underlying data sources reporting the perceptions of governance of a large number of survey respondents and expert assessments worldwide.[1]

Voice and accountability (VOIACC): Reflects perceptions about the extent to which a country's citizens are able to participate in selecting their government, as well as freedom of expression, freedom of association, and a free media.

Political stability and absence of violence/terrorism (POLSTAB): Reflects perceptions about the likelihood that the government will be destabilized or overthrown by unconstitutional or violent means including politically-motivated violence and terrorism.

Government effectiveness (GOVEFFE): Reflects perceptions about the quality of public services, the quality of civil services and the degree of its independence from political pressures, the quality of forming and implementing policies and the credibility of the government's commitment to such policies.

Regulatory quality (RQ): Reflects perceptions about the government's ability to formulate and implement sound policies and regulations that permit and promote private sector development.

Rule of law (RoL): Reflects perceptions about the extent to which agents have confidence in and abide by the rules of society, in particular, the quality of contract enforcement, property rights, the police and the courts, as well as the likelihood of crime and violence.

Control of corruption (CORR): Reflects perceptions about the extent to which public power is exercised for private gain, including both petty and grand forms of corruption as well as the 'capture' of the state by elites and private interests.

Political and institutional risk rating, as provided by the International Country Risk Guide of Political Risk Services (2015), awards the highest value to the lowest

---

[1]Details on the underlying data sources, the aggregation method, and the interpretation of the indicators, can be found in Kaufmann et al.'s (2010) WGI methodology paper.

risk and the lowest value to the highest risk and provides a means for assessing the political and institutional framework of countries. The expected signs for all the institutional variables are positive, which indicates that better quality institutions will stimulate more foreign investments.

As there is a high correlation among the political and institutional indicators and the possibility of a high degree of multi-collinearity among them, we used each of the political and institutional indicators separately and hence estimated six separate models (see Annexure 1 for the correlation matrix).

7.5 Discussion of Results

In an econometric analysis, before carrying out any estimation, a test for stationarity[2] of the variables in the model is undertaken. We found that some of the variables to be integrated were of order one-$I(1)$, while others to be integrated were of order zero-$I(0)$ (see Table 7.1).

Once checked for the unit root tests, the next step in the bounds test approach for co-integration is estimating the ARDL model using the appropriate lag length. One of the most important issues in applying ARDL is choosing the order of the distributed lag functions. Pesaran et al. (2001) have shown that the Schwarz Bayesian Criterion (SBC) should be used in preference over other model specification criteria because it often has more parsimonious specifications: the small data sample in our current study further reinforces this point. Since we had 43 annual observations, we chose two as the maximum lag length in the ARDL model.

For all the models, the bound test for co-integration with the null hypothesis of no long-run relationship among the variables is rejected as the F-statistic is greater than that of the upper bound critical value even at the one percent significance level. This proved the presence of a long-run relationship among the variables of interest in each of the models estimated (Table 7.2).

In the standard least squares model, the coefficient variance-covariance matrix is derived with a key assumption that the error terms are conditionally homoskedastic and serially uncorrelated (White White 1980). In cases where this assumption is relaxed to allow for heteroskedasticity or auto-correlation, the expression for the covariance matrix will be different and our inferences based on it will be misleading (Roecker 1991; White 1980; Wooldridge 2000, among others).

Given that the problem of heteroskedasticty and serial correlation is a customary problem in a time series analysis, it is necessary to estimate the coefficient covariance under the assumption that the residuals are conditionally heteroskedasticity and auto-correlated (Newey and West 1987). The coefficient

[2]In this study, the Augmented Dickey-Fuller unit root testing procedure (which does not take into account a structural break in the data) and the Lumsdaine and Papell (1997) unit root test (which captures two structural breaks in a series) are used. Though the latter is not reported here, both tests are in conformity.

Table 7.1 Unit root test results

Variables	At level		At first difference		Conclusion
	Intercept	Intercept and trend	Intercept	Intercept and trend	
LFDI	−0.82 (0.80)	−2.69 (0.24)	−9.49 (0.00)	−9.42 (0.00)	*I*(1)
LRGDP	−0.51 (0.88)	−1.01 (0.93)	−3.67 (0.00)	−3.72 (0.03)	*I*(1)
LRES	−1.61 (0.47)	−2.98 (0.15)	−6.88 (0.00)	−6.84 (0.00)	*I*(1)
LINF	−5.55 (0.00)	−5.57 (0.00)	−8.28 (0.00)	−8.16 (0.00)	*I*(0)
LDEBGDP	−1.94 (0.31)	−1.05 (0.93)	−4.45 (0.00)	−4.81 (0.00)	*I*(1)
LOPNES	−1.33 (0.61)	−1.89 (0.64)	−6.32 (0.00)	−6.24 (0.00)	*I*(1)
POLSTAB	−2.72 (0.08)	−3.01 (0.04)	−4.41 (0.00)	−3.77 (0.03)	*I*(0)
GOVEFFE	−0.21 (0.93)	−1.71 (0.73)	−7.64 (0.00)	−7.24 (0.00)	*I*(1)
CORR	−2.25 (0.19)	−3.51 (0.05)	−6.69 (0.00)	−6.63 (0.00)	*I*(1)
RoL	−3.54 (0.01)	−3.28 (0.08)	−7.49 (0.00)	−6.29 (0.00)	*I*(0)
RQ	−2.32 (0.17)	−1.80 (0.68)	−3.37 (0.00)	−3.54 (0.00)	*I*(1)
VOIACC	−1.26 (0.64)	−2.48 (0.33)	−6.60 (0.00)	−6.23 (0.00)	*I*(1)

Note p values in parenthesis

Table 7.2 Bound test for co-integration

Model	*F*-test statistic	Critical value bound level of significance			
		10%		1%	
		*I*0 bound	*I*1 bound	*I*0 bound	*I*1 bound
Model 1	5.08	1.99	2.94	2.88	3.99
Model 2	4.09	1.99	2.94	2.88	3.99
Model 3	4.91	1.99	2.94	2.88	3.99
Model 4	4.10	1.99	2.94	2.88	3.99
Model 5	4.19	1.99	2.94	2.88	3.99
Model 6	4.20	1.99	2.94	2.88	3.99

covariance estimator under this assumption is termed the Heteroskedasticity and Auto-correlation Consistent Covariance (HAC) or the Newey-West estimator. Note that both these approaches will change the coefficient standard errors of an equation, but not their point estimates (Newey and West 1987). Newey and West (1987) have proposed a more general covariance estimator that is consistent in the presence of both heteroskedasticity and auto-correlation of unknown form. This procedure is followed in our study. Tables 7.3 and 7.4 present the long-run and short-run determinants of FDI inflows to Ethiopia based on the ARDL approach.

(A) **The long-run model**

In line with previous empirical studies on Africa, most of the explanatory variables have their expected signs in the long run. Market size (as proxied by GDP), trade openness (as proxied by trade as a percentage of GDP), resource abundance and deprecation in the official exchange rate are found to have a significant positive impact on FDI inflows in the long run.

The significant positive long-run coefficient on the GDP variable is in line with theory and suggests the presence of market seeking FDI inflows to the country. Given that Ethiopia is home to more than 90 million people and a rising middle-class population this may not be surprising.

The positive sign of the resource abundance indicator variable, as proxied by the mining and quarrying value added, indicates the presence of resource seeking FDI inflows to the country. This is not surprising given that a good share of FDI inflows to the country found their way to this sector.

The significant positive coefficient on the exchange rate variable may indicate, as noted by Elbadawi and Mwega (1997) among others, that depreciation in Ethiopia's exchange rate is affecting the inflows of FDI positively.

On the other hand, macroeconomic instability as proxied by the inflation rate was found to affect FDI inflows negatively. The significant negative coefficient of the inflation variable in the long run implies that foreign investors prefer investing their money in countries where they perceive better macroeconomic stability. Similarly, the significant positive coefficient of the trade openness variable suggests that liberalization in the external trade sector of the country has encouraged FDI inflows; this also supports the proposition that foreign investors are more likely to invest in countries that have opened up to the outside world (see Onyeiwu and Shrestha 2004; Asiedu 2006; Anyanwu 2012; among others).

In addition, better political stability and absence of violence/terrorism, government effectiveness in forming and implementing quality policies and the credibility of the government's commitment to such policies, regulatory quality with regard to the ability of the government to formulate and implement sound policies and regulations that permit and promote private sector development, and better performance of the rule of law affect FDI inflows into the country positively.

(B) **The short-run model**

In line with previous empirical studies on Africa, most of the macroeconomic determinants of FDI inflows have their theoretical expected signs in all the models in the short run. Market size, natural resource abundance, and trade openness were found to affect FDI inflows in a significant positive way. The positive sign of the natural resource availability variable as proxied by the mining and quarrying value

Table 7.3 The long-run model's results

Dependent variable: log of net FDI inflows
Sample: 1970–2013; no. of observations: 43

Variables	Model 1	Model 2	Model 3	Model 4	Model 5	Model 6
	ARDL (1, 1, 0, 0, 0, 0, 2, 0)	ARDL (1, 1, 0, 0, 0, 0, 1, 0)	ARDL (1, 0, 0, 1, 0, 0, 1, 0)	ARDL (1, 1, 0, 0, 0, 0, 1, 0)	ARDL (1, 0, 0, 1, 0, 0, 1, 0)	ARDL (1, 1, 0, 1, 0, 0, 1, 0)
	Coefficient	Coefficient	Coefficient	Coefficient	Coefficient	Coefficient
Log of real GDP per capita	0.71**	0.98**	1.14**	0.37*	0.98**	0.16*
Log of log of natural resource abundance	2.47**	3.16**	2.00*	2.99**	2.45*	1.96*
Log of inflation	−1.93*	−2.49**	−1.9	−1.98*	−2.28*	−1.59
Log of external debt to GDP ratio	−0.27	−0.22	−0.09	−0.44	−0.19	−0.58**
Log of openness	0.18**	0.19**	0.34	0.23**	0.33	−0.33
Log of nominal exchange rate	4.53***	4.41***	3.61***	4.77**	3.92***	4.10***
Rule of law	4.60*					
Political stability		2.19**				
Government effectiveness			2.93*			
Control of corruption				−1.51		
Regulatory quality					5.09**	
Voice and accountability						2.29
Constant	23.35**	21.61**	33.47**	9.23	31.05***	3.05

Note ***, ** and * indicate 1, 5 and 10% level of significance respectively

added indicates the presence of resource seeking FDI flows to the country. This is not surprising given that a good share of FDI inflows to the country found their way to this sector.

The consistent negative coefficient of the inflation variable in all the models in the short run implies that foreign investors prefer investing their money in countries where they perceive better macroeconomic stability. Similarly, the significant positive coefficient of the trade openness variable suggests that liberalization in the

Table 7.4 The short-run model: Error correction model's (ECM) results

Dependent variable: Δ(log of net FDI inflows) Sample: 1970–2013; no. of observations: 43						
Variables	Model 1	Model 2	Model 3	Model 4	Model 5	Model 6
	ARDL (1, 1, 0, 0, 0, 0, 2, 0)	ARDL (1, 1, 0, 0, 0, 0, 1, 0)	ARDL (1, 0, 0, 1, 0, 0, 1, 0)	ARDL (1, 1, 0, 0, 0, 0, 1, 0)	ARDL (1, 0, 0, 1, 0, 0, 1, 0)	ARDL (1, 1, 0, 1, 0, 0, 1, 0)
	Coefficient	Coefficient	Coefficient	Coefficient	Coefficient	Coefficient
Δ(Log of real GDP per capita)	4.06***	3.66***	1.57*	3.93***	1.22*	2.7**
Δ(Log of natural resource abundance)	2.36**	2.50**	1.33*	2.27**	1.78*	1.46
Δ(Log inflation)	−1.28**	−2.06*	−1.75	−1.81	−2.24*	−1.38
Δ(Log of external debt to GDP ratio)	−0.29	−0.61	−0.19	−0.65	−0.23	−0.72
Δ (Log of openness)	0.19*	0.18*	0.02	0.16	0.04	0.04
Δ(Log of nominal exchange rate)	−3.36**	−0.98	−0.06	−1.52	0.44	−1.08
Δ(Rule of law)	4.38**					
Δ(Political stability)		−0.26				
Δ(Government effectiveness)			4.19***			
Δ(Control of corruption)				0.66		
Δ (Regulatory quality)					5.09**	
Δ(Voice and accountability)						4.02**
ECM_{t-1}	−0.92***	−0.88***	−0.84***	−0.79***	−0.90***	−0.78***

Note ***, ** and * indicate 1, 5 and 10% level of significance respect

external trade sector of the country has encouraged FDI inflows and also supports the proposition that foreign investors are more likely to invest in countries that have opened up to the outside world (see Onyeiwu and Shrestha 2004; Asiedu 2006; Anyanwu 2012; Geda and Yimer 2015; among others).

In addition, except for controlling corruption and political stability, all the other political and institutional indicators have their *a prior* expected significant positive signs. Among the political and institutional indicators, better regulatory quality, better performance of the rule of law, and government effectiveness have a significant positive effect on FDI inflows to the country.

As Table 7.4 shows, the expected negative sign of the error correction term (ECM) is highly significant, suggesting that deviations from the long-term trajectory are corrected very quickly. The ECM coefficient shows how quickly/slowly the relationship returns to its equilibrium path, and it should have a statistically significant coefficient with a negative sign. This holds for all the models estimated. As noted by Banerjee et al. (1998), a highly significant error correction term is further proof of the existence of a stable long-term relationship.

(C) **Diagnostic and stability tests**

As shown in Table 7.5 all the estimated models had a good fit. In addition, all the models passed all the exhaustive post-estimation diagnostic tests. Such tests included the normality test, heteroskedasticity test, test for serial correlation, model specification and stability test and a test for normality. In analyzing the stability of the long-run coefficients together with short-run dynamics, the cumulative sum (CUSUM) and the cumulative sum of squares (CUSUMQ) were applied (see Annexure 2 for the results). Following Pesaran et al. (2001), the stability of the regression coefficients was evaluated by stability tests as they can show whether or not the regression equation is stable over time. This stability test is appropriate in time series data, especially when we are uncertain about when structural change might have taken place.

As can be seen in the graphs in Annexure 2, the plots of both CUSUM and CUSUMSQ statistics moved between the critical bounds at the 5% significance level and did not cross the lower and upper critical limits. The latter implies that the estimated coefficients were stable and there was no structural break.

Table 7.5 Diagnostic and stability tests

Tests	Model 1	Model 2	Model 3	Model 4	Model 5	Model 6
R-squared	0.90	0.89	0.89	0.89	0.89	0.89
Adjusted R-squared	0.87	0.85	0.85	0.85	0.85	0.84
F-statistic	23.82	24.23	23.00	22.4	23.09	20.77
Prob(F-statistic)	0.00	0.00	0.00	0.00	0.00	0.00
Jarque–Berra	0.78	0.10	1.66	0.25	1.19	0.79
Prob(Jarque–Berra)	0.67	0.95	0.43	0.88	0.55	0.67
Breusch–Godfrey serial correlation LM test*	0.36	0.36	0.26	0.48	0.53	0.46
Heteroskedasticity test: ARCH*	0.72	0.65	0.81	0.88	0.56	0.99
Ramsey reset test*	0.04	0.10	0.47	0.18	0.76	0.12

Note *p value is reported

7.6 Conclusion

Based on the ARDL modeling approach along the lines of Dunning's (1981, 1988) 'eclectic theory,' this study identified the main determinants of FDI flows to Ethiopia for the period 1970–2013. The results of the empirical modeling exercise in this study conclusively support the hypothesis that FDI in Africa is conditional on prudent macro-policies and enabling business environments manifested through better political stability and institutional quality. Better macroeconomic conditions, political stability, institutional quality, and resource availability affect FDI flows to Ethiopia positively. The effect of depreciation in the exchange rate was also found to effect FDI inflows positively.

Prudent fiscal and monetary policies to tackle the negative impact of inflationary pressures on FDI inflows and a move toward a careful liberalization of the foreign exchange market and of external trade are important policy options that the government could work on to boost FDI inflows to the country. In addition, sustaining the current growth momentum of the economy and further strengthening political stability in the country, taking sincere steps to increase transparency, controlling corruption and improving the regulatory quality of the country's institutions are fundamental areas that the government could work on to strengthen the country's position in the FDI inflows to the continent.

Further, regarding institutional and political factors, foreign investors are attracted to those African countries that are more democratic. To attract foreign investors, the country needs to improve its political and social situation and elevate its democracy from a mere electoral level to a more liberal one. What is needed, therefore, is deep introspection and political reforms of the various institutions and political parties seeking to govern so as to promote a sustained commitment to democracy that will guarantee equal citizenship, political pluralism, freedom, human rights, general respect for others, and socio-political cum economic inclusion.

Annexure 1: Correlation Matrix of the Political and Institutional Indicators (*Polinst*)

Covariance analysis: ordinary						
Sample: 1970–2013						
Included observations: 43						
Correlation*	RoL	POLSTAB	GOVEFFE	CORR	RQ	VOIACC
RoL	1.00 –					
POLSTAB	−0.84 (0.00)	1.00 –				
GOVEFFE	0.71 (0.00)	−0.90 (0.00)	1.00 –			
CORR	0.77 (0.00)	−0.69 (0.00)	0.75 (0.00)	1.00 –		
RQ	0.71 (0.00)	−0.89 (0.00)	0.96 (0.00)	0.69 (0.00)	1.00 –	
VOIACC	−0.67 (0.00)	0.88 (0.00)	−0.84 (0.00)	−0.65 (0.00)	−0.77 (0.00)	1.00 –

Note **p* values in parenthesis
where
RoL Rule of law
POLSTAB Political stability and absence of violence/terrorism
GOVEFFE Government effectiveness
CORR Control of corruption
RQ Regulatory quality
VOIACC Voice and accountability

Annexure 2: Parameter Stability Tests

Model 1

CUSUM

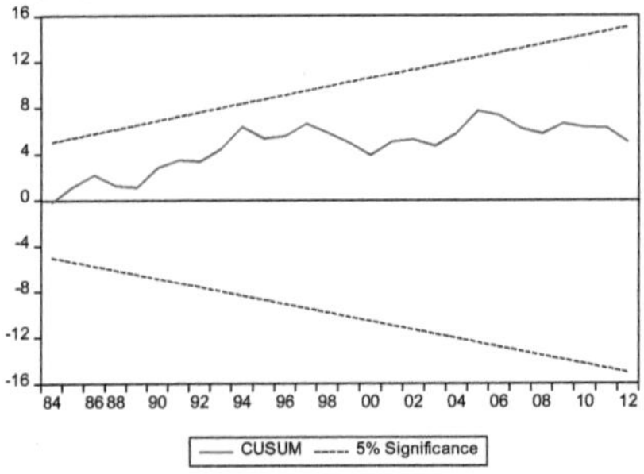

CUSUMSQ

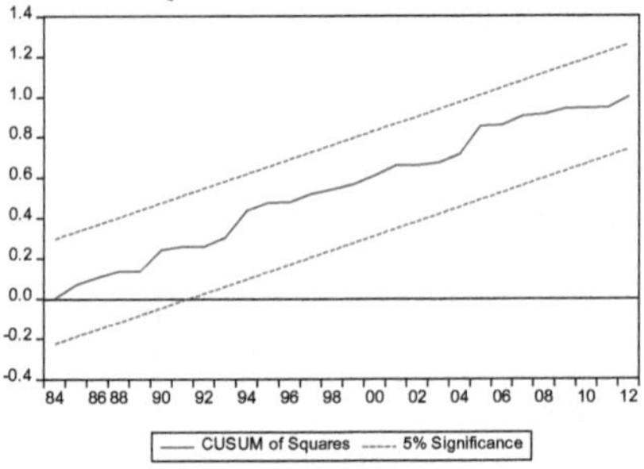

Model 2

CUSUM

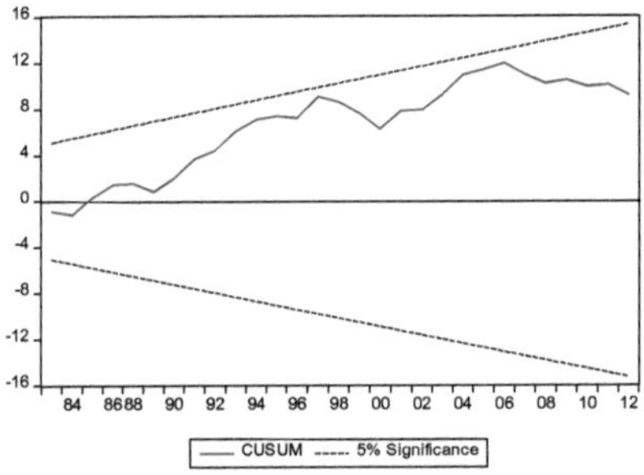

CUSUMSQ

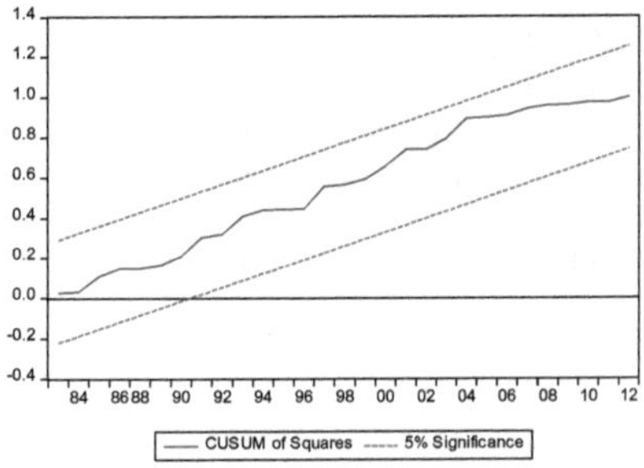

Model 3

CUSUM

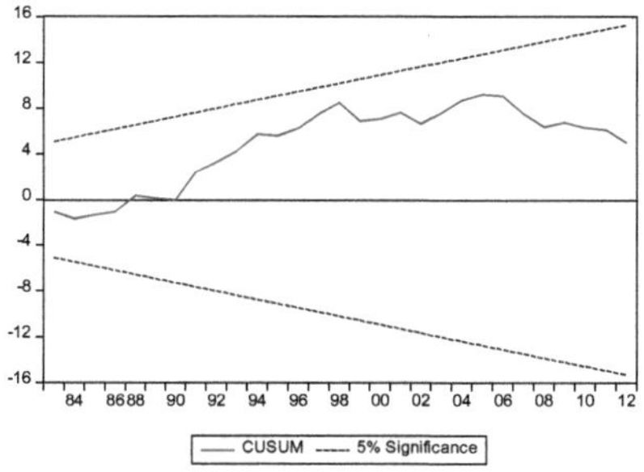

CUSUMSQ

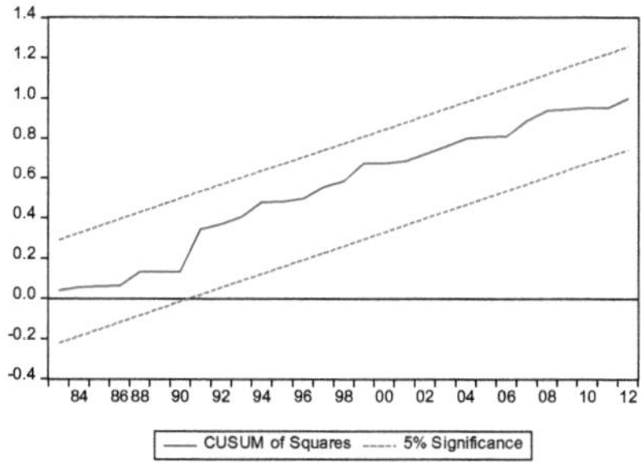

Model 4

CUSUM

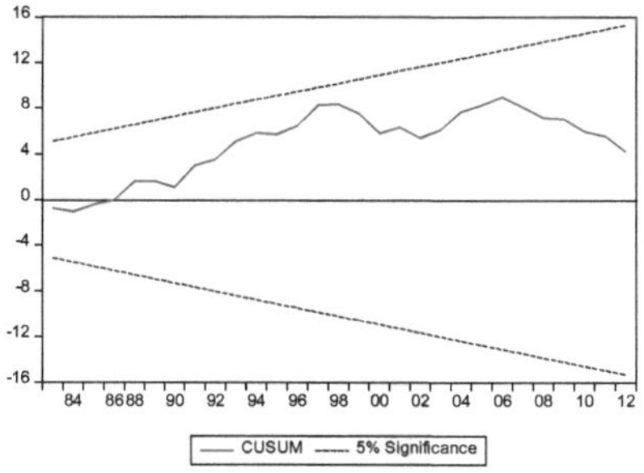

CUSUMSQ

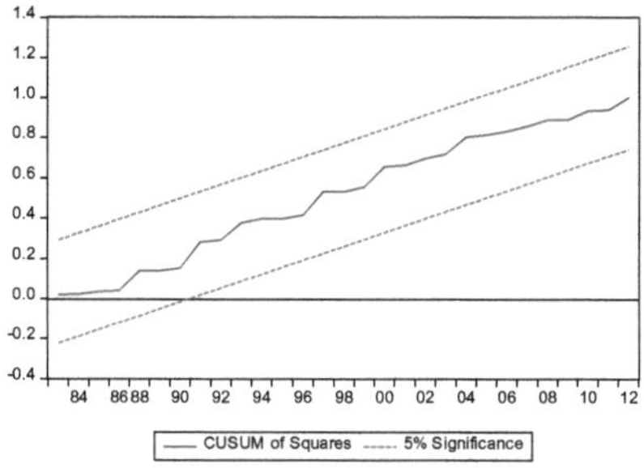

Model 5

CUSUM

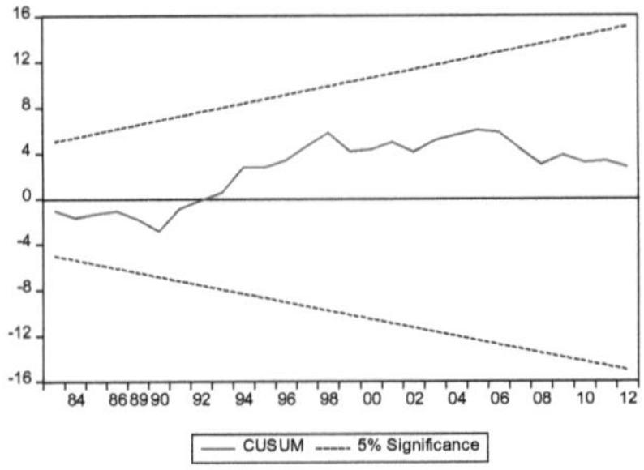

CUSUMSQ

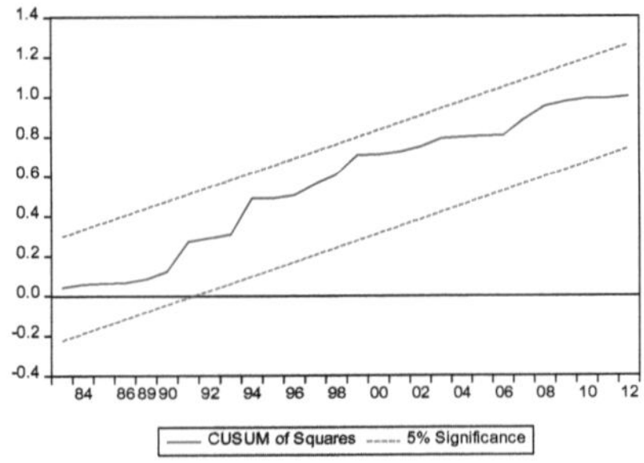

Model 6

CUSUM

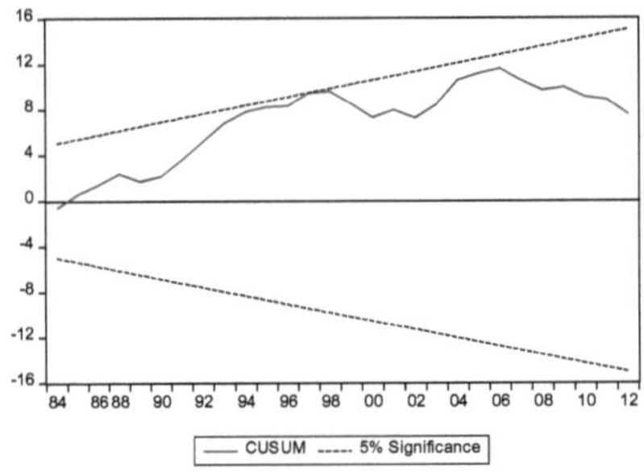

CUSUMSQ

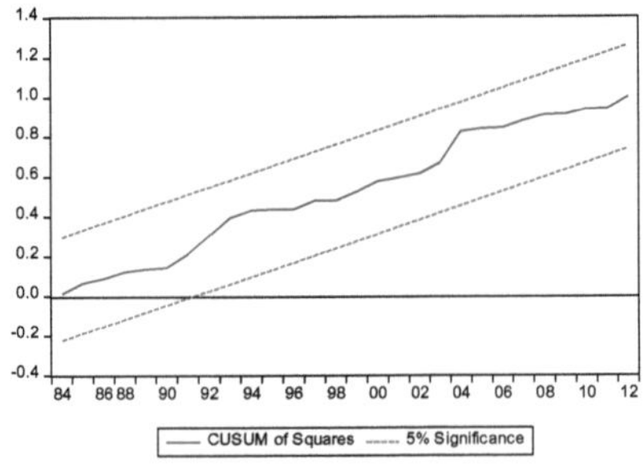

References

Abdoul GM (2012) What drives foreign direct investments in Africa? An empirical investigation with panel data. African Center for Economic Transformation (ACET), Accra

Agarwal JP (1980) Determinants of foreign direct investment: a survey. Rev World Econ 116(4):39–773

Anyanwu JC (2012) Why does foreign direct investment go where it goes? New evidence from african countries. Ann Econ Fin 13(2):433–470

Asiedu E (2002) On the determinants of foreign direct investment to developing countries: Is Africa different? World Dev 30(1):107–118

Asiedu E (2003) Foreign direct investment in Africa: the role of government policy, institutions and political instability. KS working paper No. 23, University of Kansas

Asiedu E (2006) Foreign direct investment in Africa: the role of natural resources, market size, government policy, institutions and political instability. World Econ 29(1):63–77

Asiedu E, Gyimah-Brempong K (2008) The effect of the liberalization of investment: policies on employment and investment of multination corporation corporations in Africa. African Dev Rev 20(1):49–66

Astatike G, Assefa H (2005). Determinants of foreign direct investment in Ethiopia: a time series analysis. In: Paper prepared at the 4th international conference on the Ethiopian economy, June, Addis Ababa, Ethiopia

Banerjee AJ, Dolado J, Mestre R (1998) Error-correction mechanism tests for co-integration in single-equation framework. J Time Ser Anal 19:267–283

Basu A, Srinivasan K (2002). Foreign direct investment in Africa—some case studies. IMF Working Paper No. 61

Bende-Nabende A (2002) Foreign direct investment determinants in sub-Saharan Africa: a co-integration analysis. Econ Bull 6(4):1–19

Buckley P, Casson M (1976) The future of the multinational enterprises. Macmillan, London

Caves RE (1971) Industrial corporations: the industrial economics of foreign investment. Economica 38:1–27

Coase RH (1937) The nature of the firm. Econ New Ser 4(16):386–405

Dunning JH (1981) Explaining the international direct investment position of countries toward a dynamic or development approach. Weltwirtschaftliches Archiv 117:30–64

Dunning JH (1988) The eclectic paradigm of international production: a restatement and some possible extensions. J Int Bus Stud 19(1):1–31

Dunning JH (1993) Multinational enterprises and the global economy. Wesley, Wokingham

Elbadawi I, Mwega F (1997) Regional integration, trade, and foreign direct investment in sub-Saharan Africa. In: Iqbal Z, Khan M (eds) Trade reform and regional integration in Africa. IMF, Washington, DC

Engle RF, Granger CWJ (1987) Co-integration and error correction: representation, estimation and testing. Econometrica 55:251–276

Ethiopian Investment Commission (2014) An investment guide to ethiopia. Addis Ababa, Ethiopia

Geda A (2002) Finance and trade in Africa: macroeconomic response in the world economy context. Palgrave, New York

Geda A (2008) The political economy of growth in ethiopia. In: Ndulu B, O'connell SA, Azam JP, Bates RH, Fosu AK, Gunning JW, Njinkeu D (eds) The political economy of growth in Africa: 1960–2000. Cambridge University Press, Cambridge

Geda A, Yimer A (2015) Determinants of foreign direct investment inflows to Africa: a panel co-integration evidence using new analytical country classification. AAU Dep economics working paper No. 4. Addis Ababa University

Gregory AW, Hansen BE (1996) Residual-based tests for cointegration in models with regime shifts. J Econom 70:99–126

Harvey AC (1981) Time series models. Phillip allan and atlantic highlands, Humanities Press, Oxford, NJ

Helleiner GK (1989) Transnational corporations and direct foreign investment (Ch. 27). In: Chenery H, Srinivasan TN (eds) Handbook of development economics, vol. III. Elsevier, Amsterdam

Hymer SH (1960) The international operations of national firms: a study of direct foreign investment. PhD dissertation. The MIT Press, Cambridge, MA (Published posthumously)

Hymer SH (1976) The international operation of national firms: a study of direct foreign investment. MIT Press, Cambridge

Johansen S (1988) Statistical analysis of cointegration vectors. J Econ Dyn Control 12(2–3): 231–254

Johansen S, Juselius K (1990) Maximum likelihood estimation and inference on cointegration—with applications to the demand for money. Oxf Bull Econ Stat 52(2):169–210

Jorgenson DW (1963) Capital theory and investment behavior. Am Econ Rev 53:247–259

Kandiero T, Chitiga M (2003) Trade openness and foreign direct investment in Africa. In: Paper prepared for the economic society of Southern Africa annual conference. Department of Economics, University of Pretoria

Kaufmann D, Kraay A, Mastruzzi M (2010) The worldwide governance indicators: a summary of methodology, data and analytical issues. The world bank policy research working paper no. 5430
Kindleberger CP (1969) American business abroad: six lectures on foreign direct investment. Yale University Press, New Haven
Kojima K (1973) Macroeconomic versus international business approach to direct foreign investment. Hitotsubashi J Econ 23:1–19
Krugell H (2005) The determinants of foreign direct investment in Africa in multinational enterprises. In: Gries T, Naude WA (eds) Foreign direct investment and growth in Africa, South African perspectives. Springer, Berlin, pp 49–71
Krugman PR (1979) Increasing returns, monopolistic competition and international trade. J Int Econ 9:469–479
Lumsdaine RL, Papell DH (1997) Multiple trend breaks and the unit root hypothesis. Rev Econ Stat 79(2):212–218
MacDougall GDA (1960) The benefits and costs of private investment from abroad: a theoretical approach. Econ Rec 36:13–35
Morisset J (2000) Foreign direct investment in Africa: policies also matter. Transnatl Corp 9(2):107–125
Newey W, West K (1987) A simple positive semi-definite, heteroskedasticity and autocorrelation consistent covariance matrix. Econometrica 55:703–708
Nonnenberg M, Mendonca M (2004) The determinants of direct foreign investment in developing countries. Institute of applied economic research working paper
Ocampo JA (1986) New developments in trade theory and LDCs. J Dev Econ 22:129–170
Ohlin B (1933) Interregional and international trade. Harvard University Press, Cambridge, MA
Okpara GC (2012) An error correction model analysis of the determinant of foreign direct investment: evidence from Nigeria, MPRA paper no. 36676
Onyeiwu S, Shrestha H (2004) Determinants of foreign direct investment in Africa. J Dev Soc 20 (1/2):89–106
Pattichis CA (1999) Price and income elasticities of disaggregated import demand: results from UECMs and application. J Appl Econom 31:1061–1071
Pesaran MH, Shin Y (1999) An autoregressive distributed-lag modeling approach to co-integration analysis. Econom Soc Monographs 31:313–371
Pesaran MH, Shin Y, Smith RJ (1996) Testing for the existence of a long-run relationship, DAE working paper no. 9622
Pesaran MH, Shin Y, Smith RJ (2001) Bounds testing approaches to the analysis of level relationships. J Appl Econom 16:289–326
Political Risk Services (2015) International country risk guide. The Political Risk Services Group Inc., East Syracuse
Roecker EB (1991) Prediction error and its estimation for subset-selection models. Technometrics 33:459–469
Saikkonen P, Lütkepohl H (2000) Testing for the cointegrating rank of a VAR process with structural shifts. J Bus Econ Stat 18:451–464
Seetanah B, Rojid S (2011) The determinants of FDI in Mauritius: a dynamic time series investigation. Afr J Econ Manag Stud 2(1):24–41
Schneider F, Frey BS (1985) Economic and political determinants of foreign direct investment. World Dev 13(2):161–175
Sunday AK, Lydie TB (2006) An analysis of foreign direct investment flows to cameroon. In: IbiAjayi S (ed) Foreign direct investment in sub-Saharan Africa: origins, targets, impact and potential. African Economic Research Consortium, Nairobi (Chapter 5)
The World Bank (2015a) African development indicators. The World Bank, Washington DC
The World Bank (2015b) World development indicators. The World Bank, Washington DC
UNCTAD (1998) World investment report: trends and determinants. In: United Nations conference on trade and development. United Nations, New York and Geneva

UNCTAD (2013) World investment report: trends and determinants. In: United Nations conference on trade and development. United Nations, New York

UNDP (2011) Illicit financial flows from the least developed countries: 1990–2008, UNDP discussion paper

Vernon R (1966) International investment and international trade in the product cycle. Quart J Econ 80:190–207

Wheeler D, Mody A (1992) International investment location decisions: the case of US firms. J Int Econ 33:57–76

White H (1980) A heteroskedasticity-consistent covariance matrix and a direct test for heteroskedasticity. Econometrica 48:817–838

Wooldridge JM (2000) Introductory econometrics: a modern approach. South-Western College Publishing, Cincinnati, OH

Part III
Capital Structure and Bank Loan Growth Effects

Chapter 8
Firm-Specific Determinants of Insurance Companies' Capital Structure in Ethiopia

Yitbarek Takele and Daniel Beshir

Abstract This study examines the impact of firm-specific characteristics on capital structure (CS) decisions of the Ethiopian insurance industry. The study used panel-fixed effects robust standard error regression models, the DEBT model, and the DE model using financial statements of eight insurance companies covering the period from 2005 to 2014. To validate the results, it conducted normality, multicollinearity, heteroskedasticity, autocorrelation, and robustness tests. We found pecking order, static trade-off, and agency cost theories as the most important in explaining CS decisions of insurance companies in Ethiopia though the pecking order theory appeared to be dominant. The empirical findings of the models indicate that profitability and liquidity are significant in determining Ethiopian insurance companies' financing decisions, while business risk and size of the firm are insignificant in shaping their behavior. On the other hand, firms' asset tangibility and growth opportunities had a significant impact on the total debt ratio, while these factors were insignificant for the debt–equity ratio.

Keywords Ethiopia · Capital structure · Firm-specific · Insurance · Leverage

8.1 Introduction

Capital structure (CS) is a mix of long-term debt, specific short-term debt, common equity, and preferred equity. It shows how a firm finances its overall operations and growth by using different sources of funds. While looking at what constitutes CS, debt comes in the form of bond issues or long-term notes payable and equity as common stock, preferred stock, or retained earnings. It is in insurance companies'

Y. Takele (✉)
College of Business and Economics, Addis Ababa University,
Addis Ababa, Ethiopia
e-mail: yitbarekt87@gmail.com

D. Beshir
Libya Oil Ethiopia Ltd, Addis Ababa, Ethiopia

A. Heshmati (ed.), *Studies on Economic Development and Growth in Selected African Countries*, Frontiers in African Business Research,
DOI 10.1007/978-981-10-4451-9_8

interest to know about their CS patterns as they need funds to settle claims or pay damages at the time of loss. This helps insurance companies to be sustainable because of the nature of risks involved in their businesses and the inherent impracticality of retaining all risks that they face during operations.

The paper is structured as follows. Section 8.2 gives a brief overview of the Ethiopian insurance sector. Section 8.3 discusses major theoretical underpinnings of the subject. The next section addresses the link between theoretical lenses and the variables chosen along with empirical reviews and the conceptual framework. Section 8.5 explains the relationship among the variables, the methodology, and data, while Sect. 8.6 analyzes the empirical results. Section 8.7 gives a conclusion.

The determinants of CS have been debated for many years and still represent one of the unresolved issues in the corporate finance literature. Though a few of the theories that have been developed have been empirically tested, their findings have led to different, anomalous, and sometimes conflicting results and conclusions. This also suggests that the different theories are not mutually exclusive making the debates on CS more exciting (Rajan and Zingales 1995). Moreover, Morri and Beretta (2008) emphasize the lack of a fully supported and commonly accepted theory of CS decisions and the unfolding nature of its determinant factors.

The different studies have made immense contributions to the theory of CS. However, these studies are inclined toward the developed economies, and less developed countries have received little attention. This has raised concerns about the generalizability of such works, for example, where capital markets are not well developed or are underdeveloped. Consequently, research designs, methodologies, and theoretical frameworks that best fit such contexts are worth undertaking. In previous studies, antecedent variables, commonly regarded as determinants of CS decisions, include profitability, age, agency cost, business risk, asset tangibility, growth, non-debt tax shields, liquidity, political risks, and size. These variables, among others, are related to firm value and risk exposure in one way or another.

Our study, therefore, investigates the determinants of decisions about CS in the insurance industry in Ethiopia during 2005–2014. Our research identified six hypotheses (H_{ai}):

H_{a1}: There is a negative relationship between leverage and profitability in Ethiopian insurance companies.
H_{a2}: There is a positive relationship between leverage and asset tangibility in Ethiopian insurance companies.
H_{a3}: There is a positive relationship between leverage and growth in Ethiopian insurance companies.
H_{a4}: There is a negative relationship between leverage and business risk in Ethiopian insurance companies.
H_{a5}: There is a positive relationship between leverage and size of the firm in Ethiopian insurance companies.
H_{a6}: There is a negative relationship between leverage and liquidity in Ethiopian insurance companies.

8.2 An Overview of the Insurance Industry in Ethiopia

The emergence of modern insurance in Ethiopia can be traced back to the establishment of the Bank of Abyssinia in 1905. The bank acted as an agent for foreign insurance companies to underwrite fire and marine policies. The first domestic private insurance company was established in 1951 with a share capital of Eth Br 1,000,000, and in the 1960s, the number of domestic private companies was started increasing (Zeleke 2007).

At present, there are 15 insurance companies that are operational in Ethiopia that provide general insurance services, except one, which provides life insurance. One of the insurance companies, the Ethiopian Insurance Corporation (EIC), is state-owned, while the rest are private. Ethiopian insurance companies' investment activities are heavily constrained by the restrictions imposed by the National Bank of Ethiopia's investment proclamation which requires them to invest a majority of their funds in government securities and bank deposits at negative real interest rates. Moreover, lack of infrastructure, especially a stock market, has constrained investment activities of Ethiopian insurance companies (Mezgebe 2010). Following this, competition has become stiff in the industry and some of the private insurance companies that want to increase their sales volumes have been granting unfair and huge discounts to attract clients, thus attaining sales targets. This aggressive pricing policy has led to an unhealthy spiral of premium cutting which significantly undermines the growth and prospects of the insurance industry in Ethiopia.

8.3 Theoretical Underpinnings

Since the publication of Modigliani and Miller's (1958) 'irrelevance theory of capital structure,' the theory of corporate CS has been a study of interest for finance economists. Researchers of this study believe the relevance of CS arguments and theories that take into account market imperfections as witnessed in the 2008 financial crisis. Researchers also hold the assumption that it is possible to find an 'optimal' CS after accounting for market imperfections such as taxes, bankruptcy, and agency costs. In their later work, Modigliani and Miller (1963) considered some of the criticisms and deficiencies of their theory and relaxed the assumption that neglected corporate taxes.

Major theories of CS have emerged that diverge from the assumption of perfect capital markets in which the 'irrelevance model' is promoted. The first in the irrelevance model is the trade-off theory. The original version of the trade-off theory grew out of a debate over the Modigliani–Miller theorem. When corporate income tax was added to the original irrelevance theory, it validated the use of debt as it provides a tax shield. It proposes that optimal CS is achieved when the marginal present value of the tax shield on additional debt is equal to the marginal present value of the financial distress cost on additional debt (Myers 1984).

The dynamic trade-off theory, on the other hand, recognizes the role of time that requires specifying a number of aspects that are typically ignored in a single-period model. Of particular importance are the roles of expectations and adjustment costs. In a dynamic model, the correct financing decision typically depends on the financing margin that a firm anticipates in the next period (Goldstein et al. 2001). Thus, an optimal financial choice today depends on what is expected to be optimal in the next period.

Agency cost is another theory that predicts that CS choice is dependent on agency cost. It advocates an investigation of the conflicting interests of managers and equity and debt holders and its impact on CS decisions. It argues that managers who are well placed to access superior information as compared to both debt and equity holders, mainly due to ex-post asymmetric information (Jensen and Meckling 1976; Jensen 1986), may make CS decisions that maximize their interests but destroy the firm's value.

Yet another interesting theory is the pecking order theory developed by Myers and Majluf (1984) which states that CS is driven by a firm's desire to finance new investments, first internally and then with low-risk debt and finally, if all fails, with equity. Its main thesis is an association of asymmetric information and signaling problems with external financing.

Finally, Baker and Wurgler (2002) have suggested another theory of CS: the 'market timing theory of CS.' Market timing implies that firms issue new shares when they perceive they are overvalued and that firms repurchase their own shares when they consider these to be undervalued.

What we can deduce from these theories is that they are not mutually exclusive and do not stand on their own; rather, there exists a thread connecting them: information asymmetry. The exception to this could be the trade-off theory which mainly bases itself on tax shield advantages and bankruptcy costs.

8.4 Empirical Review and Conceptual Framework

By summarizing previous studies, profitability, tangibility, growth, risk, size, and liquidity of assets were selected and included as explanatory variables in our study and a firm's CS (leverage) was used as the dependent variable. Though there are different measures of leverage, our paper used two ratios as a proxy of leverage. The first was the debt ratio (total debt to total assets), and the second was the debt–equity ratio (debt to equity). In both these, total debt was calculated as the sum of short-term and long-term liabilities.

The pecking order theory (Myers 1984) argues that profitable firms with access to retained profits can rely on them as opposed to outside sources such as debt. On the other hand, the static trade-off theory (Myers 1984; Myers and Majluf 1984) provides a contradictory view and argues that profitable firms have greater needs to shield income from corporate tax to increase profits and should borrow more as compared to less profitable firms. In contrast to Myers and Majluf (1984) and

Myers' (1984) views, empirical evidence from financial and non-financial firms (Ahmed et al. 2010; Gill et al. 2009; Najjar and Petrov 2011; Rajan and Zingales 1995; Sharif et al. 2012; Teker et al. 2009) found that profitable firms used less debt financing in line with the pecking order theory, while studies by Kumar et al. (2012) and Sayeed (2011) found that profitable firms used more debt finance. As a proxy for the measure of profitability, our study used the ratio of operating income to total assets (return on assets) used by Booth et al. (2001), Cassar and Holmes (2003), Mohammed Amidu (2007), and Adesola (2009).

According to Jensen and Meckling's (1976) agency cost theory, there is a conflict between lenders and shareholders due to the possibility of moral hazard on the part of borrowers. This conflict creates incentives for shareholders to invest in a suboptimal way, and lenders require tangible assets as collateral to protect themselves. The agency cost of debt increases when firms cannot collateralize their debts. The outsized proportion of a firm's assets can be used as collateral to fulfill lenders' requirements. In the trade-off theory, Modigliani and Miller (1963) argue a reduction in financial distress costs for those firms with more tangible assets because of a better chance to get debt financing. Empirical studies by Najjar and Petrov (2011); Noulas and Genimaks (2011); Rajan and Zingales (1995); and Titman and Wessels (1988) found that firms with more proportion of tangible assets raised more debt using the same as collateral. As indicated in the studies by Mohammed Amidu (2007) and Adesola (2009), our study also used the ratio of fixed assets over total assets as a proxy measure of tangibility.

The pecking order theory argues that firms prefer debt financing over equity due to its riskiness, and hence, a positive relationship between leverage and growth is expected. However, in the static trade-off theory, growing firms face financial distress and prefer to use equity financing. Empirical studies by Ahmed et al. (2010); Noulas and Genimaks (2011); Kumar et al. (2012); and Sharif et al. (2012) have found that growing firms used more debt to finance their businesses. Contrary to this, studies by Rajan and Zinglas (1995); Shah and Khan (2007); and Titman and Wessels (1988) show that growing firms used equity financing instead of debt. In our study, sharing the argument given by Dawood et al. (2011) and Onaolapo and Kajola (2010) growth was measured as annual percentage change in total assets.

The static trade-off theory (Myers 1984) argues that risky firms can borrow less as compared to less risky firms because the costs of financial distress offset the tax shields of debt. The riskier a firm, the greater the chance of defaulting and being exposed to such costs. That is, high-volatile earning firms face a risk of the earnings level dropping below their debt servicing commitments, thereby incurring higher costs of financial distress. Hence, such firms should reduce their leverage levels to avoid the risk of bankruptcy. As indicated in Song (2005), income variability is a measure of business risk. In our study, it is measured as the ratio of the standard deviation of operating income over total assets.

Theoretically, the static trade-off theory states that for large companies the risk of bankruptcy is minimized due to the economies of scale. The assets of a company will be financed more through debt, as optimality of CS can be reached by balancing the benefits and costs of debt (Modigliani and Miller 1958). The empirical results of Ahmed et al. (2010); Kumar et al. (2012) and Najjar and Petrove's (2011) studies support the argument that the size of a firm and its leverage are positively related. According to the pecking order theory, however, informational asymmetry for large firms is smaller, and as a result, they prefer to be financed by equity instead of debt (Myers and Majluf 1984) because this reduces the chances of undervaluation of the new issued equity and thus encourages the large firms to use equity financing. In our study, such as Booth et al. (2001) and Cassar and Holmes (2003), the natural log of total assets is used to measure the size of the firm.

There are two different opinions about the association between liquidity and CS. The first view, as explained in the trade-off theory, argues that firms with more liquidity tend to use more external borrowings because of their ability to pay off their liabilities. On the contrary, the pecking order theory believes that firms with financial slack will prefer internal sources than debt or equity to finance future investments (Myers 1984). Most previous studies confirm the negative relation. Harris and Raviv (1991); Najjar and Petrov (2011); and Sharif et al. (2012) found that firms with high liquidity ratios or more liquid assets preferred using these assets to finance their investments and discouraged raising external funds (either equity or debt). But Bayeh found an insignificant effect of liquidity on leverage usage by insurance companies. But Bayeh found an insignificant effect of liquidity on leverage usage by insurance companies. Like Dawood et al. (2011) in our study also, the ratio of current assets to current liabilities was used to capture liquidity (see Table 8.1).

8.5 Data and Methodology

Our study used the quantitative research approach to construct an empirical model. Multiple regression analyses were used to measure the effects of the determinants on the output variable and to examine the associative relationships between variables in terms of the relative importance of the independent variables and predicted values of the dependent variables.

Our study used secondary data from annual reports of insurance companies and the National Bank of Ethiopia (NBE). As per NBE's current information, 15 insurance companies are operating in the country. Since there are only a few insurance companies, there was no need to take a sample from them. Accordingly, based on the years of service, audited financial data of those insurance companies which were operational in 2005–2014 were included in our study. The reason behind selecting the stated period was to obtain strongly balanced data for the analysis. In order to make the panel data model structured and balanced, the same regular frequency of the cross-sectional data with the same start and end dates was maintained. Six insurance companies did not have the required data for the period and were excluded from the sampling frame. Moreover, one insurance company is

Table 8.1 Measurement of independent variables and expected relationships

Variable	Measurement proxy used for this study	Theoretical relationship with leverage	Theories	Expected relationship with leverage
Profitability (PF)	Operating income/total assets	(+)	Static trade-off theory	(−)
		(−)	Pecking order theory	
Tangibility of assets (TN)	Fixed asset/total assets	(−)	Agency cost theory	(+)
		(+)	Static trade-off theory	
Growth (GR)	Annual change in total assets	(+)	Pecking order theory	(+)
		(−)	Static trade-off theory	
Risk (RK)	Standard deviation of operating income	(−)	Static trade-off theory Pecking order theory	(−)
Firm size (SZ)	Natural logarithm of total assets	(+)	Static trade-off theory	(+)
		(−)	Pecking order theory	
Liquidity (LQ)	Current asset/current liability	(+)	Static trade-off theory	(−)
		(−)	Pecking order theory	

Source Own summary

government-owned and so was excluded as it was not possible to obtain complete audited financial statements for the whole period. Finally, 10 consecutive years' information and data from eight insurance companies for 2005–2014 were used in our study.

The general model for this study is presented as follows:

$$Y_{i,t} = \beta_0 + \beta X_{i,t} + \varepsilon_{i,t}$$

The subscript i represents the cross-sectional dimension, and t denotes the time series dimension. The left-hand side in the equation, $Y_{i,t}$, represents the dependent variable in the model, which is a firm's leverage. On the right side, $X_{i,t}$ represents the set of independent variables in the estimated model. Therefore, the expanded forms of both models built in line with the hypothesis of the study are as follows:

DEBT model: debt ratio (total debt/total asset) as the dependent variable

(1) $TD/TA_{it} = \beta_0 + \beta_1(PF_{it}) + \beta_2(TN_{it}) + \beta_3(GR_{it}) + \beta_4(RK_{it}) + \beta_5(SZ_{it}) + \beta_6 (LQ_{it}) + \varepsilon$ DE Model: debt–equity ratio as the dependent variable

(2) $D/E_{it} = \beta_0 + \beta_1(PF_{it}) + \beta_2(TN_{it}) + \beta_3(GR_{it}) + \beta_4(RK_{it}) + \beta_5(SZ_{it}) + \beta_6(LQ_{it}) + \varepsilon$

where

TD/TA	Total debt to total assets
D/E	Debt to equity
PF	Profitability
TN	Tangibility
GR	Growth
RK	Risk
SZ	Size of the firm
LQ	Liquidity
ε	Error term

The models were tested for the classical linear regression model's (CLRM) assumptions. Accordingly, Shapiro–Wilk, the correlation matrix, and Breusch–Pagan tests were conducted to test normality, multi-collinearity, and heteroskedasticity, respectively. We found no multi-collinearity problem which would exist if the correlation between the two independent variables was more than 0.75 (Malhotra 2008). Moreover, Shapiro–Wilk showed that normality had been established. See Annexure 2 for diagnostic tests.

We used the regression models and applied different tests (Breusch and Pagan Lagrangian multiplier (LM) test, Hausman test) to choose the best model for the panel data under the study:

- Pooled OLS (POLS) model regression,
- Pooled OLS with dummy variable (least square dummy variable: LSDV) model regression or fixed effects regression model, and
- Random effects GLS (generalized lease square) model regression.

8.6 Results and Discussion

Before explaining the results of the regression analysis, the results of the descriptive statistics and Pearson's correlation coefficient matrix are briefly explained.

The mean of debt ratio (total debt to total assets) of the 80 observations was 66.8% with a standard deviation of 8.3% indicating that more than 66% of the balance sheets of insurance companies in Ethiopia were debt-financed, while the mean debt ratio in the USA and in the UK is 58 and 54%, respectively (Rajan and

Table 8.2 Descriptive summary statistics

Variable	Obs.	Mean	Std. dev.	Min	Max
TD/TA	80	0.668	0.083	0.453	0.822
D/E	80	0.755	0.405	−0.189	1.669
gro	80	0.231	0.157	−0.066	0.670
tang	80	0.194	0.110	0.026	0.542
pr	80	0.082	0.049	−0.047	0.182
risk	80	0.141	0.099	0.025	0.432
size	80	18.914	0.843	16.965	20.294
lq	80	1.022	0.264	0.543	2.306

Source Structured review of annual financial report (generated from STATA)

Zingales 1995) (Table 8.2). Though theoretically it is argued that firms in developed countries are levered as compared to their developing country counterparts mainly due to their well-developed bond markets, the findings of our study show otherwise. This could be related to the absence of stock markets in developing country which makes equity financing more unattractive. What is interesting about the descriptive statistics of our results is the presence of high variability in the growth, tangibility, size, and liquidity of insurance companies in Ethiopia which may stress the need to consolidate the sector through mergers and acquisitions.

8.6.1 Model Selection

Annexure 1 presents all model selection tests including the results for the POLS model regression, the fixed effects (or LSDV) regression model, and the random effects model regression. We used the Breusch and Pagan Lagrangian multiplier (LM) test to decide between random effects and POLS and the Hausman test to decide between random effects and fixed effects models.

The results of Breusch and Pagan LM test for the DEBT model revealed that there was very strong evidence (p-value 0.0006) at the 1% level of significance against the null hypothesis; POLS is appropriate. This result suggests the random effects model's estimation over the pooled OLS model. The same LM test for the DE model showed indifference between POLS and the random effects model's estimations. Moreover, the results of the Hausman test showed very strong evidence (p-value 0.0085 for the DEBT model and p-value 0.0012 for the DE model) against the null hypothesis at the 1% level of significance suggesting fixed effects estimates rather than random effects estimates. Accordingly, the analysis and discussion of results are based on the fixed effects estimates.

In order to make the fixed effects estimation results robust, the modified Wald group-wise heteroskedasticity test in the fixed effects regression model was undertaken. The results for both the DEBT and DE models revealed very strong evidence (p-value 0.0000) against the null hypothesis of homoscedasticity. Hence, there was group-wise heteroskedasticity in fixed effects regression in both the models. Accordingly, a robust standard error estimation in the fixed effects model was used to tackle the group-wise heteroscedasticity problem of the fixed effects estimates in both the models.

8.6.2 Estimation Results of the DEBT Model with a Robust Standard Error in Fixed Effects

The results of the fixed effects model with a robust standard error regression for the DEBT model are presented in Table 8.3. The results show that asset tangibility, profitability, risk, and liquidity had a negative relation with debt ratio, while growth and firm size had a positive association with leverage. The results also indicate that growth and tangibility were statistically significant at 5%. Moreover, profitability and liquidity were significant at 1%, while risk and firm size were insignificant. In

Table 8.3 Fixed effects estimates with a robust standard error for the DEBT model's regression

Fixed effects (within) regression: DEBT MODEL			Number of obs.	80
Group variable: ID			Number of groups	8
R^2	Within	0.7165	Obs. per group: min	10
	Between	0.8782	avg	10.0
	Overall	0.7918	max	10
			F (6,7)	1792.72
cor ($\mathbf{u_i}$, xb)		0.4602	Prob > F	0.0000
			(Std. Err. adjusted for 8 clusters in ID)	

lev	Coeff.	Robust std. err.	T	$p > \|t\|$	[95% conf. Interval]	
gro	0.757	0.022	3.44	0.011	0.024	0.128
tang	−1.366	0.045	−3.04	0.019	−0.243	−0.030
Pr	−0.583	0.100	−5.80	0.001	−0.821	−0.345
risk	−0.319	0.198	−1.61	0.151	−0.787	0.148
size	0.016	0.024	0.68	0.521	−0.014	0.074
lq	−0.120	0.016	−7.61	0.000	−0.157	−0.083
_cons	0.582	0.490	1.19	0.274	−0.577	1.741
Sigma$_u$	0.032					
Sigma$_e$	0.029					
rho	0.554	(Fraction of variance due to $\mathbf{u_i}$)				

Source Structured review of annual financial report (generated using STATA)

addition, the value of R^2-within = 0.7165 and adjusted R^2 = 0.6931 for the DEBT model. Hence, 69.31% of the variability in leverage is explained by selected firm-specific factors.

8.6.3 Estimation Results of DE Model with a Robust Standard Error in Fixed Effects

The results of the fixed effects model with a robust standard error regression for the DE model are given in Table 8.4. The results show that profitability, risk, and liquidity had a negative relation with the debt–equity ratio, while asset tangibility, growth, and firm size had a positive association with the debt–equity ratio. The results also indicate that only profitability and liquidity were statistically significant at 5%. The other explanatory variables were insignificant. In this model, the value of R^2-within was 0.5199 and adjusted R^2 was 0.4804. This shows that only 48% of the variability in the debt–equity ratio is explained by selected firm-specific factors.

Table 8.4 Fixed effect estimates with a robust standard error for the DE model regression

Fixed effects (within) regression: DE MODEL			Number of obs.		80	
Group variable: ID			Number of groups		8	
R^2	Within	0.5199	Obs. per group: min		10	
	Between	0.7077	avg		10.0	
	Overall	0.6022	max		10	
				F (6,7)	74.13	
cor (u_i, xb)		0.2470		Prob > F	0.0000	
			(Std. Err. adjusted for 8 clusters in ID)			

lev	Coeff.	Robust std. err.	t	$p > \|t\|$	[95% conf. interval]	
gro	0.283	0.189	1.49	0.179	−0.165	0.731
tang	0.061	0.731	0.08	0.936	−1.669	1.791
Pr	−2.128	0.569	−3.74	0.007	−3.475	−0.781
risk	−0.802	0.803	−1.00	0.351	−2.700	1.096
size	0.220	0.114	1.93	0.095	−0.050	0.490
lq	−0.345	0.116	−2.98	0.020	−0.619	−0.072
_cons	−2.848	2.192	−1.30	0.235	−8.032	2.336
Sigma$_u$	0.179					
Sigma$_e$	0.215					
rho	0.410	(Fraction of variance due to u_i)				

Source Structured review of annual financial report (generated using STATA)

8.7 Discussion of Results

8.7.1 *Profitability and Leverage*

H_{a1}: There is a negative relationship between leverage and profitability in Ethiopian insurance companies.

The results of the fixed effects model with a robust standard error for both models indicated that profitability had a negative relationship with leverage, and highly significant (*p*-value = 0.001 for the DEBT model; and *p*-value = 0.007 for the DE mode). Thus, the null hypothesis is rejected, and the alternative is supported. The results are consistent with the pecking order theory which argues that profitable firms with access to retained profits can rely on internal sources instead of external ones. Moreover, the negative association between profitability and leverage is in line with the pecking order and agency theories. It also supports the findings of Rajan and Zingales (1995) and Cassar and Holmes (2003) but contradicts the static trade-off theory (Myers 1984; Myers and Majluf 1984) which argues that profitable firms have greater needs to shield their incomes from corporate tax to increase their profits and should borrow more as compared to less profitable firms.

8.7.2 *Asset Tangibility and Leverage*

H_{a2}: There is a positive relationship between leverage and asset tangibility in Ethiopian insurance companies.

A priori positive relationship was hypothesized and expected between tangibility and leverage. The results of the DE model show that tangibility had a positive but insignificant impact on leverage. The results indicate that the Ethiopian insurance sector holds less fixed assets and relies less on debt financing. Nonetheless, the positive correlation is in line with the static trade-off and pecking order theories.

On the other hand, the DEBT model's results showed that tangibility had a negative relationship and a significant (*p*-value = 0.019) impact on leverage. Consistent with the findings of previous studies (Ebru 2011), the relationship between tangibility and short-term debt was negative and significant. With respect to short-term debt, it is generally expected that firms tend to match the maturity of their debts with assets. This means that firms with more fixed assets rely more on long-term debt, while those with more contemporary assets depend more on short-term financing (Abor 2005).

The negative relationship between tangibility and leverage in our study conforms with the agency cost theory though it is not consistent with the findings of Hassan (2011); Najjar and Petrov (2011); Noulas and Genimaks (2011); Rajan and Zingales (1995); and Titman and Wessels (1988) who found that firms with a higher proportion of tangible assets used more debt using it as collateral.

8.7.3 Growth and Leverage

H_{a3}: There is a positive relationship between leverage and growth in Ethiopian insurance companies.

The results of the relationship between growth and leverage for both the DEBT and DE models' regressions show a positive association. The finding of a positive association could be for the reason that growing insurance firms rely more on external borrowings to seize market opportunities. This argument is supported by the pecking order theory.

Growth opportunities for insurance companies exhibit a significant (*p*-value = 0.011 for the DEBT model) impact on the debt ratio. The probable reason could be that growing insurance companies need to expand their branches to reach additional customers prompting them to absorb more debt. This finding is in conformity with Ahmed et al. (2010); Kumar et al. (2012); Noulas and Genimaks (2011); and Sharif et al.'s (2012) studies who found that growing firms were mainly financed by debt.

However, the results obtained from the DE model regression show that there exists no significant relationship (*p*-value = 0.179 for the DE model) between expected growth and the debt-to-equity ratio. This finding is in conformity with studies by Hassen (2011); Najjar and Petrove (2010); Olayinka (2011); Rajan and Zinglas (1995); Shah and Khan (2007); and Titman and Wessle (1988) which showed that growing firms were financed more by equity instead of debt. This positive insignificant result indicates that growth is not considered a proper explanatory variable of leverage in the Ethiopian insurance sector. One possible explanation could be that the measure used in our study, the percentage change in total assets, did not reflect future growth possibilities enough. Thus, other more significant results might be obtained by using another measure (proxy) for growth, for instance annual change in sales or the market-to-book ratio. In addition, the adjusted R^2 for the DE model's regression revealed that only 48% of the variability in the debt–equity ratio was explained by the selected firm-specific variables in our study.

8.7.4 Risks and Leverage

H_{a4}: There is a negative relationship between leverage and business risk in Ethiopian insurance companies.

Business risks are insignificant for both the DEBT model (*p*-value = 0.151) and the DE model (*p*-value = 0.351) in explaining CS decisions of Ethiopian insurance companies. This result contradicts Kindie (2011) and Solomon's (2012) studies. However, it is in line with the argument of the trade-off theory which suggests that less risky insurance firms can take more debt as their ability to pay interest payments without delay is reliable. The results of both the models are also in line with the pecking order theory, which predicts a negative relationship between leverage and the earning volatility of a firm.

8.7.5 Size of the Firm and Leverage

H_{a5}: There is a positive relationship between leverage and the size of a firm in Ethiopian insurance companies.

The size of the insurance firms is insignificant in explaining capital decision behaviors for both the DEBT model (*p*-value = 0.521) and the DE model (*p*-value = 0.095) at the 5% significance level. The reason could be that lending organizations give less emphasis to the size of the firm while performing a credit risk analysis. However, the results of both the models confirm that the size of an Ethiopian insurance company positively affected leverage even if it was insignificant. This is in line with the trade-off and agency theories and is similar to Rajan and Zingales (1995) and Kindie (2011).

8.7.6 Liquidity and Leverage

H_{a6}: There is a negative relationship between leverage and liquidity in Ethiopian insurance companies.

For both models, liquidity had a negative relationship with leverage and was significant (*p*-value = 0.000) for the DEBT model and (*p*-value = 0.020) for the DE model at the 5% significance level. This negative strong significant relationship implies that Ethiopian insurance firms with liquid assets such as cash and marketable securities prefer internal sources than debt or equity to finance future investments which are consistent with the pecking order theory. The results, however, contradict the trade-off theory, which argues that firms with more liquidity tend to use more external borrowings because of their ability to pay off their liabilities. The results also deviate from Kindie's (2011) empirical study.

8.8 Conclusion and Future Research Direction

The empirical findings of both the models indicate that profitability and liquidity were significant in determining Ethiopian insurance companies' financing decisions, while business risk and size of a firm were found to be insignificant in shaping the behavior of the firm. On the other hand, asset tangibility and growth opportunities for firms had a significant impact on the total debt ratio. However, these factors were insignificant for the debt–equity ratio. Insurance companies in Ethiopia rely on short-term debt due to the absence of a stock market in the country. They also depend more on external borrowings to expand their markets.

Based on previous studies and an extensive literature review, the major theories of CS including the static trade-off theory, the pecking order theory, and the agency theory were selected and an attempt was made to identify the theory that best explained the financial decision behavior of insurance companies in Ethiopia. The results revealed that pecking order, information asymmetry, and the static trade-off theories were all important in explaining the CS of insurance companies in Ethiopia, even if the pecking order theory appeared to be dominant.

Considering the current growth opportunities for insurance companies in Ethiopia, internal sources of funding might not be enough. Therefore, it is advisable not to depend only on internal sources of funds. Having a reasonable proportion of long-term debt in CS is considered a priority for growth in developing countries as this helps them utilize available market opportunities. Moreover, the industry should keep in touch with the trade-off theory since it has strong practical appeal; it rationalizes moderate debt ratios and sets a target debt-to-equity ratio.

Future Research Direction

Macroeconomic factors (such as inflation, GDP, and interest rate), other qualitative factors (management quality of each insurance company, policies, and procedures), and the ownership structures of the companies which might have an impact on CS choice and the effect of regulation on solvency and CS of insurance companies are recommended as area for further research. Moreover, there is a need to thoroughly study why pecking order happens to be the dominant theory in explaining the financing behavior of insurance companies in Ethiopia.

Annexure 1: Model Selection

POLS model regression, fixed effects (or LSDV) regression model, and the random effects model regression results of the DEBT model regression

Variable	POLS	LSDV	Fixed effects	Random effects
gro	0.119***	0.076**	0.076**	0.089***
tang	−0.280***	−0.137*	−0.137*	−0.204***
pr	−0.755***	−0.583***	−0.583***	−0.645***
Risk	−0.409***	−0.319**	−0.319**	−0.328***
size	0.003	0.014	0.014	0.015
lq	−0.183***	−0.120***	−0.120***	−0.147***
ID				
2		−0.015		
3		−0.65*		
4		0.014		
5		−0.019		
6		−0.489***		

(continued)

(continued)

Variable	POLS	LSDV	Fixed effects	Random effects
7		−0.073***		
8		−0.0566**		
_cons	0.949***	0.615*	0.582	0.651**
N	80	80	80	80

Note *p < 0 0.05; **p < 0.01; ***p < 0.001
Source Structured review of annual financial report (generated using STATA)

POLS model regression, fixed effects (or LSDV) regression model, and the random effects model regression results of the DE model regression

Variable	POLS	LSDV	Fixed effects	Random effects
gro	0.496*	0.283	0.283	0.496*
tang	−0.833**	0.061	0.061	−0.833**
pr	−3.220***	−2.128**	−2.128**	−3.220***
Risk	−1.530**	−0.802	−0.802	−1.530**
size	0.119	0.220	0.220	0.119
lq	−0.674***	−0.345*	−0.345*	−0.674***
ID				
2		−0.157		
3		−0.335		
4		−0.099		
5		0.093		
6		−0.189		
7		−0.467***		
8		−0.244		
_cons	−0.273	−2.673	−2.673	−0.273
N	80	80	80	80

Legend *p < 0 0.05; **p < 0.01; ***p < 0.001
Source Structured review of annual financial report (generated using STATA)

Breusch and Pagan LM test for DEBT model

Breusch and Pagan Lagrangian multiplier test for random effects: DEBT model		
lev [ID, t] = xb + u[ID] + e[ID, t]		
Estimated results:		
	Var	sd = sqrt (var)
lev	0.0069	0.0832
e	0.0008	0.0291
u	0.0003	0.0180
Test: var (u) = 0		
Chi²(01) = 10.63		
prob > Chi² = 0.0006		

Source Structured review of annual financial report (generated using STATA)

Breusch and Pagan LM test for DE Model

Breusch and Pagan Lagrangian multiplier test for random effects: DE model		
lev[ID, t] = xb + u[ID] + e[ID, t]		
Estimated results:		
	var	sd = sqrt (var)
lev	0.164	0.405
e	0.046	0.215
u	0	0
Test: var(u) = 0		
Chi²(01) = 0.00		
prob > Chi² = 1.0000		

Source Structured review of annual financial report (generated using STATA)

Hausman LM test for DEBT model

Coefficients				
	(b)	(B)	(b − B)	Sqrt (diag(v_b − v_B))
	Fixed effects	Random effects	Difference	S.E
gro	0.076	0.089	−0.13	.
tang	−0.137	−0.206	0.069	0.370
pr	−0.583	−0.645	0.062	0.014

(continued)

(continued)

Coefficients				
	(*b*)	(*B*)	(*b* − *B*)	Sqrt (diag(*v_b* − *v_B*))
	Fixed effects	Random effects	Difference	S.E
risk	−0.319	−0.329	0.087	0.067
size	0.016	0.015	0.001	0.009
lq	−0.120	−0.147	0.027	0.012
b = consistent under H_0 and H_a; obtained from xtreg				
B = inconsistent under H_a *and* efficient under H_0; obtained from xtreg				
Test: H_0 : difference in coefficiens not systematic				
*Chi*²(6) =	(*b* − *B*)'[(*v_b* − *v_B*) ^ (−1)] (*b* − *B*)			
=	17.21			
prob > *Chi*² =	0.0085			

Source Structured review of annual financial report (generated using STATA)

Hausman LM test for DE Model

	Coefficients			
	(*b*)	(*B*)	(*b* − *B*)	Sqrt (diag(*v_b* −*v_B*))
	Fixed effects	Random effect	Difference	S. E
gro	0.283	0.496	−0.213	.
tang	0.061	−0.834	0.893	0.358
pr	−2.128	−3.222	1.094	0.329
risk	−0.802	−1.530	0.728	0.639
size	0.220	0.119	0.102	0.0903
lq	−0.345	−0.674	0.329	0.115
b = consistent under H_0 and H_a; obtained from xtreg				
B = inconsistent under H_a and efficient under H_0; obtained from xtreg				
Test: H_0 : difference in coefficiens not systematic				
*Chi*²(6) =	(*b* − *B*)'[(*v_b* −*v_B*) ^ (−1)] (*b* − *B*)			
=	22.10			
prob > *Chi*² =	0.0012			

Source Structured review of annual financial report (generated using STATA)

Modified Wald test for group-wise heteroscedasticity in fixed effects regression: DEBT model

H_0 : sigma$(i)^2$ = sigma^2 for all i
$Chi^2(8) = 49.00$
prob > $Chi^2 = 0.000$

Source Structured review of annual financial report (generated using STATA)

Modified Wald test for group-wise heteroscedasticity in fixed effects regression: DE model

H_0 : sigma$(i)^2$ = sigma^2 for all i
$Chi^2(8) = 1129.25$
prob > $Chi^2 = 0.000$

Source Structured review of annual financial report (generated using STATA)

Annexure 2: Diagnostic Tests

Test of normality for DEBT model: Shapiro–Wilk Test

H_0: The distribution is normal					
Variable	Obs.	W	V	z	Prob > z
lev	80	0.980	1.339	0.640	0.261

Source Structured review of annual financial report (generated using STATA)

Test of normality for DE model: Shapiro–Wilk test

H_0: The distribution is normal					
Variable	Obs.	W	V	z	Prob > z
lev	80	0.990	0.682	−0.838	0.799

Source Structured review of annual financial report (generated using STATA)

Tests of multi-collinearity: correlation matrix between explanatory variables

	Gro	Tang	pr	Risk	Size	Lq
gro	1.000					
tang	−0.246	1.000				
pr	0.328	−0.100	1.000			
risk	−0.101	0.043	−0.367	1.000		
size	0.027	−0.213	0.449	−0.731	1.000	
lq	0.306	−0.243	0.1429	0.238	−0.289	1.000

Source Structured review of annual financial report (generated using STATA)

References

Abor J (2005) The effect of capital structure on profitability: empirical analysis of listed firms in Ghana. J Risk Financ 6:438–445

Adesola WA (2009) Testing static tradeoff theory against pecking order models of capital structure in Nigerian quoted firms. Glob J Soc Sci 8(1):51

Ahmed N, Ahmed Z, Ahmed I (2010) Determinants of capital structure: a case of life insurance sector of Pakistan. Eur J Econ Financ Adm Sci 24:7–12

Amidu M (2007) Determinants of capital structure of banks in Ghana: an empirical approach. Balt J Manag 2(1):67–79

Baker M, Wurgler J (2002) Market timing and capital structure. J Finance 57(1):1–32

Booth L, Aivazian V, Demirguc-Kunt A, Maksimovic V (2001) Capital structures in developing countries. J Finance 56(1):87–130

Cassar G, Holmes S (2003) Capital structure and financing of SMEs: Australian evidence. Account Finance 43(2):123–147

Dawood MHAK, Moustafa ESI, El-Hennawi M (2011) The determinants of capital structure in listed Egyptian corporations. Middle East Finance Econ 9:83–99

Ebru Ç (2011) An empirical investigation on the determinants of capital structures of Turkish firms. J Finance Econ 9:35–42

Gill A, Biger N, Pai C, Bhutani S (2009) The determinants of capital structure in the service industry: evidence from United States. Open Bus J 2:48–53

Goldstein R, Ju N, Leland H (2001) An EBIT-based model of dynamic capital structure. J Bus 74 (4):483–512

Harris M, Raviv A (1991) The theory of capital structure. J Finance 46(1):297–355

Jensen MC (1986) Agency cost of free cash flow, corporate finance, and takeovers. Corporate Finance, and Takeovers. Am Econ Rev 76(2):323–329

Jensen MC, Meckling WH (1976) Theory of the firm: managerial behavior, agency costs and ownership structure. J Financ Econ 3(4):305–360

Kindie AB (2011) Determinants of capital structure on Ethiopian insurance companies. Thesis Addis Ababa University, Addis Ababa

Kumar MS, Dhanasekaran M, Sandhya S, Saravanan R (2012) Determination of financial capital structure on the insurance sector firms in India. Eu J Soc Sci 29(2):288–294

Malhotra NK (2008) Marketing research: an applied orientation, 5th edn. Pearson Education India

Mezgebe M (2010) Assessment of the reinsurance business in Developing Countries: Case of Ethiopia. MA thesis, Graduate School of Business, University of South Africa

Modigliani F, Miller MH (1958) The cost of capital, corporation finance and the theory of investment. Am Econ Rev 48(3):261–297
Modigliani F, Miller MH (1963) Corporate income taxes and the cost of capital: a correction. Am Econ Rev 53(3):433–443
Morri G, Beretta C (2008) The capital structure determinants of REITs. Is it a peculiar industry? J Eur Real Estate Res 1(1):6–57
Myers SC (1984) The capital structure puzzle. J Finance 39(3):574–592
Najjar N, Petrov K (2011) Capital structure of insurance companies' in Bahrain. Int J Bus Manag 6 (11):138
Noulas A, Genimakis G (2011) The determinants of capital structure choice: evidence from Greek listed companies. Appl Financ Econ 21(6):379–387
Onaolapo AA, Kajola SO (2010) Capital structure and firm performance: evidence from Nigeria. Eur J Econ Finance Adm Sci 25:70–82
Rajan RG, Zingales L (1995) What do we know about capital structure? Some evidence from international data. J Finance 50(5):1421–1460
Sayeed MA (2011) The determinants of capital structure for selected Bangladeshi listed companies. Int Rev Bus Res Pap 7(2):21–36
Shah A, Khan S (2007) Determinants of capital structure: evidence from Pakistani panel data. Int Rev Bus Res Pap 3(4):265–282
Sharif B, Naeem MA, Khan AJ (2012) Firm's characteristics and capital structure: a panel data analysis of Pakistan's insurance sector. Afr J Bus Manage 6(14):4939
Solomon MA (2012) Characteristics and capital structure: a panel data analysis from Ethiopian insurance industry. Int J Commer Manag 3(12):21–27
Song HS (2005) Capital structure determinants an empirical study of Swedish companies. CESIS Electronic Working Paper Series 2005–25
Teker D, Tasseven O, Tukel A (2009) Determinants of capital structure for Turkish firms: a panel data analysis. Int Res J Finance Econ 29:179–187
Titman S, Wessels R (1988) The determinants of capital structure choice. J Finance 43(1):1–19
Zeleke H (2007) Insurance in Ethiopia: historical development, present status and future challenges. Master Printing Press, Addis Ababa, Ethiopia

Chapter 9
Income Distribution and Economic Growth

Atnafu Gebremeskel

Abstract This paper links access to bank loans and income distribution to productivity growth. Its main focus is on examining how functional income distribution can influence the evolution of productivity and thereby promote economic growth. We obtained key variables and their evolution from the Ethiopian Central Statistical Agency dataset on medium and large scale manufacturing firms. The paper uses the evolutionary economic framework and the evolutionary theory jointly with its evolutionary econometric approach. This sees economic growth as an open-ended process. The major findings and conclusions of this paper are lack of strong evidence of evolution (intra-industry selection) to foster productivity growth and reallocation (structural change). The employment share of each firm within an industry entered the model with a negative sign but a significant coefficient. In economic terms, the positive and negative coefficients of labor share within a firm and employment share of each firm within the industry give us important information about structural changes within the manufacturing sector. The key policy lesson is that access to bank loans is of great importance to firms. This is particularly so for industries such as spinning, tanning and publishing in which all firms that had access to bank loans revealed movements in their employment shares. This is evidence of structural transformation. It is desired that future research includes economy-wide modeling, estimation and more formalization of evolutionary economic models to study the link between access to bank loans and its effects on income distribution and inclusive economic growth.

Keywords Income distribution · Evolutionary economics · Evolutionary econometrics · Productivity · Growth

A. Gebremeskel (✉)
Department of Economics, Addis Ababa University, Addis Ababa, Ethiopia
e-mail: atnafuga@gmail.com

A. Heshmati (ed.), *Studies on Economic Development and Growth in Selected African Countries*, Frontiers in African Business Research,
DOI 10.1007/978-981-10-4451-9_9

9.1 Introduction

Income distribution remains one of the few unanswered questions in economics. Mincer's (1958) thinking is that economists have long theorized about the nature or causes of inequalities in personal incomes. In contrast, the vigorous development of empirical research in the field of personal income distribution is of recent origin. For nearly 200 years, Anglophone economics followed Ricardo (1815) and conceived of distribution as referring to a functional role in economic production.

The functional approach to income distribution has survived a marginal revolution in economics, an industrial revolution, the development of welfare economics, the great depression, the advent of macroeconomics, the creation of a welfare state, the mathematizing of neo-classical economics and several generations of prominent economists arguing that economics should rightly be concerned with the distribution of well-being across individuals and the erosion of the sharp class divisions that gave Ricardo his distribution theory (Goldfarb and Leonard 2005).

While who gets what refers to personal distribution of income across individuals, functional distribution is across suppliers of productive factors because of the distributive consequences and their wider implications are more important than the causes.

Moreover, the emphasis of contemporary research has almost completely shifted from a study of the causes of inequalities to the study of the facts and of their consequences for various aspects of economic activities. One such activity is productivity growth and economic growth.

The question of how inequalities are generated and how they evolve over time has been a major concern of economics for more than a century. Yet, the relationship between inequalities and the process of economic development is far from being an agreed area of research. In developing economies, it is a challenge for both academic and policy circles. There is demand for academicians to investigate this and it is an issue that also needs to be dealt with by policymakers.

Thus, a study of income distribution should not be undertaken for the sake of a study but for its wider implications on economic performance. Economic growth is effected by economic performance because the growth-inequality linkage is both important and controversial.

It is important because policymakers need to understand the way in which an increase in output will be shared among different groups within an economy and the constraints that this sharing may put on future growth. Its controversial aspects arise from the fact that it has been difficult to reconcile the different theories, especially since empirical evidence has been largely inconclusive (Cecilia 2010). For example, Barro (1990) and Persson and Tabellini (1994) argue that moderate redistribution promotes growth whereas a high degree of redistribution will have a negative impact on growth.

The conventional textbook approach on the effect of inequality on growth is that inequality is good for incentives and therefore good for growth, even though incentive and growth considerations might be traded off against equity goals. On the other hand, development economists have long expressed counter-arguments.

For example, Todaro (1997) provides four general arguments why greater equality in developing countries may in fact be a condition for self-sustaining economic growth: (a) dissaving and/or unproductive investments by the rich; (b) lower levels of human capital held by the poor; (c) demand pattern of the poor being more biased toward local goods; and (d) political rejection by the masses.

Overall, the view that inequality is necessary for accumulation and that redistribution harms growth has faced challenges from many fronts. For example, Alesina and Rodrik (1994) and Persson and Tabellini (1994) combine political economy arguments with the traditional negative incentive effect of redistribution. These authors maintain that inequalities affects taxation through the political process when individuals are allowed to vote in order to choose the tax rate (or, equivalently, vote to elect a government whose programs include a certain redistributive policy). If inequalities determine the extent of redistribution, then this will have an indirect effect on the rate of growth of the economy.

In their paper 'Social Conflict, Growth and Income Distribution,' Benhabib and Rustichini (1996) explore the effect of social conflict arising due to income distribution on both short-run and long-run economic growth rates. According to them, despite the predictions of the neo-classical theory of economic growth, poor countries were observed to invest at lower rates and have not grown faster than rich countries. They studied how the level of wealth and the degree of inequalities affected growth and show how lower wealth can lead to lower growth and even to stagnation when the incentives to domestic accumulation are weakened by redistributive considerations.

Perotti (1996) contends that equality has a positive impact on growth while Rehme (2006) argues that redistributing governments may have a relatively stronger interest in technological advances or high economic integration. He observes a positive association between redistribution and growth across countries.

While we can find vast literature on income inequalities and economic growth similar to the studies mentioned earlier, they exclude the role of firms and the mechanisms behind them for the creation and evolution of the links between income distribution and economic growth. However, the existence of firms and their actions are recognized in economic theory.

Thus, our introduction of firms in such an analysis is not arbitrary. Firms play a central role in shaping the path of economic theory and as sources of growth in the process of economic evolution. This argument is theoretically consistent with one of the questions in economics (Coase 1937). Thus, any analysis which omits the role of firms in the creation and evolution of income distribution in the growth process cannot make a complete description. More specifically, empirical evidence on how firms' financial structures can influence their productivity and thereby drive economic growth is scarce. This study bridges this gap.

Two crucial questions arise for policymakers which have policy relevance. The first is whether inequality is a prerequisite for growth. And the second concerns the effects of growth promoting policies on inequalities, and in particular under which circumstances a conflict between the two objectives may emerge.

Thus, our paper takes firms as a hub for generating macroeconomic regularities. Firms generate a link between sources and uses of funds, productivity, income distribution and structural transformation in the market process. We explore the dependence of macroeconomic productivity growth on firm-level productivities. We examine how firms' access to bank loans can influence an aggregate rate of growth. Growth in productivity, output and employment is determined mutually and endogenously. More specifically, this paper answers the following questions:

(a) How do firm-level sources and use of funds (investments from bank loans) influence economic growth?
(b) Does access to bank loans affect intra- and inter-firm reallocation of labor?
(c) Can we find evidence of structural change, that is, reallocation of labor from less productive to more productive industries?
(d) Can we draw some theoretical results and what policy lessons can we draw from this?

The rest of the paper is organized as follows. Section 9.2 discusses economic growth theories. Section 9.3 deals with evolutionary economics and economic growth from an evolutionary perspective. Section 9.4 discusses econometric modeling in the presence of evolutionary change; it also presents empirical evidence and is followed by Sect. 9.5 which presents empirical results from Ethiopia. Section 9.6 gives a conclusion.

9.2 Theory of Economic Growth

Economic growth is a dominant area of theoretical and empirical research in economics in general and in macroeconomics in particular. For example, Nelson (1996: 7) points out that from the beginning of modern economics as a field of study, economic growth has often been the central area of inquiry, but on and off. During the early decades, Hahn and Matthews (1964) presented the most comprehensive survey on the contributions that had been made to the theory of economic growth beginning with Harrods's article in 1939. Salavadori (2003) emphasizes that an interest in the study of economic growth has experienced remarkable ups and downs in the history of economics. It was the central issue in classical political economy from Adam Smith to David Ricardo, and then in the critique by Karl Marx (Nelson 1996; Salavadori 2003).

Then, the growth theory waned (Nelson 1996) and moved to the periphery during the so-called marginal revolution (Salavadori 2003). Undoubtedly, one of the reasons for this was that formal theory had developed which focused on market equilibria. The concern was with what lay behind demand and supply curves and how these jointly determined the observed configuration of outputs, inputs and prices. The troubled economic times after World War I, in particular the great depression, also pulled the attention of economists toward analyzing shorter-run phenomena such as balance of payment disequilibria, inflation and unemployment.

There was a renaissance of interest in long-run economic growth after World War II. One reason for this was that new national product data was first available for USA and later for other advanced industrial nations. This for the first time allowed economists to measure economic growth at the national level (Nelson 1996).

In modern times, the starting point for any study of economic growth is the neo-classical growth model which emphasizes the role of capital accumulation. This model, first constructed by Solow (1956) and Swan (1956), shows how economic policy can raise an economy's growth rate by inducing people to save more. But the model also predicts that such an increase in growth cannot last indefinitely. In the long run, a country's growth rate will revert to the rate of technological progress, which neo-classical theory takes as being exogenous. Underlying this long-run result is the principle of diminishing marginal productivity which puts an upper limit on how much output a person can produce simply by working with more and more capital given the state of technology. Aghion and Howitt (1992, 1998) provide a presentation on this.

9.2.1 The Neo-Classical Growth Theory

In the neo-classical framework, the notion of growth as increased stocks of capital goods was codified as the Solow–Swan growth model, which involves a series of equations that show the relationship between output, labor-time, capital and investment. This was the first attempt to model long-run growth analytically. According to this theory, the role of technological changes was crucial and even more important than the accumulation of capital.

This theory assumes that countries use their resources efficiently and that there are diminishing returns to capital and labor. From these two premises, the neo-classical model makes three important predictions: first, increasing capital relative to labor creates economic growth since people can be more productive given more capital. Second, poor countries with less capital per person grow faster because each investment in capital produces a higher return than in rich countries with ample capital. Third, because of diminishing returns to capital, economies eventually reach a point where any increase in capital no longer creates economic growth.

The model also notes that countries can overcome this steady state and continue growing by inventing new technologies. In the long run, output per capita depends on the rate of saving, but the rate of output growth should be equal to any saving rate. In this model, the process by which countries continue growing despite diminishing returns is 'exogenous' and represents the creation of new technology that allows production with fewer resources. As technology improves, the steady state level of capital increases and the country invests and grows.

The strengths of the neo-classical approach for economic growth are considerable. The neo-classical theory has provided a way of thinking about the factors behind long-run economic growth in individual sectors and in the economy as a whole. The theoretical structure has called attention to historical changes in factor proportions and has focused an analysis of the relationship between those changes and factor prices. These key insights and the language and formalism associated with them have served to effectively guide and to give coherence to research that has been done by many different economists around the globe. The weakness of the theoretical structure is that it provides a grossly inadequate vehicle for analyzing technical change.

The fundamental problems with neo-classical explanations of economic growth are: (1) despite much empirical efforts at the neo-classical production function, the model still faces problems in explaining considerable inter-plant and international differences in productivity as well as differences between developed economies. Even more striking is evidence for single industries, showing big sectoral productivity gaps between different countries (Hodgson 1996); and (2) increasing capital creates a growing burden of depreciation. It is also noted that the economic life of capital assets has been declining. In particular, the orthodox formulation offers no possibility of reconciling analyses of growth undertaken at the level of the economy or the sector with what is known about the processes of technical changes at the microeconomic level. Hodgson (1996) has a detailed account of this and similar arguments.

9.2.2 The Endogenous Growth Theory

In response to some of the problems in the standard neo-classical growth theory, the idea of an endogenous growth theory emerged in the works of Romer (1986, 1987, 1990, 1994), Lucas (1988) and a second generation variant pioneered by Aghion and Howitt (1992, 1998). They developed the endogenous growth theory which includes a mathematical explanation of technological advancement.

This broke from the preceding neo-classical thinking by encompassing learning by doing and knowledge spillover effects. In these models, cumulative divergence of national output and productivity becomes more likely than convergence and thus seems to correspond more adequately to available data.

However, the amended aggregate production function is still at the conceptual foundation of the endogenous growth models, typically embodying features such as increasing marginal productivity of knowledge but diminishing returns in the productivity of knowledge (Hodgson 1996).

Therefore, overall, there are constant returns to capital and economies never reach a steady state. Growth does not slow as capital accumulates, but the rate of growth depends on the type of capital that a country invests in. Research done in this area has focused on what increases human capital (for example, education) or technological change (for example, innovation).

9.3 Economics as an Evolutionary Science and Economic Growth from an Evolutionary Perspective

9.3.1 Why an Evolutionary Approach in Economics?

The basic paradigm in mainstream economic theory, namely that individuals take decisions in isolation using only the information received through some general market signals such as prices, is built on the general equilibrium model. However, as is well known, this model guarantees neither stability nor uniqueness of equilibrium. Since the latter is essential for macroeconomists who wish to use comparative statistics, they have had to avoid this fundamental problem by resorting to what has become the standard paradigm in modern macroeconomics, that is, the representative agent (RA) framework.

The basic assumption is that the behavior of the aggregate can be treated as the behavior of an average individual. The use of such an approach has been frequently contested and has several obvious disadvantages. Firstly, it means that one has to ignore communication and direct interaction among agents and ultimately defines away the problem of coordination (Hahn and Solow 1995; Leijonhufvud 1992). In this setting, interaction and coordination occur only through prices. The role of prices is undoubtedly important, but the price mechanism alone can work only if information is complete; in such a case, one can ignore the influence of other coordination and interaction mechanisms. Here, again, these difficulties can be sidestepped by assuming that a sector of the economy can be described by a RA.

There is no simple, direct, correspondence between individual and aggregate regularities. It may be that in some cases, aggregate choices correspond to those that can be generated by an individual. However, even in such exceptional cases, the individual in question cannot be thought of as maximizing anything meaningful from the point of view of society's welfare. Our approach is exactly the opposite from the representative individual approach. Instead of trying to impose restrictions on aggregate behavior, by using, for example, the first-order conditions obtained from the maximization program of the representative individual, the claim is that the structure of aggregate behavior (macro) actually emerges from the interaction between the agents (micro). In other words, statistical regularities emerge as a self-organized process at the aggregate level: complex patterns of interacting individual behavior may generate a certain regularity at the aggregate level. The idea of representing a society by one exemplar denies the fact that the organizational features of the economy play a crucial role in explaining what happens at the aggregate level.

The way in which markets are organized is assumed to have no influence on aggregate outcomes. Thus, aggregate behavior, unlike that of biological or physical systems, can be reduced to that of a glorified individual. Such an idea has, as a corollary, the notion that collective and individual rationality are similar. What we suggest is that collective outcomes be thought of as a result of an interaction between agents who may have rather simple rules of behavior and who may adapt rather than optimize. Once one allows for direct interaction among agents, macrobehavior cannot, in general, be thought of as reflecting the behavior of a 'typical' or 'average' individual.

The key assumption behind the construction of the aggregate production function is that all factor markets are perfect in the sense that individuals can buy or sell as much as they want at a given price. With perfect factor markets (and no risk), the market must allocate the available supply of inputs to maximize total output (extensively found in Gatti et al. 2007 and the literature cited there).

Evolutionary theory in economics is as old as economics itself. It was pioneered by Veblen (1898) when he asked, 'Why is economics not an evolutionary science?' and suggested that the only rational approach for economists was to assume that economies evolve. Otherwise, he argued, we can describe an economy but have no effective theory of change and development.

Veblen started his argument by asserting that all modern sciences are evolutionary sciences (1898: 374) while Alchian (1950) brought out the evolutionary approach as an alternative framework in economics. He started by proposing a suggestion for a modification of economic analyses to incorporate incomplete information and uncertain foresight as axioms. In the words of Alchian, this approach dispensed with 'profit maximization' and it did not rely on predictable individual behavior that is usually assumed as a first approximation in standard textbook treatment.

The suggested approach embodies the principles of biological evolution and natural selection by interpreting economic systems as an adaptive mechanism which chooses among exploratory actions generated by the adaptive pursuit of 'success' or 'profit.'

Krugman (1996) articulates economics as it is about what *individuals* do: not classes, not 'correlations of forces' but individual actors. This is not to deny the relevance of higher levels of analyses, but they must be grounded in individual behavior. Methodological individualism is of the essence. He further notes that individuals are *self-interested.* He extends his argument by saying that there was nothing in economics that inherently prevented us from allowing people to derive satisfaction from others' consumption, but the predictive power of economic theory came from the presumption that normally people care about themselves.

Individuals are *intelligent;* they do not neglect obvious opportunities for gain. It is often asserted that economic theory draws its inspiration from physics, and that it should become more like biology. If that is what you think, you should do two things. First, read a text on evolutionary theory, like John Maynard Smith's *Evolutionary Genetics*. You will be startled at how much it looks like a textbook on microeconomics. Second, try to explain a simple economic concept, like supply and demand, to a physicist. You will discover that our whole style of thinking, of building up aggregative stories from individual decisions, is not at all the way they think (Krugman 1996). Veblen and Krugman's suggestion is that 'evolutionary economics is the only rational proposition' (Boulton 2010).

The renaissance in evolutionary economics in the past two decades has brought with it a great deal of theoretical developments and interdisciplinary import (Dopfer and Potts 2004).

Inspired by Veblen's theory, evolutionary economics has become one alternative approach to economic analyses involving complex economic interactions. Recent contributors include Nelson's (1974), *Neo-classical vs Evolutionary Theories of Economic Growth: Critique and Prospectus*. More importantly, Richard Nelson and Sidney Winter's seminal work *An Evolutionary Theory of Economic Change* (1982), Dopfer's *The Evolutionary Foundations of Economics* (2005) and Beinhocker's *The Origin of Wealth, Evolution, Complexity and the Radical Remarking of Economics* (2006) are advancements in the theory of evolutionary economics.

The questions to be answered before using an evolutionary theoretical framework to understand how economies grow are: What is evolutionary economics? Why evolutionary economics? What are the theoretical foundations of evolutionary economics? Where do economies come from? (Beinhocker 2006). How do the behaviors, relationships, institutions and ideas that underpin an economy form, and how do they evolve over time?

Beinhocker has argued that questions about origins play a prominent role in most sciences because like it will be difficult to imagine modern cosmology without the Big Bang or biology without evolution, it would be hard to believe that economics could ever truly succeed as a science if it were not able to answer the question 'Where do economies come from?'

Yet, the question about the origin of economies has not played a central role in traditional economics which has tended to focus on how an economy's output is allocated rather than how it got there in the first place. The process of economy formation presents us with a first-class scientific puzzle and one of the sharpest distinctions between traditional economics and what is described as Complexity Economics (Beinhocker 2006).

But what is evolution in economic science? A relatively narrow definition of evolution is change in the mean characteristics of a population (Andersen 2004). Economic growth, that is, the aggregate change in real output per person, is a consequence of increasing the productivity of the factors of production and of technological changes in a very wide sense. For a constant participation rate, it can be modeled as a change in firm-level mean real output per employee weighted by the firm's employment share in the total number of firms in the economy. In Holm (2014) this is referred to as the evolution of labor productivity.

The key ideas of evolutionary theory are that firms at any time are viewed as possessing various capabilities, procedures and decision rules that determine what they do given external conditions. They also engage in various 'search' operations whereby they discover, consider and evaluate possible changes in their ways of doing things. Firms, whose decision rules are profitable, given the market environment, expand; those firms that are unprofitable contract. The market environment surrounding individual firms may be in part endogenous to the behavioral system taken as a whole; for example, product and factor prices may be influenced by the output of the industry and the demand for inputs (Nelson and Winter 1982).

According to Holm (2014), economic evolution is an open-ended process of novelty generation and the reallocation of resources. Selection is the sorting of a population of agents (firms) that is implicit to their differential growth rates. Firms perform innovations and develop knowledge in attempts to gain decisive competitive advantages over competitors, but firms are intentionally rational agents with limited information and innovation; so more generally, learning may also lead to decreased productivity. Firms prosper or decline as a result of the interaction between their own learning activities, the learning activities of competitors and the external factors that set the premises for the interaction. We can find more on this in Dosi and Nelson (2010) and Metcalfe (1998). Safarzyńska (2010) also has an excellent survey.

Holm (2014) explores how the evolution of productivity or any other characteristic in a population of firms can be described. According to him, evolution can be understood as the sum of two effects, which is referred to by different names in literature: inter-firm or reallocation or selection effect and intra-firm or learning or innovation effect. To this, the effects of entry and exit are added but as far as entry is the introduction of new knowledge by entrepreneurs and exit is the disappearance of an inferior firm, these effects are also learning and selection. As a stylized depiction of economic evolution Holm (2014) expresses evolution as the total effect of selection, learning, entry and exit.

Whereas inter-firm selection is driven by the process of competition, inter-industry selection is driven by the process of structural change, which is somewhat different. Productivity understood as physical efficiency is important in competition among firms which produce homogenous products, for example, within industries. This is less the case with heterogeneous outputs because computing physical efficiency for heterogeneous products does not make sense because as the composition of demand changes over time, not least as a consequence of economic growth in itself, relative prices change as well and this affects inter-industry selection (Holm 2014).

Holm has emphasized the importance of indicating the basic differences between standard growth theories and growth theories in evolutionary economics. Evolutionary economists (for example, Richard Nelson, Eric Beinhocker, Geoffrey Hodgson and John Foster) strongly argue that an evolutionary framework is more encompassing than standard approaches. Carlsson and Eliasson (2003) note that economic growth can be described at the macrolevel but never explained at that level. Economic growth is basically a result of experimental project creation and selection in a dynamic market and in hierarchies of the capacity of the economic system to capture winners and losers. Castellacci (2007) gives a review on the evolution of evolutionary theories in economics which is presented in Table 9.1.

Metcalfe et al. (2006) explored an evolutionary theory of adaptive growth. They supposed economic growth as a product of structural change and economic self-transformation based on processes that were closely connected with but not reducible to the growth in knowledge.

Table 9.1 Contrast between new growth theories and evolutionary growth

Issues	New growth theories	Evolutionary theories
What is the main level of aggregation?	Aggregate models based on neo-classical micro-foundations (methodological individualism)	Toward a co-evolution between micro-levels and macrolevels of analysis ('non-reductionism')
Representative agent or heterogeneous individuals?	Representative agent and typological thinking	Heterogeneous agents and population thinking
What is the mechanism of creation of innovation?	Learning by doing and searching activity by: the R&D sector; radical innovations; and general purpose technologies	Combination of various forms of learning with radical technological and organizational innovations
What is the dynamics of the growth process? How is history conceived?	History is a uniform-speed transitional dynamics	Toward a combination of gradualist and dynamics: history is a process of qualitative change and transformation
Is the growth process deterministic or unpredictable?	'Weak uncertainty' (computable risk): stochastic but predictable process	'Strong' uncertainty: non-deterministic and unpredictable process
Toward equilibrium or never ending	Toward the steady state	Never ending and ever changing

The dominant connecting theme is enterprise, the innovative variations it generates and the multiple connections between investment, innovation, demand and structural transformation in the market process. Metcalfe and Foster (1998) explored the dependence of macroeconomic productivity growth on the diversity of technical progress functions and income elasticities of demand at the industry level and the resolution of this diversity into patterns of economic change through market processes. They show how industry growth rates are constrained by higher-order processes of emergence that convert an ensemble of industry growth rates into an aggregate rate of growth. The growth in productivity, output and employment is determined mutually and endogenously, and its value depends on variations in the primary causal influences in the system.

9.3.2 Econometric Modeling in the Evolutionary Economic Framework

Evolutionary economics in general and evolutionary econometrics in particular are not an arbitrarily choice. They are both relevant and have theoretical foundations. The theoretical basis for such a modeling is drawn from a self-organization approach and analyzed by the logistic diffusion growth model.

Evolutionary economics and the subsequent developments of its estimation techniques have enabled researchers to explore the advantages of evolutionary economics. This methodology is offered to construct an econometric model in the prescience of a structural change of an evolutionary type. In its various approaches, evolutionary economics has been concerned with economic processes that arise from systems which are subject to on-going structural changes in historical time. Foster and Wild (1999a) identified three characteristics that all evolutionary representations of economic processes seem to share:

1. A system that is undergoing a cumulative process of structure building, which results in increasing organization and complexity, cannot easily reverse its structure;
2. In the face of this time irreversibility, structure can change in non-linear and discontinuous ways in the face of exogenous shocks, particularly when the relevant evolutionary niche is filled; and
3. An evolutionary process of on-going structural changes introduces an increasing degree of fundamental uncertainty. Thus, a great deal of structure building involves the installation of protective repair and maintenance sub-systems.

Based on this discussion on evolutionary economics and the underlying theory of the functional income distribution and its implications on economic impact such as growth in productivity, our study tests if there is an indication for structural transformation. This is achieved by investigating the evolution of key variables, that is, evolution of employment share, evolution of market share, evolution of output share at the industry level and the evolution of productivity growth. This is done in two ways. First, by developing and estimating evolutionary econometrics to learn if there is an indication for evolution and second by conducting a graphical simulation.

Based on this background, we use a logistic diffusion equation (LDE) offered by Foster and Wild (1999b) as a theory of historical process. In real terms, it is rooted in the Bernoulli Differential Equation of the type shown in the equation in Annexure 1. The last line in this equation is a Logistic Differential Equation of First Order (LDEFO). Thus, based on the equation in Annexure 1, Foster and Wild (1999b) have developed an econometric model in the presence of evolutionary change as:

$$\frac{\mathrm{d}X}{\mathrm{d}t} = b\left(1 - \frac{X}{K}\right) \tag{9.1}$$

In Eq. 9.1, b is the net, that is, it allows for deterioration or deaths, firm entry-exit rate or diffusion coefficient, and K is the carrying capacity of the environment, for example, total industry or economy's market size, employment or output over which each firm will compete to capture as much of it. K is a constraint, for example, the total sales of an industry and X could be a firm's sales so that X/K is the firm's market share.

Two points must be raised about Eq. 9.1. First X/K can be understood as any share. If we are to work at the macrolevel, we may interpret X/K as the ratio of GDP to capital stock. This ratio is less than 1 because at any point in time the total national output is some fraction of inputs, the magnitude of the fraction depending on the productivity of the economy.

Equation 9.1 can be expanded to employ the existing econometric framework for estimation. Foster and Wild (1999b) have acknowledged that the application of the LDE of this type has been common in literature on the economics of innovation, following Griliches's (1957) pioneering work. However, economists have tended to view LDE in terms of disequilibrium adjustments from a stable equilibrium state to another in economics of the evolutionary growth theory.

As it stands, Eq. 9.1 depicts a smooth process tending toward infinite time. Only in a discrete interval version of LDE, we can generate the kinds of discontinuities that we can see in historical data. However, discrete interval dynamics are not pronounced features of most aggregated economic data. Thus, it is unlikely that we can generate a discontinuity endogenously in most cases.

Now, it is convenient for the purposes of an econometric investigation to rearrange Eq. 9.1 in the following way to obtain the Mansfield (1981) variant, employed in many such studies. Dividing both sides of Eq. 9.1 by K and rearranging, we arrive at:

$$\begin{aligned} X_t - X_{t-1} &= X_{t-1} b\left(1 - \frac{X_{t-1}}{K}\right) + u_t \\ \text{In} X_t - \text{In} X_{t-1} &= b - bX_{t-1}/K + e_t \quad \text{where } e_t = u_t/K \end{aligned} \tag{9.2}$$

The transformation into approximation in Eq. 9.2 allows the logistic equation to be estimated linearly and the error term is corrected for bias because of the upward drift of the mean of the X-series.

Equation 9.2 offers a representation of the endogenous growth of a self-organizing system subject to time irreversibility and constrained by boundary limits. To come up with the complete econometric model, Foster and Wild qualified their argument in the following ways:

(a) Regulation in the economic system can restrict economic agents and their organizations to particular market niches. This means, again, that the principle of competitive exclusion is significantly weakened. For example, governments restrict the issue of bank licenses, which preserves a niche which non-bank financial institutions have difficulty entering. Typically, competition in the economic sphere is overlaid by 'public interest' regulations that attempt to limit competition;
(b) Economic sub-systems rely on an interaction with the wider economic system in order to engage in trade. Thus, the K limit for a particular system will tend to rise continually in line with the general expansion of economic activity; and
(c) Increasing politicization of an economic system will lead to more predator–prey type interactions. This will tend to occur in saturation phases of LD growth. Thus, we do not always witness smooth transitions from one LD growth path to another but, instead, Schumpeterian 'creative destruction', dominated by

conflict and discontinuous dissipation of an accumulated structure (that is, a rapid fall in *K*).

Taking into account these qualifications, we arrived at the following LDE which is suitable for application in economics:

$$\text{In}X_t - \text{In}X_{t-1} = [b(\cdot)]\left[1 - \left\{\frac{X_{t-1}}{K(\cdot)} - a(\cdot)\right\}\right] + e_t \tag{9.3}$$

Thus, *b* and *K* are now themselves functions of other variables. The function (·) allows for factors that affect the diffusion coefficient, rendering it non-constant over time and *K*(·) takes into account the factors in the greater system that expand or contract the capacity limit faced by the system in question. The resource competition term, *a*(·), is now a more general functional relationship than the simple mechanism containing, for example, relative prices and existing demand for a particular product, the general economic condition in the environment.

A potential problem with Eq. 9.3 is that as *X* tends to its limit, growth in *X* will tend to zero so that the impact of factors in *b*(·) will also tend to zero. This is unlikely to be the case, so it is more appropriate to allow exogenous variables that affect the diffusion rate to influence the rate of growth of *X* with the same strength at all points on the logistic diffusion:

$$\text{In}X_t - \text{In}X_{t-1} = [b(\cdot)]\left[1 - \left\{\frac{X_{t-1}}{K(\cdot)} - a(\cdot)\right\}\right] + b(\cdot) + e_t \tag{9.4}$$

As it stands, Eq. 9.4 could be viewed as a disequilibrium process tending to an equilibrium defined in terms of *K*(·) and *a*(·). However, such an equilibrium interpretation differs from that in conventional usage. The non-stationary process modeled by Eq. 9.4 represents neither a mean reversion process in the presence of a deterministic trend, nor a co-integrated association between *X* and variables in *K*(·) and *a*(·), in the presence of a stochastic trend.

The stationary state to which the logistic trajectory tends is the limit of a cumulative, endogenous process, not a stable equilibrium outcome of an unspecified disequilibrium mechanism following an exogenous shock. The functions *K*(·) and *a*(·) allow for measurable shocks to the capacity limit and (·) encompasses the effect of exogenous shocks which alter the diffusion rate.

One final development is necessary. Although an equilibrium correction mechanism is inappropriate in this type of a model, homeostasis will occur in the short period around what can be viewed as a moving equilibrium.

Equation 9.4 relates to the momentum of a process and, as such, some path dependence is likely to exist in the sense that the system in question will still have a (decelerating) velocity even if all endogenous and exogenous forces impinging on the system cease to have an effect.

This is likely to be stronger the more non-stationary the variable in question is and the shorter the observation interval. Imposing a simple AR (1) process, we get:

$$\text{In}X_t - \text{In}X_{t-1} = [b(\cdot)]\left[1 - \left\{\frac{X_{t-1}}{K(\cdot)} - a(\cdot)\right\}\right] + b(\cdot) + c(\text{In}X_t - \text{In}X_{t-1})_{t-1} + e_t \tag{9.5}$$

In conventional treatments of path dependence in time-series data, constructs like the 'partial adjustment hypothesis,' concerning the presumed disequilibrium movements of levels of variables, are used to rationalize the use of lagged dependent variables. Inclusion of a lagged dependent variable requires upward revision of the estimated coefficients on explanatory variables in order to obtain their 'equilibrium' values. Here, the interpretation is different, but related. Instead of viewing a lagged dependent variable as evidence of sluggishness, we view its presence in our growth specification as evidence of momentum in the process (Foster and Wild 1999b). In Eq. 9.5, we can note that the left hand side is equivalent to the growth rate of series X. In our paper, it could be the growth rate of productivity.

9.3.3 Empirical Evidence of Evolutionary Econometrics

Empirical literature on evolutionary economics is scarce. However, there are some works which focus on the macrolevel, for example, Foster (1992, 1994) and Hodgson (1996).

Foster (1992) looked into a new perspective on the determination of sterling M3 using econometric modeling under the presence of evolutionary change. First, he obtained a logistic diffusion model from the first-order differential equation. Next, he modeled the evolution of M3 in log-linear specification in the form of evolutionary econometrics. He noted the ordinary least squares (OLS) and recursive least squares (RLS) as favored estimation methods in such a condition. He estimated datasets over 1963–1988 obtained from the UK monetary authority. He concluded that it was possible to understand the determination of M3 by viewing it as money supply, rather than money demand magnitude which is an outcome of a historical process. Such a process has been modeled as institutionally driven and subject to evolutionary change.

In Foster (1994), we can also find an evolutionary macroeconomic approach stressing institutional behavior used for estimating a model for Australian dollar M3. The conclusion is that since Australia and UK have the same cultural and institutional heritage, evolutionary econometrics captured a similar M3 creation process in both countries implying the appropriateness of an evolutionary approach for studies involving the diffusion process.

The most interesting out of these is Hodgson (1996) as it is the most direct theoretical and empirical research in long-term economic growth. He argues that his work is in part inspired by works on institutional economics such as those by Nelson and Winter and Thorstein Veblen (who was the first to suggest the use of economics as an evolutionary analogy taken from biology). His empirical estimation starts by placing major stress on institutional disruptions such as wars or revolutions and on the existence of political institutions such as multiparty systems.

Hodgson used a regression analysis to provide some preliminary empirical validation for his ideas. He admitted that it was not a fully fledged macroeconomic model, saying that the available data was crude and limited for providing a more ambitious and adequate test. He used real GDP per worker-hour as the index of productivity from Madison's data and summarized his findings as: first, two kinds of disruptions (disruption of extensive foreign occupation of home soil and revolution) seemed to be significant in determining and eventually advancing productivity growth. Second, there was evidence that the growth trajectory was determined by the timing of industrialization. Third, a relatively stable international order was found to be significant and positively related to growth.

Stockhammer et al. (2008) estimated the relationship between functional income distribution and aggregate demand (AD) in the Euro area. They modeled AD as: AD is the sum of consumption (*C*), investment (*I*), net exports (NX) and government expenditure (*G*). All variables are in real terms. In their general formulation, consumption, investment and net exports are written as a function of income(*Y*), the wage share (Ω) and some other control variables (summarized as *z*). The latter are assumed to be independent of output and distribution. Government expenditure is considered to be a function of output (because of automatic stabilizers) and exogenous variables (such as interest rates). However, as our paper focuses on the private sector, this will play no further role in our analysis. AD thus is:

$$\mathrm{AD} = C(Y,\Omega) + I(Y,\Omega,z_1) + \mathrm{NX}(Y,\Omega,z_{NX}) + G(Y,z_G) \tag{9.6}$$

Stockhammer et al.'s (2008) basic assertion for the inclusion of income distribution in consumption, investment and net export and government expenditure terms in Eq. 9.6 is: in the consumption function wage incomes (*W*) and profit incomes (*R*) are associated with different propensities to consume. The Kaleckian assumption is that the marginal propensity to save is higher for capital incomes than for wage incomes; consumption is therefore expected to increase when the wage share rises. They argue that Keynesian as well as neo-classical investment functions depend on output (*Y*) and the long-term real interest rate or some other measure of the cost of capital. The latter is part of z_1. The authors further argue that in addition to output and interest rate, investments are expected to decrease when the wage share rises because future profits may be expected to fall. Moreover, it is often argued that retained earnings are a privileged source of finance and may thus influence investment expenditures.

They claim that first, the policy implications of their findings are that wage moderation in the EU is unlikely to stimulate employment. They suggest that wage moderation leads to a (moderate) contraction in output. Since an expansion in output can be regarded as a necessary (but not sufficient) condition for an expansion in employment, wage moderation (at the EU level) is not an 'employment-friendly' wage policy. Their second implication refers to wage coordination; they contend that their findings suggest that demand is wage-led in the Euro area. This finding does not extend to individual Euro member states.

Our paper takes advantage of the formalization of evolutionary economics by Foster (1994, 2014) and Foster and Wild (1999a, b).

9.4 Empirical Results

9.4.1 The Data and Variables

This section examines if firms' access to bank loans has any effect on growth through[1] its effects on functional income distribution. The dataset is the medium and large manufacturing industries as compiled by the Central Statistical Agency (CSA) of Ethiopia. The available panel data covers 1996–2009 with 611 and 1943 firms in 1996 and 2009, respectively.

If access to bank loans first affects functional income distribution and if functional income distribution affects productivity growth that would imply that facilitating access to bank loans might ultimately foster growth in the economy. To achieve this objective, we first explore the real firms over the period on some key variables and econometrically estimate Eq. 9.5 using the generalized method of moments (GMM). Finally, alternative policy simulation scenarios are performed to understand the full effect of bank loans, income distribution and productivity growth linkage.

First, from firm-level data, the parameters of interest are computed for each firm for each year:

- Employment share (EMPSHAFIRM): Is supposed to capture if there is an indication of a structural change, that is, the movement of labor from less productive to more productive sectors;
- Market share (MKTSHARE): This is the available resource over which firms have to compete. It is through this competition process that decisions to invest in productivity fostering factors are undertaken;
- Output share (OUSHA): Firms can also compete over industry output; and
- Productivity growth (GROWTHPRO): Is the main variable of interest. Its growth rate is understood as the growth of mean characteristics in evolutionary economics. Thus, growth is perceived to mean growth in productivity.

Based on these variables, our paper draws some inferences about the connection between access to bank loans, functional income distribution and productivity growth.

[1]In the evolutionary growth framework, growth is mainly understood as growth of any mean characteristics (in our case productivity growth).

9.4.2 Results from Data Exploration

The evolution of employment shares, market shares, output shares and growth in productivity are shown in Figs. 9.1, 9.2, 9.3 and 9.4 in Annexure 2. The purpose of these figures is to learn if there is any indication of a structural transformation process within the manufacturing sector. If there is a change in the structure of production in the manufacturing sector, we expect the labor share to be continuously shifting within the industry. The shift should take place from low productivity to high productivity industries. This would mean higher labor productivity and consequently higher labor incomes which will form a positive feedback loop with productivity.

In Fig. 9.1, we observe movements for employment share within the industries only for 11 industries. We identified these industries from the data as:

- Production, processing and preserving of meat, fruits and vegetables
- Manufacture of animal feed
- Manufacture of non-metallic NEC
- Manufacture of basic iron and steel
- Manufacture of other fabricated metal products
- Manufacture of pumps, compressors, valves and taps
- Manufacture of other general purpose machinery
- Manufacture of batteries
- Manufacture of bodies of motor vehicles
- Manufacture of parts and accessories
- Manufacture of furniture.

From the firm-level dataset, it was possible to learn that most of the firms within these industries had access to bank loans. For example, overall, the 105 firms within the production, processing and preserving of meat, fruits and vegetables industries had access to bank loans. In the manufacture of animal feed industry, out of 98 firms, 37 had access to bank loans. Generally, all the indicated firms had access to bank loans during the years of observation. In Fig. 9.1, we can observe that in these industries, there is a significant movement (fluctuation) in employment shares. The only exceptions are spinning, tanning and publishing industries in which all firms had access to bank loans. However, any indication of movement in their employment share is not displayed.

One can argue that the employment share must be within the same sector (industries) and not across industries. If the reallocation of labor was taking place across industries, we could have observed variations in the employment share in the rest of the industries, but this is not evidenced.

Whether these industries are high productivity sectors and hence growth and equality promoting can be another area of enquiry. But looking at their face value alone, we may tentatively conclude that those industries which are related to metallic manufacturing in particular are connected to the government (see Fig. 9.1 in Annexure 2).

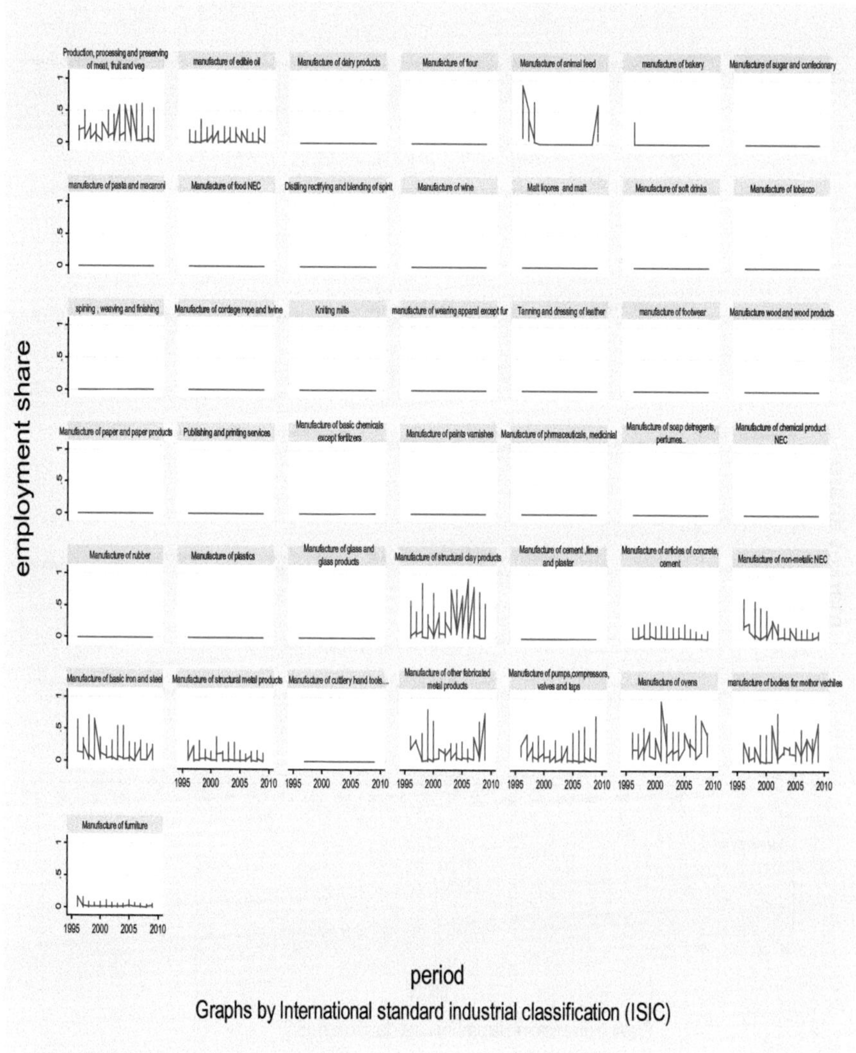

Fig. 9.1 Evolution of employment share

Referring to Fig. 9.3, firms' shares in total industry output are more pronounced than their market shares. This tells us the underlying market structure, which may subsequently have an effect on functional income distribution and productivity growth (see Fig. 9.3 in Annexure 2).

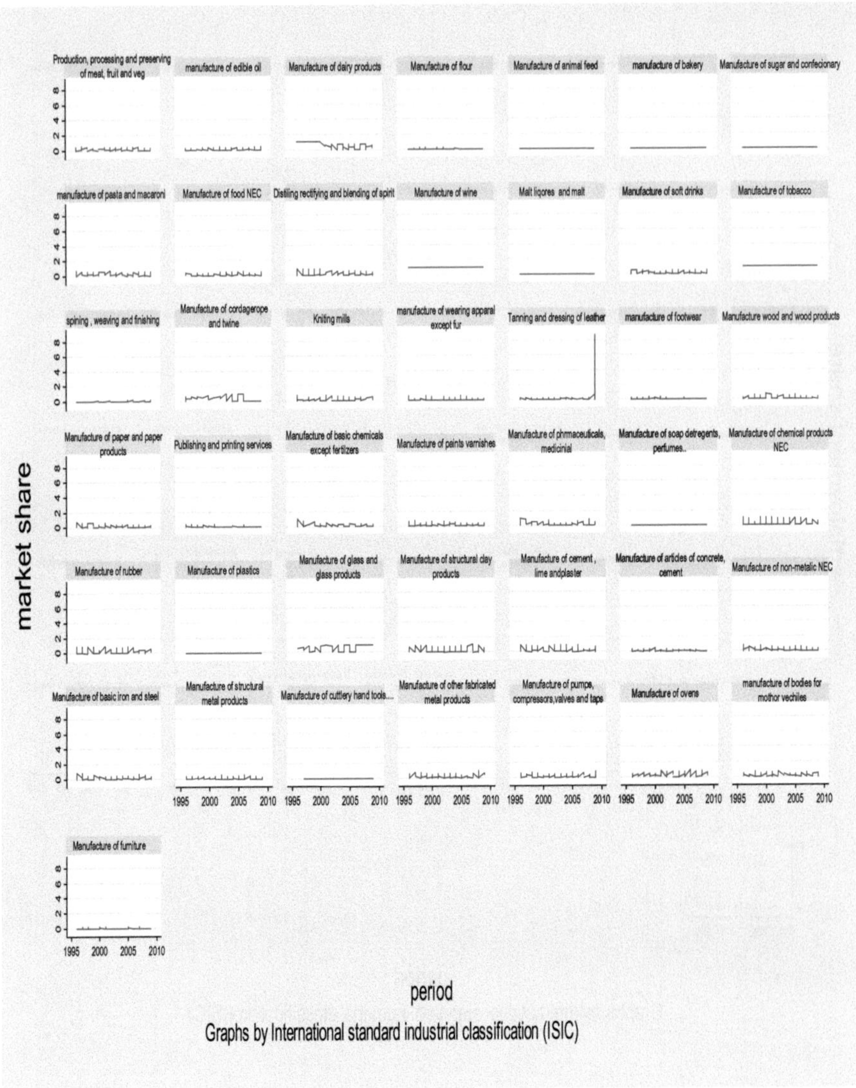

Fig. 9.2 Evolution of market share

It has been discussed that firms are at the heart of an evolutionary approach to economic growth and growth in productivity at the firm level is a key to economic growth. We can see from Fig. 9.4 that there are fluctuations in the productivity growth rate (from −20 to 10%). We also note that, for example, the productivity growth for production, processing and preserving of meat, fruits and vegetables remained positive, which might be an indication of the effect of access to bank loans (see Fig. 9.4 in Annexure 2).

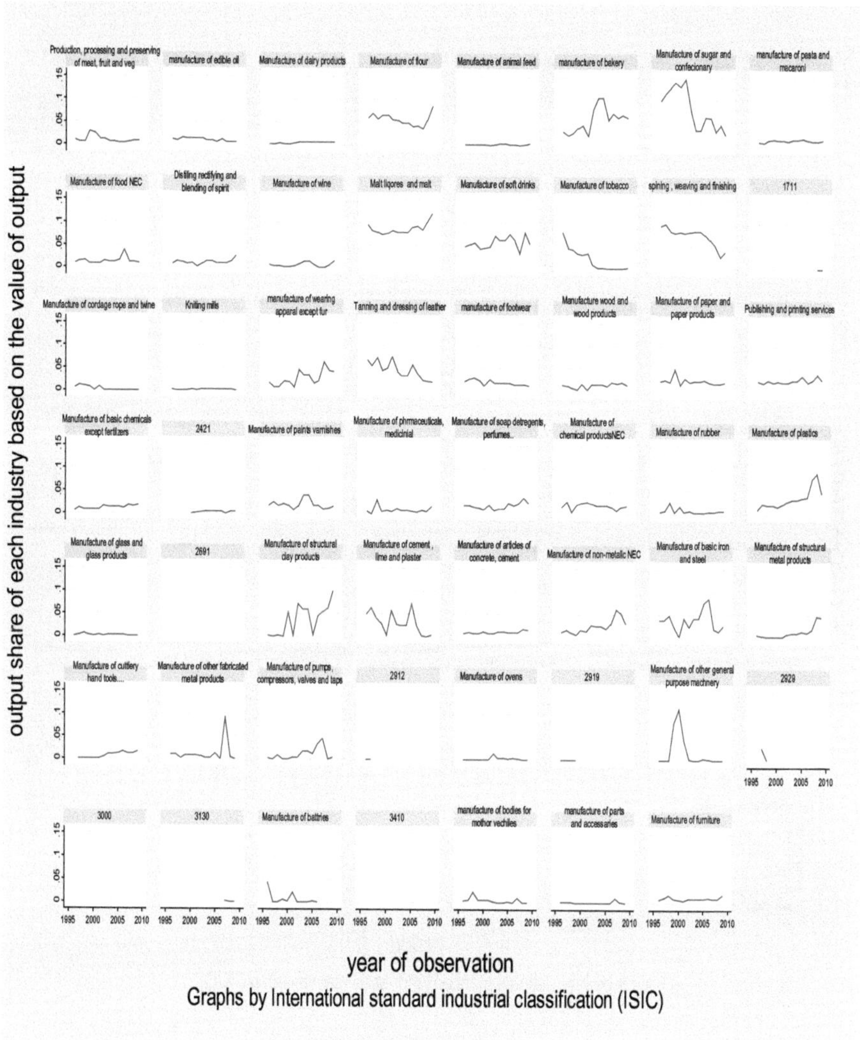

Fig. 9.3 Evolution of output share at the industry level

9.4.3 Econometric Results

This section deals with the econometric estimation of the logistic differential equation in Eq. 9.5. The variables entering the model are two natured: the evolutionary component and the exogenous component.

We estimated Eq. 9.5 using firm-level panel data. To achieve this, the data was transformed (logarithms, growth rates, lags and differences) so that the transformed data was consistent with the evolutionary econometric framework.

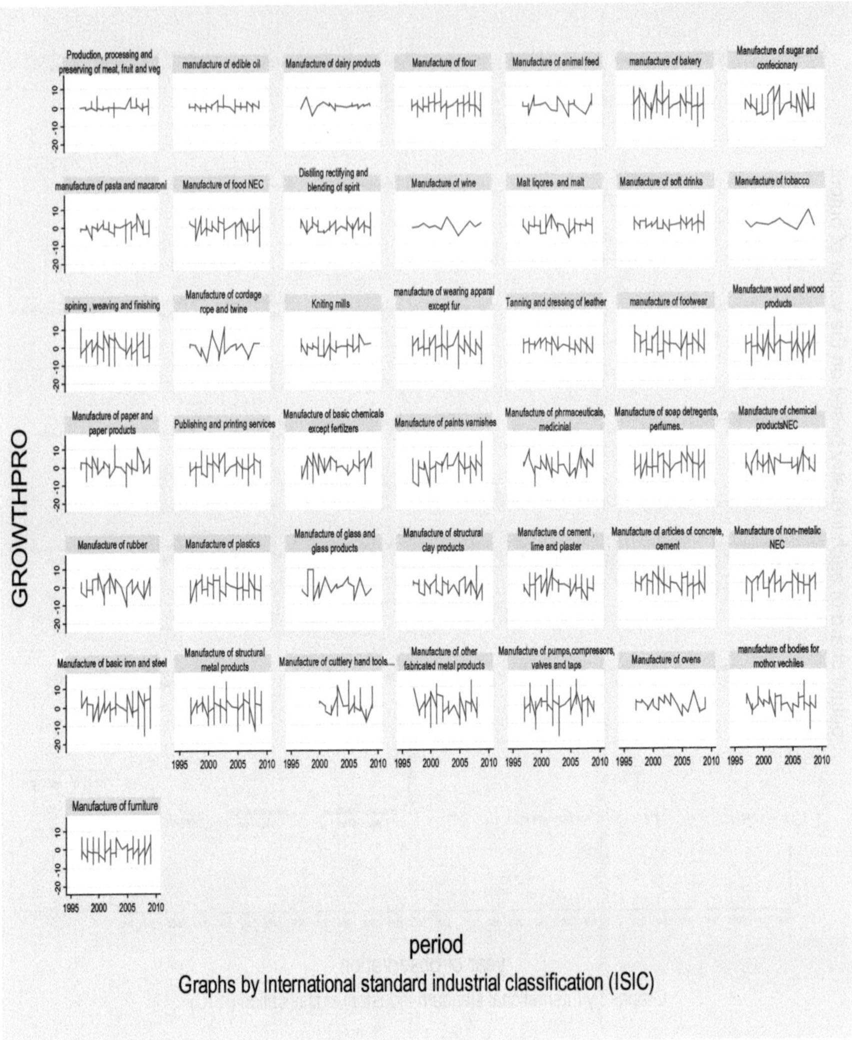

Fig. 9.4 Evolution of productivity growth

The dependent variable is change in the mean characteristics (growth in productivity). The explanatory variables are growth in labor share (GRWTHLSHARE*)*, the complement[2] of output share (COMPVOUSHA*)*, technically one minus output share to fit the first term in Eq. 9.5, complementary market share (COMPMKTSHARE), again the same interpretation as before so that it is consistent with Eq. 9.5, lagged

[2]Here the complement of variable x is equal to $(1 - x)$ (see the first term on the right hand side in Eq. 9.5).

Table 9.2 Estimation results (GMM): dependent variable: growth in productivity

Variable	Coeff.	Std. error	Z	P > [Z]
GRWTHLSHARE	0.00052	0.0001	3.47	0.001
COMPVOUSHA	−5.626	0.409	−13.75	0.000
COMPMKTSHARE	4.251	0.456	9.32	0.000
LAGDELTFP	−0.412	0.0203	−20.20	0.000
EMPSHAFIRM	−4.068	1.556	−2.61	0.009
cons	0.9196	0.421	2.18	0.029

change in labor productivity (LAGDELTFP) which represents the last term of Eq. 9.5 and finally, employment share of each firm (EMPSHAFIRM).

For the evolutionary approach, once the logistic differential in Eq. 9.5 is formulated, it can be estimated using standard panel data econometric techniques (random effects, fixed effects or GMM) which do not require separate treatment here. The reported results are with a Wald Chi-square value of 773.57 with six degree of freedom and probability value of ($p > X^2$) of 0.0000 (Table 9.2).

The estimated results indicate that all explanatory variables entered the estimation with statistically significant estimates. As expected, productivity was positively affected by the growth in labor share. However, the employment share entered with a negative and statistically significant coefficient. We may interpret this as lack of labor movement from low productive to high productive industries.

9.5 Summary, Conclusions, Policy Recommendations and Future Areas of Research

The basic research question in this paper was explaining how firm-level labor share affects firm and industry level productivity and how it affects aggregate productivity in an economy taking the case of Ethiopia.

The most direct interpretation of the estimated results is that evolution and change in mean characteristics (change in productivity) are positively affected by the growth of functional income distribution (the growth in labor share: even if the economic sign of the coefficient is of small order), its statistical significance is quite acceptable.

The other variable of interest here is employment share of each firm within an industry, which entered the model with a negative sign but a significant coefficient. In economic terms, the positive and negative coefficients of labor share within a firm and the employment share of each firm within the industry tell us very important information about structural changes in the manufacturing sector.

If structural change was evident, the employment share would have entered with a positive effect. However, it did not do this. Therefore, this does not support the popular view of a structural bonus hypothesis which postulates a positive relationship between structural change and economic growth. This hypothesis was based on the assumption that during the process of economic development, economies upgrade from industries with comparatively low to those with a higher value added per labor input. For example, Timmer and Szirmai (2000) have a detailed explanation on this.

This result is supported by an almost opposite mechanism, where structural change has a negative effect on aggregate growth; this is revealed by Baumol's hypothesis of unbalanced growth. Intrinsic differences between industries in their opportunities to raise labor productivity (for a given level of demand) shift ever larger shares of the labor force away from industries with high productivity growth toward stagnant industries with low productivity growth and accordingly higher labor requirements. In the long-run, the structural burden of increasing labor shares getting employed in the stagnant industries tends to diminish the prospects for aggregate growth of per capita income. Baumol (1967) is key literature on this.

When the complement of firms' market share enters the regression result with a positive sign, the actual market share would have entered with a negative sign which has a direct and clear economic meaning, that is, since firms may try to capture the market through nominal ways (for example, price competition or advertising or any other institutional arrangements) this will harm productivity. Our major conclusion is lack of strong evidence for intra-industry selection.

The policy lesson is that access to bank loans is of great importance to firms. Particularly those industries (spinning, tanning and publishing) in which all firms had access to bank loans revealed movements in employment share, which is evidence of structural transformation.

There are reasons why it is important to introduce appropriate public loan policies, that is, ensuring a lending channel of monetary policy to work without breaks. First, a credit aggregate can be a better indicator of monetary policy than an interest rate or a monetary aggregate in Ethiopia. Second, monetary tightening that reduces loans to firms can have negative distributional consequences. Particularly for those firms for whom bank loans are a primary source of finance, ease of access to bank loans can have economy-wide distributional consequences. More specifically, the credit policy should be such that manufacturing firms get better access to banks.

It is desired that the future research direction includes economy-wide modeling, estimation and more formalization of evolutionary economic models to study the link between access to bank loans and its effects on income distribution and inclusive economic growth.

Acknowledgments This research is supported by the Jönköping International Business School, Jönköping University (Sweden), in collaboration with Addis Ababa University for doctoral studies in economics, a project supported by the Swedish International Development Cooperation Agency (SIDA).

The author would like to thank Professor Almas Heshmati, Professor Andreas Stephan, Dr Tadele Ferede and other participants of a seminar at the Jonkoping International Business School for their comments and suggestions on an earlier version of this research.

Annexure 1: Basic Logistic Differential Equation

$$\dot{X} + a(t)X = b(t)X^r, \text{ if } r = 1, \text{ it is easily separable and becomes}$$
$$\dot{X} + a(t)X = b(t)X^{\mathrm{r}} \text{ and introducing } Z = X^{1-r}$$
$$\dot{Z} = (1-r)X^{-\mathrm{r}}\dot{X}$$
$$\text{But } \frac{\dot{X}}{X} + a(t) = b(t)X^{r-1} \Rightarrow \dot{X} = \left(b(t)X^{r-1} - a(t)\right)X$$

Therefore,

$$\dot{Z} = (1-r)X^{-r}\dot{X} = (1-r)X^{-r}\left(b(t)X^{r-1} - a(t)\right)X$$
$$\text{(Eq A2)} \quad Z + (1-r)\,a(t) = (1-r)\,b(t)$$

Annexure 2: Evolution of Key Variables

See Figs. 9.1, 9.2, 9.3 and 9.4.

References

Aghion P, Howitt P (1992) A model of growth through creative destruction. Econometrica 60 (2):323–351
Aghion P, Howitt P (1998) Endogenous growth theory. MIT Press, Cambridge
Alchian A (1950) Uncertainty, evolution, and economic theory. J Polit Econ 58(3):211–221
Alesina A, Rodrik D (1994) Distributive politics and economic growth. Quart J Econ 109(2):465–490
Andersen E (2004) Population thinking, price's equation and the analysis of economic evolution. Evol Inst Econ Rev 1(1):127–148
Barro RJ (1990) Government spending in a simple model of endogamous growth. J Polit Econ 98 (5):103–125
Baumol WJ (1967) Macroeconomics of unbalanced growth: the anatomy of urban crisis. Am Econ Rev 57(3):415–426
Beinhocker, ED (2006). The Origin of Wealth, Evolution, Complexity, & the Radical Remarking of Economics. Random House Business Books, Boston
Benhabib J, Rustichini A (1996) Social conflict, growth and income distribution. J Econ Growth 1:125–142
Boulton J (2010) Why is economics not an evolutionary science? Quart J Econ 12(2):41–69
Carlsson B, Eliasson G (2003) Industrial dynamics and endogenous growth. Ind Innov 10(4):435–455
Castellacci F (2007) Evolutionary and new growth theories. Are they converging? J Econ Surv 21 (3):585–627
Cecilia G (2010) Income distribution, economic growth and European integration. J Econ Inequal 8(3):277–292
Coase RH (1937) The nature of the firm. Economica 4(16):386–405

Dopfer K (2005) The evolutionary foundations of economics. Cambridge University Press, Cambridge
Dopfer K, Potts J (2004) Evolutionary realism: a new ontology for economics. J Econ Method 11 (2):195–212
Dosi G, Nelson RR (2010) Technical change and industrial dynamics as evolutionary processes. In Hall B, Rosenberg N (eds) Handbook of the economics of innovation. Academic Press, Amsterdam, pp 51–127
Foster J (1992) The determination of sterling M3, 1963–88: an evolutionary macroeconomic approach. Econ J 102(412):481–496
Foster J (1994) An evolutionary macroeconomic model of Australian dollar M3 determination: 1967–93. Appl Econ 26(11):1109–1120
Foster J (2014) Energy, knowledge and economic growth. J Evol Econ 24(2):209–238
Foster J, Wild P (1999a) Detecting self-organizational change in economic processes exhibiting logistic growth. J Evol Econ 9(1):109–133
Foster J, Wild P (1999b) Econometric modeling in the presence of evolutionary change. Camb J Econ 23(6):749–770
Gatti Domenico, Gaffeo D, Gallegati E, Giulion M, Kirman G, Palestrini A, Russo A (2007) Complex dynamics and empirical evidence. Inf Sci 177:1204–1221
Goldfarb RS, Leonard TC (2005) Inequality of what among whom: rival conceptions of distribution in the 20th Century. In Samuels WJ, Biddle J, Emmett Ross B (eds) Research, in the history of economic thought and methodology, vol 23-A. Emerald Group Publishing Limited, Amsterdam, pp 79–123
Griliches Z (1957) Hybrid corn: an exploration in the economics of technological change. Econometrica 25(4):501–522
Hahn F, Matthews R (1964) The theory of economic growth: a survey. Econ J 74(296):779–902
Hahn F, Solow R (1995) A critical essay on modern macroeconomic theory. MIT Press, Cambridge
Hodgson G (1996) An evolutionary theory of long-term economic growth. Int Stud Quart 40 (3):391–440
Holm J (2014) The significance of structural transformation to productivity growth: how to account for levels in economic selection. J Evol Econ 24(5):1009–1036
Krugman P (1996) What economists can learn from evolutionary theorists. A talk given to the European Association for Evolutionary Political Economy. November 1996. http://web.mit.edu/krugman/www/evolute.html
Leijonhufvud A (1992) Keynesian economics: past confusions, future prospects. In: Vercelli A, Dimitri M (eds) Macroeconomy: a survey of research strategies. Oxford University Press, Oxford
Lucas R (1988) On the mechanics of economic development. J Monet Econ 22(1):3–42
Mansfield E (1981) Composition of R and D expenditures: relationship to size of firm, concentration, and innovative output. Rev Econ Stat 63(4):610–615
Metcalfe JS (1998) Evolutionary economics and creative destruction. Routledge, London
Metcalfe JS, Foster J, Ramlogan R (2006) Adaptive economic growth. Camb J Econ 30:7–32
Mincer J (1958) Investment in human capital and personal income distribution. J Polit Econ 66 (4):281–302
Nelson RR, Winter SG (1974). Neoclassical vs. evolutionary theories of economic growth: critique and prospectus. Economic Journal 84:886–905
Nelson R (1996) The sources of economic growth. Harvard University Press, Cambridge
Nelson R, Winter S (1982) An evolutionary theory of economic change. Harvard University Press, Cambridge
Perotti R (1996) Growth, income distribution, and democracy: what the data say. J Econ Growth 1 (2):149–187
Persson T, Tabellini G (1994) Is inequality harmful for growth? Am Econ Rev 84(3):600–621
Rehme G (2006) Redistribution and economic growth in integrated economies. J Macroecon 28 (2):392–408

Ricardo D (1815) Essay on The influence of a low price of corn upon the profits of stock, 2nd edn. John Murray, London

Romer P (1986) Increasing returns and long-run growth. J Polit Econ 94(5):1002–1037

Romer P (1987) Crazy explanations for the productivity slowdown. NBER Macroecon Annu 2:163–202

Romer P (1990) Endogenous technological change. J Polit Econ 98(5):71–102

Romer P (1994) The origins of endogenous growth. J Econ Perspect 8(1):3–22

Safarzyńska K, van den Bergh JCJM (2010) Evolutionary models in economics: a survey of methods and building blocks. J Evol Econ 20(3):329–373

Salvadori N (2003) The theory of economic growth. Edward Elgar, Cheltenham

Solow R (1956) A contribution to the theory of economic growth. Q J Econ 70(1):65–94

Stockhammer E, Onaran O, Ederer S (2008) Functional income distribution and aggregate demand in the Euro area. Camb J Econ 33(1):139–159

Swan TW (1956) Economic growth and capital accumulation. Econ Rec 32(2):334–361

Timmer M, Szirmai A (2000) Productivity growth in Asian manufacturing: the structural bonus hypothesis examined. Struct Change Econ Dyn 11(4):371–392

Todaro MP (1997) Economic development. Longman, London

Veblen T (1898) Why economics is not an evolutionary science? Quart J Econ 12(4):373–397

Part IV
Trade, Mineral Exports and Exchange Rate

Chapter 10
Determinants of Trade with Sub-Saharan Africa: The Secret of German Companies' Success

Johannes O. Bockmann

Abstract This paper evaluates the degree to which internal, micro and macro-environmental variables explain why some small- and medium-sized enterprises (SMEs) based in Germany export more successfully to sub-Saharan Africa (SSA) than other firms in the same category. It derives explanatory factors specific to the region from experts. A bivariate correlation analysis identifies relations between (in)dependent export performance (EP) measurements. Stepwise multiple regression equations for firms' overall EP and overall export profitability in the last three years highlight factors with the most significant correlations. As evaluated in previous research and as mentioned by experts, it applies a multidimensional approach, investigating variables according to the resource-based view and the contingency paradigm. This study indicates that SSA has specific requirements for successful exports which differ from other regions. Knowledge about these particular characteristics of the market will enable managers and policymakers to improve trade relations. By focusing on the EP of German SMEs in SSA, this study fills a research gap since no previous study has concentrated on this specific aspect.

Keywords German small- and medium-sized enterprises · Export performance · Comparative advantages · Internal · Micro and macro-environmental factors · Sub-Saharan Africa

---

J.O. Bockmann (✉)
Department of Economics and Logistics, International School of Management Hamburg, Hamburg, Germany
e-mail: johannesbockmann@gmail.com

A. Heshmati (ed.), *Studies on Economic Development and Growth in Selected African Countries*, Frontiers in African Business Research,
DOI 10.1007/978-981-10-4451-9_10

10.1 Introduction

Exports represent the preferred method for entry into foreign markets (Lado et al. 2004; Sousa et al. 2014; Zhao and Zou 2002) since they offer firms a comparatively high level of flexibility with relatively small necessary investments thus permitting a fast entry into new markets (Katsikea et al. 2007; Leonidou 1995; Sousa and Novello 2014). Research on export modalities is of high interest to three major stakeholders: public policymakers, managers, and researchers (Katsikea et al. 2000; Sousa 2004).

Scholars explain the increasing interest in exports on the basis of its positive effect on a country's growth alongside the business opportunities that it offers individual firms (Dean et al. 2000). Public policymakers encourage export activities since they foster the accumulation of foreign exchange reserves, support the development of national industries, create new jobs, and improve productivity (Czinkota 1994). Developed countries see cross-border economic relationships as a necessary instrument for maintaining their standard of living (Baldauf et al. 2000).

A detailed review of 33 articles published between 2000 and May 2015 looking at export performance (EP), we identified 65 internal and 35 external determinants. However, none of them focused on sub-Saharan Africa (SSA). This is surprising since these markets offer great business opportunities. According to data from the World Bank (Catalog Sources World Development Indicators 2015), the region's total GDP grew by 5.72% per year on average from 2000 to 2013. Further, imports of goods and services increased by an average of 12.05% per year from 2010 to 2012 (Catalog Sources World Development Indicators 2015; United Nations Statistics Division 2011, 2014). In 2012, SSA countries imported US$496.50 billion worth of goods and services (United Nations Statistics Division 2014). The increasing demand for foreign products together with a relatively high level of uncertainty in the region makes SSA predestined for exports rather than alternative market entry methods such as foreign direct investment (Boly et al. 2014; Riddle 2008; Sousa and Novello 2014).

Regarding the exporter's home country, only three papers concentrated on Germany although the country was one of the top three merchandise exporters with a share of 7.7% of world trade in 2013 and a trade surplus of US$264 billion (WTO 2014). The main drivers of this success are Germany's small- and medium-sized enterprises (SMEs) (MoAE 2015), a situation which is similar to that in most European countries (Bijmolt and Zwart 1994). According to an EU definition, SMEs include all firms with a maximum of 250 employees (Sousa et al. 2014). However, Katsikea et al. (2007) argue that SMEs are not just smaller versions of large firms but that they operate differently because of their size. Therefore, an insight into the success factors of German SMEs may be relevant for German policymakers and executives interested in the guarantors of EP (Baldauf et al. 2000).

Between 2000 and 2013, exports from Germany to all SSA countries grew on average by 8.8% to US$13.51 billion. 89% of German exporters with experience in Africa plan to expand on their commitments, especially in West and Central Africa (Foly 2013). Politicians too, including the German Chancellor Angela Merkel are showing an increasing interest in Africa. For example, during conferences such as the EU–Africa summit a steady cross-sectoral rise in demand is expected thanks to a growing middle class (Merkel 2014). Consequently, a deeper insight into the factors which influence German EP in SSA is necessary.

Scholars argue that further research is needed to investigate the possible predictors of EP (Baldauf et al. 2000; Fevolden et al. 2015; Navarro-García et al. 2015). A focus on the EP of SMEs is specifically important since they in particular profit from a combination of flexibility with limited resource commitments (Sousa et al. 2014), while their significant contributions to national economies underline their relevance for policymakers (Sousa and Novello 2014). Further, there is a need to investigate the specifics of EP in selected regions/countries (Navarro-García et al. 2015; Rambocas et al. 2015). Concerning Germany, Wagner (2014) maintains that detailed company characteristics should be worked out. Sousa et al. (2008) and Sung (2015) have identified a strong demand for more research on developing countries (DC), such as the ones in SSA, since their share in world trade is increasing thus offering significant opportunities in the present and future global economic order.

In summary, the quoted views substantiate the need for additional research in the field of EP, covering individual regions and explanatory variables. To provide evidence if SSA requires different or additional internal, micro and macroeconomic variables, this study concentrates on the factors relevant for German SMEs targeting this region. The rest of this paper is organized as follows. It first gives a literature review which is followed by a section on methodology. The next section gives the findings and analysis of the semi-structured interviews and questionnaire. The last section gives the conclusions and discusses possible areas for further research.

10.2 Literature Background

Research about EP goes back to Tookey's (1964) work about factors associated with success in exporting. In a wider context, it addresses the outcomes of export activities, mostly at the firm or export venture level (Kahiya and Dean 2014). Nowadays, EP is the mostly studied in the field of export marketing (Leonidou and Katsikea 2010). Multiple aspects arise from the fact that the 'Export performance dialogue is spread over a large pan-discipline research landscape which includes

International Businesses, International Marketing, International Entrepreneurship, Small Business Management and International Trade' (Kahiya and Dean 2014: 378).

10.2.1 Measuring EP

Approaches for measuring EP are fragmented and uncoordinated (Kahiya and Dean 2014; Katsikea et al. 2000) and no single view prevails (Sousa 2004). An almost philosophical approach points out that for most export start-ups pure survival is already some measurement of success (Kahiya and Dean 2014). Indicators reflect objective and subjective facts. While objective measures deal with absolute performance, subjective ones are concerned with a firm's expectations or its perceived performance as compared to its competitors (Akyol and Akehurst 2003). Scholars have identified 42 (Katsikea et al. 2000: 497) or even 50 (Sousa 2004: 9) indicators for EP. Since no individual indicator adequately captures the phenomenon of EP (Kahiya and Dean 2014; Lages and Lages 2004; Zou et al. 1998), there is general agreement in favor of a multidimensional approach. Many researchers such as Baldauf et al. (2000) and Papadopoulos and Martín-Martín (2010) prefer a multiple approach.

10.2.2 Determinants of EP

Two major theoretical approaches to classify the determinants of EP stand out. The resource-based view emphasizes a firm's individual competencies as its unique bundles of assets (Conner and Prahalad 1996; Nalcaci and Yagci 2014; Stoian et al. 2011). Accordingly, the success of a company is a result of its acquiring and exploiting its own unique resources such as competence, experience, and size (Zou and Stan 1998). Research also identifies how higher performance can be achieved in comparison with other firms (Barney 2002; Dhanaraj and Beamish 2003; Singh and Mahmood 2014).

On the other hand, the contingency paradigm proposes that environmental factors affect the companies' strategies and EP which is then the result of a specific company context (Sousa et al. 2008). Consequently, exports are considered an organization's strategic response to the interaction of external and internal factors (Robertson and Chetty 2000; Sousa et al. 2008; Yeoh and Jeong 1995).

In the meantime, there is a general agreement that a multidimensional approach including a range of determinants such as managerial, organizational, and environmental aspects is most appropriate (Baldauf et al. 2000; Katsikea et al. 2000; Rambocas et al. 2015). This is confirmed by Morgan et al. (2004) who synthesized the different views into a robust theoretical model.

10.2.3 Internal and Microenvironmental Factors

Thirty-three papers published between 2000 and May 2015 were analyzed and 65 variables were identified. International experience measured in years (21.21% of the reviewed papers), firm size as represented by the number of employees (18.18%), adapting the price strategy to market conditions (15.15%), and the number of foreign markets served by a firm (12.12%) are mostly applied to explain a business' EP.

10.2.4 Macro-environmental Factors

Most scholars extend their research scope by using qualitative and quantitative determinants. In the 33 papers published between 2000 and May 2015, 21 studies covered external variables, identifying 35 external factors. An increasing level of competition in the foreign market influences EP, but there is no consensus if it is positive (9.09% of reviewed papers) or negative (6.06%). Scholars are equally inconsistent regarding the influence of distance. Two papers (6.06%) show that an increasing distance has a positive impact, whereas one paper presents a negative result. Also, the foreign exchange rate plays a multifaceted role: in one paper it has a positive influence, whereas three papers (9.09%) found no significant effect. Customs and tariffs (9.09%) and regulations (15.15%) are frequently named as impacting EP negatively, while one study claimed that they were irrelevant.

10.3 Methodology

10.3.1 Research Philosophy

Our research applies pragmatism, which is not committed to any single philosophy. The lack of studies about EP of German SMEs in SSA leads to pragmatism since it allows a researcher to consider different points of view to get a holistic picture. Consequently, multiple approaches are necessary to gain quantitative and qualitative data (Collis and Hussey 2014; Saunders 2012). Actually, many EP studies (e.g., Freeman and Styles 2014; Rambocas et al. 2015) have applied this philosophy.

10.3.2 Research Approach

Our study is abductive since it combines both deductive and inductive elements. The initial semi-structured interviews aimed at expanding knowledge about EP from experts without reference to the existing theory. The respective results were merged with the findings from existing literature into one questionnaire. Thus, for German SMEs targeting SSA, the existing theory could be tested and modified by new insights (Collis and Hussey 2014; Saunders 2012).

10.3.3 Research Purpose

To answer the research question, a varied approach (multiple methods) rather than one method was chosen achieving a broader view (e.g., by Freeman and Style 2014; Rambocas et al. 2015; Wagner 2014). First semi-structured interviews were carried out which mainly resulted in qualitative data. Subsequently, a questionnaire survey was done to gain primarily quantitative, but also qualitative data.

The aim of exploratory research is to 'seek new insights into phenomena, to ask questions, and to assess the phenomena in a new light' (Saunders 2012: 670). Consequently, this study started with semi-structured interviews examining the factors known to influence EP as well as searching for additional ones prior to developing a questionnaire. A good reason to include exploratory research as a first step is the positive experience of Freeman and Styles (2014), Lacka and Stefko (2014), and Nalcaci and Yagci (2014) who gained new insights about EP for other regions by conducting interviews.

Explanatory research has its emphasis on clarifying the relationship between variables. The questionnaire supports this purpose by enabling the identification of interrelations between dependent and independent factors of EP and the development of casual relationships between them (Saunders 2012). It tests the interaction between existing measurements for EP relevant in other countries identified during the literature review. The fact that researchers such as Singh and Mahmood (2014) and Sousa and Novello (2014) have applied explanatory research in their EP studies underlines the value of this approach.

10.3.4 Research Strategy

Based on a detailed literature study to gain secondary data and information about the current status of research activities, semi-structured interviews were chosen to extract new insights from experts concerning the factors which influence a firm's EP, thus getting answers to specific key questions while providing the flexibility to react to the flow of conversation (Saunders 2012). Freeman and Styles (2014) have previously used a similar approach.

Subsequently, a self-completion questionnaire (Collis and Hussey 2014) was developed to collect data for empirical tests. The nature of this questionnaire was mainly quantitative and explanatory since the participants were asked to grade the influence of different variables on their firm's EP. By evaluating the data with a bivariate correlation and multiple regression, the relationships were identified, as previously done, for example, by Castellacci and Fevolden (2014), Fevolden et al. (2015) and Stoian et al. (2011). Moreover, the participants were encouraged to explain their grading and to suggest additional factors influencing EP.

The applied semi-structured interviews and questionnaire fall in the survey strategy which is mostly applied to gain quantitative data, but qualitative information can also be accumulated this way. A questionnaire allows an efficient collection of standardized data from a large population enabling comparisons and further analysis. Moreover, it helps define the relationship between EP's independent and dependent factors. This strategy is generally perceived as authoritative, comparatively easy to explain and understandable for participants.

10.3.5 Semi-structured Interviews

At first, general information about the participants and their firms was derived from answers to closed questions, followed by an inquiry regarding target markets in SSA. Closed questions were used since the participants were surveyed on a specific issue. In the second part, participants elaborated freely on internal and external factors which were perceived to influence their firm's EP (Saunders 2012).

As a sampling technique, a non-probability sample was chosen because 'the probability of each case being selected from the total population is not known' (Saunders 2012: 261). More specifically, purposive sampling based on the scholar's judgment was applied. Although all participants had been in charge of exports to SSA for several years and were therefore a good fit, this approach is not statistically representative. Therefore, it was followed by a questionnaire survey (Saunders 2012). The response rate of 40% was fairly high compared to Sousa's reviews with 30 and 25% (Sousa et al. 2008).

Table 10.1 summarizes the general information, which has been changed to ensure confidentiality about the participants.

10.3.6 Questionnaire Survey

Based on the literature review and the interviews, a Web-based questionnaire was developed. For Easterby-Smith et al. (2015), this is an efficient way to collect data from a large number of people, which was also important for our analysis (Collis and Hussey 2013). First, general information about the respondents was gathered, which was followed by questions regarding their target markets in SSA. Later, the participants were asked to grade their EP and the respective determinants. Finally, they could enter personal data to receive an executive summary of the findings.

The seven-point Likert scale: Answers were graded on a seven-point Likert scale because this allows the gathering of perceptions (Navarro-García et al. 2015).

Table 10.1 Participants of the semi-structured interview

Firm	A	B	C	D
Industry	Trading house, incl. finance	Medical turnkey projects	Medical turnkey projects	Textiles and advertising industry
Interviewee	Senior Executive Project Manager for SSA	Director turnkey projects	Chief Executive Officer	Chief Executive Officer
Employed (years)	4	27	5	9
Target countries (years of export activities)	Ghana (4.5) Kenya (4.5) South Africa (4.5) Angola (4.5) Mozambique (1) Tanzania (1)	Congo (7) Senegal (6) South Africa (1) Zimbabwe (25) Nigeria (4) Ghana (7) Guinea (1)	Ghana (50) Nigeria (35) South Sudan (10)	Several countries in SSA such as South Africa, Congo, Namibia, Liberia, and South Sudan (56)

Further, this extended scale 'has been shown to process valid psychometric measure properties' (Singh and Mahmood 2014: 88) and has been successfully used in previous EP studies (e.g., Rambocas et al. 2015; Singh and Mahmood 2014; Ward and Duray 2000).

Subjective self-reporting was employed because of the expectation (and experience) that firms are unwilling to disclose full data (Leonidou et al. 2002; Singh and Mahmood 2014) and because of a proven correlation between subjective and objective measures (Akyol and Akehurst 2003; Dess and Robinson 1984; Matanda and Freeman 2009; Stoian et al. 2011).

Dependent variables of EP: Since there is no generally accepted definition for EP (Sousa 2004; Sousa et al. 2008; Stoian et al. 2011; Wheeler et al. 2008), the measurements for our study were developed on the basis of existing literature which guaranteed success and facilitated comparisons with previous results.

First, the respondents were encouraged to rate their overall perceived satisfaction with EP in SSA in the last three years on a seven-point Likert scale, ranging from 'extremely dissatisfied' to 'extremely satisfied' (similarly applied, e.g., by Akyol and Akehurst 2003; Cadogan et al. 2012; Freeman and Style 2014; Lee and Griffith 2004; Navarro-García et al. 2015; Sousa and Novello 2014; Sousa et al. 2014). They were told that the overall satisfaction about EP should include the areas of international sales growth, export business profitability, the firm's image in foreign markets, international expansion, and market share (Cavusgil and Zou 1994; Navarro-García et al. 2015; Navarro et al. 2010).

Second, they were asked about their overall satisfaction with their company's performance in terms of export profitability in SSA in the last three years (similar to, e.g., Cadogan et al. 2002; Dean et al. 2000; Nalcaci and Yagci 2014; Robertson and Chetty 2000; Singh and Mahmood 2014; Sousa and Novello 2014; Stoian et al.

2011). The time frame was adapted from Cadogan et al. (2012) and Navarros-García et al. (2015). Sousa and Novello's (2014) and Sousa et al.'s (2014) approaches to ask for the overall satisfaction with EP and export profitability was employed.

Independent variables of EP: The items applied to measure each construct were based on the earlier interviews with professionals as well as existing literature. Participants were again asked to grade internal, micro and macro-factors on a seven-point Likert scale.

Questionnaire sampling: Only German SMEs exporting to at least one SSA country in the last three years were considered. Following most researchers in the field of EP such as Nalcaci and Yagci (2014), Sousa et al. (2014), and Sousa and Novello (2014), only CEOs and managers with decision making responsibilities regarding exports to SSA were accepted. As shown in Table 10.2, the response rate, when compared with Sousa was quite low, possibly because the authors only/or additionally sent out the questionnaire via post or called all potential participants (Sousa 2008).

To ensure representative sampling, the number of participants should be as large as possible (Cooper and Schindler 2014; Saunders 2012). According to Saunders et al. (2012), a relatively low response rate, however, is not necessarily bad as a sample size of 30 or more represents a high degree of accuracy and reliability. With a useable sample size of 41, this was a given. Moreover, Armstrong and Overton's (1977) extrapolation procedure was applied to ensure that no differences existed between early and late responses (the basic details of the participants in the questionnaire are given in Table 10.3).

10.4 Findings and Analysis: Semi-structured Interviews

10.4.1 Method of Analysis

A content analysis was done to quantify the orally given data. Using this widely applied method, items of qualitative data were systematically converted into numerical data (Collis and Hussey 2014; Easterby-Smith et al. 2015).

10.4.2 Evaluated Macro-environmental Factors

The factors mentioned in an open question to influence EP are given in Table 10.4.

Table 10.2 Comparison of response rates

Sousa's (2000) review of EP papers	Sousa's (2008) review of EP papers	This study
30%	25%	10.96%

Table 10.3 Basic data of questionnaire participants

Total number of participants	58
Number of analyzed participants	41
Company size, range (number of full-time employees)	247.00
Company size, mean (number of full-time employees)	129.62
Industries	Advertising Materials/Textiles; Agriculture; Architecture; Automation Technology; Automotive; Building; Business Services; Cables and Wires; Commodities Trading; Construction; Consulting; Consumer Goods; Energy (Services); Engineering; Export Trade; Finance; Food; Health Services; Healthcare/Medical; ICT/Consulting; IT; Management Consultancy; Manufacture of Welding Consumables; Metalwork; Refrigeration and Air Conditioning; Shipping; Solar energy; Toys; Trading
Key informants	Area Sales Director—Africa and Middle East; Authorized Officer; Chief Executive Officer; Export Manager; General Coordinator Africa; Head of Department International; Head of Sales Department Africa and Asia; Head of Sales Department EMEA; International Business Development; Managing Director; Market Development Manager Africa; Marketing Director/Manager; President Region Africa; Regional (Sales) Manager, Sales Director; Sales Manager; Senior Manager; Shareholder; Speaker; VP International Sales
Head offices	All over Germany
Unit of analysis	Firm
Company age, range (years)	174.00
Company age, mean (years)	63.02

Besides other factors such as export promotion programs and the prohibition of bribery, German politics and the legal environment were also considered to have an impact on EP. A survey by Transparency International (Hardoon 2013) shows that bribe is a serious matter in Africa and that decision makers are willing to accept such payments. For example, 54% of the 2207 households questioned in Ghana in 2013 said that they had paid bribes; politicians were described as corrupt by 76% (Hardoon 2013). A participant in one of the studies stated that for this reason his firm concentrated on private customers. Two others argued that contributions were illegal in all European countries, but Germany was the only country where the law was strictly enforced. France, besides others, was said not to apply existing legislations. In cultures where expensive presents express esteem and where decision makers depend on special payments to support their families and tribes, German companies have no chances of getting contracts. This supports O'Cass and Julian's study (2003) stating that legal and political decisions influence EP. Dean et al. (2000) confirm that governmental agencies may support exports.

Table 10.4 Macro-factors which influence EP

Positive influence	Negative influence
Made in Germany (four times) Export promotion by the German government (once) Local conditions: Some countries are not able to coordinate projects by themselves so they need companies specializing in offering turnkey projects (once)	Difficulties in finding partners to finance big projects (once) Contributions to decision makers are illegal in Germany, but especially offered by firms based in other countries (three times) German politics does not consider the special characteristics of the region, information level does not correspond with the current situation (once) German politics should support German producers by financing exports to the region (once) Competition from China and other countries with cheaper products (twice)

The country of origin referred to by all interviewees as influencing EP has been previously mentioned to be relevant by Lacka and Stefko (2014). The difficulties in finding partners to finance big projects have been addressed by Felbermayr and Yalcin (2013). Identified competition from other countries matches the factor 'market competitiveness' recorded to be significant, for example, by Cadogan et al. (2012), Lages and Montgomery (2005), and Navarros-García et al. (2015).

10.4.3 Evaluated Internal and Microenvironmental Factors

The variables mentioned in an open question to influence EP are given in Table 10.5.

The relevance of product quality falls in line with the importance of the product strategy. Previously, O'Cass and Julian (2003) and Shoham et al. (2002) have identified its significance for Australian firms, Lee and Griffith (2004) for South Korea, and Piercy et al. (1997) for Britain.

The influence of price has been highlighted by various scholars such as Lado et al. (2004), Morgan et al. (2004), and Sousa et al. (2014). However, Sousa and Novello's study (2014) found that there was no influence of the price strategy.

Factor market knowledge or rather know-how and social competencies emerged significant in studies by Kahiya and Dean (2014) and Ling-yee (2004).

Also, company size matters. Besides others, Kahiya and Dean (2014) and Lado et al. (2004) describe it as fundamental and Lee, and Griffith (2004) mention that a certain size is necessary to export successfully. For example, one participant mentioned that his firm as a medium-sized company concentrated on smaller projects. There is no consensus, however, about its relevance. For instance, Lee and Griffith (2004) and Stoian et al. (2011) could not prove any influence.

Table 10.5 Internal and micro-factors which influence EP

Positive influence	Negative influence
Concept of sustainability, for example, not only building a hospital but also training employees and finding qualified staff (once) Continuous physical presence in the target market (twice) Network in the industrial sector in the firm's home country (once) As a medium-sized company concentration on smaller projects (once) General willingness of the firm to deal with risks in Africa caused by insufficient experience in the region (once) Cooperation with local partners (once) High local market knowledge (once) Company image (once) Employees: Know-how and social competence (twice) Competence not only to offer good quality, but also good prices (twice) Product quality (once)	Initially mistrust toward the region, it was necessary to build trust in different departments such as risk control and accounting (once)

General willingness of firms to deal with the aspect of risk in Africa has not been mentioned in previous studies.

Two participants said that time spent in abroad or rather continuous physical presence in the target country was essential. However, Stoian et al. (2011) could not prove any relevance of this for Spanish exporters.

Employees' principle mistrust toward SSA was mentioned as influencing EP negatively. The attitude of employees toward a target market has been previously researched by Nalcaci and Yagci (2014).

10.5 Findings and Analysis: Questionnaire

10.5.1 Method of Analysis

Data were imported from the online questionnaire provider into IBM SPSS. From 58 given datasets, 41 emerged as valid, once they were edited following Brase and Brase (2010) and Pallant (2013). The included datasets fulfilled the mathematical requirements for analysis and fit into the target group:

- Except firms larger than 250 employees (SME threshold),
- Except unfinished datasets, and
- Including individuals who are involved with their firms in exports to SSA.

First, a none-response bias was ensured by an extrapolation procedure. To isolate those regions of SSA where the results of the analysis were applicable, the information provided by the participants was evaluated by means of descriptive statistics. EP's dependent variables were studied regarding their frequency and possible bivariate correlations to ensure their validity for further analysis. Then the independent variables were looked at with the Pearson correlation and Spearman. Later, for both EP measurements a stepwise multiple regression analysis was carried out.

10.5.2 Target Regions

Figure 10.1 gives the regions served by at least 20% of the participants' firms.

Countries colored green (Ghana, Nigeria, and South Africa) enjoyed the patronage of more than 60% of the German SMEs exporting to SSA. However, this was almost equally true for the orange zone (Cameroon, Angola, Namibia, Mozambique, Tanzania, Kenya, and Ethiopia), with a total of 50–60% of the companies having export activities there.

Obviously, all areas colored in green and orange (except Ethiopia) are located by the sea. German SMEs prefer exporting to countries that are easily accessible and they avoid landlocked markets.

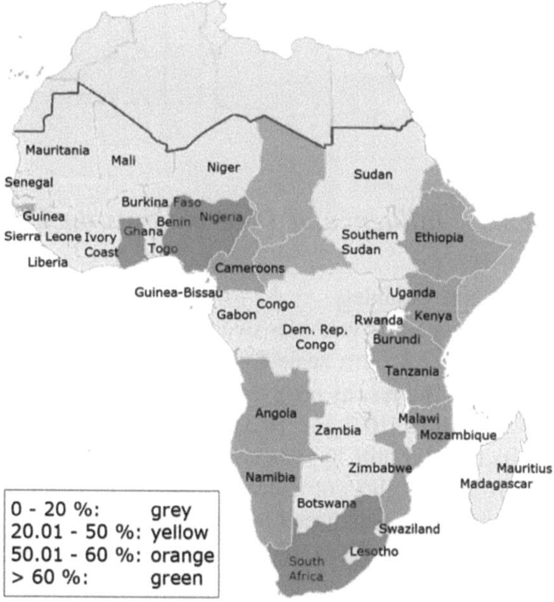

Fig. 10.1 Markets served by participants' firms in SSA

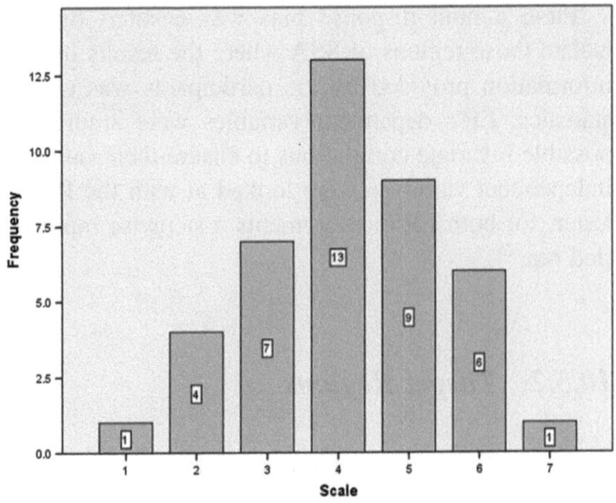

Fig. 10.2 Overall EP–frequency distribution ($n = 41$)

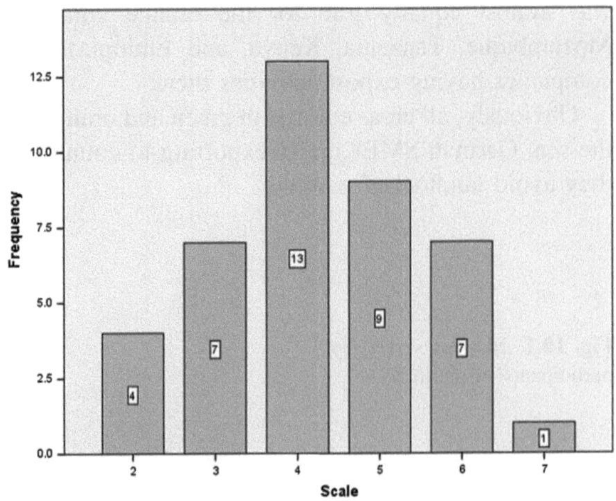

Fig. 10.3 Export profitability–frequency distribution ($n = 41$)

10.5.3 Influence of Determinants on EP

Dependent variables

The dependent variables over all of EP and export profitability were graded by all participants on a scale from one (extremely dissatisfied) to seven (extremely satisfied). The results are symmetrically bell-shaped thus representing normal distribution (Figs. 10.2 and 10.3).

To test the null hypothesis if there is no correlation between overall EP and export profitability of German SMEs, a Pearson product-moment correlation coefficient was established following Anderson et al. (2014). Since the significance (2-tailed) is less than 0.05, the correlation is significant. The Pearson correlation actually shows a strong positive relationship between the variables (0.682), that is,

Table 10.6 Pearson correlation with overall EP and export profitability

		Overall EP	Export profitability
Overall EP	Pearson correlation	1	0.682**
	Sig. (2-tailed)		0.000
	N	41	41
Export profitability	Pearson Correlation	0.682**	1
	Sig. (2-tailed)	0.000	
	N	41	41

Note *Correlation is significant at the 0.01 level (2-tailed)

higher levels in one variable are associated with higher values in the other. A shared variance of 46.51% can explain each other's variance. In view of these results, there is significant evidence to reject the formulated null hypothesis (Pallant 2013) (Table 10.6).

Independent variables

The participants were asked to grade the influence of different macro-factors on their company's EP in SSA from one (none) to seven (substantial). Internal and microenvironmental factors were graded from one (much worse) to seven (much better) in comparison with major competitors in the market.

Both measurements for EP were tested with each factor by a bivariate correlation to describe the strength and direction of their relationship following Anderson et al. (2014) and Pallant (2013). The following hypotheses were tested:

H0a: There is no correlation between overall EP and the 'independent variable.'
H1a: There is a significant correlation between overall EP and the 'independent variable.'
H0b: There is no correlation between export profitability and the 'independent variable.'
H1b: There is a significant correlation between export profitability and the 'independent variable.'

In case of $p < 0.05$, the correlation is significant at the 0.05 level (2-tailed) and H0 can be rejected. If $p < 0.01$, the correlation is even significant at the 0.01 level (2-tailed) and H0 can be rejected (Pallant 2013). The relationships were characterized depending on '*r*' (Table 10.7).

Table 10.8 summarizes the results on internal and microenvironmental factors.

Table 10.9 summarizes the results on macro-environmental factors.

Table 10.7 Guidelines for interpreting the correlation coefficient based on Pallant (2013)

Small positive relation	$r = 0.10$ to 0.29
Medium positive relation	$r = 0.30$ to 0.49
Large positive relation	$r = 0.50$ to 1.0
Small negative relation	$r = -0.10$ to −0.29
Medium negative relation	$r = -0.30$ to 0.49
Large negative relation	$r = -0.50$ to −1.0

Table 10.8 Pearson correlation/Spearman of internal and microenvironmental factors with overall EP/export profitability

		Overall EP	Export profitability
Age of firm in years	Pearson correlation	0.010	−0.052
	Sig. (2-tailed)	0.948	0.748
Total number of full-time employees	Pearson correlation	−0.008	−0.009
	Sig. (2-tailed)	0.959	0.954
Years your firm has been exporting in general	Pearson correlation	0.074	−0.020
	Sig. (2-tailed)	0.646	0.901
Years your firm has been exporting to sub-Saharan Africa	Pearson correlation	0.161	0.041
	Sig. (2-tailed)	0.314	0.797
Number of languages spoken in the export department (fluently or better)	Pearson correlation	0.019	0.093
	Sig. (2-tailed)	0.905	0.562
Number of countries in the sub-Saharan Africa region that your company serves	Pearson correlation	0.183	0.178
	Sig. (2-tailed)	0.253	0.266
Adaptation of product strategy to the markets of sub-Saharan Africa	Pearson correlation	0.333*	0.470**
	Sig. (2-tailed)	0.034	0.002
Adaptation of price strategy to the markets of sub-Saharan Africa	Pearson correlation	0.168	0.317*
	Sig. (2-tailed)	0.294	0.044
Adaptation of promotion strategy to the markets of sub-Saharan Africa	Pearson correlation	0.280	0.456**
	Sig. (2-tailed)	0.076	0.003
Adaptation of distribution strategy to the markets of sub-Saharan Africa	Pearson correlation	0.338*	0.491**
	Sig. (2-tailed)	0.031	0.001
Firm characteristics: federal state the company is located in	Spearman's rho Correlation coefficient	0.066	−0.135
	Sig. (2-tailed)	0.681	0.399
Firm characteristics: company's image in sub-Saharan Africa is …	Pearson correlation	0.219	0.357*
	Sig. (2-tailed)	0.169	0.022
Firm characteristics: willingness to deal with risks in sub-Saharan Africa caused by insufficient experience in the region is …	Pearson Correlation	0.463**	0.542**
	Sig. (2-tailed)	0.002	0.000
Firm characteristics: product/service quality	Pearson Correlation	−0.001	0.187
	Sig. (2-tailed)	0.996	0.241
Firm characteristics: product/service sustainability	Pearson correlation	0.034	0.157
	Sig. (2-tailed)	0.831	0.326
Firm characteristics: our firm keeps up to date with relevant export market information	Pearson correlation	0.322*	0.282
	Sig. (2-tailed)	0.040	0.074
Firm characteristics: research and development	Pearson correlation	0.076	0.119
	Sig. (2-tailed)	0.635	0.458

(continued)

Table 10.8 (continued)

		Overall EP	Export profitability
Firm characteristics: resources in managerial, financial, and staff endowments	Pearson correlation	0.093	0.257
	Sig. (2-tailed)	0.564	0.105
Managerial characteristics and relationships: network in the industrial sector in the home country	Pearson correlation	0.033	0.135
	Sig. (2-tailed)	0.837	0.401
Managerial characteristics and relationships: export commitment and support	Pearson correlation	0.086	0.319*
	Sig. (2-tailed)	0.591	0.042
Managerial characteristics and relationships: international business knowledge	Pearson correlation	0.100	0.350*
	Sig. (2-tailed)	0.533	0.025
Managerial characteristics and relationships: social competencies	Pearson correlation	0.356*	0.426**
	Sig. (2-tailed)	0.022	0.006
Managerial characteristics and relationships: access to information about foreign market/opportunities	Pearson correlation	0.242	0.399**
	Sig. (2-tailed)	0.128	0.010
Managerial characteristics and relationships: attitude toward the region in involved departments	Pearson correlation	0.267	0.518**
	Sig. (2-tailed)	0.091	0.001
Relationship with foreign intermediaries: commitment/cooperation with intermediaries	Pearson correlation	0.377*	0.198
	Sig. (2-tailed)	0.015	0.216
Relationship with foreign intermediaries: trust in intermediaries	Pearson correlation	0.359*	0.245
	Sig. (2-tailed)	0.021	0.123
Relationship with foreign intermediaries: information exchange	Pearson correlation	0.311*	0.142
	Sig. (2-tailed)	0.048	0.377
Relationship with foreign intermediaries: output control	Pearson correlation	0.290	0.094
	Sig. (2-tailed)	0.066	0.557
Relationship with foreign intermediaries: process control	Pearson correlation	0.289	0.147
	Sig. (2-tailed)	0.067	0.358
Relationship with foreign intermediaries: flexibility	Pearson correlation	0.423**	0.296
	Sig. (2-tailed)	0.006	0.060
Relationship with foreign intermediaries: relative dependence on intermediaries	Pearson correlation	0.058	−0.044
	Sig. (2-tailed)	0.720	0.786
Relationship with foreign intermediaries: integration	Pearson correlation	0.267	0.088
	Sig. (2-tailed)	0.092	0.584
Relationships with customers and customer characteristics: need of bribery to get contracts	Pearson correlation	0.018	−0.033
	Sig. (2-tailed)	0.913	0.836

(continued)

Table 10.8 (continued)

		Overall EP	Export profitability
Relationships with customers and customer characteristics: continuous physical presence in the foreign market	Pearson correlation	0.353*	0.387*
	Sig. (2-tailed)	0.024	0.012
Relationships with customers and customer characteristics: price sensitivity of customers regarding product/service	Pearson correlation	0.332*	0.479**
	Sig. (2-tailed)	0.034	0.002
Relationships with customers and customer characteristics: customer sensitivity concerning product origin/image of company's home country …	Pearson correlation	0.141	0.483**
	Sig. (2-tailed)	0.380	0.001
Relationships with customers and customer characteristics: power of customers	Pearson correlation	−0.135	0.156
	Sig. (2-tailed)	0.399	0.330
Relationships with customers and customer characteristics: developing and maintaining relationships with export customers	Pearson correlation	0.263	0.496**
	Sig. (2-tailed)	0.096	0.001
Concerning your exports to sub-Saharan Africa: do you sell more proactively or reactively?	Spearman's rho Correlation coefficient	−0.239	−0.242
	Sig. (2-tailed)	0.132	0.128
Do you provide after sales services?	Spearman's rho correlation Coefficient	0.305	0.384*
	Sig. (2-tailed)	0.052	0.013

Note
**Correlation is significant at the 0.01 level (2-tailed)
*Correlation is significant at the 0.05 level (2-tailed) $n = 41$

10.5.4 *Multiple Regression Analysis with Dependent Factor of Overall EP*

Stepwise multiple regressions were carried out using SPSS. As suggested by Anderson et al. (2014), for all multiple regressions a 0.05 alpha was used to add and 0.10 to remove determinants. Further, an appropriate procedure was guaranteed thanks to a sample size of at least 40 participants, multi-collinearity and singularity, ensuring no influence of outliers as well as normality and linearity (Pallant 2013).

Table 10.10 gives details about the variables selected for the stepwise multiple regression analysis. Three different models with either one, two or three independent variables were constructed.

Table 10.9 Pearson correlation/Spearman of macro-environmental factors with overall EP/export profitability

		Overall EP	Export profitability
Germany: availability of export financing programs	Pearson correlation	−0.186	−0.046
	Sig. (2-tailed)	0.244	0.776
Germany: availability of export guarantees	Pearson correlation	−0.310*	−0.053
	Sig. (2-tailed)	0.048	0.741
Germany: offset agreements between Germany and SSA	Pearson correlation	0.044	0.215
	Sig. (2-tailed)	0.786	0.176
Germany: export assistance	Pearson correlation	−0.101	−0.061
	Sig. (2-tailed)	0.530	0.705
Germany: home country's legal environment	Pearson correlation	0.027	−0.162
	Sig. (2-tailed)	0.867	0.312
Germany: home country's political influence	Pearson correlation	−0.035	−0.119
	Sig. (2-tailed)	0.826	0.459
SSA: environmental turbulences	Pearson correlation	−0.233	−0.212
	Sig. (2-tailed)	0.143	0.183
SSA: local partners to finance projects	Pearson correlation	0.020	0.075
	Sig. (2-tailed)	0.899	0.641
SSA: bribery to fulfill contract obligations	Pearson correlation	−0.089	−0.283
	Sig. (2-tailed)	0.578	0.073
SSA: customs and tariffs	Pearson correlation	−0.138	−0.417**
	Sig. (2-tailed)	0.390	0.007
SSA: ecological environment	Pearson correlation	−0.326*	−0.220
	Sig. (2-tailed)	0.037	0.167
SSA: economic policies	Pearson correlation	−0.153	0.068
	Sig. (2-tailed)	0.338	0.674
SSA: foreign exchange rate	Pearson correlation	0.174	0.301
	Sig. (2-tailed)	0.275	0.056
SSA: legal influences	Pearson correlation	−0.025	0.161
	Sig. (2-tailed)	0.875	0.316
SSA: political influences	Pearson correlation	0.100	0.238
	Sig. (2-tailed)	0.536	0.134
SSA: social environment	Pearson correlation	−0.043	−0.036
	Sig. (2-tailed)	0.789	0.825
SSA: technical environment	Pearson correlation	−0.095	−0.155
	Sig. (2-tailed)	0.554	0.334
SSA: GDP	Pearson correlation	0.018	−0.083
	Sig. (2-tailed)	0.910	0.604
SSA: infrastructure	Pearson correlation	0.118	0.083
	Sig. (2-tailed)	0.462	0.605
SSA: level of competition	Pearson correlation	0.391*	0.074
	Sig. (2-tailed)	0.011	0.646

(continued)

Table 10.9 (continued)

		Overall EP	Export profitability
SSA: psychic distance	Pearson correlation	0.021	0.119
	Sig. (2-tailed)	0.899	0.457
SSA: market distance	Pearson correlation	−0.087	0.013
	Sig. (2-tailed)	0.588	0.937
SSA: mining/export of oil and rare earth elements	Pearson correlation	0.081	0.069
	Sig. (2-tailed)	0.613	0.670
SSA: regulations	Pearson correlation	0.157	0.089
	Sig. (2-tailed)	0.327	0.579

Note
**Correlation is significant at the 0.01 level (2-tailed)
*Correlation is significant at the 0.05 level (2-tailed) $n = 41$

Table 10.10 Variables entered/removed during the stepwise multiple regression analysis (dependent factor overall EP)

Model	Variables entered	Variables removed	Method
1	Firm characteristics: willingness to deal with risks in sub-Saharan Africa caused by insufficient experience in the region is …	.	Stepwise (criteria: probability-of-*F*-to-enter $\leq$ 0.050, Probability-of-*F*-to-remove $\geq$ 0.100)
2	SSA: level of competition	.	
3	SSA: ecological environment	.	

As recommended by Pallant (2013), for relatively small sample sizes the model summary is evaluated regarding the adjusted R square which helps understand the degree to which each model represents the variance of the dependent variable. It turns out that Model 1 explains 19.4%; Model 2, 31.9%; and Model 3, 41.1% of the variance of overall EP. See Table 10.11.

To determine the statistical significance of the three models, the ANOVA tables were checked. All three models reached an overall statistical significance since in each case $p < 0.01$ (Pallant 2013). In each of the three models, all independent variables had a significance value of <0.05. This indicates that all variables made a significant statistical contribution to the prediction of overall EP (Pallant 2013).

According to Pallant (2013), an adjusted R square of 0.411 for Model 3 is quite a respectable result since it explains 41.1% of the variance in overall EP. The Mastery Scale of the third-factor ecological environment in SSA has a part-correlation coefficient of −0.32. The squared value 0.1024 indicates that 10.24% of the variance in overall EP is attributable to the ecological environment. The same procedure shows that the level of competition makes a unique contribution of 11.09% and that of willingness to deal with risks in SSA 22.09% (Pallant 2013; Tabachnick and Fidell 2013).

Table 10.11 Model summary of stepwise multiple regression analysis with dependent factor overall EP

Model	R	R^2	Adjusted R^2	Std. error of the estimate
1	0.463[a]	0.215	0.194	1.214
2	0.594[b]	0.353	0.319	1.116
3	0.675[c]	0.455	0.411	1.038

Note Significant at 1% (a), 5% (b) and 10% (c) levels of significance

Following Tabachnick and Fidell (2013), the regression equation was formulated using the unstandardized coefficient B selected from Model 3. Regression equation for overall EP is obtained from:

$$Y = \beta_1 x_1 + \beta_2 x_2 - \beta_3 x_3$$

where

Y Overall EP (seven-point Likert scale)
x_1 Willingness to deal with risks in SSA (seven-point Likert scale)
x_2 Level of competition in SSA (seven-point Likert scale)
x_3 Ecological environment in SSA (seven-point Likert scale)

$$\begin{aligned} \text{Overall EP} = {} & 1.111 \\ & + 0.501 * \text{Willingness to deal with risks in SSA} \\ & + 0.281 * \text{Level of competition in SSA} \\ & - 0.233 * \text{Ecological environment in SSA} \end{aligned}$$

With values entered on a seven-point Likert scale, the results are shown on this scale as well. The equation demonstrates that the willingness of the managers to deal with risks had the greatest positive influence on overall EP. A change of one point in the Likert scale increased overall EP by 0.501 Likert points. Since this factor has not been researched before, no comparisons with existing literature can be done.

Also, the level of competition in SSA had a positive influence on the dependent factor. A change of one point led to a change of 0.281 Likert points. This confirms Matanda and Freeman (2009) and Sousa and Novello's (2014) works who identified a positive relation. However, Cadogan et al. (2012), Lee and Griffith (2004), and Navarro-García et al. (2015) found a negative relation in their research.

The ecological environment had the smallest (yet negative) influence. Higher ecological standards resulted in a lower overall EP; an improvement by one Likert point was associated with a decrease of 0.233. Again, a comparison with existing literature is not possible since this factor, which emerged during the semi-structured interviews, has not been researched before.

10.5.5 Multiple Regression Analysis with Dependent Factor Export Profitability

Table 10.12 shows the variables that were selected during the stepwise multiple regression analysis.

To ensure that the statistical significance is given, the ANOVA was checked again. Model 11, explaining 80.4% of the variance in export profitability, was selected since it had the highest adjusted *R* square (Pallant 2013) (Table 10.13).

Following Tabachnick and Fidell (2013), the subsequent regression equation was formulated based on the unstandardized coefficient B. Regression equation for export profitability:

$$Y = \beta_1 x_1 - \beta_2 x_2 + \beta_3 x_3 + \beta_4 x_4 - \beta_5 x_5 + \beta_6 x_6 + \beta_7 x_7 + \beta_8 x_8 + \beta_9 x_9$$

where

Y Export profitability (seven-point Likert scale)
x_1 Customer sensitivity for product origin (seven-point Likert scale)
x_2 Customs and tariffs in SSA (seven-point Likert scale)
x_3 Psychic distance (seven-point Likert scale)
x_4 Adaptation of product strategy (seven-point Likert scale)
x_5 Network in industrial sector in home country (seven-point Likert scale)
x_6 Updating with market information (seven-point Likert scale)
x_7 Foreign exchange rate (seven-point Likert scale)
x_8 Research and development (seven-point Likert scale)
x_9 Dependence on intermediaries (seven-point Likert scale)

$$\begin{aligned}
\text{Export Profitability} = {} & -2.228 \\
& + 0.420 * \text{Customer sensitivity for product origin} \\
& - 0.402 * \text{Customs and tariffs in SSA} \\
& + 0.351 * \text{Psychic distance} \\
& + 0.580 * \text{Adaptation of product strategy} \\
& - 0.566 * \text{Network in industrial sector in home country} \\
& + 0.388 * \text{Updating with market information} \\
& + 0.271 * \text{Foreign exchange rate} \\
& + 0.181 * \text{Research and development} \\
& + 0.172 * \text{Dependence on intermediaries}
\end{aligned}$$

The positive influence of customer sensitivity to product origin previously mentioned during the interview has been confirmed by Lacka and Stefko (2014) for Poland before.

Table 10.12 Variables entered/removed during stepwise multiple regression analysis (dependent factor export profitability)

Model	Variables entered	Variables removed	Method
1	Firm characteristics: willingness to deal with risks in sub-Saharan Africa caused by insufficient experience in the region is …	.	Stepwise (criteria: probability-of-F-to-enter ≤ 0.050, probability-of-F-to-remove ≥ 0.100)
2	Relationships with customers and customer characteristics: customer sensitivity concerning product origin/image of company's home country …	.	
3	SSA: customs and tariffs	.	
4	SSA: psychic distance	.	
5	Adaptation of product strategy to the markets of sub-Saharan Africa	.	
6	Managerial characteristics and relationships: network in the industrial sector in home country	.	
7	Firm characteristics: our firm keeps up to date with relevant export market information	.	
8	SSA: foreign exchange rate	.	
9	.	Firm characteristics: willingness to deal with risks in sub-Saharan Africa …	
10	Firm characteristics: research and development	.	
11	Relationship with foreign intermediaries: Relative dependence on intermediaries	.	

The negative influence of customs and tariffs in SSA confirms the results from the semi-structured interviews. Although Baldauf et al. (2000) consider this factor to have a neutral influence, most researchers (e.g., Fugazza and McLaren 2014; Jordan 2014; Kahiya and Dean 2014) have proved a negative influence.

Table 10.13 Model summary of stepwise multiple regression analysis with dependent factor export profitability

Model	*R*	*R* square	Adjusted *R* square	Std. error of the estimate
1	0.542[a]	0.294	0.276	1.094
2	0.637[b]	0.406	0.375	1.016
3	0.713[c]	0.509	0.469	0.936
4	0.776[d]	0.602	0.558	0.854
5	0.808[e]	0.652	0.603	0.810
6	0.834[f]	0.695	0.641	0.770
7	0.877[g]	0.769	0.720	0.680
8	0.894[h]	0.799	0.749	0.644
9	0.889[i]	0.790	0.745	0.648
10	0.907[j]	0.823	0.779	0.605
11	0.921[k]	0.848	0.804	0.569

Note Significant at 1% (a), 5% (b) and 10% (c) levels of significance

According to the regression equation, psychic distance has a positive influence on export profitability. The same effect has been established for other regions, for example, by Lee and Griffith (2004), Sousa et al. (2014) and Stoian et al. (2011).

The positive influence of the adaptation of product strategy confirms Lado et al. (2004), Lee and Griffith (2004), and Shoham et al.'s (2002) results. For the regions they researched, they found a positive influence of this factor. However, Freeman and Styles' (2014) research about Australian firms showed a neutral influence. This indicates that the factor adaptation of product strategy may have a positive influence in some regions and is relevant for German SMEs which target SSA.

The negative impact of networking activities in the industrial sector cannot be explained. Since this factor, mentioned during the semi-structured interviews, has not been researched before no comparisons with existing literature are possible.

In the regression equation updating with market information has a positive influence. Lately, Freeman and Styles (2014) have also proved its positive effect on EP.

The positive influence of research and development falls in line with Kahiya and Dean's (2014) findings.

Wierts et al. (2014) substantiated a positive influence of the foreign exchange rate on EP. The regression equation related to export profitably confirms this. However, Baldauf et al. (2000), Lacka and Stefko (2014), and Jordan (2014) came to the conclusion that the foreign exchange rate had no significant influence.

Among all the positive relations, the positive influence of a dependence on intermediaries is interesting. According to Porters' five-forces, an increasing dependence on intermediaries should rather be negative (Porter 2014). In SSA, however, there is an unpredictable environment where local partners safeguard and increase the chances of getting business. The price to pay is dependence (Foly 2013).

Similar to the regression equation for overall EP, all values were entered and presented on a seven-point Likert scale.

10.5.6 Comparison of Multiple Regression Analyses Results on Overall EP and Export Profitability

Both analyses indicate that the willingness to deal with risks in SSA has a high impact on the dependent variables. All three models constructed with overall EP as a dependent variable include this factor, whereas models relating to export profitability exclude this factor from Model 8 onwards. Otherwise, all other variables included in the various models differ. Therefore, decision makers wanting to influence EP need to differentiate between the targets to overall EP or export profitability and choose suitable strategies. These findings tally with suggestions made by, for example, Sousa et al. (2008), Stoian et al. (2011), and Wheeler et al. (2008), that different measurements for EP are necessary for adequate results.

10.6 Conclusion

Sousa et al. (2008) name EP as one of the most widely researched but least understood areas of international marketing. Our paper, specifically analyzing the EP of German SMEs targeting SSA, contributes to know-how in this field and fills a research gap. It carried out and evaluated a comprehensive literature review, semi-structured interviews, and a questionnaire survey. New questions were identified like why German SMEs tend to prefer exporting to countries with direct access by sea.

The results prove that SSA has specific requirements for successful exports which differ from other regions. This knowledge enables managers and policy-makers to improve trade relations and to enhance their businesses.

10.7 Further Research

In order to generalize the findings, like in cases of Sousa et al. (2014), Stoian et al. (2011), and Styles (2014), we suggest that the scope of work be extended to additional home markets as well as foreign countries/regions. Since our paper evaluated the whole of SSA without considering country specifics, additional research focusing on individual target markets within SSA is desirable. Another shortcoming of this paper lies in the fact that it covers only a specific time frame. Longitudinal studies about German SMEs targeting SSA would be useful for gaining further insights into their EP. It would also be useful to research individual industries instead of multi-industries to find out if particular criteria need to be considered (Stoian et al. 2011). Although there is no academic limit to the number of independent and dependent variables for further analysis, two concrete ideas can be derived from the suggestions made by respondents. They said that ‘area competitiveness of German industry should be analyzed more deeply, also with regard to raw materials' and the aspect of 'local content.' However, in our study, these valuable aspects were not included since the respective questionnaires were received after data collection had been completed.

The collected data indicate that German SMEs have a tendency to export to limited countries in SSA. They seem to be attracted to regions with direct access to the sea. Additional research should be done to identify the reasons for this preference.

References

Akyol A, Akehurst G (2003) An investigation of EP variations related to corporate export market orientation. Eur Bus Rev 15(1):5–19

Anderson DR, Sweeney DJ, Williams TA, Freeman J, Shoesmith E (2014) statistics for business and economics. Cengage Learing, Hampshire, p 3

Armstrong JS, Overton TS (1977) Estimating non-response bias in mail surveys. J Mark Res 14 (3):396–402

Baldauf A, Cravens DW, Wagner U (2000) Examining determinants of EP in small open economies. J World Bus 35(1):61–79

Barney J (2002) Gaining and sustaining competitive advantage. Prentice Hall, New Jersey

Bijmolt THA, Zwart PS (1994) The impact of internal factors on the export success of Dutch small and medium-sized firms. J Small Bus Manage 32(2):69–83

Boly A, Coniglio N, Prota F, Seric A (2014) Diaspora investments and firm EP in selected sub-Saharan African countries. World Dev 59:422–433

Brase CH, Brase CP (2010) Understanding basic statistics. Brooks/Cole Cengage Learning, Belmont

Cadogan JW, Diamantopoulos A, Siguaw J (2002) Export market-oriented activities: Their antecedents and performance consequences. J Int Bus Stud 33(3):615–626

Cadogan JW, Sundqvist S, Puumalainen K, Salminen RT (2012) Strategic flexibilities and EP: the moderating roles of export market-oriented behavior and the export environment. Eur J Mark 46(10):1418–1452

Castellacci F, Fevolden A (2014) Capable Companies or changing markets? Explaining the EP of firms in the defence industry. Def Peace Econ, pp. 1–27

Catalog Sources World Development Indicators (2015) GDP (current US$). The World Bank Group

Cavusgil ST, Zou S (1994) Marketing strategy-performance relationship: an investigation of the empirical link in export market ventures. J Marketing 58(1):1–21

Collis J, Hussey R (2013) Business research: a practical guide for undergraduate and postgraduate students, 4th edn. Palgrave Macmillan, Basingstoke

Collis J, Hussey R (2014) Business research: a practical guide for undergraduate and postgraduate students, 4. Palgrave Macmillan, Basingstoke

Conner KR, Prahalad CK (1996) A resource based theory of the firm: knowledge versus opportunism. Organ Sci 7:477–501

Cooper DR, Schindler PS (2014) Business research methods, vol 12. McGraw-Hill Education, New York

Czinkota MR (1994) A national export assistance policy for new and growing businesses. J Int Marketing 2(1):91–101

Dean DL, Mengüç B, Myers CP (2000) Revisiting firm characteristics, strategy, and EP relationship. Ind Mark Manage 29(5):461–477

Dess GG, Robinson RB (1984) Measuring organizational performance in the absence of objective measures: the case of privately-held firm and conglomerate business unit. Strateg Manag J 5:265–273

Dhanaraj C, Beamish PW (2003) A resource-based approach to the study of EP. J Small Bus Manage 41(3):242–261

Easterby-Smith M, Thorpe R, Jackson P (2015) Management research, 5th edn. Sage Publications Ltd, London

Felbermayr GJ, Yalcin E (2013) Export credit guarantees and EP: an empirical analysis for Germany. World Econ 36(8):967–999

Fevolden AM, Herstad SJ, Sandven T (2015) Specialist supplier or systems integrator? The relationship between competencies and EP in the Norwegian defence industry. Appl Econ Lett 22(2):153–157

Foly C (2013) Chancenkontinent Afrika. Bundesverband der Deutschen Industrie e.V, Berlin. Available at: http://www.bdi.eu/images_content/GlobalisierungMaerkteUndHandel/BDI-Umfrage_SSA.pdf (online)

Freeman J, Styles C (2014) Does location matter to EP? Int Mark Rev 31(2):181–208

Fugazza M, Mclaren A (2014) Market access, EP and survival: evidence from Peruvian Firms. Rev Int Econ 22(3):599–624

Hardoon H (2013) Global corruption barometer. Transparency International, Berlin

Jordan AC (2014) The impact of trade facilitation factors on South Africa's exports to a selection of African countries. Dev Southern Afr 31(4):591–605

Kahiya ET, Dean DL (2014) EP: multiple predictors and multiple measures approach. Asia Pac J Marketing Logistics 26(3):378–407

Katsikea CS, Leonidas S, Leonidou C, Morgan NA (2000) Firm-level EP assessment: review, evaluation, and development. J Acad Mark Sci 28(4):493–511

Katsikea E, Theodosiou M, Morgan RE (2007) Managerial, organizational, and external drivers of sales effectiveness in export market ventures. J Acad Mark Sci 35(2):270–283

Lacka I, Stefko O (2014) Key factors for development of export in Polish food sector. Organizacija 47(2):107–115

Lado N, Martínez-Ros E, Valenzuela A (2004) Identifying successful marketing strategies by export regional destination. Int Mark Rev 21(6):573–597

Lages LF, Lages CR (2004) The 'STEP' scale. A measure of short term EP improvement. J Int Marketing 12(1):36–56

Lages LF, Montgomery DB (2005) The relationship between export assistance and performance improvement in Portuguese export ventures: an empirical test of the mediating role of pricing strategy adaptation. Eur J Mark 39(7/8):755–784

Lee C, Griffith D (2004) The marketing strategy-performance relationship in an export-driven developing economy: a Korean illustration. Int Mark Rev 21(3):321–334

Leonidou LC (1995) Export barriers: non-exporters' perceptions. Int Mark Rev 12:4–25

Leonidou LC, Katsikea CS (2010) Integrative assessment of exporting research articles in business journals during the period 1960–2007. J Bus Res 63(8):879–887

Leonidou LC, Katsikea CS, Samiee S (2002) Marketing strategy determinants of EP: a meta-analysis. J Bus Res 55:51–67

Ling Yee L (2004) An examination of the foreign market knowledge of exporting firms based in the People's Republic of China: its determinants and effect on export intensity. Ind Mark Manage 33(7):561–572

Matanda MJ, Freeman S (2009) Effect of perceived environmental uncertainty on exporter-importer inter-organisational relationships and EP improvement. Int Bus Rev 18 (1):89–107

Merkel A (2014) Speech by Federal Chancellor Angela Merkel at the reception for the diplomatic corps at the federal chancellery. In Federal Chancellor of Germany. The Press and Information Office of the Federal Government, Berlin, p. 1

MoAE (2015). German Mittelstand: Motor der deutschen Wirtschaft. Bundesministerium für Wirtschaft und Energie (BMWi) [Federal Ministry for Economic Affairs and Energy],

Öffentlichkeitsarbeit. Available at: http://www.bmwi.de/BMWi/Redaktion/PDF/Publikationen/factbook-german-mittelstand,property=pdf,bereich=bmwi2012,sprache=de,rwb=true.pdf (online)
Morgan NA, Kalek A, Katsikea CS (2004) Antecedents of export venture performance: a theoretical model and empirical assessment. J Marketing 68(1):90–108
Nalcaci G, Yagci MI (2014) The effects of marketing capabilities on EP using resource-based view: assessment on manufacturing companies. Proc Soc Behav Sci 148:671–679
Navarro A, Acedo FJ, Robson MJ, Ruzo E, Losada F (2010) Antecedents and consequences of firms' export commitment: an empirical study. J Int Marketing 18(3):41–61
Navarro-García A, Schmidt ACM, Rey-Moreno M (2015) Antecedents and consequences of export entrepreneurship. J Bus Res 68(7):1532–1538
O'Cass A, Julian C (2003) Examining firm and environmental influences on export marketing mix strategy and EP of Australian exporters. Eur J Mark 37(3/4):366–384
Pallant J (2013). SPSS survival manual—a step by step guide to data analysis using IBM SPSS, vol 5. Mc Graw-Hill, Berkshire
Papadopoulos N, Martín-Martín P (2010) Toward a model of the relationship between internationalization and EP. Int Bus Rev 19(4):388–406
Piercy NF, Cravens DW, Katsikea S (1997) Examining the role of buyer-seller relationships in EP. J World Bus 32(1):73–86
Porter ME (2014) Wettbewerbsvorteile—Spitzenleistungen erreichen und behaupten, 3rd edn. Campus Verlag, Frankfurt
Rambocasa M, Menesesb R, Monteiroc C, Brito PQ (2015) Direct or indirect channel structures. Evaluating the impact of channel governance structure on EP. Int Bus Rev 24(1):124–132
Riddle L (2008) Diasporas: exploring their development potential. ESR Rev 10:28–35
Robertson C, Chetty SK (2000) A contingency-based approach to understanding EP. Int Bus Rev 9(2):211–235
Saunders M (2012) Choosing research participants. In: Symons G, Cassell C (eds) The practice of qualitative organizational research: core methods and current challenges. Sage Publications, London, pp 37–55
Shoham A, Evangelista F, Albaum G (2002) Strategic firm type and EP. Int Mark Rev 19(3):236–258
Singh H, Mahmood R (2014) Aligning manufacturing strategy to EP of manufacturing small and medium enterprises in Malaysia. Proc Soc Behav Sci 130:85–95
Sousa CMP (2004) EP measurement: an evaluation of the empirical research in the literature. Acad Marketing Sci Rev 2004(9):1–22
Sousa CMP, Martínez-López FJ, Coelho F (2008) The determinants of EP: a review of the research in the literature between 1998 and 2005. Int J Manag Rev 10(4):343–374
Sousa CMP, Novello S (2014) The influence of distributor support and price adaptation on the EP of small and medium-sized enterprises. Int Small Bus J 32(4):359–385
Sousa CMP, Lengler JFB, Martínez-López FJ (2014) Testing for linear and quadratic effects between price adaptation and EP: the impact of values and perceptions. J Small Bus Manage 52 (3):501–520
Stoian MC, Rialp A, Rialp J (2011) EP under the microscope: a glance through Spanish lenses. Int Bus Rev 20(2):117–135
Sung B (2015) Public policy supports and EP of bioenergy technologies: a dynamic panel approach. Renew Sustain Energy Rev 42:477–495
Tabachnick BG, Fidell LS (2013). Using multivariate statistics, vol 7. Pearson, Boston, p. *138*
Tookey DA (1964) Factors associated with success in exporting. J Manage Stud 1(1):48–66
United Nations Statistics Division (2011) World Statistics pocketbook. Department of Economic and Social Affairs, Statistics Division, USA
United Nations Statistics Division (2014). World statistics pocketbook. Department of Economic and Social Affairs, Statistics Division
Wagner J (2014) Is export diversification good for profitability? First evidence for manufacturing enterprises in Germany. Appl Econ 46(33):4083–4090

Ward PT, Duray R (2000) Manufacturing strategy in context: environment, competitive strategy and manufacturing strategy. J Oper Manag 18(2):123–138

Wheeler C, Ibeh K, Dimitratos P (2008) UK EP research: review and implications. Int Small Bus J 26(2):207–239

Wierts P, Van Kerkhoff H, De Haan J (2014) Composition of exports and EP of Eurozone countries. J Common Market Stud 52(4):928–941

WTO (World Trade Union) (2014). International trade statistics 2014. World Trade Organization International Trade Statistics, pp 178–179

Yeoh PL, Jeong I (1995) Contingency relationships between entrepreneurship, export channel structure and environment: a proposed conceptual model of EP. Eur J Mark 29:95–115

Zhao H, Zou S (2002) The impact of industry concentration and firm location on export propensity and intensity: an empirical analysis of Chinese manufacturing firms. J Int Marketing 10(1):52–71

Zou S, Stan S (1998) The determinants of EP: a review of the empirical literature between 1987 and 1997. Int Mark Rev 15:333–356

Zou S, Taylor C, Osland G (1998) The EXPERF scale: a cross-national generalized EP measure. J Int Marketing 6(3):37–58

Chapter 11
An Assessment of the Contribution of Mineral Exports to Rwanda's Total Exports

Emmanuel Mushimiyimana

Abstract In 2012, the International Council on Mining and Metals (ICMM) proved that mineral exports can be an alternative for increasing exports for agrarian, low- and middle-income countries and that in the past two decades their contribution to total exports increased from 30 to 60%. Based on this theory, we use an econometric model and work with data techniques to test whether Rwanda maintained this pace from 1998 to 2014. Our results show that Rwanda did not manage to reach that level since she only averaged 29.1%. Our findings show that if mineral exports increase at 10%, total exports will increase at 7%. This implies that the Government of Rwanda needs to bring in a lot of reforms in the mining sector and take Botswana and Namibia as its role models.

Keywords Mineral export · Governance · Mining sector · Resources · Rwanda

11.1 Introduction

Modern mining started in Rwanda in the 1930s even though before colonialism Rwandans heated tin for the production of traditional hoes, machetes, spears, and other domestic material. The mining sector in Rwanda was started by Belgians who got mining experience in southeastern DRC, in Katanga. Then, two companies

International Council on Mining and Metals was formed in 2001 to catalyze improved performance and enhance the contribution of mining, minerals, and metals to sustainable development.

E. Mushimiyimana (✉)
Department of Political Science and International Relations, College of Arts and Social Sciences, University of Rwanda, Butare, Rwanda
e-mail: manemanu12@yahoo.fr

A. Heshmati (ed.), *Studies on Economic Development and Growth in Selected African Countries*, Frontiers in African Business Research,
DOI 10.1007/978-981-10-4451-9_11

emerged—MINETAIN[1] and SOMUKI.[2] The two remained important in the mining sector in Rwanda until its independence in 1962. In 1985, SOMIRWA became bankrupt. In 1988, COPIMAR (Mining Cooperative of Artisan Miners) started operations. In 1989, the government created another company REDEMI[3] with an investment of almost 100 million RWF. However, this company collapsed due to the genocide.

After the genocide against the Tutsi in 1994, REDEMI continued to function but without enough capacity since its infrastructure base was almost fully destroyed. In 2001, mineral exports recovered and reached 45.7% of Rwanda's total exports. Mineral revenue increased gradually: 'In 2006, the Rwandan Minerals Industry set revenue targets of $54 million and $63 million for 2007 and 2008 respectively. The targets were exceeded with revenues of $71 million in 2007 and $93 million in 2008. In 2011, the export revenue reached to $156 million and $136 million in 2012 and US$228 million in 2013. The performance of this sector is due to strengthened supervision regulation, availability of new data for investor's interest and the support for value addition in metallic ores and quarries. The main issue with Rwanda's mineral exports is to increase the scale at which the current mineral exports are produced' (RNRA 2014: 1).

In 2007, the Office of Geology and Mines replaced REDEMI. The government was in a period of privatizing most of its companies. In 2008, the Government of Rwanda contracted South African company, New Resolutions Geophysics (NRG), to carry out an aerial survey covering almost the whole country to acquire gravity and new magnetic data for further understanding the subsurface and its possible associated mineral potential. In 2011, OGMR changed its name and become the Geology and Mines Department. Through the privatization process, the Rutongo Mining Company replaced most of the public shares and organizational parts of the mining sector of cassiterites (tin ore). Mining deposits were liberalized to include private firms. Actually, the government privatized mining concessions for improving performance.

The Government of Rwanda sets up prospective target areas (PTAs) to delineate and quantify mineral resources. The government has invested in exploration works in PTAs to generate geology data to be used by mineral exploration companies (RNRA 2014). It has also enacted a mining law allowing the right to exploit three categories of mines—artisanal, small scale, and large scale—to any person/company with proven technical expertise and financial capacity to develop and run a mining project (RNRA 2014). Industrial mining is yet to intensify in Rwanda since what exists right now is artisan mining. There is a need for modern technology and mechanization in this sector. Among, the needed equipments are drillers, bulldozers, and gravity table shakers. There is no value addition to Rwanda's mineral exports since they are exported as raw materials and not as metals in the

[1]Société des Mines d'Etain du Ruanda-Urundi.

[2]Société Minière de Muhinga-Kigali.

[3]Régie d'Exploitation et de Développement des Mines.

case of metal resources such as tin and tungsten. ‘The establishment of processing plants to smelt cassiterite into tin, refining wolframite and tantalite into tungsten and tantalum respectively is open to private investors’ (RDB 2014: 1). The government is committed to supporting over 400 local mining companies, and 30 cooperatives are opened to consider partnerships and joint ventures, covering financing, capital equipment, technical support, and competitive mineral trade contracts (RDB 2014). Besides, there is a need to boost the exploitation of gemstones: ‘Rwanda possesses a variety of gemstones including; beryl (aquamarine), amblygonite, corundum (ruby and sapphire), tourmalines and different types of quartz and granites. Setting up cutting and polishing plants of gemstones is also an opportunity’ (RDB 2014).

Trading of minerals is carried out by ‘holders of mining and mineral trading licenses and owners of smelting and screening companies’ (RDB 2014: 2). Rwanda’s target is ‘trading in minerals, including cassiterite, wolframite and niobium—tantalite must contain at least 30% value added’ (RDB 2014). There is a need to develop industrial minerals in order to meet the ‘demand for construction materials especially tiles, slabs sculptures, paints, bricks and concrete aggregates. Rwanda possesses a variety of minerals such as good quality silica sands, kaolin, vermiculite, diatomite, clays, limestone, talcum, gypsum and pozzolan’ (RDB 2014). However, as compared to other countries, Rwanda’s performance in mineral exports is yet to improve.

Botswana, for instance, used mineral resources as a source of income to finance her expenditure for her independence. ‘Botswana’s success appears so exceptional because the driving force behind Botswana’s economy has been its mineral sector’ (Dougherty 2011: 9). On the contrary, Rwanda considered the mining sector as a subsidiary. Its main source of income has been aided and mineral exploitation has remained weak since independence. However, due to the developmental needs of the country in the twenty-first century, the policy is changing and the mining sector is considered one of the strategic inputs that will help the country to sustain growth, independence, and self-reliance. One does wonder about the means and way forward to bring about positive changes though.

In comparison, Botswana’s strategy was to attract foreign direct investment (FDI) and protect investors from any failures or to compensate them when they failed. This helped the country to be FDI friendly, and it accumulated more and more resources from abroad. Botswana’s openness to foreign assistance was also reflected in its export-oriented productive structure. Initially, Botswana produced beef and diamonds for export, but over time it diversified into non-traditional export crops, mostly to South Africa (Dougherty 2011). The government was able to retain a significant portion of the wealth generated by Botswana’s diamond mines through a policy which rather than retaining a fixed percentage of the sales involved profit-sharing agreements and a portion of equity in mining operations. This policy allowed the government to retain significant shares of profitable ventures and fewer shares of less profitable ventures; such a policy also did not deter new investors (Dougherty 2011).

Further, interest in mining investments needs to be underpinned by an open market economy. Restricted trade halts competitiveness. However, there should be a sense of control of the mining sector since it is based on natural resources and has both embedded advantages and risks. One of the mechanisms of controlling mining companies is framing proper agreements.

Botswana signed an agreement with De Beers, a heavy investor in the country in a contract based on production sharing. In this regard, there are four types of contracts: license agreements, production-sharing agreements, joint ventures, and service agreements. License agreements give more rights to a contracting firm such as right to a mining concession, production, and exports. Production-sharing agreements state that the state cedes all production and exporting authority to the firm, but this usually involves an equity arrangement and higher returns to the government in the long run. Under these two types of agreements, the government does not shoulder any risks (Dougherty 2011). However, in the license agreement, the government can lose total control of mining concessions. In joint ventures and service agreements, a firm gets a limited right to mineral exploitation and trading and the government controls the concessions and the trading of the production. The consequences are that political elites who control the government use political power to mismanage production. Consequently, the firm that works with the government gets over-tightened. It is worth knowing the type of contracts that Rwanda has signed with key mining companies as improvements in mineral exports not only depend on the type of contract and natural resource endowments, but also depend on the diversification of mineral products for exports.

Namibia is a sound example of successful mining of gold and dimension stones such as granite and marble; Rwanda too has potential in these minerals. Some minerals that have been left behind are currently important given the fact that Africa is modernizing with both styles and sizes. For instance, Rwanda has a new industry that processes granite—the East African Granite Industry Ltd. Namibia exports granite. It has gold in Miyove in the Northern Province. In 2011, Simba Gold Corp. of Canada engaged in soil and rock sampling at its Miyove Gold project. In November, Desert Gold Ventures Inc. of Canada purchased the Byumba concession, which had resources of 5.55 million metric tons at a grade of 1.48 g per metric ton gold. Desert Gold and Simba planned to drill at Byumba and Miyove Gold, respectively, in 2012 (Desert Gold Ventures Inc. 2012). Since gold is a precious and lucrative metal worldwide, its exports can yield enough money for Rwanda once it is well exploited.

In short, Namibia and Botswana are role models for sub-Saharan African countries as they have enhanced their economic development by strengthening their mining sectors. Though unlike some other sub-Saharan countries, Rwanda has not extracted diamonds and oil as yet she has gold, cassiterite, and tantalum in addition to methane gas, granite, and other types of dimension stones. The necessary thing is to boost production and attract more foreign direct investment in order to generate more income from mineral exports.

Our research hinges on the hypothesis that the exports of mineral resources can contribute significantly and progressively to Rwanda's total export revenue as has happened in other low- and middle-income countries. In our research, we use econometric methods to investigate the contribution of Rwanda's mineral exports to total exports from 1998 to 2014. The literature review discusses recent theories developed by ICMM that argue that mineral exports increased in value from 2005 to 2010 and this has proven to have played a significant role in enhancing sustainable economies and reducing poverty in developing nations. The contribution of our research is in testing whether this ICMM theory is applicable to Rwanda from 1998 to 2014. It also looks at different perspectives that Botswana and Namibia have used to reach high levels of mineral production and exports and thus highlight the way that Rwanda can follow these African role models in the mining sector.

The research outcomes show that if mineral exports increase by 10%, then total exports will increase by 7%. The probability calculated Pr = 0.00 is inferior (<) to 0.05. Therefore, there is a significant contribution of mineral exports (MINEX) to total exports (TOTEX), considering the significance level of 5%. The recommendation is that the Government of Rwanda can set up mechanisms to boost mineral exploitation both at her domestic mineral sites and in neighboring countries through private companies or public-private joint ventures. The government should respect the legalization standards set up regionally and internationally so that the revenue from mining empowers the state and the region instead of destroying it (Collier and Hoeffler 2002).

Our study concludes that Rwanda did not reach the minimum average level of contribution of mineral exports to total exports which was between 30 and 60% according to ICMM. It is also argued that the pace is still slow for the country to reach other low- and middle-income countries because even if Rwanda increases mineral exports by 10%, *ceteris paribus*, total exports will only increase by 7%. Instead, Rwanda needs to increase her mineral exports to at least 50% in order to have a 35% increase in total exports or achieve a 100% increase in mineral exports in order to have a 70% increase in total exports. Therefore, there is a need to reform the mining sector by referring to role models such as Botswana and Namibia.

11.2 Literature Review

Our research hinges on the ICMM theory that mineral exports increase rapidly to become a major share of total exports in low-income agrarian economies even when they start from a low base. Developing countries' exports are less than their imports, and this implies that the LDCs[4] balance of payments is always in deficit. Increasing exports is a good way of boosting the economy. Increasing exports implies that the government earns more foreign currency to be able to purchase the commodities that the country needs to import for economic sustainability and the welfare of its citizens. In a framework of self-reliance, the government of Rwanda is

[4]Less developed countries or developing nations with GDP less than US$5000 per capita.

looking at lowering its aid dependency and building an economy based on production, accumulation of FDI, and expansion of other sectors such as services and industries. The key sectors in Rwanda have been mainly agriculture, industry, and services. According to Minister Gatete, the service sector was the main contributor to the country's GDP in 2011: 'The Service sector contributed 45% of GDP compared to 33 and 16% of agriculture and industrial sectors respectively. The Service sector had the highest growth of 12% followed by Industry 7% and agriculture 3%.' Based on the Prebisch–Singer hypothesis: '(a country) with high export dependence on primary products[5] stands to lose out from a worsening of the terms of trade' (Riley 2012), ICMM posits that the contribution of mineral resources to the accumulation of FDI and to total exports is high at a level of 60–90 and 30–60%, respectively, while it is limited and very low to government revenue (2–20%), national income (3–10%), and total employment (1–2%) in low- and middle-income countries.

On the one hand, mining FDI often dominates total FDI flows in low-income economies that have only limited other attractions for international capital; on the other hand, mineral exports can increase rapidly to become a major share of total exports (ICMM 2012). These are the domains in which mineral resources have provided considerable outputs in the last two decades. However, without a considerable increase in government revenue, income, and employment, no one can assure the role of the mining sector in a more sustainable economy in a developing nation. The mining sector has contributed to the growth of countries such as Botswana and Namibia (Dougherty 2011), while it has also led to a reverse outcome, namely a resource curse or put the countries at high risk (Collier and Hoeffler 2002; Global Witness 2010). In sub-Saharan Africa, the countries endangered by mineral resources are Sierra Leone, Zimbabwe, DRC, and Angola. Therefore, accumulation of FDI and increase in total exports go hand in hand with strategies for the government to get a considerable share in mining revenue, otherwise minerals will only raise profits for companies rather than for states and societies.

Mineral taxation has become a very significant source of tax revenue in many low-income economies with limited tax-raising capacities (2–20%) (ICMM 2012). However, this is not high because of lack of institutional capacity to tax mineral exploiters and having mining concessions that are dominated by informal trade. Moreover, some low- and middle-income nations have corrupt tax systems or inefficiencies in managing collected money and other resources.

Mineral exports of some developing nations lack value addition since they export raw materials. The modern mineral process technology is sophisticated and requires intensive capital (ICMM 2012) and skilled labor to be more effective for total exports. Wright and Czelusta (2004) argue that it is no coincidence that countries' exports of minerals and metals tend to emerge across multiple

[5]Goods with low levels of processing, diversification and raw materials.

commodities in concert. Davis (2009) has argued that many countries have multiple and various mineral endowments that are there for the taking, and mineral extraction is a matter of domestic public interest, supported by sufficient country-specific technological knowledge and in some cases technological advances that lead to production and exports across a broad range of endowments. According to Davis (2009), a mining policy is important for potential augmentation of endowments. For instance, Chile was a major exporter of copper in the 1800s, which then fell away as its high grade deposits got exhausted and there was no national consensus for supporting the industry. Production surged again in the mid-1900s as government support for mining was renewed (Davis 2009: 5). In actual fact, the main difficulties lay in the link between mineral income profitability and the welfare of citizens.

Mining employment on its own is usually small relative to the total national labor force (ICMM 2012) because the mining sector is developing and using more machines than man power. This means that for minerals to be profitable for the people and the economy in general, economic distribution is important. Other findings also show that countries with mineral endowments become poorer than those without mining concessions. Zimbabwe and Nigeria are an illustration of this. 'Zimbabwe is a country tremendously blessed with vast and diverse precious stones ranging from gold, chrome, lithium, asbestos, and cesium, as well as high-quality emeralds and other minerals and metals' (Mahonye and Mandishara 2015: 1–2). Since independence, the mining sector has contributed an average of about 40% to total exports (Hawkins 2009) with the major share coming from gold and other minerals such as ferrochrome, nickel, and platinum. This, however, still falls in the range of low-income countries with many people under the poverty line. In another case, Mills (2010) highlights that Nigeria despite having earned an estimated US$400 billion from oil in the past 40 years has the number of Nigerians living under US$1 per day increasing consistently. Says Mills (2010: 171b): 'Nigeria would have been better- by some estimates the economy would have been 25% bigger- if the Niger delta had no oil.' Table 11.1 shows that not only have the countries in the Great Lakes region misused natural resources for their economic growth but also that the contribution of mineral exports was very poor in the other countries in the same sub-Saharan region. This implies that mining policies in the Great Lakes region in general and in Rwanda in particular should be taken seriously.

Our research uses the ICMM theory that mineral resources can rapidly contribute to total exports even if the economy of that country is agrarian. Therefore, we rely on ICMM's measurable data highlighted earlier besides Davis' (2009) theory referred to earlier which argues that the development of mineral exports does not depend on an abundance of natural reservoirs but mostly on policy choices to develop an added value for minerals for export and increasing their endowments in the national economy. The contribution of our research is that it tests the applicability of the existing knowledge to the Rwandan situation and tests the position and pace of Rwanda as one of the low-income countries in the area.

Table 11.1 Mineral resources and the GDP PPP per capita of GLR countries as compared to advanced countries in the mining sector in the sub-Saharan region

Great lakes region			Other sub-Saharan countries with mining efficiency		
Country name and her natural resources	GDP PPP per capita 2012	GDP PPP per capita 2013	Country name	GDP PPP per capita 2012	GDP PPP per capita 2013
Burundi: nickel, uranium, rare earth oxides, peat, cobalt, copper, platinum, vanadium, arable land, hydropower, niobium, tantalum, gold, tin, tungsten, kaolin, limestone	$600	$600	Botswana: diamonds, copper, nickel, salt, soda ash, potash, coal, iron ore, silver	$15,900	$16,400
DRC: cobalt, copper, niobium, tantalum, petroleum, industrial and gem diamonds, gold, silver, zinc, manganese, tin, uranium, coal, hydropower, timber	$400	$400	The Republic of the Congo: petroleum, timber, potash, lead, zinc, uranium, copper, phosphates, gold, magnesium, natural gas, hydropower	$4700	$4800
Rwanda: gold, cassiterite (tin ore), wolframite (tungsten ore), methane, hydropower, granites, sand, and arable land	$1500	$1500	Namibia: diamond, copper, uranium, gold, silver, lead, tin, lithium, cadmium, tungsten, zinc, salt, hydropower	$7900	$8200

Source CIA world fact book (data value in US$ 2013)

11.3 Methods

Our research used quantitative methods, especially econometrics. Econometrics is a statistical and mathematical application to economic variables for testing and predicting future outcomes. Econometrics was coined by Ragnar Frisch (1895–1973) of Norway, through the foundation of the Econometric Society and the Journal *Econometrica*. Frisch described an economic society as an international society for the advancement of economic theory in its relation to statistics and mathematics. Frisch explained that statistics, economic theory, and mathematics were necessary but were not sufficient conditions by themselves for a real understanding of the quantitative relations in modern economic life. It is the unification of all three which is powerful, and it is this unification that constitutes econometrics (Bjerkholt 1995). Methods alone cannot be useful without use of research instruments employed in data collection and analysis.

Our research used a triangulation of techniques such as documentary approach and working with data to support the econometric analysis of Rwanda's mineral exports to total exports from 1998 to 2014. Our research also used a comparative analysis of Rwandan mineral exports with other sub-Saharan countries like Botswana and Namibia. The Eviews tool was used in econometrics to calculate the contribution of mineral exports to total exports and to see whether there was a significant effect of the former on the latter. The method critically assessed whether Rwandan mineral exports were moving at the pace of other low- and middle-income countries that are performing very well in mining exports as highlighted by ICMM.

11.4 Data

Our research used secondary data, official documents, and discourses related to Rwandan exports. It also compared data from known sources such as the CIA World Fact Book, the National Bank of Rwanda (BNR), and the Rwanda Natural Resource Authority (RNRA). We visited BNR for a field visit and data gathering.

Table 11.1 gives information about mineral resources and GDP per capita of the countries in the Great Lakes region (GLR) as compared to advanced countries in the mining sector in the sub-Saharan region. From the table, it is clear that GLR's mineral resources did not contribute to the countries' GDPs. Though our research did not measure the rate of contribution of the mining sector to the rest of the countries highlighted earlier due to the limitation of the scope of the research, it is clear that countries such as Botswana and Namibia benefitted from good policies in the mining sector to help them overcome poverty. Besides, Rwanda and GLR in general have different mineral endowments. Development of Rwanda's mineral exports during 1999–2003 is shown in Table 11.2.

Table 11.2 Rwanda's mineral exports (1999–2013)

Year	Volume (tons)	Value (US$ million)
1999	943	6.9
2000	1.012	12.6
2001	2.102	42.6
2002	2.083	15.9
2003	2.599	11.1
2004	5.082	29.3
2005	6.465	37.3
2006	6.187	37.0
2007	8.283	70.6
2008	7.364	94.0
2009	7.960	54.6
2010	8.406	71.0
2011	9.697	158.0
2012	7.588	136.3
2013	7.639	226.2

Source RNRA (2014)

Table 11.3 shows Rwanda's annual export earnings and annual contribution of mineral exports during 1995–2013. There is a strong and positive trend in both indicators over time.

Table 11.3 shows that the contribution of mineral exports to total exports, calculated in percentages, increased from 1995 to 2001, and went downward and upward in a U-shaped curve from 2001 to 2005. It increased again in 2008 to take a stable position in 2010 and 2013 (see also Table 11.4). However, though there was a positive increase in general, mineral exports were in a sharp upward move from 1995 to 2001 while positively uneven from 2002 to 2012 (see Fig. 11.1).

Table 11.3 Annual contribution of mineral exports to total export of Rwanda since 1995 (in %)

Year	Export earnings (US$ million)	Contribution of mineral exports (%)
1995	1.5	3.0
1996	2.3	3.7
1997	3.8	4.1
1998	4.7	7.3
1999	6.9	11.2
2000	12.6	18.2
2001	42.6	45.6
2002	15.9	23.6
2003	11.1	17.5
2004	29.3	29.9
2005	37.3	29.9

(continued)

Table 11.3 (continued)

Year	Export earnings (US$ million)	Contribution of mineral exports (%)
2006	37.0	24.8
2007	70.6	40.0
2008	94.0	40.0
2009	54.6	30.0
2010	71.0	30.0
2011	158.0	30.0
2012	136.3	28.3
2013	226.2	31.0
Average in %		29.1

Source RNRA (2014)

Table 11.4 Mineral exports contribution and total exports

Year	MINEX (US$)	TOTEX (US$)
1998	4,690,000	64,140,000
1999	6,930,000	62,010,000
2000	12,580,000	69,040,000
2001	42,630,000	93,550,000
2002	15,870,000	67,360,000
2003	11,080,000	63,030,000
2004	29,280,000	98,110,000
2005	37,300,000	124,980,000
2006	36,570,000	147,380,000
2007	70,620,000	176,770,000
2008	92,350,000	264,820,000
2009	55,430,000	234,970,000
2010	67,850,000	297,280,000
2011	151,430,000	464,240,000
2012	136,070,000	590,750,000
2013	225,700,000	703,010,000
2014	203,320,000	723,090,000

Source BNR (2015)

11.5 Empirical Results

11.5.1 Calculation of Predictability of Increase in Mineral Resource Export Value

Figure 11.1 shows the increase in mineral revenues from 1998 to 2014 (drawn from Table 11.2). There is a prediction that in 2020, mineral exports will be equal to or

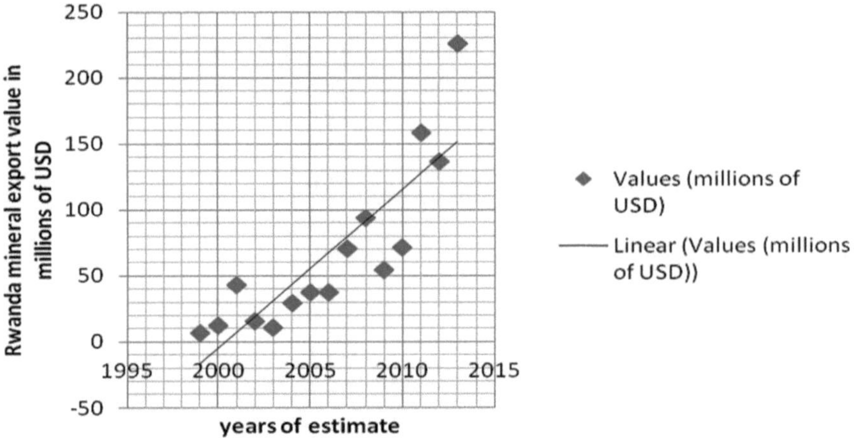

Fig. 11.1 Prediction of increase in revenue from mineral exports in Rwanda

more than US$300 million. A scatter plot of mineral export data for Rwanda was done between 1999 and 2013 to find the progress in generating revenue.

The results as shown in Table 11.4 and Fig. 11.1 are that the revenue accrued was almost US$20 million to US$250 million in 2013. This shows how progressive mineral income has been for Rwanda's total revenue in the last 15 years. The linear shape of the scatter plot shows that Rwanda will continue to get more and more mineral revenue in the coming years, if other factors remain constant.

Though revenues from mineral exports increased positively from 2000 to 2013, Fig. 11.2 shows that there were some downfalls in 2003, 2009, and 2012 and the effect on total revenue, in percentage, decreased little by little in 2003 and 2006, to be constant at almost 30% from 2009 to 2013. The effect in percentage is still low

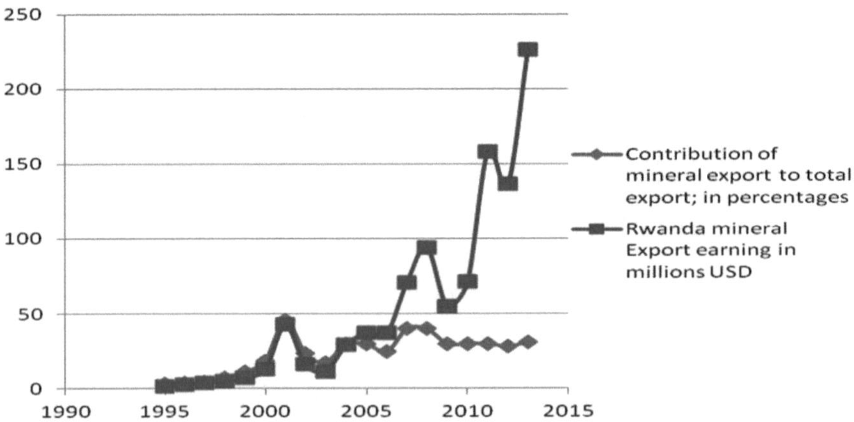

Fig. 11.2 Contribution of mineral exports to total exports and earnings for Rwanda (in %)

though the real income from mineral exports increased sharply due to improvements of other sectors in Rwanda's GDP; this was mainly the service sector which has taken the lead in the last few years. This is also quite similar to the Rwanda Development Board's (RDB 2014) position and prediction: 'In the last three years, mineral exports recorded USD 96.4M (2010), USD 15.4M (2011) and USD 136.1M (2012). The sub-sector's contribution to GDP is to increase from 1.2 to 5.27% (10% growth rate per each year) up to 2017/2018.'

11.5.2 Specification of the Econometric Model

This model refers to the fact that the more the mineral export revenue (LMINEX) increases, the more it significantly increases Rwanda's total exports (LTOTEX). If the total export revenue increases at a high pace, then Rwanda's balance of payments will be positive and the country will be able to finance most of its imports and other public expenditure. Therefore, the econometric model will define the contribution of mineral exports to total exports:

(1) $LTOTEX = (b_1 + b2LMINEX + e_t)$

From Table 11.4 we get an econometric table, set in logarithmic data in order to ease an interpretation of percentages (Table 11.5).

The estimation is that LTOTEX = 6.4318 + 0.71423 * LMINEX. This means if mineral exports increase at 10%, total exports will increase at 7%. The probability calculated $Pr = 0.00 < 0.05$. Therefore, there is a significant effect of mineral revenue LMINEX to total export revenue LTOTEX, considering the level of significance at the 5% level, but this pace is very slow considering the level of other

Table 11.5 Econometric model and results

Dependent variable: LTOTEX				
Method: Least Squares				
Date: 05/27/16 Time: 23:20				
Sample: 1998, 2014				
Included observations: 17				
Variable	Coefficient	Std. Error	*t*-statistic	Prob.
C	6.431831	1.184529	5.429862	0.0001
LMINEX	0.714291	0.067415	10.59542	0.0000
R-squared	0.882134	Mean-dependent variable		18.95617
Adjusted R-squared	0.874276	S.D-dependent variable		0.890265
S.E. of regression	0.315667	Akaike info criterion		0.641871
Sum of squared residuals	1.494681	Schwarz criterion		0.739896
Log likelihood	−3.455902	F-statistic		112.2628
Durbin-Watson[aut]Watson, J. stat	0.775939	Prob. (F-statistic)		0.000000

Source Eviews data

performing low- and middle-income states as stipulated by ICMM. The estimation of parameters of this model is very reliable and significant since the R-squared is 0.88 which means that this model explains the contribution of mineral exports to total exports at 88%. Table 11.3 supports this by providing the average contribution of 29.1% which is less but almost close to the worldwide average contribution of mineral exports to total exports of 30–60% as highlighted by ICMM. This means that though Rwanda is making some progress, like other low- and middle-income countries she is still following a low pace in terms of the contribution of mineral exports to total exports.

11.6 Summary and Conclusion

Rwanda is far away from Botswana and Namibia, which have average percentage contribution of mineral exports to total exports of 83.7 and 53.4%, respectively (ICMM 2012). The results of our econometric model show that if Rwanda wants to reach the levels of these role models, she has to increase her mining sector's performance to 80 or 120%.

Based on the model used, our research recommends that the mining policy of Rwanda should focus on: (1) setting up a main strategy to boost exports of minerals, (2) structure and industrialize the mining sector so that the exploitation and production of minerals stay smooth and increase instead of being uneven with decreases and increases in years and to add value especially by setting up refineries, (3) determine the types of contracts that the government signs with firms. We recommend production-sharing agreements instead of license agreements or any other type of contract. Production-sharing agreements maximize the government's revenue while giving all rights of exploitation and exports to private firms, (4) the Government of Rwanda needs to reallocate mineral incomes to other pro-development policies such as education and infrastructure starting from where mining concessions are given as collateral to local environment damage, (5) the mining sector should go hand in hand with other public reforms such as good governance and politics that decrease the gaps between the rich and the poor. Once the government has accrued mining revenue, it can also help other sectors such as manufacturing, agriculture, and industry to develop, (6) the mining sector needs more modern technology and market openness to be more effective and efficient—attracting efficient investors could be an added value, and (7) Rwanda needs to develop not only cassiterite or tantalum production but also gold exploitation, methane gas, and the processing of dimension stones such as granite like Namibia did.

Our research concludes that mineral exports have not contributed considerably to Rwanda's total export revenues. However, Rwanda had a significant increase in revenues from mineral resources between 1998 and 2014 but did not reach the average contribution of mineral exports to total exports of 30–60% as highlighted by ICMM. Minerals only contributed 29.1% to her total exports, and this implies that Rwanda still has a lot to do in terms of improving its mining sector. We have also seen that Botswana and Namibia in Africa took off due to strategic and wise exploitation of resources. Rwanda can learn from them.

The econometric model proves that if mineral revenues from exports increase by 10%, then total export revenues will increase by 7%. Rwanda needs to multiply its existing efforts by 8–12 times if like Namibia and Botswana she needs a more significant effect of mineral exports on its economy.

The Government of Rwanda can set up mechanisms to boost mineral exploitation so that this sector contributes significantly to its economy. She can come up with policy measures to attract foreign companies to invest heavily in the exploitation of gold, methane gas, and dimension stones such as granite and marble, as happened in Namibia, and not only focusing on cassiterites or tantalum. The contractual frameworks with companies should be based on production-sharing agreements like Botswana did in order to liberalize the mining sector with the state maximizing its profits.

References

Bjerkholt O (1995) The economic society. Econometrica 63(4):755–765

CIA (2015) Natural resources. The world fact book. Available online, https://www.cia.gov/library/publications/the-world-factbook/fields/2111.html, last consulted on 02 June 2016

Collier P, Hoeffler A (2002) On the incidence of civil War in Africa. J Conflict Resolut 46(1): 13–28

Davis, Graham A (2009) Extractive economies, growth and the poor. In: Richards Jeremy (ed) Mining society, and a sustainable world. Verlag, Berlin, Springer, pp 37–60

Desert Gold Ventures Inc. (2012) Desert gold announces encouraging results at its Rubaya project located in Rwanda: Vancouver, British Columbia, Canada, Desert Gold Ventures Inc. press release, January 26, p 8. Available online at http://www.desertgold.ca/news/February%206%202012.pdf, last consulted, 02 June 2016

Dougherty ML (2011) A policy framework for new mineral economies: lessons from Botswana, Illinois State University. Available online: http://www.uvm.edu/ieds/sites/default/files/Botswana_Minerals.pdf, last consulted 01 June 2016

Witness Global (2010) The hill belongs to them—the need for international action on Congo's conflict minerals trade: London. United Kingdom, Global Witness 31 p

Hawkins T (2009) The mining sector in Zimbabwe and its potential contribution to recovery. United Nations Development Programme, Working paper Series No 1

ICMM (2012) The role of mining in national economies. Available online: http://www.icmm.com/the-role-of-mining-in-national-economies, last consulted 01 June 2016

Mahonye N, Mandishara L (2015) Mechanism between mining sector and economic growth in Zimbabwe, is it a resource curse? Economic Research Southern Africa, South Africa. Available online: http://www.econrsa.org/system/files/publications/working_papers/working_paper_499.pdf, last consulted 01 June 2016

Mills G (2010) Why Africa is poor and what African can do about it. Penguin Books, South Africa

RDB (2014) Mining. Available online: http://www.rdb.rw/rdb/mining.html, last consulted 24 Oct 2014

Riley G (2012) Economic growth-prebisch-singer hypothesis. Available online at http://www.tutor2u.net/economics/revision-notes/a2-macro-economic-growth-prebisch-singer-hypothesis.html, last consulted on 14 Oct 2014

RNRA (2014) Mining in Rwanda. Available online at http://rnra.rw/fileadmin/user_upload/Mining_in_Rwanda_.pdf, last consulted 30 May 2016
Wright G, Czelusta J (2004) The myth of the resource curse. Challenge 47(2):6–38

Chapter 12
Testing the Balassa Hypothesis in Low- and Middle-Income Countries

Fentahun Baylie

Abstract This study analyses the long-run relationship between economic growth and real exchange rate for a group of 15 low- and middle-income countries for the period 1950–2011. Co-integration between growth and exchange rate is established by means of an augmented pooled mean group estimation method (which controls for heterogeneity and cross-sectional dependence). Unlike previous studies, cross-sectional dependence is accounted for which implies that the productivity effect of the Balassa term is expected to be estimated consistently and without bias. Moreover, our results indicate that the effect of the Balassa term depends more on the income group (level of per capita income) than the rate of economic growth. In general, the power of the effect is stronger for higher income countries in the long run. The study clearly indicates that the Balassa hypothesis holds for middle-income countries, while this is not the case for low-income countries. However, fiscal policy and exchange rate volatility rather clearly explain the variations in the real exchange rate.

Keywords Productivity · Growth · Real exchange rate · Balassa hypothesis · Panel data

12.1 Introduction

The Balassa hypothesis tests the impact of productivity growth on the real exchange rate. It states that for a growing economy, the real exchange rate is expected to appreciate in the long run. Our study is based on a finding by Baylie (2008). The real effective exchange rate is an important policy parameter and among the most determining factors of growth in Ethiopia (Baylie 2008). Though Baylie recommends depreciation of the domestic currency for promoting economic growth in the short run, the author discovered that it is healthier to allow appreciation in the long

F. Baylie (✉)
Department of Economics, Addis Ababa University, Addis Ababa, Ethiopia
e-mail: fbaylie@yahoo.com

A. Heshmati (ed.), *Studies on Economic Development and Growth in Selected African Countries*, Frontiers in African Business Research,
DOI 10.1007/978-981-10-4451-9_12

run to encourage sustainable economic growth. Hence, he provided (an exchange rate) policy recommendations which promote appreciation of the domestic currency for sustainable growth in the long run.

Both depreciation and appreciation are not welcomed effortlessly by the monetary authority. As suggested by Baylie (2008), depreciation in particular is not favored by the monetary authority as it increases the burden on the importing capacity for a developing country like Ethiopia. In contrast, by the time it is recommended that a country allows appreciation, all advantages of depreciation have been exhausted while prospects of appreciation are pending. Depreciation may initially help promote exports and generate sufficient foreign earnings. Once this objective is met, there arises a need to promote imports of capital goods by allowing appreciation to establish import-substituting industries to transform the economy. The only issue to consider in this case is the 'timing' of switching policy. The solution to this dilemma is provided by the Balassa hypothesis.

At the time when the Balassa hypothesis holds in a particular economy, depreciation is not gainful. In short, it states that if economic growth is accompanied in appreciation of the domestic currency (Balassa hypothesis), the monetary authority should not constrain the appreciation for the simple reason that it may discourage exports. If economic growth by itself brings appreciation, it can be sustained as the latter further puts inertia on the former. There is a possibility of one driving the other in the long run when the hypothesis holds.

In short, the hypothesis states that the impact of growth on the exchange rate is positive; that is, there is appreciation of the domestic currency. The main purpose of our study, therefore, is to show whether this analysis can be extended to a group of low- and middle-income countries on various continents. While there is evidence in favor of the hypothesis, there are also some anti-Balassa results in some studies. The negative results could be associated with different reasons specific to each study.

Tica and Druzic's (2006) survey shows that since its discovery in 1964, the hypothesis has been tested 58 times in 98 countries in time series or panel analyses and in 142 countries in cross-country analyses. In these analyzed estimates, country-specific Balassa hypothesis coefficients have been estimated 164 times. The first empirical test of the theory was carried out by Balassa (1964) himself. Kravis and (1983) and Bhagwati (1984) were also among the forerunners. The conclusions from all these studies confirm the difficulty in ignoring the significance of the hypothesis in general. The strongest empirical support in favor of the relationship between productivity and exchange rate is found in cross-sectional and panel empirical studies.

Chuoudhri and Kahn (2004) found evidence of Balassa–Samuelson effects in a panel of 16 developing countries. They found the traded and non-traded productivity differential to be a significant determinant of the relative prices of non-traded goods, and the relative price in turn exerted a significant effect on the real exchange rate. Similarly, Guo and Hall (2010) and Jabeen et al. (2011) also show that productivity differences directly explained changes in the real exchange rate by using the Johansen co-integration approach for China and Pakistan, respectively.

A positive relationship between productivity and the real exchange rate is not, however, a common fact in all studies. There are a number of studies that show anti-Balassa results. Drine and Rault (2002, 2004), for example, tested the Balassa hypothesis for 20 Latin American (middle-income) and six Asian (low-income) developing countries separately. They applied Pedroni's co-integration techniques in both the studies. Though they were able to find evidence for the hypothesis in the first study for middle-income countries, they failed to replicate the result in the second study for low-income countries. The reason given for the failure is a break in the relationship between productivity and relative price, one of the assumptions of the hypothesis. Asea and Mendoza (1994a, b), Harberger (2003), Hassan (2011), Isard and Symansky (1996), Miyajima (2005), and Wilson (2010) also found anti-Balassa results in their studies on developing countries.

The study that comes the closest to our study is Chuah's (2012). This study found mixed results from a panel study of 142 developing (middle- and low-income) and developed (high-income) countries. The estimation of the fixed effect model showed that productivity growth in developed economies resulted in real appreciation of domestic currencies, while the relationship was nonlinear in developing economies. In the latter group, the real exchange rate initially depreciated and then appreciated after per capita income jumped to a higher level (above $2200), the main reason being a level of development.

Our study makes three improvements over Chuah's (2012) study in terms of data quality, methodology, and variables. First, our study uses data from the latest version of the Penn World Table (PWT), version 8. Data from this version address shortcomings associated with previous versions. In particularly, Chuah (2012) used an expenditure-based measure of GDP from version 7, while our study uses the output-based measure of GDP from version 8. Feenstra et al. (2013) suggested using the second measure for studies interested in an economy's productive capacity. Second, our study accounts for cross-sectional dependence and heterogeneity by applying the common correlated effect approach of Pesaran (2013) and pooled mean group estimation, respectively. Third, our study controls for important supply- and demand-side factors.

The remaining paper is organized as follows. Section 12.2 provides the theoretical background of the hypothesis. Section 12.3 discusses the methodology. The findings are presented in Sects. 12.4 and 12.5 gives the conclusion and policy implications derived from the findings.

12.2 Theoretical Framework of the Model: The Balassa–Samuelson Hypothesis[1]

The Balassa hypothesis demonstrates the relationship between exchange rate, purchasing power parity (PPP), and inter-country income comparisons in general. The hypothesis emanates from the PPP theory. It explains the reason why the PPP theory of exchange rate is imperfect. In the absence of all frictions, the prices of a common basket of goods in two countries measured in the same currency should be the same at all times for absolute PPP to hold, that is, $P/\varepsilon P^{*} = 1$. The Balassa–Samuelson effect, first formulated by Harrod in 1934 and later by Balassa and Samuelson in 1964 separately, says that distortions in purchasing power parity are the result of international differences in relative productivity growth between the tradable goods sector (mainly manufacturing and agriculture) and the non-tradable goods sector (mainly services) (Herberger 2003; Tica and Druzic 2006). In contrast to the PPP theory, price levels are higher in rich countries than poor ones when converted to a common currency. This may be associated with higher productivity growth in the tradable sector in rich countries (Rogoff 1996).

A nation's prosperity is mainly associated with productivity growth in the tradable goods sector. This has an effect of reducing costs in the same sector and increasing real wages in the economy and puts an upward pressure on relative prices of non-tradable goods where productivity has not grown by the same magnitude. This distorts the PPP relationship and results in appreciation of the real exchange rate. The same effect holds true across nations. A more prosperous nation experiences higher productivity growth in the tradable goods sector than a poor nation. Thus, an increase in the prices of non-tradable goods will be higher in a rich country. As a result, a rich country's real exchange will appreciate compared to a poor's nation currency (Asea and Corden 1994a, b).

The Balassa hypothesis may be tested in two forms: external and internal versions. The external version analyzes the impact of productivity growth on the real exchange rate. The internal version analyzes the impact of productivity on relative prices. If one fails to prove a relationship between productivity and the real exchange rate, it is most likely that the hypothesis is functioning through the internal version; that is, the relationship between relative prices and the real exchange rate or relative prices and productivity growth should be tested. The main objective of our study is to examine the validity of the external version of the hypothesis.

The core idea of the Balassa hypothesis is related to the concept of convergence (beta-β-convergence) in growth theories. Both describe features of developing economies. Convergence between economies may be roughly defined as the

[1]Though the idea has been mentioned by several authors (like Ricardo 1911; Harrod 1933; Viner 1937), the contribution of other authors is not as bold as Paul A. Samuelson and Bela Balassa and hence the name Balassa-Samuelson hypothesis (Tica and Druzic 2006). The term 'Balassa hypothesis' is used in this study.

tendency for levels of per capita income or productivity to equalize over time. Growth theories[2] state that countries with low capital-to-labor ratios (high marginal productivity of capital) in general and with advantages of elements such as innovation ability, human capital formation, technical progress, and economies to scale in particular grow faster than others (Kumo 2011; Orlik 2003; Soukiazis 1995).

According to these growth theories, there is a tendency for developing countries to grow faster than developed countries if some conditions in particular are satisfied. Given that the Balassa hypothesis is related to the impact of economic (productivity) growth on the real exchange rate, there should be a greater probability of finding evidence for the hypothesis in converging economies as compared to developed ones. The convergence process, thus, may be used as a criterion for identifying candidate countries for a sample study.

12.3 Methodology

12.3.1 Data Type and Collection Methods

Data for all countries and variables are from Penn World Table for the period 1950–2011. The variables include exchange rate, per capita GDP, and government expenditure. While the choice of the study period for each country depends on data availability, countries are selected on the basis of the convergence criterion which suggests that the fastest growing economies are mainly the developing economies.

According to IMF's World Economic Outlook Report (2015), all 15 countries in our sample are developing countries. However, for comparison purposes, the sample is divided into two categories on the basis of the size of economies (relative GDP). The first group represents the top five largest economies in the sample—BRICS (Brazil, Russia, India, China, and South Africa). They are from the (upper) middle-income countries' category (except India) which together nearly represent 90% of the US economy. The second group consists of 10 low-income countries (Angola, Ethiopia, Ghana, Indonesia, Kenya, Nigeria, the Philippines, Rwanda, Tanzania, and Uganda). Lower middle-income countries (with per capita income lower than $4125) are included in the second group in our sample.

[2]There are three main theoretical approaches to explain the convergence phenomenon: the neoclassical approach, endogenous growth theory, and demand-orientated approach. While (absolute) convergence is the inherent nature of diminishing returns to reproducible capital in the first approach, it is conditional on different factors and elements such as innovation ability, human capital formation, technical progress, and economies to scale in the second and third approaches (Soukiazis 1995).

12.3.2 Model Specification

The original Balassa model was designed for a fully employed small open economy; a 2 × 2 × 2 system (two countries, two commodities, two factors); an inter-sector mobile labor (scarce factor) and inter-nation mobile capital; law of one price for factors within a nation and for tradables across nations; a constant return to scale production frontier; perfect competition in both markets (goods and factors); neural technical progress; and constant terms of trade (Podkaminer 2003).

A derivation of the Balassa–Samuelson model may be considered as a three-stage process. The first is to derive the relationship between the productivity differential and relative price. The second is to derive the relationship between relative price and exchange rate. The third is to derive the relationship between productivity differential and exchange rate.

STEP 1: The original Balassa–Samuelson model is framed on the basis of the traditional Ricardian trade model (Asea and Corden 1994a, b). It is a supply-side model defined by constant return to scale Cobb-Douglas style production functions in two sectors as (Podkaminer 2003):

$$Y_T = A_T L_T^{\alpha} K_T^{1-\alpha} \tag{12.1}$$

$$Y_N = A_N L_N^{\beta} K_N^{1-\beta} \tag{12.2}$$

where T and N refer to traded and non-traded sectors, and α and β represent the share of labor in each sector, respectively, with $\beta \geq \alpha$.

In a perfectly competitive market, factor prices must equal their respective value of marginal products at equilibrium for both sectors:

$$P_T A_T \alpha \left(\frac{K_T}{L_T}\right)^{1-\alpha} = w \tag{12.3}$$

$$P_T A_T (1-\alpha) \left(\frac{K_T}{L_T}\right)^{-\alpha} = r \tag{12.4}$$

$$P_N A_N \beta \left(\frac{K_N}{L_N}\right)^{1-\beta} = w \tag{12.5}$$

$$P_N A_N (1-\beta) \left(\frac{K_N}{L_N}\right)^{-\beta} = r \tag{12.6}$$

Combing the two factor markets for each sector independently and taking the logarithm of both sides for each equation yields:

$$\log(P_T) = (1-\alpha)\log(\mathrm{r}) - (1-\alpha)\log(1-\alpha) + \alpha\log(\mathrm{w}) - \log(A_T) \quad (12.7)$$

$$\log(P_N) = (1-\beta)\log(\mathrm{r}) - (1-\beta)\log(1-\beta) + \beta\log(\mathrm{w}) - \log(A_N) \quad (12.8)$$

Recalling the assumption that price of tradables (*numeraire*) and interest rate (not technology) are the same across boundaries, differentiation of the above with respect to time yields:

$$\frac{\left(\frac{\mathrm{d}P_T(\tau)}{\mathrm{d}\tau}\right)}{P_T(\tau)} = 0 = \frac{\alpha\left(\frac{\mathrm{dw}(\tau)}{\mathrm{d}\tau}\right)}{\mathrm{w}(\tau)} - \frac{\left(\frac{\mathrm{d}A_T(\tau)}{\mathrm{d}\tau}\right)}{A_T(\tau)} \quad (12.9)$$

$$\frac{\left(\frac{\mathrm{d}P_N(\tau)}{\mathrm{d}\tau}\right)}{P_N(\tau)} = \frac{\beta\left(\frac{\mathrm{dw}(\tau)}{\mathrm{d}\tau}\right)}{\mathrm{w}(\tau)} - \frac{\left(\frac{\mathrm{d}A_N(\tau)}{\mathrm{d}\tau}\right)}{A_N(\tau)} \quad (12.10)$$

Substituting Eq. (12.9) into Eq. (12.10) helps define the relative price of non-tradables in terms of productivity differentials for home and foreign country ($\hat{A}$ represents growth rate):

$$\frac{\left(\frac{\mathrm{d}P_N(\tau)}{\mathrm{d}\tau}\right)}{P_N(\tau)} = \frac{\beta}{\alpha}\frac{\left(\frac{\mathrm{d}A_T(\tau)}{\mathrm{d}\tau}\right)}{A_T(\tau)} - \frac{\left(\frac{\mathrm{d}A_N(\tau)}{\mathrm{d}\tau}\right)}{A_N(\tau)} \quad (12.11)$$

$$\hat{p}_N = \left(\frac{\beta}{\alpha}\right)\hat{A}_T - \hat{A}_N \quad (12.12)$$

$$\hat{p}_N^* = \left(\frac{\beta}{\alpha}\right)^* \hat{A}_T^* - \hat{A}_N^* \quad (12.13)$$

The difference between Eqs. (12.12) and (12.13) defines price differentials across countries:

$$\hat{p}_N - \hat{p}_N^* = \left[\left(\frac{\beta}{\alpha}\right)\hat{A}_T - \hat{A}_N\right] - \left[\left(\frac{\beta}{\alpha}\right)^* \hat{A}_T^* - \hat{A}_N^*\right] \quad (12.14)$$

This means that the price differential between sectors and across countries can be explained by productivity differentials between sectors and across nations.

STEP 2: We follow Ahn (2009) to link the exchange rate and productivity differential through the price index. The real exchange rate is defined in a log-linear form as (increase shows appreciation):

$$Q = P/\varepsilon P^*$$
$$q = p - e - p^* \tag{12.15}$$

Price indices are defined as weighted averages of prices in tradable and non-tradable sectors in both domestic and foreign markets:

$$P = P_N^{\delta} P_T^{1-\delta} \quad \text{and} \quad P^* = P_N^{*\theta} P_T^{*(1-\theta)}$$

In log-linear form:

$$p = \delta p_N + (1 - \delta) p_T \tag{12.16}$$

$$p^* = \theta p_N^* + (1 - \theta) p_T^* \tag{12.17}$$

δ and θ represent the share of non-tradables in the consumer basket at home and abroad, respectively. Substituting Eqs. (12.16) and (12.17) into Eq. (12.15) helps define the real exchange rate as a function of price differential:

$$q = \left[\delta(p_N - p_T) - \theta\left(p_N^* - p_T^*\right)\right] + p_T - e - p_T^* \tag{12.18}$$

Since $p_T = e + p_T^*$ (law of one price for tradables), Eq. (12.18) will be:

$$q = \left[\delta(p_N - p_T) - \theta\left(p_N^* - p_T^*\right)\right] \tag{12.19}$$

STEP 3: Eq. (12.19) defines the real exchange rate as a function of the relative price differential between countries. Substituting Eq. (12.14) into Eq. (12.19) helps define the exchange rate as a function of the productivity differential. We assume that the share of non-tradables in the foreign consumer basket (θ) is the same as home (δ). Hence:

$$\hat{q} = \delta\left(\left[\left(\frac{\beta}{\alpha}\right)\hat{A}_T - \hat{A}_N\right] - \left(\frac{\beta}{\alpha}\right)^* \hat{A}_T^* - \hat{A}_N^*\right) \tag{12.20}$$

If the home market grows faster than the foreign one, then the domestic currency appreciates and vice versa.

In order to avoid the assumption of neutral technical progress, we introduced an intercept in the econometric model (Kohler 1998). We also introduced demand-side factors as the Balassa model is not complete by itself (De Gregorio and Wolf 1994).

Therefore, the econometric model used in our study is derived from Eq. (12.20) (see Annexure 1 for derivation). It includes two more factors (demand and supply sides):

$$(\mathrm{lnQ})_{it} = \alpha_i + \beta_{1i}\ln(\mathrm{Y}/\mathrm{Y}^*)_{it} + \beta_{2i}\ln(\mathrm{G}/\mathrm{G}^*)_{it} + \beta_{3i}\mathrm{vol}(\mathrm{E})_{it} + e_{it} \tag{12.21}$$

where Q and E are real and nominal exchange rates.

$(\mathrm{lnQ})_{it}$ is log of the real exchange rate of each country measured against the US dollar. Increase implies appreciation. '*it*' refers to *i*th country in period *t*. $\ln(\mathrm{Y}/\mathrm{Y}^*)_{it}$ is log of real GDP per capita relative to the US economy. It is a proxy for the productivity growth differential in each country. The Balassa hypothesis declares that productivity growth has a positive impact on the real exchange rate.

$\ln(\mathrm{G}/\mathrm{G}^*)_{it}$ is log of relative real government expenditure. It is a proxy for fiscal policy. Kohler (1998) argues that government expenditure accounts for demand shifts toward non-tradables which results in appreciation of the real exchange rate in the short run. In the long run, it does not have an impact unless financed by distortionary taxes. Distortionary taxes reduce real wages and relative prices of non-tradables, and this leads to the depreciation of the real exchange rate in the long run.

$vol(\mathrm{E})_{it}$ is exchange rate volatility measured as the absolute value of percentage change in the nominal exchange rate. It is a supply-side factor. The impact of volatility on the real exchange rate may be positive or negative; it depends on the time horizon and type of regime. Kohler (1998) shows that the impact of volatility is smaller in the short run and in poor countries due to greater nominal rigidities. In relatively fixed exchange rate regimes (mainly poor economies), movements in nominal exchange rate are restricted. In this case, growing economies experience inflation in both sectors with relative prices of non-tradables falling. This leads to a depreciation of the real exchange rate. In contrast, there is smaller rigidity in freely floating exchange rate regimes (mainly rich economies). With productivity growth, inflation in the non-tradable sector is balanced by deflation in the tradable sector (as a result of a nominal appreciation). Relative prices of non-tradables increase, and this leads to the real exchange rate appreciation.

12.3.3 Cross-sectional Dependence Test

Cross-sectional dependence is a problem associated with panel data that mixes information from different cross sections and leads to a difficulty in interpreting the individual effects of each section. It may be caused by socioeconomic network effects, spatial effects, or the influence of a dominant unit or common unobserved factors. When the problem is ignored, estimates are badly biased and the tests may be misleading (Shin 2014). Factor models are used to filter out cross-sectional dependence due to unobserved common factors. We used the Pesaran cross-sectional independence test in our study as it is the most powerful test (Eberhardt 2011). It is given by CD (cross-sectional dependence) which is $N(0, 1)$.

$$CD = \sqrt{\left(\frac{2}{N(N-1)}\right)}\left(\sum_{i=1}^{N-1}\sum_{j=i+1}^{N}\sqrt{T_{ij}}\hat{\rho}_{ij}\right) \tag{12.22}$$

12.3.4 Panel Unit Root Tests

Six types of panel unit root tests are available: Levin-Lin-Chu (LLC), Hariss-Tzavalis (HT), Breitung, Im-Pesaran-Shin (IPS), Fisher type, and Hadri LM. The panel data for our study are unbalanced, and N is fixed and smaller relative to T. It also assumes that the auto-regressive parameter, ρ, is panel specific. Hence, the candidate panel unit root tests that fit these criteria are the IPS and Fisher-type tests. Another advantage of these tests is that they can be used to test a series which is not serially independent across cross sections.

(a) **The Im–Pesaran–Shin test**

The following is a panel unit root test as proposed by Pesaran (2007) which accounts for cross-sectional dependence. The standard Augmented Dickey–Fuller (ADF) regressions are further augmented with cross-sectional averages of lagged levels and first differences of individual series. Let $y_{i,t}$ be the observation on the ith cross-sectional unit at time t, and suppose that it is generated according to the simple dynamic linear heterogeneous panel data model:

$$y_{i,t} = (1-\phi_i)\mu_i + \phi_i y_{i,t-1} + e_{it} \tag{12.23}$$

$$\text{where} \quad e_{it} = \gamma_i f_t + \varepsilon_{it};\, i = 1\ldots N; \quad t = 1\ldots T.$$

The initial value, $y_{i,0}$, has a given density function with a finite mean and variance, and the error term, e_{it}, has a single-factor structure. f_t is the unobserved common effect, and ε_{it} is an individual-specific (idiosyncratic) error. The unit root hypothesis of interest is expressed as:

$$H_0\colon \phi_i = 1 \text{ for all } i \text{ against the possibly heterogeneous alternatives}$$

$$H_1\colon \phi_i < 1, i = 1, 2, \ldots .N_1, \phi_i = 1, i = N_1 + 1, N_2 + 2, \ldots ., N$$

N_1/N, a fraction of the individual processes that are stationary, is nonzero and tends to the fixed value δ such that $0 < \delta < 1$ as $N \to \infty$. This condition is necessary for the consistency of unit root tests.

(b) **Fisher-type tests**

Maddala and Wu (1999) provide a Fisher-type panel unit root test which accounts for cross-sectional dependence. Like the IPS test, the Fisher-type test is a way of combining evidence on the unit root hypothesis from the N unit root tests performed on N cross-sectional units. The fisher-type test makes this approach more explicit. It combines p values from panel-specific unit root tests using four methods. Three of the methods differ in whether they use inverse chi-square, inverse-normal, or inverse-logit transformation of p values, and the fourth is a modification of the inverse Chi-square transformation. The inverse-normal Z statistic offers the best trade-off between size and power.

Let G_{i,T_i} be a unit root test statistic for the *ith* group, and assume that as $T_i \to \infty$, then $G_{i,T_i} = > G_i$. Let p_i be the p value of a unit root test for cross section i, that is, $p_i = 1 - F(G_{i,T_i})$, where $F(\cdot)$ is the distribution function of random variable G_i. In Chen (2013), the Fisher-type test is given as:

$$P = -2\sum_{i=1}^{N} \ln p_i \tag{12.24}$$

P is distributed as χ^2 with $2N$ degrees of freedom as $T \to \infty$ for all N. p_i value closer to zero ($\ln p_i$ closer to $-\infty$) implies large value of P, and then, the null hypothesis of the existing panel unit root is rejected. p_i value closer to 1 ($\ln p_i$ closer to zero) implies that the panel unit root does exist.

12.3.5 Panel Co-integration Tests

There are two possibilities to deal with nonstationary variables in a given model after the stationarity test. First, to test whether the linear combination of nonstationary variables is stationary by using the co-integration test. If they are co-integrated, then we proceed to a long-run analysis with the nonstationary variables. Otherwise, we difference the stationary variables for a short-run analysis.

Engle and Granger (1987) noted that 'a test for co-integration can be thought as a pretest to avoid "spurious regression" situations.' If regression of one nonstationary variable over another nonstationary variable yields a stationary series, it is known as a co-integrating regression and the slope parameter in such a regression is known as a co-integrating parameter.

We employ a residual-based Pedroni co-integration test which is simply a unit root test applied to the residuals obtained from a co-integrating regression. If variables are co-integrated, then the residuals should be $I(0)$. If the variables are not co-integrated, then the residuals are not $I(0)$ (Pedroni 2004). The test allows for heterogeneous intercepts and trend coefficients across cross sections. It is based on a residual obtained from a regression:

$$y_{it} = \alpha_i + \delta_i t + \beta_{1i} x_{1i,t} + \beta_{2i} x_{2i,t} + \cdots + \beta_{Mi} x_{Mi,t} + e_{i,t} \tag{12.25}$$

for $t = 1, \ldots, T$; $i = 1, \ldots, M$; $m = 1, \ldots, M$; and x and y are assumed to be integrated of order 1, $I(1)$. The parameters α_i and δ_i are individual and trend effects. Pedroni proposes seven different statistics to test panel data co-integration: panel v-statistic, panel rho-statistic, panel PP-statistic, panel ADF-statistic, group rho-statistic, group PP-statistic, and group ADF-statistic. The first four are based on pooling or the 'within' dimension, and the last three are based on the 'between' dimension. The null hypothesis is no co-integration for both. However, the alternative hypothesis is $\rho_i = \rho < 1$ for all i in the former, and it is $\rho_i < 1$ for all i in the latter (Pedroni 2004).

12.3.6 Estimation Method

The choice of estimation method mainly depends on the results of preliminary tests of data. In our case, we looked for a method that helped an analysis of nonstationary variables which were co-integrated. We considered a method that provides estimated coefficients for individual countries. Therefore, we are not supposed to consider traditional estimators such as Pooled OLS, fixed effect, and first-difference OLS models which assume homogeneous technology parameters and factor loadings (common slope). Eberhardt et al. (2011) and others have suggested using the *pooled mean group estimation* method for analyzing nonstationary variables which are co-integrated in a long panel setting. This method is helpful for heterogeneous technology parameters and factor loadings in particular.

The pooled mean group (PMG) estimator involves averaging and pooling. It restricts long-run coefficients to be homogenous over cross sections, but allows for heterogeneity in intercepts, short-run coefficients (including the speed of adjustment), and error variances. It is argued that country heterogeneity is particularly relevant in short-run relationships given that countries may be affected by over-lending, borrowing constraints and financial crises in short-time horizons. Homogenous long-run relationships may be assumed for reasons such as budget or solvency constraints, arbitrage conditions, or common technologies (Cavalcanti et al. 2011).

The relationship in pooled mean group estimation may be defined by an ARDL model as:

$$\Delta q_{it} = \alpha_i + \beta_i \Delta x_{it} + \lambda_i \left(q_{i,t-1} - \theta x_{i,t-1} \right) + e_{it} \tag{12.26}$$

where $q = lnQ$ and $x = lnX$. β_i are short-run parameters, which like σ_i^2 differ across countries. Error correction term, λ_i, also differs across i, long-run parameter; θ, however, is constant across the groups. This estimator is quite appealing when studying small sets of arguably 'similar' countries. In $I(1)$ panels, this estimator allows for a mix of co-integration $(\lambda_i > 0)$ and non-co-integration $(\lambda_i = 0)$. $x_{i,t}$ represents the set of explanatory variables defined in Eq. (12.21).

To account for cross-sectional dependence which may result from any common unobserved factor incorporated in the error term, we follow Pesaran's (2013) common correlated effect approach. Unlike de-meaning, the approach handles multiple factors which can be correlated with regressors and serial correlation in errors and lagged dependent variables (Shin 2014). It does not require prior knowledge of the number of unobserved common factors and can be applied to dynamic panels with heterogeneous coefficients and weakly exogenous regressors (Pesaran 2013). The procedure consists of approximating the linear combinations of unobserved common factors by cross-sectional averages of the dependent and explanatory variables and then running standard panel regressions augmented with these cross-sectional averages.

The PMG estimator for a cross-sectionally dependent series may be explicitly defined as:

$$\Delta q_{it} = \alpha_i + \beta_i \Delta x_{it} + \lambda_i \left(q_{i,t-1} - \theta x_{i,t-1}\right) + \gamma_{it} f_t + \varepsilon_{it} \tag{12.27}$$

$$\text{where } \gamma_i' f_t + \varepsilon_{it} = e_{it}$$

f_t is a vector of unobserved common shocks which captures the source of error term dependencies across countries. It may be stationary or nonstationary. The impacts of these factors on each country are governed by the idiosyncratic loadings in γ_{it}. The individual-specific errors, ε_{it}, are distributed independently across i and t; they are not correlated with the unobserved common factors or the regressors; and they have zero mean, variance greater than zero, and finite fourth moments (Cavalcanti et al. 2011). The augmented pooled mean group estimator is, therefore, defined by substituting cross-sectional averages for the unobserved common factors, f_t.

$$\Delta q_{it} = \alpha_i + \beta_i \Delta x_{it} + \lambda_i \left(q_{i,t-1} - \theta x_{i,t-1}\right) + \frac{1}{N} \sum_{l=1}^{PT} \delta \bar{z}_{w,t-l} + \varepsilon_{it} \tag{12.28}$$

where $\bar{z}_{w,t}$ represents a set of cross-sectional averages of the dependent and independent variables and their lagged values which approximate/proxy the unobserved common factors (f_t). The focus of this estimator is on obtaining consistent estimates of parameters related to observable variables, while the estimated coefficients on cross-sectionally averaged variables are not interpretable in a meaningful way: They are merely present to alter the biasing impact of unobservable common factors (Eberhardt 2012).

12.3.7 Error Correction Mechanism (ECM)

If two/more variables are co-integrated or prove to have a long-run relationship, then one needs to go for an error correction mechanism. The error correction mechanism (ECM) is a method used to correct any short-run deviations of variables from their long-run equilibrium; that is, it corrects for short-run disequilibrium. An important theorem, the Granger representation theorem, states that if two variables *Y* and *X* are co-integrated, then the long-term or equilibrium relationship that exists between the two can be expressed as ECM (Engle and Granger 1987). This means that one shall go for the construction of an error correction model if the two variables are co-integrated. ECM is given as follows in Bhattarai (2011) for ARDL (1,1) with $\beta_i = 0$:

$$q_{it} = \alpha_i + \gamma_i q_{it-1} + \beta_i x_{it} + \theta_i x_{i,t-1} + \varepsilon_{it}$$

$$\Delta q_{it} = \alpha_i + \beta_i \Delta x_{it} + \lambda_i u_{i,t-1} + \varepsilon_{it} \tag{12.29}$$

Δ denotes the first-difference operator, ε_{it} is a random error term, and $u_{i,t-1} = \left(q_{i,t-1} - \theta x_{i,t-1}\right)$ is one-period lagged value of error term from a co-integrating regression.

This ECM equation states that δq_{it} depends on δx_{it} and also on the equilibrium error term. If the error term is nonzero, the model is out of equilibrium. Suppose δx_{it} is zero (Bhattarai 2011) and $u_{i,t-1}$ is positive, it means q_{it-1} is too high (above) to be in equilibrium. Since λ_i is expected to be negative, the term $\lambda_i u_{i,t-1}$ is negative, and therefore, δq_{it} will be negative to restore equilibrium. That is, if q_{it} is above its equilibrium value, it will start falling in the next period to correct the equilibrium error. Similarly, if $u_{i,t-1}$ is negative (i.e., q_{it} is below its equilibrium value), $\lambda_i u_{i,t-1}$ will be positive, which causes δq_{it} to be positive, leading q_{it} to rise in the next period. The absolute value of λ_i determines how quickly the equilibrium is restored (Engle and Granger 1987).

12.4 Empirical Results

12.4.1 Test Results

This analysis begins by performing different econometric tests. Since not all unit roots provide the appropriate results, a cross-sectional independence test was performed to decide the type of panel unit root test to be considered. Using the Pesaran CD test, and possibly all other tests, the null hypothesis of cross-sectional independence was rejected for the original data. Hence, the series for our data was initially cross-sectionally dependent. However, after the data were augmented for cross-sectional averages to eliminate unobserved common factors, the Pesaran CD test, and possibly two other tests, failed to reject the null hypothesis of cross-sectional independence. The test results are given in Annexure 2.

IPS and Fisher-type tests are panel unit root tests which account for cross-sectional dependence. The results of the tests with different assumptions are given in Annexure 2. All the variables are nonstationary at the 1% level of significance.

The next step is to test for co-integration—whether there is a long-run relation between our nonstationary variables. The test for co-integration is residual based. We used two Pedroni type tests (ADF and PP tests) and the IPS test. In all the cases, we strongly reject the null hypothesis of no co-integration for both types of models (augmented and non-augmented) (see Annexure 2). Augmented models include cross-sectional averages of dependent and independent variables to account for cross-sectional dependence.

We propose three types of augmented models for the model selection criterion: models I, II, and III with one, two, and three explanatory variables, respectively. Even though the model selection criterion suggests that a model with three variables is our 'best model' in terms of log-likelihood ratio and Akaike information criteria (see Annexure 2), we present the results of the other models as well for comparison.

12.4.2 Estimation Results

Unlike most previous studies, the results of our study were not uniform across all developing countries. The impact of productivity growth on the real exchange rate differed by income group or per capita income. Productivity growth led to an appreciation in middle-income countries and depreciation in low-income countries in the long run. Our results substantiate the findings of Drine and Rault (2002, 2004) and Chuah (2012). Drine and Rault (2002, 2004) found evidence for the hypothesis in a study for middle-income countries (MICs) in 2002 and failed to arrive at the same conclusion for low-income countries (LICs) in another study in 2004. Our findings also seem to be in implicit confirmation of Chuah's (2012) results. He calculated a turning point ($2200) below which change in income resulted in depreciation of the real exchange rate. Almost all LICs in our study had a per capita income less than $2200. The conclusions of Chuah's (2012) study coincide with our conclusions for LICs such as Indonesia, Kenya, Nigeria, Tanzania, and Uganda.

Table 12.1 shows the long-run results of the panel co-integration estimation using the augmented PMG estimator for different groups of countries and models in the sample. We follow the tradition of presenting estimated coefficients of only observable variables as cross-sectionally averaged variables are not directly interpretable in a meaningful way. Estimated coefficients of full models (with observable and unobservable variables) are reported in Annexure 3.

Basically, we consider three types of models in comparing three types of groups: the *all countries* group (15 countries), country groups by income (middle-income countries (*MICs*), 5 countries; low-income countries (*LICs*), 10 countries), and

Table 12.1 Panel co-integration estimation: the augmented PMG estimator

Sample [# of countries]	Type of model	Long-run coefficients		
		$\ln Q$ = dependent variable		
		$\ln(Y/Y^{*})$	$\ln(G/G^{*})$	vol(E)
All countries [15]	Model I	0.378296*** (0.108540)		
	Model II	0.246642*** (0.075056)	0.170621*** (0.037414)	
	Model III	0.388355*** (0.092802)	0.110547** (0.045996)	−0.021531** (0.010345)
MICs (BRICS) [5]	Model I	0.109014 (0.151776)		
	Model II	0.382324** (0.160930)	0.220887* (0.120288)	
	Model III	0.344657** (0.149000)	0.252061*** (0.092608)	0.024845** (0.012602)
LICs [10]	Model I	0.320488* (0.132415)		
	Model II	0.211173** (0.098594)	0.140663*** (0.041793)	
	Model III	−0.287286*** (0.086673)	0.010920 (0.049502)	−3.21610*** (0.419248)
Africa [9]	Model I	0.366216** (0.144702)		
	Model II	0.239056** (0.103439)	0.168407*** (0.043046)	
	Model III	−0.247591*** (0.071625)	0.077565** (0.038439)	−2.56978*** (0.285754)
Asia [4]	Model I	0.248016 (0.258474)		
	Model II	0.519768** (0.216328)	−0.179409** (0.078622)	
	Model III	0.771434* (0.439197)	−0.339890 (0.207397)	−7.71735*** (2.826821)

Note Q and E are real and nominal exchange rates, Y/Y^{*} = real GDP of home relative to foreign (US), G/G^{*} = real government expenditure of home relative to foreign (US), and vol(E) exchange rate volatility

***, **, and * refer to significance level at 1, 5, and 10%. Standard errors in parentheses

MICs refers to middle-income countries of the BRICS group (Brazil, Russia, India, China, and South Africa)

LICs refers to low-income countries (Angola, Ethiopia, Ghana, Indonesia, Kenya, Nigeria, the Philippines, Rwanda, Tanzania, and Uganda)

Africa refers to African countries (Angola, Ethiopia, Ghana, Kenya, Nigeria, Rwanda, Tanzania, Uganda, and South Africa)

Asia refers to Asian countries (China, India, Indonesia, and the Philippines)

country groups by region (*Africa*, 9 countries; *Asia*, 4 countries). For each group in Table 12.1, the first row shows a model with one explanatory variable (productivity); the second row shows a model with two explanatory variables (productivity and government expenditure); and the third row shows a model with three explanatory variables (productivity—$\ln(Y/Y^{*})$, government expenditure —$\ln(G/G^{*})$, and exchange rate volatility—$\mathrm{vol}(E)$). The center of our discussion is Model III (shaded rows) for each group below.

In general, the results in Table 12.1, in general, show that the Balassa hypothesis holds for *all countries* as a group in the sample in the long run; that is, a 1% improvement in productivity leads to an appreciation of domestic currencies in the developing countries in the group by 0.388% on average. We find a different result, however, when the sample is categorized into different groups. When categorized by level of per capita income, the results show that the Balassa hypothesis holds only for middle-income countries (*MICs*). The same fact holds when countries are categorized by region; that is, the Balassa hypothesis holds only for *Asian* countries. This may be related to the fact that in our sample, most middle-income countries are from Asia and poor countries are from Africa. In both the cases, a 1% increase in productivity appreciates the domestic currencies of countries in *MICs* and *Asia* groups nearly by 0.34 and 0.77%, respectively (though only at the 10% level of significance for the latter). For *LICs* and *Africa* groups, a 1% increase in productivity depreciates domestic currencies of countries in the groups by nearly 0.287 and 0.247%, respectively.

The long-run relationship between government expenditure and the real exchange rate shows that expansionary fiscal policies result in appreciation of domestic currencies in all cases except for the *LICs* and *Asia* groups. This may not be surprising as the major countries with 'big economies' in both the groups are almost similar (Indonesia and the Philippines are members of both groups). The results of these groups are in line with Kohler's (1998) argument who states that government expenditure does not have an impact in the long run unless financed by distortionary taxes.

Exchange rate volatility has the impact of depreciating the real exchange rate for all countries in all groups except the middle-income group in the long run. This confirms theoretical arguments which associate relatively fixed or highly managed exchange rate systems (mainly in poor countries) to depreciation and flexible regimes to appreciation in the real exchange rate.

Table 12.2 presents the results of short-run dynamics of the same groups of countries and models as given in Table 12.1. The discussion that follows focuses on Model III (the shaded rows). Short-run dynamics show that the impact of change in productivity on change in the real exchange rate is significant but negative; that is, it has the impact of depreciating the real exchange rate for all countries in all groups in the short run.

Fiscal policy does not significantly explain the variations in the real exchange rate. Exchange rate volatility has an impact only in *MICs* and *all countries* groups. It negatively impacts the real exchange rate in the short run. This may be due to greater rigidity in the short run.

Table 12.2 Short-run dynamics of panel co-integration estimation: the augmented PMG estimator

Sample [# of countries]	Type of model	Adjustment coefficient	Short-run coefficients		
			$\Delta \ln Q$ = dependent variable		
			$\Delta \ln(Y/Y^*)$	$\Delta \ln(G/G^*)$	$\Delta\,\mathrm{vol}(E)$
All countries [15]	Model I	−0.109894*** (0.022462)	−0.327721*** (0.081918)		
	Model II	−0.142981*** (0.032498)	−0.359401*** (0.091545)	−0.046910* (0.027791)	
	Model III	−0.122432*** (0.037203)	−0.397465*** (0.082479)	−0.057736* (0.030909)	−0.161279*** (0.038693)
MICs (BRICS) [5]	Model I	−0.167326*** (0.068251)	−0.300195*** (0.082509)		
	Model II	−0.193645*** (0.102726)	−0.408364*** (0.133144)	−0.082710 (0.073367)	
	Model III	−0.12243*** (0.037203)	−0.3974*** (0.082479)	−0.057736* (0.030909)	−0.161279*** (0.038693)
LICs [10]	Model I	−0.111716*** (0.027206)	−0.352239*** (0.118025)		
	Model II	−0.141304*** (0.036735)	−0.364848*** (0.136587)	−0.042973 (0.032613)	
	Model III	−0.086261*** (0.024822)	−0.423972*** (0.099213)	−0.016775 (0.028716)	−0.020308 (0.031332)
Africa [9]	Model I	−0.098028*** (0.031963)	−0.427619*** (0.104199)		
	Model II	−0.131601*** (0.041812)	−0.427570*** (0.122564)	−0.058400** (0.031572)	
	Model III	−0.107015*** (0.032358)	−0.408247*** (0.100776)	−0.032190 (0.029437)	−0.034526 (0.046803)
Asia [4]	Model I	−0.127473*** (0.041693)	−0.213683 (0.193959)		
	Model II	−0.165803* (0.092356)	−0.229174 (0.192154)	0.035224 (0.067468)	
	Model III	−0.052518*** (0.019297)	−0.458148*** (0.162181)	−0.013347 (0.067688)	−0.044258* (0.023795)

Note $\Delta \ln Q$ = log of real exchange rate differenced, $\Delta \ln Y/Y^*$ = log of real GDP relative to foreign (US) differenced, $\Delta \ln G/G^*$ = log of real government expenditure relative to foreign (US) differenced, and vol(E) exchange rate volatility differenced

***, **, and * refer to the significance level at 1, 5, and 10%. Standard errors in parenthesis

MICs refers to middle-income countries of the BRICS group (Brazil, Russia, India, China, and South Africa)

LICs refers to low-income countries (Angola, Ethiopia, Ghana, Indonesia, Kenya, Nigeria, the Philippines, Rwanda, Tanzania, and Uganda)

Africa refers to African countries (Angola, Ethiopia, Ghana, Kenya, Nigeria, Rwanda, Tanzania, Uganda, and South Africa)

Asia refers to Asian countries (China, India, Indonesia, and the Philippines)

The (negative) signs and statistical significance of the error correcting terms show that the system is stable. A stable co-integrating relationship adjusts short-run deviations by the extent of the error correcting term. The rate of adjustment is, however, higher (12%) in *MICs* than *LICs* (8%). This means *MICs* have a faster rate of adjustment and achieve equilibrium earlier than *LICs*. This may be associated with better conditions to fulfill assumptions of the model in the former group.

Tables 12.3 and 12.4 present the short-run dynamics for individual countries in two income groups (*MICs* and *LICs*), respectively. The results are for Model III.

The short-run dynamics show that the impact of productivity on the real exchange rate was significant and negative for all countries except Brazil and South Africa. Productivity did not have an impact on the real exchange rate in these countries in the short run. Expansionary fiscal policies resulted in depreciation of the real exchange rate in Brazil, Russia, and China. The role of exchange rate volatility was significant in all countries. However, the effect was exceptionally positive in Russia.

The rate of adjustment was the highest in Russia (56.25%) followed by Brazil (22.76%). This may be associated with the size and features of these economies. These are the two biggest economies in the group which account for 40 and 20% of the US economy, respectively. A faster rate of adjustment means that they can achieve equilibrium earlier than others.

Table 12.4 presents the short-run dynamics for *LICs*. The short-run dynamics shows that the impact of productivity on the real exchange rate was significant and negative for all countries except Indonesia and Uganda. Productivity did not impact

Table 12.3 Short-run dynamics by country: middle-income group (BRICS): Model III

Cases	Adjustment coefficient	Short-run coefficients		
		$\Delta \ln Q$ = dependent variable		
		$\Delta \ln(Y/Y^*)$	$\Delta \ln(G/G^*)$	$\Delta\, \mathrm{vol}(E)$
All countries	−0.12243*** (0.037203)	−0.3974*** (0.082479)	−0.057736* (0.030909)	−0.161279*** (0.038693)
Brazil	−0.227627*** (0.004377)	0.228636* (0.096920)	−0.088359*** (0.006094)	−0.002061*** (1.62E−05)
China	−0.064666*** (0.000587)	−0.5913*** (0.012107)	−0.101536*** (0.006333)	−0.354891*** (0.007472)
India	−0.046854*** (0.000797)	−0.4483*** (0.026819)	0.015571 (0.008586)	−0.301000*** (0.006721)
Russia	−0.562507*** (0.015174)	−0.4439*** (0.045163)	−0.451463*** (0.010053)	0.006537*** (3.27E−05)
South Africa	−0.078684*** (0.001472)	−0.194967 (0.151551)	0.039537 (0.058783)	−0.373313*** (0.009758)

Note $\Delta \ln Q$ = log of real exchange rate differenced, $\Delta \ln Y/Y^*$ = log of real GDP relative to foreign (US) differenced, $\Delta \ln G/G^*$ = log of real government expenditure relative to foreign (US) differenced, and vol(E) exchange rate volatility differenced

MICs refers to middle-income countries of the BRICS group (Brazil, Russia, India, China, and South Africa)

Table 12.4 Short-run dynamics by country: low-income group

Cases	Adjustment coefficient	Short-run coefficients		
		$\Delta \ln Q$ = dependent variable		
		$\Delta \ln(Y/Y^*)$	$\Delta \ln(G/G^*)$	$\Delta \text{vol}(E)$
All countries	−0.086261*** (0.024822)	−0.423972*** (0.099213)	−0.016775 (0.028716)	−0.020308 (0.031332)
Angola	−0.001548*** (4.27E−07)	−0.372509*** (0.025896)	−0.171725** (0.003968)	−0.005968*** (7.06E−06)
Ethiopia	−0.136337*** (0.000650)	−0.816907*** (0.015748)	−0.03830*** (0.002945)	0.065656*** (0.007485)
Ghana	−0.094831*** (0.000562)	−0.691301*** (0.035033)	0.03351*** (0.002317)	−0.042398*** (0.002733)
Indonesia	−0.000108*** (1.02E−05)	−0.006073 (0.086557)	0.06723*** (0.010901)	−0.017159 (5.17E−05)
Kenya	−0.248868*** (0.001492)	−0.121422*** (0.012865)	0.11217*** (0.000995)	0.164651*** (0.003452)
Nigeria	−0.042414*** (0.000194)	−0.632917*** (0.009143)	−0.02030*** (0.000807)	−0.125337*** (0.002453)
The Philippines	−0.145762*** (0.000584)	−0.647025*** (0.022619)	0.05421*** (0.003975)	−0.089533*** (0.002379)
Rwanda	−0.075394*** (0.000518)	−0.345743*** (0.005333)	−0.012847** (0.002458)	−0.028748*** (0.002997)
Tanzania	−0.107271*** (0.000337)	−0.665093*** (0.013354)	−0.04128*** (0.002109)	−0.177574*** (0.003046)
Uganda	−0.010293*** (5.76E−05)	0.059272 (0.032875)	−0.15042*** (0.007855)	0.053328*** (0.002087)

Note $\Delta \ln Q$ = log of real exchange rate differenced, $\Delta \ln Y/Y^*$ = log of real GDP relative to foreign (US) differenced, $\Delta \ln G/G^*$ = log of real government expenditure relative to foreign (US) differenced, and vol(E) exchange rate volatility differenced
***, **, and * refer to significance level at 1, 5, and 10%. Standard errors in parentheses
LICs refers to low-income countries (Angola, Ethiopia, Ghana, Indonesia, Kenya, Nigeria, the Philippines, Rwanda, Tanzania, and Uganda)

the real exchange rate in the short run in these countries. The role of fiscal policy was significant in all countries even though the effect was different. The increase in government expenditure resulted in a depreciation of the real exchange rate in all countries except in Ghana, Kenya, Indonesia, and the Philippines. The strongest impact of the fiscal policy was shown by Uganda (0.15%). The impact of exchange rate volatility was significant in all countries except Indonesia.

The rate of adjustment was the highest in Kenya (24.89%) followed by the Philippines (14.58%) and Ethiopia (13.63%). These three countries may achieve equilibrium earlier than others in the group.

12.5 Conclusions and Policy Implications

12.5.1 Conclusions

Unlike most previous studies, the results of our study are not uniform across all the developing countries in our sample. The impact of productivity growth on the real exchange rate varied by income group or per capita income. Productivity growth led to an appreciation of the real exchange rate in middle-income countries and depreciation of the real exchange rate in low-income countries in the long run. In general, the results of our study confirm that the relationship between the real exchange rate and productivity does exist and is stronger for higher income countries in the long run. Real per capita income matters more than the rate of economic growth in explaining the effects of the Balassa term in our study.

In the short run, however, we find almost uniform results across income groups. Productivity growth (possibly of non-tradables), expansionary fiscal policies, and high exchange rate volatility result in the real exchange rate depreciation. More specifically:

- Improvements in productivity and expansionary fiscal policies both have the impact of depreciating the real exchange rate in almost all the countries, both middle and low incomes.
- The impact of exchange rate volatility is significant only in m*iddle-income countries*. This may be associated with the type of exchange rate policy/regime adopted. It is mainly fixed (unchanged) in *low-income countries* in which case it may not be useful to explain variations in the real exchange rate in the short run.

The reasons for the anti-Balassa hypothesis results in low-income countries in our study may be associated with a failure to satisfy the basic assumptions of the model. The relationship between the real exchange rate and productivity in the external version of the hypothesis assumes a positive relationship between productivity and relative prices as well as relative prices and the real exchange rate in the internal version. In addition, the law of one price must hold in the tradable sector.

12.5.2 Policy Implications

On the basis of our findings, we recommend the following policy options for MICs and LICs:

- The Balassa hypothesis holds for *middle-income countries* in our sample. Economic growth leads to an appreciation in the real exchange rate in these countries. Hence, countries in this group may promote growth by increasing productivity in the tradable sector.

- Since the Balassa hypothesis does not hold for *low-income countries* in our sample, economic growth does not lead to the real exchange rate appreciation in these countries. Hence, countries in this group may continue to grow by promoting productivity growth in the non-tradable sector.
- Depreciation of the real exchange rate can be associated with improvements in the productivity of the non-tradable sector for *low-income countries* and should be used accordingly.
- The role of fiscal policy may not last long in *low-income countries* and so should be used accordingly.

Acknowledgements I am grateful for all comments and contributions of Professor Scott Hacker, Professor Par Sjolander, and Dr. Girma Estiphanos for this work. It was a great pleasure to have their say in my paper.

Annexure 1

1.1 Model Derivation (Scott Hacker's Contribution)

Suppose that the growth rate of the real exchange rate is defined as a function of productivity differential between the non-tradable and tradable sectors as in:

$$\hat{Q} = \delta\left(\left[\left(\frac{\beta}{\alpha}\right)\hat{A}_T - \hat{A}_N\right] - \left(\frac{\beta}{\alpha}\right)^{*}\hat{A}_T^{*} - \hat{A}_N^{*}\right) \tag{1}$$

with $\hat{Q} \equiv \hat{p} - \hat{p}^{*}$.

This is the same as:

$$\hat{Q} = \delta\left(\left[\left(\frac{\beta}{\alpha}\right)\hat{A}_T - A_T^{*}\right] - \hat{A}_N - \hat{A}_N^{*}\right) \tag{1.1}$$

If we let $\hat{M}_0 = -\delta(\hat{A}_N - \hat{A}_N^{*})$ and $m_1 = \delta\left(\frac{\beta}{\alpha}\right)$, then:

$$\hat{Q} = \hat{A}_0 + m_1(\hat{A}_T - \hat{A}_T^{*}) \tag{1.2}$$

In levels form, this is equivalent to:

$$Q = M_0 \left(A_T/A_T^*\right)^{m_1} \tag{1.3}$$

and in log-levels, it is

$$q = m_0 + m_1 ln\left(A_T/A_T^*\right) \tag{1.4}$$

where $q \equiv \ln Q \, and \, m_0 \equiv \ln M_0$

We proxy A_T/A_T^* with Y/Y^* where Y is the home real GDP per capita and Y^* is the foreign (US) real GDP per capita, so we get Eq. (2.23).

$$q = m_0 + m_1 (lnY/Y^*) \tag{1.5}$$

Annexure 2

See Tables 12.5, 12.6, 12.7, 12.8, 12.9, and 12.10

Table 12.5 Descriptive statistics (all countries)

Statistics	$\ln(Q)$	$\ln(Y/Y^*)$	$\ln(G/G^*)$	$\text{vol}(E)$
Mean	−0.6737	−2.7011	0.9462	0.4726
Median	−0.6646	−2.7219	1.1813	0.0424
Maximum	0.4235	−0.4348	2.8605	45.552
Minimum	−1.6263	−4.6914	−2.2488	0.0000
Std. dev.	0.3675	0.7907	0.9795	2.8547
Skewness	0.2293	0.0585	−0.7068	11.761
Kurtosis	2.7686	2.5192	2.9466	164.64
Jarque–Bera	9.1598	8.4988	69.465	909407
Probability	0.0102	0.0143	0.0000	0.0000
Sum	−561.22	−2250.0	788.16	386.62
Sum sq. dev.	112.38	520.19	798.28	6658.1
Observations	833	833	833	818

Table 12.6 Descriptive statistics (by country)

Country	ln(Q)		ln(Y/Y^*)		ln(G/G^*)		Vol(E)		Obs.
	Mean	Std. dev.	Mean	Std. dev.	Mean	Std. dev.	Mean	Std. dev.	
Angola	−0.4650	0.2996	−2.2869	0.4128	1.5568	0.5088	3.4174	10.3081	41
Brazil	−0.3824	0.3295	−1.8292	0.2390	0.4919	0.6321	1.8454	4.5140	61
China	−0.8927	0.3308	−2.7127	0.4237	1.4123	0.2741	0.0474	0.0861	59
Ethiopia	−0.6491	0.3398	−3.8203	0.3501	1.0952	0.4464	0.0434	0.1172	61
Ghana	−0.4949	0.2539	−2.7498	0.4530	−0.0584	1.0071	0.2148	0.2427	56
India	−0.9066	0.2218	−2.9414	0.2323	1.1495	0.5007	0.0528	0.0688	61
Indonesia	−0.9281	0.2891	−2.5105	0.1529	1.0049	0.7692	0.6411	2.5342	51
Kenya	−0.6909	0.2801	−2.8806	0.3690	0.5182	0.6943	0.0628	0.1158	61
Nigeria	−0.4329	0.5292	−2.7153	1.0063	0.9769	1.0085	0.1322	0.2678	61
The Philippines	−0.6683	0.3533	−2.3381	0.1450	0.7938	0.7134	0.0769	0.1468	61
Russia	−0.9519	0.2779	−1.1607	0.3472	1.7785	0.3746	1.5517	3.5475	21
Rwanda	−0.9272	0.2395	−3.3872	0.3605	1.5705	0.9514	0.0867	0.1667	51
South Africa	−0.4349	0.1711	−1.4829	0.2699	−0.8529	0.4004	0.0757	0.1007	61
Tanzania	−0.7518	0.2005	−3.3301	0.4605	2.0835	0.4700	0.1328	0.2058	51
Uganda	−0.7283	0.3749	−3.4294	0.4039	1.6334	0.2242	0.2552	0.4379	61
All	−0.6737	0.3675	−2.7011	0.7907	0.9462	0.9795	0.4726	2.8547	818

Table 12.7 Cross-sectional dependence tests

Tests	Non-augmented model	Augmented model
Breusch-Pagan LM	235.4183***	145.5989***
Pesaran scaled LM	7.964616***	1.766490*
Bias-corrected scaled LM	7.837498***	1.639371
Pesaran CD	11.56950***	−0.781383

Note Null hypothesis: no cross-sectional dependence (correlation)
Note ***, and * refer to significance level at 1, and 10%.

Annexure 3

See Tables 12.11 and 12.12

Table 12.8 Panel unit root tests (IPS and Fisher-type tests)

Variables	Specifications	Pesaran statistics	Fisher statistics	Order of integration
$\ln(Q)$	Constant	−1.0567	32.73	$I(1)$
	Constant and trend	1.6161	21.13	
$\Delta \ln(Q)$	Constant	−21.07***	401.23***	$I(0)$
	Constant and trend	−20.07***	344.39***	
$\ln(Y/Y^*)$	Constant	−0.3133	34.84	I(1)
	Constant and trend	3.3929	21.69	
$\Delta \ln(Y/Y^*)$	Constant	−16.22***	296.62***	$I(0)$
	Constant and trend	−19.43***	327.62***	
$\ln(G/G^*)$	Constant	−0.9245	32.50	$I(1)$
	Constant and trend	0.6120	26.57	
$\Delta \ln(Y/Y^*)$	Constant	−19.99***	377.62***	$I(0)$
	Constant and trend	−19.23***	350.83***	
$\mathrm{vol}(E)$	Constant	−13.74***	246.72***	$I(0)$
	Constant and trend	−16.07	230.49	

Note *** indicates the rejection of the null hypothesis (unit root) at 1%

Table 12.9 Results of co-integration tests

Model	IPS test		ADF test		PP test	
	Non-augmented	Augmented	Non-augmented	Augmented	Non-augmented	Augmented
Model I	−19.15***	−22.18***	356.99***	427.72***	353.95***	430.16***
Model II	−18.13***	−22.00***	339.99***	426.95***	351.52***	499.48***
Model II	−17.36***	−20.75***	314.36***	392.64***	317.27***	409.21***

Note *** indicates rejection of the null hypothesis (unit root/no co-integration) at 1%

Table 12.10 Model selection criteria

Model type	Log *L*	AIC*	BIC	HQ	Specification
I	822.9247	−1.8213	−1.3725	−1.6491	ARDL (1, 1)
II	858.6465	−1.8304	−1.1975	−1.5875	ARDL (1, 1, 1)
III	920.9778	−1.9800	−1.2444	−1.6975	ARDL (1, 1, 1, 1)

Note * refer to significance level at 10%.

Table 12.11 Panel co-integration estimation: pooled mean group estimator (*MICs* = 5 countries)

Cases	Model type	Adjustment coefficient	Long-run coefficients					
			$\ln(Q)$ = dependent variable					
			$\overline{\ln(Q)}$	$\ln(Y/Y^*)$	$\overline{\ln(Y/Y^*)}$	$\ln(G/G^*)$	$\overline{\ln(G/G^*)}$	vol(E)
All countries	I		0.7986 (0.3929)	0.1090 (0.1518)	−0.2792 (0.4087)			
	II		2.5721*** (0.6182)	0.3823** (0.1609)	−2.0355** (0.7849)	0.2209* (0.1203)	−1.0014*** (0.2819)	
	III		3.0730*** (0.5858)	0.3447** (0.1490)	−2.2913*** (0.7061)	0.2521*** (0.0926)	−0.8858*** (0.2532)	0.0248** (0.0126)
Short-run coefficients								
			$\Delta\ \ln(Q)$ = *dependent variable*					
			$\overline{\Delta\ln(Q)}$	$\Delta\ \ln(Y/Y^*)$	$\overline{\Delta\ \ln(Y/Y^*)}$	$\Delta\ \ln(G/G^*)$	$\overline{\Delta\ \ln(G/G^*)}$	Δ vol(E)
All countries	I	−0.1673*** (0.0682)	1.1840*** (0.2976)	−0.3002*** (0.0825)	0.1930 (0.1433)			
	II	−0.1936*** (0.10272)	0.9115*** (0.1791)	−0.4084*** (0.1331)	0.2804 (0.2339)	−0.0827 (0.0734)	0.1863*** (0.0612)	
	III	−0.1224*** (0.0372)	0.8424*** (0.1041)	−0.3974*** (0.0825)	0.1953** (0.0869)	−0.0577* (0.0309)	0.0648 (0.0663)	−0.1613*** (0.0387)
Brazil	I	−0.0940*** (0.0026)	1.5177*** (0.0929)	0.0801 (0.0812)	−0.1346 (0.0974)			
	II	−0.1458*** (0.0044)	1.2512*** (0.1148)	0.0152 (0.0927)	−0.1126 (0.0964)	−0.0096 (0.0059)	0.0453 (0.0435)	
	III	−0.2276*** (0.0044)	1.0306*** (0.1047)	0.2286* (0.0969)	−0.0875 (0.0865)	−0.0883*** (0.0060)	0.2952** (0.0529)	−0.0021*** (0.0001)

(continued)

Table 12.11 (continued)

Cases	Model type	Adjustment coefficient	Long-run coefficients					
			$\ln(Q)$ = dependent variable					
			$\overline{\ln(Q)}$	$\ln(Y/Y^*)$	$\overline{\ln(Y/Y^*)}$	$\ln(G/G^*)$	$\overline{\ln(G/G^*)}$	vol(E)
China	I	−0.0625*** (0.0012)	0.7314*** (0.0440)	−0.5448*** (0.0166)	0.1722* (0.0610)			
	II	−0.0933*** (0.0011)	0.5149*** (0.0416)	−0.5655*** (0.0143)	0.1126 (0.0523)	−0.1301*** (0.0076)	0.2787*** (0.0293)	
	III	−0.0647*** (0.0006)	0.5464*** (0.0344)	−0.5913*** (0.0121)	0.1947** (0.0438)	−0.1015*** (0.0063)	0.2244*** (0.0242)	−0.3549*** (0.0075)
India	I	−0.0883*** (0.0019)	0.6518*** (0.0235)	−0.4247*** (0.0294)	0.1166** (0.0267)			
	II	−0.0488*** (0.0011)	0.6234*** (0.0301)	−0.3918*** (0.0327)	0.1173** (0.0271)	0.0029 (0.0091)	0.1059*** (0.0129)	
	III	−0.0468*** (0.0008)	0.5813*** (0.0267)	−0.4483*** (0.0268)	0.1445*** (0.0229)	0.0156 (0.0086)	0.0836*** (0.0112)	−0.3010*** (0.0067)
Russia	I	−0.4328*** (0.0122)	2.2026*** (0.1078)	−0.2004*** (0.0308)	0.7271* (0.3085)			
	II	−0.5998*** (0.0173)	1.4202*** (0.2234)	−0.7845*** (0.0570)	1.2003** (0.3171)	−0.3464*** (0.0124)	0.3769** (0.1013)	
	III	−0.5625*** (0.0152)	1.3547*** (0.1719)	−0.4439*** (0.0452)	1.1735** (0.3029)	−0.4515*** (0.0100)	0.3237** (0.0646)	0.0065*** (0.0001)
South Africa	I	−0.1589*** (0.0051)	0.8167*** (0.0582)	−0.2509* (0.1060)	0.0837 (0.0756)			
	II	−0.0806*** (0.0015)	0.7475*** (0.0622)	−0.3152 (0.1463)	0.0843 (0.0773)	0.0696 (0.0426)	0.1248** (0.0356)	
	III	−0.0787*** (0.0015)	0.6452*** (0.0548)	−0.1949 (0.1515)	−0.0028 (0.0679)	0.0395 (0.0588)	0.2259*** (0.0306)	−0.3733*** (0.0097)

Note ***, **, and * refer to significance level at 1, 5, and 10%. Standard errors in parentheses

Table 12.12 Panel co-integration estimation: pooled mean group estimator (*LICs* = 10 countries)

Cases	Model type	Adjustment coefficient	Long-run coefficients					
			$\ln(Q)$ = dependent variable					
			$\overline{\ln(Q)}$	$\ln(Y/Y^*)$	$\overline{\ln(Y/Y^*)}$	$\ln(G/G^*)$	$\overline{\ln(G/G^*)}$	vol(E)
All countries	I		0.3168 (0.2237)	0.3205* (0.1324)	0.8329*** (0.2129)			
	II		0.6872*** (0.2259)	0.2112** (0.0986)	0.3854 (0.2512)	0.1407*** (0.0418)	−0.3507*** (0.0959)	
	III		1.0669*** (0.2127)	−0.2873*** (0.0867)	0.2720 (0.2552)	0.0109 (0.0495)	−0.0182 (0.1282)	−3.2161*** (0.4192)
			Short-run coefficients					
			$\Delta \ln(Q)$ = *dependent variable*					
			$\overline{\Delta \ln(Q)}$	$\Delta \ln(Y/Y^*)$	$\overline{\Delta \ln(Y/Y^*)}$	$\Delta \ln(G/G^*)$	$\overline{\Delta \ln(G/G^*)}$	Δ vol(E)
All countries	I	−0.1117*** (0.0272)	0.7647*** (0.1003)	−0.3522*** (0.1180)	0.2879** (0.1313)			
	II	−0.1413*** (0.0367)	0.7635*** (0.1032)	−0.3648*** (0.1366)	0.2653** (0.1351)	−0.0429 (0.0326)	−0.0144 (0.1094)	
	III	−0.0863*** (0.0248)	0.5631*** (0.1294)	−0.4239*** (0.0992)	0.1896 (0.1162)	−0.0168 (0.0287)	0.0173 (0.0951)	−0.0203 (0.0313)
Angola	I	−0.1021*** (0.0129)	0.8559** (0.2088)	−0.2539** (0.0445)	0.6178** (0.3376)			
	II	−0.1835*** (0.0105)	1.0438*** (0.1673)	−0.2890*** (0.0349)	0.6206** (0.2624)	−0.1326*** (0.0049)	−0.7164*** (0.0993)	
	III	−0.0015*** (0.0001)	0.9369*** (0.1255)	−0.3725*** (0.0259)	0.4225 (0.1812)	−0.1717** (0.0039)	−0.5855** (0.0886)	−0.0059*** (0.0001)

(continued)

Table 12.12 (continued)

Cases	Model type	Adjustment coefficient	Long-run coefficients					
			$\ln(Q)$ = dependent variable					
			$\overline{\ln(Q)}$	$\ln(Y/Y^*)$	$\overline{\ln(Y/Y^*)}$	$\ln(G/G^*)$	$\overline{\ln(G/G^*)}$	vol(E)
Ethiopia	I	−0.3364*** (0.0034)	0.5018*** (0.0332)	−0.9714*** (0.0187)	0.3830*** (0.0419)	0.3830*** (0.0419)		
	II	−0.4113*** (0.0031)	0.4470*** (0.0291)	−1.1079*** (0.0161)	0.4443*** (0.0334)	−0.1390*** (0.0028)	0.1123*** (0.0161)	
	III	−0.1363*** (0.0006)	0.3654*** (0.0279)	−0.8169*** (0.0157)	0.3477*** (0.0343)	−0.038*** (0.0029)	0.1337*** (0.0192)	0.0657*** (0.0075)
Ghana	I	−0.1228*** (0.0032)	0.3116** (0.0722)	−0.7780*** (0.0433)	0.7832*** (0.0938)			
	II	−0.2304*** (0.0046)	0.2622** (0.0696)	−0.8854*** (0.0518)	0.6431*** (0.0870)	−0.0894*** (0.0034)	0.1710** (0.0427)	
	III	−0.0948*** (0.0006)	0.0931 (0.0470)	−0.6913*** (0.0350)	0.3100** (0.0622)	0.0335*** (0.0023)	−0.079616* (0.025340)	−0.0424*** (0.0027)
Indonesia	I	−0.1386*** (0.0043)	0.8098*** (0.1281)	0.2978** (0.0631)	0.5774** (0.1625)			
	II	−0.1571*** (0.0050)	0.8070*** (0.1307)	0.3864** (0.0765)	0.4926* (0.1635)	0.0454** (0.0103)	−0.0530 (0.0744)	
	III	0.0001*** (0.0001)	0.8071*** (0.1249)	−0.0061 (0.0866)	0.6202** (0.1609)	0.0672*** (0.0109)	0.0295 (0.0685)	−0.0172 (0.0001)
Kenya	I	−0.1036*** (0.0025)	1.0582*** (0.0396)	−0.4606*** (0.0340)	0.1793** (0.0450)			
	II	−0.1197*** (0.0033)	1.0269*** (0.0374)	−0.4043*** (0.0334)	0.1692** (0.0443)	0.0740*** (0.0037)	−0.1535*** (0.0211)	
	III	−0.2489*** (0.0015)	0.2617*** (0.0133)	−0.1214*** (0.0129)	−0.0381* (0.0124)	0.1122*** (0.0009)	−0.0537*** (0.0074)	0.1646*** (0.0034)

(continued)

Table 12.12 (continued)

Cases	Model type	Adjustment coefficient	Long-run coefficients					
			$\ln(Q)$ = dependent variable					
			$\overline{\ln(Q)}$	$\ln(Y/Y^*)$	$\overline{\ln(Y/Y^*)}$	$\ln(G/G^*)$	$\overline{\ln(G/G^*)}$	vol(E)
Nigeria	I	−0.0364*** (0.0002)	0.8468*** (0.0885)	−0.4929*** (0.0112)	0.8597*** (0.1219)			
	II	−0.0277*** (0.0002)	0.7961*** (0.0832)	−0.5074*** (0.0106)	0.9467*** (0.1138)	−0.0155*** (0.0011)	0.5019*** (0.0436)	
	III	−0.0424*** (0.0002)	0.7329*** (0.0613)	−0.6329*** (0.0091)	0.7799*** (0.0850)	−0.0203*** (0.0008)	0.5929*** (0.0378)	−0.1253*** (0.0024)
The Philippines	I	−0.1089*** (0.0036)	0.6733*** (0.0759)	−0.2433** (0.0713)	−0.1986* (0.0830)			
	II	−0.1138*** (0.0045)	0.7101*** (0.0724)	−0.3810** (0.0716)	−0.1423 (0.0821)	0.1328*** (0.0141)	−0.3828*** (0.0469)	
	III	−0.1458*** (0.0006)	0.3199*** (0.0226)	−0.6470*** (0.0226)	0.1060** (0.0239)	0.0542*** (0.0039)	−0.0446* (0.0158)	−0.0895*** (0.0024)
Rwanda	I	−0.0665*** (0.0008)	0.8509*** (0.0487)	−0.4273*** (0.0069)	−0.0079 (0.0531)			
	II	−0.1001*** (0.0018)	0.7458*** (0.0559)	−0.4331*** (0.0071)	−0.0645 (0.0540)	−0.0098* (0.0035)	−0.0204 (0.0313)	
	III	−0.0754*** (0.0005)	0.7087*** (0.0363)	−0.3457*** (0.0053)	−0.1616** (0.0416)	−0.0128** (0.0024)	0.0278 (0.0235)	−0.0287*** (0.0029)
Tanzania	I	−0.0505*** (0.0019)	0.3739*** (0.0578)	−0.2922*** (0.0151)	−0.0059 (0.0659)			
	II	−0.0359*** (0.0024)	0.4408*** (0.0572)	−0.0900** (0.0263)	−0.0628 (0.0658)	−0.1428*** (0.0058)	0.1009** (0.0306)	
	III	−0.1073*** (0.0003)	0.0668** (0.0195)	−0.6651*** (0.0133)	−0.1276** (0.0238)	−0.0412*** (0.0021)	−0.1234*** (0.0102)	−0.1776*** (0.0030)

(continued)

Table 12.12 (continued)

Cases	Model type	Adjustment coefficient	Long-run coefficients					
			$\ln(Q)$ = dependent variable					
			$\overline{\ln(Q)}$	$\ln(Y/Y^*)$	$\overline{\ln(Y/Y^*)}$	$\ln(G/G^*)$	$\overline{\ln(G/G^*)}$	vol(E)
Uganda	I	−0.0512*** (0.0005)	1.3649*** (0.0555)	0.0995* (0.0325)	−0.3089** (0.0661)			
	II	−0.0335*** (0.0004)	1.3547*** (0.0526)	0.0635 (0.0314)	−0.3939*** (0.0651)	−0.1529*** (0.0069)	0.2964*** (0.0228)	
	III	−0.0103*** (0.0001)	1.3388*** (0.0542)	0.0593 (0.0329)	−0.3629** (0.0673)	−0.1504*** (0.0078)	0.2763*** (0.0276)	0.0533*** (0.0021)

$\ln(Q)$ = log of real exchange rate, $\ln(Y/Y^*)$ = log of real GDP relative to foreign (US), $\ln(G/G^*)$ = log of real government expenditure relative to foreign (US), vol(E) exchange rate volatility, $\overline{\ln(Q)}$ = log of real exchange rate demeaned, $\overline{\ln(Y/Y^*)}$ = log of real GDP relative to foreign (US) demeaned, and $\overline{\ln(G/G^*)}$ = log of real government expenditure relative to foreign (US) demeaned

***, **, and * refer to significance level at 1, 5, and 10. Standard errors in parentheses

References

Ahn M (2009) Looking for the Balassa-Samuelson effect in real exchange rate changes: Andong National University. J Econ Res 14:219–237

Asea K, Corden M (1994a) The Balassa-Samuelson model: an overview. USA

Asea K, Mendoza G (1994b) The Balassa-Samuelson model: a general equilibrium appraisal. Review of International Economics, Working Paper #709

Balassa B (1964) The purchasing power parity doctrine: a reappraisal. J Polit Econ 72(6):584–596

Baylie F (2008) The impact of real effective exchange rate on the economic growth of Ethiopia. Master thesis, Addis Ababa University, Ethiopia

Bhagwati N (1984) Why are services cheaper in the poor countries? The Econ J 94(374)

Bhattarai K (2011) Co-integration and error correction models: econometric analysis. Hull University, Business School, England

Cavalcanti V, Mohaddes K, Raissi M (2011) Commodity price volatility and the sources of growth. IMF Working Paper, Middle East and Central Asia Department

Chen M (2013) Panel unit root and co-integration tests. National Chung Hsing University, USA

Chuah P (2012) How real exchange rate move in growing economies: Anti-Balassa evidence in developing countries. Malaysia

Chuoudhri E, Kahn S (2004) Real exchange rate in developing countries: are Balassa-Samuelson effect present? IMF Working Papers WP/04/188

De Gregorio J, Wolf H (1994) Terms of trade, productivity and the real exchange rate. NBER Working Paper No. 4407

Drine I, Rault C (2002) Do panel data permit to rescue the Balassa-Samuelson hypothesis for latin American countries? An empirical analysis using panel data co-integration tests. William Davidson Working Paper Number 504

Drine I, Rault C (2004) Does the Balassa-Samuelson hold for Asian countries? An empirical analysis using panel data co-integration tests. Appl Econ Int Dev 4(4):000

Eberhardt M (2011) Panel time-series modelling: new tools for analyzing xt-data. University of Nottingham, Case Business School, England

Eberhardt M (2012) Estimating Panel Time Series Models with Heterogeneous Slopes. Stata Journal 12 (1):61–71

Engle R, Granger C (1987) Co-integration and error correction: representation, estimation, and testing. Econometrica 55(2):251–276

Feenstra R, Inklaar R, Timmer M (2013) The next generation of the penn world table. Am Econ Rev 105(10):3150–3182

Guo Q, Hall G (2008) A test of the Balassa-Samuelson effect applied to Chinese regional data. Rom J Econ Forecast 2:57–78

Hassan F (2011) The Penn-Balassa-Samuelson effect in developing countries: price and income revisited. London School of Economics and Political Science, London

Herberger C (2003) Economic growth and the real exchange rate: revising the Balassa-Samuelson effect. University of California, Los Angeles

IMF (2015) World Economic Outlook Report. IMF

Isard P, Symansky S (1996) Long-run movements in real exchange rates. IMF Occasional Paper No. 145

Jabeen S, Malik S, Haider A (2011) Testing the Harrod-Balassa-Samuelson hypothesis: the case of Pakistan. Quaid-i-Azam University, Islamabad

Kohler M (1998) The Balassa-Samuelson effect and monetary targets. Centre for Central Banking Studies, Bank of England

Kravis B, Lipsey E (1983) Towards an explanation of national price levels. Princeton Studies in International Finance, No. 52, Princeton University, USA

Kumo W (2011) Growth and macroeconomic convergence in Southern Africa. African Development Bank Group, Working Paper No. 130

Maddala S, Wu S (1999) A comparative study of unit root tests with panel data and a new simple test. Oxford Bull Econ Stat 61:631–652

Miyajima K (2005) Real exchange rates in growing economies: how strong is the role of the nontradables sector? IMF Working Paper No. 05/233

Orlik A (2003) Real convergence and its different measures; lessons to be learnt by EMU applicant countries

Pedroni P (2004) Panel co-integration; asymptotic and finite sample properties of pooled time series tests with an application to the PPP hypothesis. Econ Theor 28:597–625

Pesaran H (2007) A simple panel unit root test in the presence of cross-section dependence. J Appl Econ 22(2):265–312

Pesaran H (2013) Large panel data models with cross-sectional dependence: a survey. Unpublished, Cambridge, UK

Podkaminer L (2003) Analytical notes on the Balassa-Samuelson effect. BNL Q Rev 226

Rogoff K (1996) The purchasing power puzzle. J Econ Lit XXXIV: 647–668

Shin Y (2014) Dynamic panel data workshop. University of Melbourne

Soukiazis E (1995) The endogeneity of factor inputs and the importance of balance of payments on growth: an empirical study for the OECD countries with special reference to Greece and Portugal. unpublished PhD dissertation, University of Kent, Canterbury

Tica J, Druzic I (2006) The Harrod-Balassa-Samuelson effect: a survey of empirical evidence. University of Zagreb, Zagreb

Wilson E (2010) European real effective exchange rate and total factor productivity: an empirical study. Victoria University of Wellington, New Zealand

Part V
Growth, Productivity and Efficiency in Various Industries

Chapter 13
Agricultural Tax Responsiveness and Economic Growth in Ethiopia

Hassen Azime, Gollagari Ramakrishna and Melesse Asfaw

Abstract Of late, the pattern of tax revenues and its nexus with economic growth in developing countries become an increasing concern for policy framers and researchers. Since tax revenue is one of the important sources of government revenue, a tax policy assumes significance as a vehicle for a viable and long-term source of revenue and economic growth. Similarly, economic growth has augmenting effects on the tax revenue of a country. This study investigates tax responsiveness to the changes in gross domestic product in Ethiopia in the period 1981–2014. It mainly focuses on the components of agricultural tax revenue: agricultural income tax and land use fee. In addition, it also studies personal income tax and business profit income. Understanding and analyzing the level of sensitivity of tax revenue to discretionary policy measures and GDP are essential in formulating fiscal policy. The empirical evidence on Ethiopia suggests that the trends in agricultural income tax and land use fee collection are highly inconsistent. Agricultural income tax and land use fee are not buoyant, indicating that the growth of the agricultural sector has no statistically significant impact on agricultural income tax buoyancy. However, personal income tax revenue, business profit revenue, and total direct tax revenue are responsive to changes in non-agricultural GDP in Ethiopia. In light of these findings, some policy interventions for improving tax revenue are suggested.

Keywords Tax buoyancy · Tax elasticity · Agricultural tax revenue · Direct tax revenue

---

H. Azime (✉)
Institute of Tax and Customs Administration, Department of Public Finance
Ethiopian Civil Service University, Addis Ababa, Ethiopia
e-mail: azimeadem@gmail.com

G. Ramakrishna · M. Asfaw
School of Graduate Studies, Ethiopian Civil Service University, Addis Ababa, Ethiopia
e-mail: profgrk@gmail.com

M. Asfaw
e-mail: drmelesse@gmail.com

A. Heshmati (ed.), *Studies on Economic Development and Growth in Selected African Countries*, Frontiers in African Business Research,
DOI 10.1007/978-981-10-4451-9_13

13.1 Introduction

Several studies have emphasized the importance of tax revenue in promoting economic development. In a recent study, Feger and Asafu-Adjaye (2014) conclude that in order to advance development, governments are required to spend more on public services and this can be achieved by improving tax revenue mobilization. A similar opinion was expressed by Besley and Ghatak (2006) when they wrote, ‘the different public goods such as availability of clean drinking water, sewage disposal, transportations, health care, and primary and secondary schools are the necessity for well-being as well as an input for increasing the productivity.’ Even though the main purpose of taxation is financing public goods and services, the tax policy should be based on certain fiscal principles. In this connection, Tanzi and Zee (2000) emphasize that a tax system should be guided by the equity principle that stipulates that taxpayers should only pay what is deemed to be their fair share of taxes. Additionally, the tax administration should have certain efficiency objectives whereby the government collects sufficient revenues to carry out its welfare and development goals. Therefore, while designing a tax system, it is important that the equity principle and the efficiency objectives do not come in direct conflict with each other.

Economic development, particularly rural development in countries such as Ethiopia, requires substantial financial investments in infrastructure, education, health, and other social services. A fiscal policy instrument of an economic system needs to fund public expenditure from the domestic economy in a larger proportion. One important source for meeting these investment needs is tax revenue.

Sub-Saharan African countries are facing several challenges in augmenting their tax collections (Sanjeev and Tareq 2008). Rural development in these countries largely depends on the contribution of the agricultural sector, and thus, the tax revenue raised in this sector also plays a major role in economic development. The main purpose of our study is to examine the responsiveness of agricultural tax revenue to growth in the agricultural component of Ethiopia’s GDP. This revenue is the legal levy imposed on farmers on their incomes generated through agricultural activities as well as the fee imposed on the land owned. Empirical evidence on this issue, more particularly on Ethiopia, is limited as well as mixed and does not provide comprehensive and conclusive evidence. Our paper tries to fill this gap.

Tax revenue responsiveness to changes in the economic activity of a country affects its revenue mobilization efforts. In theory, tax revenue is said to increase with economic growth based on the assumption that the tax base grows as GDP increases (Milwood 2011). Increase in revenue during a particular fiscal year may occur either due to an effect of changes in the tax policy or as a result of a natural increase in tax revenue because of an increase in GDP. The responsiveness of tax revenue to changes in GDP is usually measured by two concepts: tax elasticity and tax buoyancy. The first concept measures the extent to which a tax structure generates revenue in response to increases in taxpayer incomes without a change in statutory tax rates (Bunescu and Comaniciu 2013; Craig and Heins 1980).

The second concept is defined as the overall reaction of tax revenue to changes in GDP and discretionary changes in the tax policy over time. It is a measure of how tax revenue varies with changes in GDP. Tax revenue is therefore expected to increase as the economy grows, that is, the level of estimation is how far the tax revenue reacts to changes in GDP. Tax buoyancy measures can be used to assess the efficiency of a given tax system regarding its revenue generation capacity (Jenkins et al. 2000). Knowledge of this measure is important in decision making about the fiscal policy of a country because it allows us to determine the evolution of the tax revenue collected by the government (Bunescu and Comaniciu 2013; Moreno and Maita 2014). Hence, tax buoyancy is a valuable method for analyzing the tax policy and examining the composition of a tax system.

The tax structures in developing countries should be responsive enough so as to enable the countries to meet their government spending for development. Thus, the main objective of our study was to examine the responsiveness of agricultural tax revenue and other tax revenues to the changes in economic growth in Ethiopia. More specifically, the paper has the following objectives:

- To estimate and analyze the responsiveness of agricultural income tax revenue and land use fee to changes in the agricultural component of GDP, and
- To estimate the responsiveness of personal income tax and business income tax revenue to changes in non-agricultural GDP.

The rest of the paper is organized as follows: The next section gives a brief overview of the tax structure in Ethiopia. In Sect. 13.3, a conceptual model and a brief review of earlier studies are presented. The data collection methods and the variables are presented in Sect. 13.4. Section 13.5 gives the data analysis and empirical findings. The last section gives a summary and conclusion.

13.2 An Overview of the Tax Structure in Ethiopia

This section presents an overview of the tax structure in Ethiopia across its two economic regimes: the state-led liberalized regime (1991 onward) and the socialist regime (1974–91) called the Derg regime. Under both the regimes, the Ethiopian tax system consisted of direct and indirect taxes. Direct taxes include agricultural income, land use fee, personal income, rental income, business profit, interest income, and capital gain tax while indirect taxes include value-added tax (VAT), turnover tax, excises, stamp duties, customs duties, and export taxes.

During the socialist regime, the government controlled all economic spheres including agriculture. The land reform policy of 1975 nationalized land and took another step of distributing land equally among peasants. Consequently, the peasants were forced to establish and organize themselves into peasant associations (Prichard 2015). Smallholder farmers in Ethiopia depend on small acres of land that is owned or rented to generate income. The term 'agricultural taxation' used in our study includes only taxes paid by the farmers. So the smallholder farmers' burden of taxes is from agriculture income tax and land use fee.

During the socialist regime, the objective of agricultural tax was transferring a substantial portion of the agricultural surplus to industry. As a result, the government taxed the agricultural sector heavily. In particular, the agricultural income tax rate was progressive and was as high as 89% in the highest income bracket. Taxation on exports of the main crop reached as high as 100% of the farm gate price (Rashid et al. 2007).

Because of the change of government in Ethiopia in 1991, the country witnessed a shift in the policy regime. Different reforms were initiated in 1992. These included new legislations for earnings tax, business income tax, rural land, and agricultural income tax (Alemayehu and Shimeles 2005). During 1992, agricultural taxes were not collected because of the transition period and difficulties in collecting taxes from farmers. Since 1992, IMF and the World Bank have supported Ethiopia in liberalizing its economy and implementing structural adjustment programs (SAPs) to address the internal and external imbalances in the economy.

The government has initiated different reforms to liberalize its economy. It undertook comprehensive tax reforms encompassing most of the principal revenue sources. Along with the reforms in the tax system, the liberalization policies were also extended to monetary policy tools, foreign and domestic trade, production, and distribution (Geda and Shimeles 2005). The major goals of the tax reforms initiated during this regime included increasing the tax base, improving tax collection, tax incentives for the private sector, and dealing with equity in taxation.

13.2.1 The Current Agricultural Tax Structure in Ethiopia

Agricultural income tax is one of the most sensitive features of income taxation in general. In most developing countries, governments impose taxes on agricultural income, but it is hard to determine the income of smallholder farmers and to reach income earners. These difficulties are due to the large number of small units of income generation, the absence of accounting procedures suited to income taxation, the fluctuating nature of agricultural productivity and profits, and low levels of education.

Ethiopia amended its 1978 agricultural income tax rates in 1995 and 1997. Moreover, annual revenue exceeding birr[1] 1200 was subjected to a progressive tax rate. Agricultural income tax rates imposed by the regional states with the provision of the constitution were wide ranging from 5 to 40%. Agricultural income taxation was based on the size of the landholding rather than the amount of annual agricultural production. For instance, the Oromia regional state (the largest and most populous region in Ethiopia) initially adopted a progressive agricultural income tax system but replaced it with an agricultural income tax system based on the size of the landholding, rather than the amount of agricultural produce (ONRS 2002, 2005).

[1]Birr is the currency used in Ethiopia. Currently, one (1) USD is equal to about 22.24 birr.

The agricultural income tax rate, exemption limits, and assessment differ slightly across regions. Each region levying the tax has its statutes with specific provisions for determining taxable incomes.

13.2.2 Land Use Fee

In principle, land taxes are less complex as compared to agricultural income tax because assessment of land tax requires the total area of the land, its location, and type of land grade; suitability for irrigation; land fertility; and rural transportation for a market. As Newbery (1987) has suggested, this information might not be too costly to collect. Based on this information, it would be possible to design a simple presumptive tax structure for land tax (Sarris 1994).

According to the amended proclamation number 77/1997 of income tax for land use and agricultural activities, smallholder farmers in the regional states are taxed birr 10 for the first hectare and birr 7.5 for each extra half hectare (Geda and Shimeles 2005). In some regions, the area of land and the land classification system that is based on relative soil fertility estimates determine the level of taxation. During 2004–14, the total rural area cultivated and expanded for agricultural purposes increased by 2.7% per year and the number of smallholder farmers increased by 3.8%. The total agricultural output level also increased during this period (Bachewe et al. 2015; Moller 2015).

13.2.3 Agricultural Tax Revenue Growth

In macroeconomic terms, the level of tax revenue is measured relative to its GDP. Measuring the tax revenue in GDP compares the level of taxes collected to the tax base; this helps in evaluating the tax performance for a given tax base. Evidently, developing countries have fewer tax ratios to GDP when compared to developed countries. According to Besley and Persson (2014), developing countries collect taxes which are 10–20% of GDP, whereas developed countries on average raise around 40% of GDP. Similar to this, Ethiopia's tax revenue to its GDP is also low. Despite the government's tax revenue mobilization efforts, the total tax revenue-to-GDP ratio was 11.4% in 2009–10, and with some small fluctuations, it rose to 11.7% in 2013–14.

Although direct taxes increased from 0.02 in 2009–10 to 0.022 in 2013–14, Fig. 13.1 indicates that the ratio of direct taxes to GDP declined steadily. Indirect tax revenues were twice as high as direct taxes in most years, and Fig. 13.1 shows that the ratio of indirect taxes to GDP increased steadily. This is in line with the findings of Feger and Asafu-Adjaye (2014), who concluded that the tax structure in sub-Saharan Africa (SSA) is skewed toward indirect taxes because the existing structural, institutional, and policy characteristics in these countries are not

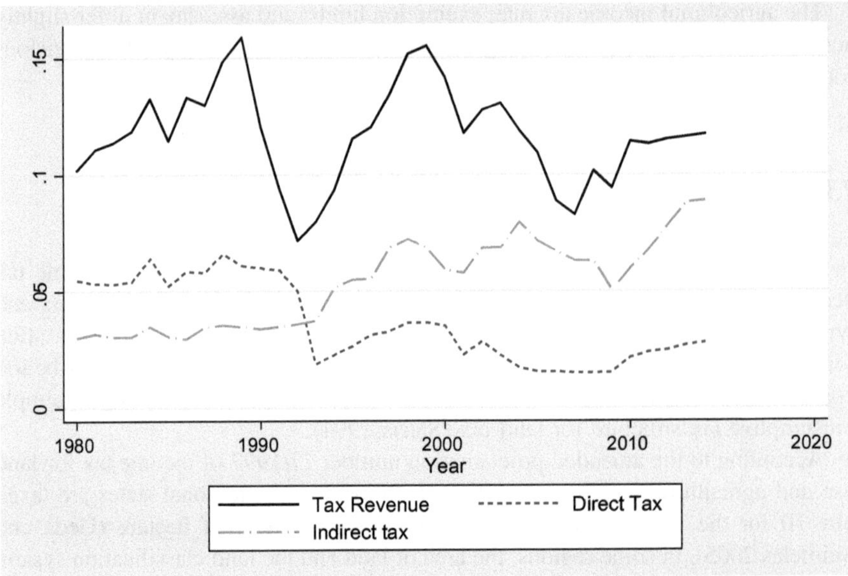

Fig. 13.1 Total tax revenue, direct and indirect tax as shares of GDP. *Source* Authors' computations using data from the Ministry of Finance and Economic Development (MOFED)

conducive to the collection of direct taxes. It is also argued that indirect taxes are less sensitive to these influences; hence, they can be collected with little effort and are relatively easy to administer (Khan 2001).

As depicted in Fig. 13.2, the agricultural tax revenue series shows a decline in revenue until 1992. Because of the change in regime during 1991–92, there was no assessment of agricultural tax revenue. The figure also shows that the tax ratio has

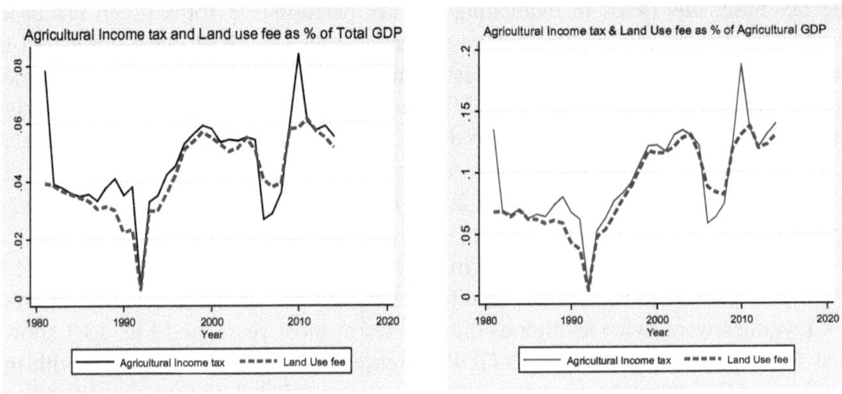

Fig. 13.2 Agricultural tax revenue as share of total GDP and agricultural GDP. *Source* Authors' computations using data from MOFED

fluctuated consistently in the last two decades in Ethiopia. In fact, the tax ratio trend is not stable, implying inconsistency in tax performance that could be due to fluctuations in GDP.

According to Feger and Asafu-Adjaye (2014), to date, total tax revenue collection in SSA countries has only averaged about 15% of GDP. However, in the case of Ethiopia, it is 11.5%, which is still below the SSA average amount. Moreover, the agricultural income tax collection efficiency in Ethiopia is not as broad-based as it should be. The efforts of the tax administration, capacity, and efficiency may have attributed to less progress in collecting the revenue generated from the agricultural tax income base. In 2003-04, the agricultural income tax revenue was 0.13% of agricultural GDP (0.06% of total GDP). It dropped to 0.07% of agricultural GDP in 2007–08 (0.03% of total GDP), but it picked up to 0.13% of agricultural GDP (0.08% of the total GDP) in the 2010–11 fiscal year.

Though agriculture remains the mainstay of the Ethiopian economy when it comes to employment and its contribution to GDP, its contribution to the total tax revenue collection is below 1%. Figure 13.3 shows the shares of personal income tax and business profit tax to GDP from 1981 to 2014. In 1981, personal income tax's revenue share was around 0.1% of GDP; its share grew to 2% of GDP in 2014. Business profit income tax also fluctuated but was still slightly higher than personal income tax until 2005. However, after this period, it increased moderately and its contribution reached a 3.5% share of GDP.

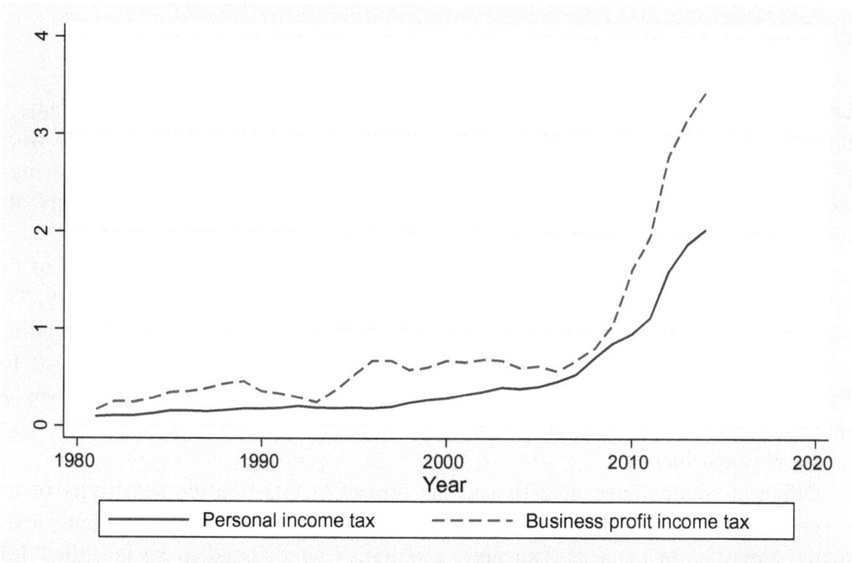

Fig. 13.3 Personal income tax and business profit income tax revenue as shares of total GDP. *Source* Authors' computations based on data from MOFED

13.3 The Conceptual Model and a Review of Earlier Studies

The need to measure tax responsiveness in relation to its revenue-generating capabilities can be seen in light of monitoring the progress of tax collections and tax revenue forecasting. Two measures for monitoring the government's revenue-generating capabilities have been formulated: tax buoyancy and tax elasticity. These two concepts measure the response of tax revenue to changes in income. According to Howard et al. (2009), this estimation of elasticity and buoyancy concepts has relevance in sub-Saharan African countries, where there is a considerable lag in tax collection and inefficiency given its potential for tax.

13.3.1 Tax Buoyancy

The buoyancy of a tax is estimated with the relative deviation in tax collection efforts, or it is a specific tax revenue item as compared to a change in the tax base. Thus, buoyancy is based on actual tax income and shows the changes in the tax structure, which may include tax rates, tax basis, and tax administration and compliance. Therefore, tax buoyancy is a measure of both the soundness of the tax base and the usefulness of tax changes regarding revenue collection.

13.3.2 Tax Elasticity

On the other hand, tax elasticity measures the automatic response of tax revenue to the evolution of the tax base. Tax elasticity does not include the effects of fiscal policy changes in the tax structure such as a change in tax rates, coverage, exemptions, and deductions or administration. Tax elasticity reflects only the built-in responsiveness of tax revenue to movements in the national income.

Both the tax buoyancy and elasticity concepts help analyze the capacity of the tax system in mobilizing revenue with and without changes in the tax policy. Tax buoyancy is a useful concept for measuring the performance of both the tax policy and tax administration over time whereas tax elasticity is a relevant factor for forecasting purposes (Jenkins et al. 2000). The tax elasticity coefficient gives an indication to policymakers on whether tax revenues will increase at the same pace as the national income.

Different studies have investigated the impact of GDP on the sensitivity of tax revenues for African countries. Among these, Osoro (1993) concluded that for the main categories of taxes in Tanzania, elasticities were found to be less than 1%. However, in comparison with buoyancy due to its discretionary changes, it became higher than the elasticity coefficient. Mawia and Nzomoi (2013) evaluated the tax buoyancy of different taxes in Kenya and found that tax revenue did not respond to economic changes except excise duty. Ahmed and Muhammad (2010) analyzed 25 countries for the period 1998–2008 and applied a pooled least squares analysis method. Their results show that growth in the agricultural sector had little impact on the efficiency of tax revenue and was also less responsive to revenue mobilization in the case of developing countries mainly due to difficulties in assessing the incomes generated and the low incomes that may not be taxed or may be under-taxed.

Other studies show that the agricultural share's contribution demonstrated a consistently negative impact on revenue collections, but tax revenue increased with trade share (Prichard 2015). Leuthold (1991) studied eight African countries by measuring the tax effort for the period 1973–81 in a panel data using the OLS estimation. The author argues that the agricultural share will affect the estimation coefficient of direct and indirect tax revenues negatively. His review suggests that evidence is not in favor of improving tax buoyancy in agriculture, and it also seems that there is no evidence available on Ethiopia. Studying the responsive elements of agricultural taxation in Ethiopia's current context is expected to provide an effective agricultural taxation system that enhances domestic revenue mobilization and rural investments, which can be used for stimulating development.

13.4 Estimation Methods and Data Collection

13.4.1 Estimation of Tax Buoyancy

Public finance policies in developing countries typically change tax parameters and structures from time to time. This affects 'revenue buoyancy.' According to Creedy and Gemmell (2001), the tax buoyancy estimation coefficient is the ratio of the observed increase in revenues to the observed increase in incomes. A tax is buoyant if revenue measures are increased in excess of 1% for a 1% increase in GDP or national income (Creedy and Gemmell 2008; McCluskey and Trinh 2013). More than 1% tax buoyancy will indicate a more proportionate increase in tax revenues compared to that of GDP. Therefore, tax buoyancy that includes discretionary changes is a measure of the efficiency of the tax base and the soundness of changes in the tax policy regarding revenue collection and mobilization.

According to Haughton (1998), tax buoyancy (TB) is formulated as the percentage change in tax revenue to the percentage change in the tax base:

$$\mathrm{TB} = \%\Delta\,\mathrm{Revenue}/\%\Delta\,\mathrm{base} \qquad (13.1)$$

where the base can be GDP, or the relative base can be considered. Revenue could refer to the different components of the total tax or individual taxes.

In our study, the focus is on two types of agricultural taxes: agricultural income tax (AgIT) and agricultural land tax or land use fee (AgLT):

$$\log \text{AgIT}_t = a_0 + a_1 + \log \text{AgrGDP}_t + \varepsilon \tag{13.2}$$

$$\log \text{AgLT}_t = a_0 + a_1 + \log \text{AgrGDP}_t + \varepsilon \tag{13.3}$$

where AgrGDP is agricultural gross domestic product and ε is a stochastic disturbance term. Since the variables are converted into their natural log forms, the coefficient estimates indicate tax buoyancy as they measure the percentage response in agricultural income tax and land use fee variables for a given 1% change in agricultural GDP.

In estimating the coefficient of buoyancy, no attempt is made to control for discretionary changes in the tax policy and administration. Discretionary tax measures refer to legal changes in tax rates, tax base, tax allowances and credits, and administrative tax efficiency. Consequently, buoyancy reflects both discretionary changes and anticipated revenue growth. It helps investigate whether growth in the agricultural sector has an impact on tax revenue.

13.4.2 Estimation of Tax Elasticity

Tax elasticity measures the extent to which a tax structure generates revenues in response to increases in taxpayer incomes without a change in statutory tax rates (Craig and Heins 1980). If a tax is to be elastic, a 1% increase in GDP may bring in a more than 1% increase in revenue from the tax, holding discretionary tax changes constant.

Singer (1968) and Ehdaie (1990) have developed an econometric model measurement for estimating the tax elasticity coefficient. The model takes into account the relations between GDP, tax revenue, the formation of the tax system, the tax base using time series data for analysis and a model based on logarithmic functions (Bunescu and Comaniciu 2013).

Accordingly, we used a dummy variable (D_i) to represent the shift in tax policy during the study period 1981–2014. From Eq. 13.2, the functional tax form is as follows:

$$\log_t(\text{AgIT}) = \log \alpha + \beta \log(\text{AgrGDP})_t + \sum \theta_i D_i + \varepsilon_t \tag{13.4}$$

where

- α Constant;
- β Elasticity coefficient;
- θ_i Impact or coefficient of the discretionary change; and

D_i Dummy variable as a proxy for the *i*th discretionary tax measures (DTM) taken during the period under review. The summation sign in Eq. 13.4 creates room for the possibility of multiple changes in the tax system during the study period

We introduced a dummy variable to represent a shift in tax policy during the administrative reforms starting from 1992. The decade of the 1990s differed from the previous period in the application of a more liberal policy. During the second half of the 1990s, tax reforms were implemented. Since 1993, the tariff structure has improved extensively and more proclamations and regulations have been introduced to streamline the old tax system.

In estimating the coefficient of tax buoyancy, annual time series data was collected from 1981 to 2013. The data comprises the following variables of interest: agricultural GDP, non-agricultural GDP, aggregated agricultural income tax, aggregated land tax, personal income tax, business profit income tax, aggregated direct tax, and consumer price index. This data is from the Ministry of Finance and Economic Development (MOFED) and the World Development Indicators' (WDI) database.

Agricultural income tax revenue, land tax revenue, personal income tax, business profit income tax, and aggregated direct tax were converted to their real values by dividing the nominal values with the consumer price index (CPI). The use of CPI as the deflator helps smoothen the data and also avoids biased results that could have resulted from inflation. CPI is used because it falls on the expenditure side of the GDP equation. According to Triplett (2001), CPI is preferable as it represents the cost-of-living index and avails appropriate guidance for measuring consumer inflation. Hence, it is best used in deflating tax revenues.

The variables used in the models are as follows:

D.ln_RealAGDP is the first differenced log of real agricultural GDP;
*D*1992 is a dummy variable to show for 1992 when there was a change in government and no collection of tax revenue;
*D*policy is a dummy variable to capture policy changes due to the tax reforms; and
t is time trend

The limitation of applying this approach is data requirement which separates tax revenue from discretionary changes. Due to lack of this data, we corrected the dataset for the effects of tax reforms and tax policy changes using dummies. This technique assumes that income elasticity is constant over the range of revenues considered.

13.5 Empirical Findings

Initially, the agricultural GDP fluctuated steadily but was followed by a period when there was a quick increase. Since 1992, the new Ethiopian regime has introduced various changes in the tax system and it is expected that real agricultural

GDP could be non-stationary. As such, to have meaningful results, the trend model with options of Dickey-Fuller test that includes a constant and a time trend and the Augmented Dickey-Fuller tests were employed to test for the presence of unit roots in the variables. Also, other methods such as Kwiatkowski–Phillips–Schmidt–Shin (KPSS) and Phillips–Perron (PP) unit root tests were also employed.

The results indicate that the real agricultural GDP exhibited unit roots at different critical levels. However, real agricultural GDP was found to be stationary after differencing once, implying that the variable was integrated of order one. However, the real agricultural income tax, the real land use fee, and the total agricultural tax variables were found to be stationary at levels (see Annexure 1). Thus, real agricultural income tax and real land use fee, as well as the total agricultural tax series, are integrated of zero. Therefore, the first difference of the real agricultural GDP (*D.* ln_RealAGDP) was used as a dependent variable in the model. The independent variables in the model include time (t); and a dummy variable $d1992$ was introduced for 1992 when real economic activity for assessing agricultural income tax and land use fee was substantially slower than the historical trend.

13.5.1 Agricultural Income Tax and Land Use Fee Buoyancy

The results suggest that agricultural GDP had some significant impact on agricultural income tax. In fact, the estimated value of revenue buoyancy is −1.13 which is significant at the 10% level. This implies that a 1% increase in agricultural GDP was associated with a 1.13% decrease in agricultural income tax in Ethiopia. The findings also suggest that agricultural GDP had no statistically significant influence on agricultural land use fee and total agricultural tax. The R^2 value is high, suggesting that the model is a good fit. Table 13.1 presents the regression results on tax buoyancy.

Table 13.1 Estimates of tax buoyancy for Ethiopia (1984–2014)

	Agricultural income tax	Agricultural land use fee	Total agricultural tax
D.ln_RealAGDP	−1.126	−0.716	−0.645
	(1.83)*	(1.16)	(1.06)
*d*1992	−3.160	−3.038	−3.103
	(10.57)***	(10.11)***	(10.54)***
_cons	4.912	4.826	5.571
	(85.42)***	(83.55)***	(98.39)***
R^2	0.79	0.77	0.79
N	33	33	33

*$p < 0.1$; **$p < 0.05$; ***$p < 0.01$
Source Authors' computations using data from MOFED

13.5.2 Agricultural Income Tax and Land Use Fee Elasticity

A further analysis was done in evaluating tax elasticity by including a dummy variable for a policy change since 1992. The basic model was extended by including time trend t and a dummy variable to capture policy changes that represent tax reforms for the period 1992–2014.

The elasticity of agricultural income tax was estimated to be −1.16, implying that a 1% increase in agricultural GDP was associated with a decrease in a 1.16% in agricultural income tax (Table 13.2). On the other hand, agricultural GDP had no statistically significant effect on agricultural land use fee and total agricultural tax. This may be due to the declining share of agriculture in GDP and employment as the economy grew over this period.

The coefficient of time is statistically significant at 5% for land use fee and significant for total agricultural tax at 1%; its *t*-value is approximately 2.54 and 2.78, respectively. However, the coefficient of time is not statistically significant for agricultural income tax at the 5% significance level; its *t*-value is approximately 1.87. This supports the observation that agricultural income tax is driven not only by agricultural GDP but also by other internal developments in the country and due to an improving tax administration. It also shows that informational requirements of land taxation affect the design of taxes in the rural sector. Thus, the case for agriculture productivity as a focus of economic growth strategies must rely on

Table 13.2 Estimate of tax elasticity (1984–2014)

	Agricultural income tax	Agricultural land use fee	Total agricultural tax
D.ln_RealAGDP	−1.156	−0.918	−0.833
	(1.89)*	(1.53)	(1.45)
*d*1992	−3.379	−3.249	−3.335
	(11.48)***	(11.21)***	(12.05)***
Dpolicy	−0.439	−0.459	−0.498
	(2.48)**	(2.63)**	(2.99)***
T	0.016	0.021	0.022
	(1.87)*	(2.54)**	(2.78)***
_cons	4.940	4.778	5.533
	(47.43)***	(46.59)***	(56.49)***
R^2	0.83	0.82	0.84
N	33	33	33

$*p < 0.1$; $**p < 0.05$; $***p < 0.01$

Source Authors' computation using data from MOFED

Table 13.3 Estimates of buoyancy and elasticity (1984–2014)

	Buoyancy	Elasticity
Agricultural income tax	−1.12	−1.15
Land use fee	−0.71	−0.91
Total agricultural tax	−0.64	−0.83

Source Authors' computation using data from MOFED

identifying a set of inter-linkages through which agricultural growth contributes to a growth in revenue sources for the effective provision of public services in the rural Ethiopian economy. See Table 13.3.

13.5.3 Buoyancy and Elasticity of Personal Income Tax and Business Income Tax

Under the category of direct taxes, non-agricultural tax revenue variables, which are real personal income tax and business profit income tax, as well as the total direct tax series, were analyzed. As the first step, a more detailed examination of the data properties and the final model specification was done and the property of the series was analyzed using the augmented Dickey–Fuller (ADF), KPSS, and Phillips–Perron (PP) unit root tests (the results are presented in Annexure 1).

Since all series were found to be $I(1)$, this required testing for co-integration to establish the relationship between personal income tax and business income tax with non-agricultural GDP. Upon realizing the existence of a unique co-integrating vector, the structural vector auto-regressive (SVAR) model was used to investigate and estimate the elasticity and buoyancy in the short run between the variables. AIC was used to select the optimum lag length of SVAR models. Based on the SVAR estimation, tax buoyancy and elasticity results are given in Table 13.4.

The results in Table 13.4 suggest that personal income tax had a buoyancy of 0.08. Estimates of the tax system yielded a 0.08% change in tax revenue as a consequence of both automatic changes and a change in the discretionary fiscal policy for a 1% change in non-agricultural GDP. In other words, a 1% increase in non-agricultural GDP led to a 0.08% increase in personal income tax during the current period even though some proportion of incremental income was transferred to the government in the form of taxes, implying that the tax system was less buoyant.

Table 13.4 Estimates of buoyancy and elasticity for personal income tax and business income tax

	Buoyancy	Elasticity
Personal income tax	0.08	0.068
Business profit income tax	0.12	0.11
Total direct tax	0.13	0.118

Source Authors' computation using data from MOFED

The results clearly show that elasticity for Ethiopia's personal income tax was 0.068%, which indicates that the developments in non-agricultural GDP over the study period spurred less than the automatic proportionate increase in tax revenue. The implication is that the tax system did yield a 0.068% change in tax revenue, resulting from economic activity for every 1% change in non-agricultural GDP. Thus, a decreasing proportion of incremental income was collected and transferred to the government in the form of tax revenue, which shows that the personal income tax system in Ethiopia was inelastic over the study period.

This also shows that a 1% increase in non-agricultural GDP led to a 0.12% increase in business profit income tax in the current fiscal year. Thus, a decreasing amount of incremental business profit income tax was collected and transferred to the government in the form of taxes, implying that the tax system was less buoyant.

When the policy change is captured as a dummy variable, the estimates of tax elasticity result in a 1% increase in non-agricultural GDP leading to a 0.11% increase in business profit income tax in the current period. Thus, a lesser proportion of incremental business profit income tax was collected and transferred to the government in the form of tax revenue. This shows that this tax was also inelastic over the study period. In general, personal income tax and business profit income tax were progressive in nature given that it was expected that their elasticities would be greater than 1.

Further, a 1% increase in non-agricultural GDP led to a 0.13% increase in total direct tax in the current period. When a policy change was included as a dummy variable, a 1% increase in non-agricultural GDP led to about a 0.12% increase in direct tax in the current period.

The overall elasticity of the tax system clearly shows that the tax system in the country is inelastic and is therefore not responsive to changes in national income. The elasticity coefficient was not much lower than buoyancy for all the variables, implying that the discretionary measures did not significantly impact own revenue. It can easily be observed that discretionary changes to personal income tax and business profit income tax made little contribution to the growth in overall direct tax revenues.

13.6 Summary and Conclusion

Our study analyzed and measured the responsiveness of agricultural tax to economic growth in Ethiopia. Agricultural tax buoyancy measures growth in agricultural tax revenue as a ratio of the growth in agricultural GDP. The study concludes that growth in agricultural GDP had a significant and negative impact on the growth in agricultural income tax collections in Ethiopia. Agriculture's share had an adverse influence on revenue collections consistently but non-agricultural direct taxes increased by an increase in personal income and business profit taxes. In general, tax buoyancy or an elasticity coefficient that is lower than unity may indicate issues related to the structure of the tax, administration or compliance in the tax system. Based on these findings, the study recommends that reviewing the tax system is crucial as and when the economic structure changes. Tax policy measures should aim at increasing the tax base by bringing in the growing agricultural sector of smallholder farmers under the tax administration of the federal government. There is also a need to improve the tax administration continuously so that tax evasion and other malpractices can be tackled. Efforts are also needed to minimize the costs of tax collection.

With inelastic tax estimates for personal income tax and profit tax, the Ethiopian government has to review its tax collection system and pursue further reforms to exploit the tax revenue potential of the economy fully. The sensitivity response of revenue to changes in the tax base for personal income tax and business profit income tax was also found to be less than unity, indicating that the possibility of enhancing revenue proceeds from these taxes remains fairly weak. This requires the implementation of discretionary measures coupled with other measures for the shortfalls in revenue.

Annexure 1

ADF, KPSS, and PP unit root test results

	ADF test					KPSS test				PP test					
Variables	Critical value			Test statics	Lag order	Critical value		Test statics	Lag order	Critical value				Test statics	Lag order
%	1	5	10			1	5	10			1	5	10		
Agricultural GDP	−4.38	−3.6	−3.24	−2.025	12	0.216	0.146	0.119	0.633	3	−23.524	−18.508	−15.984	−2.935	3
Agricultural income tax	−4.38	−3.6	−3.24	−4.817	12	0.216	0.146	0.119	0.16	3	−23.524	−18.508	−15.984	−22.573	3
Land Use fee	−4.38	−3.6	−3.24	−3.658	12	0.216	0.146	0.119	0.116	3	−23.524	−18.508	−15.984	−18.661	3
Total Agr tax	−4.38	−3.6	−3.24	−6.739	10	0.216	0.146	0.119	0.108	3	−23.524	−18.508	−15.984	−20.679	3
Non-agricultural GDP	−4.38	−3.6	−3.24	−0.079	12	0.216	0.146	0.119	0.654	3	−23.524	−18.508	−15.984	−3.274	3
Personal income tax	−4.38	−3.6	−3.24	1.406	12	0.216	0.146	0.119	0.624	3	−23.524	−18.508	−15.984	0.659	3
Business income tax	−4.38	−3.6	−3.24	1.115	12	0.216	0.146	0.119	0.384	3	−23.524	−18.508	−15.984	−4.116	3
Direct tax	−4.38	−3.6	−3.24	0.527	12	0.216	0.146	0.119	0.429	3	−23.524	−18.508	−15.984	−2.695	3
First differences															
Agricultural GDP	−4.325	−3.576	−3.226	−4.698	1	0.216	0.146	0.119	0.0634	3	−23.396	−18.432	−15.936	−23.538	3
Non-agricultural GD	−4.334	−3.58	−3.228	−3.632	2	0.216	0.146	0.119	0.041	3	−23.524	−18.508	−15.984	−23.396	3
Personal income tax	−4.325	−3.576	−3.226	−3.952	1	0.216	0.146	0.119	0.104	3	−23.396	−18.432	−15.936	−30.704	3
Business income tax	−4.316	−3.572	−3.223	−4.205	0	0.216	0.146	0.119	0.0922	3	−23.396	−18.432	−15.936	−22.889	3
Direct tax	−4.325	−3.576	−3.226	−4.427	0	0.216	0.146	0.119	0.102	3	−23.268	−18.356	−15.888	−25.549	3

Source Computed by the authors

References

Ahmed QM, Muhammad SD (2010) Determinant of tax buoyancy: empirical evidence from developing countries. Eur J Soc Sci 13(3):408–418

Alemayehu G, Shimeles A (2005) Taxes and tax reform in Ethiopia, 1990–2003. Research Paper, UNU-WIDER, United Nations University (UNU), No. 65

Bachewe FN, Guush B, Berhane B, Minten M, Taffesse AS (2015) Agricultural growth in Ethiopia (2004–2014): Evidence and drivers. International Food Policy Research Institute (IFPRI), Working Paper, Washington, DC, p 81

Besley T, Ghatak M (2006) Public goods and economic development. Oxford University Press, Oxford

Besley T, Persson T (2014) Why do developing countries tax so little? J Econ Perspect 28(4): 99–120

Bunescu L, Comaniciu C (2013) Tax elasticity analysis in Romania: 2001–2012. Proc Econ Finance 6:609–614

Craig ED, Heins AJ (1980) The effect of tax elasticity on government spending. Public Choice 35 (3):267–275

Creedy J, Gemmell N (2001) The revenue elasticity of taxes in the UK. Melbourne Institute Working Paper, No. 11/01

Creedy J, Gemmell N (2008) Corporation tax buoyancy and revenue elasticity in the UK. Econ Model 25(1):24–37

Ehdaie J (1990) An econometric method for estimating the tax elasticity and the impact on revenues of discretionary tax measures: applied to Malawi and Mauritius. Country Economics Deprtment, The World Bank, Working Paper Series, No. 334

Feger T, Asafu-Adjaye J (2014) Tax effort performance in sub-Sahara Africa and the role of colonialism. Econ Model 38:163–174

Geda A, Shimeles A (2005) Taxes and Tax Reform in Ethiopia, 1990–2003 WIDER Working Paper Series 065, World Institute for Development Economic Research (UNU-WIDER)

Haughton J (1998) Estimating tax buoyancy, elasticity and stability. United States Agency for International Development, EAGER/PSGE Excise Project

Howard M, Foucade AL, Scott E (2009) Public Sector Economics for Developing Countries. University of the West Indies Press

Jenkins GP, Kuo CY, Shukla GP (2000) Tax analysis and revenue forecasting. Harvard Institute for International Development, Harvard University, Cambridge, Massachusetts

Khan MH (2001) Agricultural taxation in developing countries: a survey of issues and policy. Agric Econ 24(3):315–328

Leuthold JH (1991) Tax shares in developing economies a panel study. J Dev Econ 35(1):173–185

Mawia M, Nzomoi J (2013) An empirical investigation of tax buoyancy in Kenya. Afr J Bus Manage 7(40):4233–4246

McCluskey WJ, Trinh HL (2013) Property tax reform in Vietnam: options, direction and evaluation. Land Use Policy 30(1):276–285

Milwood TAT (2011) Elasticity and Buoyancy of the Jamaican tax system. Bank of Jamaica

Moller LC (2015) Ethiopia's great run: the growth acceleration and how to pace it. The World Bank Group, Washington, DC

Moreno MA, Maita M (2014) Tax elasticity in Venezuela a dynamic cointegration approach. Central Bank of Venezuela

Newbery DM (1987) Taxation and development. In the theory of taxation for developing countries. Newbery DM, Stern NH (eds), pp 165–204. Published for the World Bank [by] Oxford University Press

ONRS (2002) Oromia Rural Land Use and Administration Proclamation. No. 56, (ed.), Oromia National Regional State. Finfinnee, Ethiopia

ONRS (2005) Oromia national regional Government rural land use payment and agricultural income tax amendment, 2005, Proc. No. 99, Megeleta Oromia, 13th year, No. 13. Oromia National Regional State

Osoro N (1993) Revenue productivity implications of tax reform in Tanzania. African Economic Research Consortium, Research Paper No. 20

Prichard W (2015) Taxation, responsiveness and accountability in Sub-Saharan Africa: the dynamics of tax bargaining. Cambridge University Press

Rashid S, Assefa M, Ayele G (2007) Distortions to agricultural incentives in Ethiopia. Agricultural Distortions Working Paper 43. The World Bank, Washington, DC

Sanjeev G, Tareq S (2008) Mobilizing revenue. Finance Dev 45(3):44–47

Sarris AH (1994) Agricultural taxation under structural adjustment. Food and Agriculture Organization of the United Nations

Singer NM (1968) The use of dummy variables in estimating the income-elasticity of state income-tax revenues. National Tax J 21(2):200–204

Tanzi V, Zee HH (2000) Tax policy for emerging markets: developing countries. National Tax J 53(2):299–322

Triplett JE (2001) Should the cost-of-living index provide the conceptual framework for a consumer price index? Econ J 111(472):311–334

Chapter 14
Improving Agricultural Productivity Growth in Sub-Saharan Africa

Olaide Rufai Akande, Hephzibah Onyeje Obekpa and Djomo-Raoul Fani

Abstract Improved agricultural productivity is central to achieving inclusive development, reducing poverty, and enhancing the living standards of most people in sub-Saharan Africa. Concerned by the declining state of agricultural productivity in this region, we pursue the question whether agro-processing activities and exports of raw agricultural materials have a backward linkages effect on agricultural production activities. And if the relationship exists how can it be more effectively used? The regression results indicate that increases in export of raw agricultural materials negatively influence productivity growth in agriculture. Consistent with the findings of other studies that agro-industrial growth in the sub-Saharan region faces several challenges, the response of agricultural production to agro-industrial activities was positive but inelastic. To overcome these challenges, improving the value of agricultural exports and thereby improving agricultural productivity growth are needed in policy, regulatory, and institutional frameworks across countries in the region that will enable agro-industrial development to become stronger; lead to the creation of opportunities for increased private sector engagement including through the formation of public–private partnerships for developing synergies; provide access to credit for participants along the agricultural value chain; provide rural infrastructure that reduces postharvest losses and transport costs and shorten transit time, while increasing overall rural mobility; support innovations and technology for developing competitive value chains; provide access to value-responsive markets; provide access to timely information for improving bargaining powers; establish organizations to reduce transaction costs; and lead to inclusion of women, poor, and/or marginal groups in the value chains. Overall, this strategy will be optimal when it concomitantly and yearly increases agro-industrial activities and decreases agricultural raw material exports by 2.5% of their existing values, given 1981 as the base year.

O.R. Akande (✉) · H.O. Obekpa · D.-R. Fani
Department of Agricultural Economics, University of Agriculture, Makurdi, Nigeria
e-mail: akande.olaide@uam.edu.ng

A. Heshmati (ed.), *Studies on Economic Development and Growth in Selected African Countries*, Frontiers in African Business Research,
DOI 10.1007/978-981-10-4451-9_14

Keywords Total factor productivity · Agricultural production · Inclusive development agro-processing · Export of agricultural raw materials · Panel data · Simulation

14.1 Introduction

Growth theories emphasize the influential role of nonconventional inputs in accounting for productivity and income differences among output producing units. However, in contrast to the neoclassical growth theory, arguments based on the endogenous growth theory (Aghion and Howitt 1992; Grossman and Helpman 1991; Romer 1990) assume that differences in growth among economic entities using the same or similar inputs are accounted for by factors and disturbances within the growth model. By implication, therefore, policy interventions can be used to adjust suboptimal production.

In sub-Saharan Africa (SSA), agriculture remains the major occupation of most people, contributing to the population's food security and providing rural dwellers livelihood option. In many countries in the region, agriculture is the key source of foreign exchange and revenue for the government. If properly developed, agriculture also has the potential of stemming the current dangerous trend of rural-urban migration, reducing the numerous social problems in cities and spurring sustainable inclusive development. However, as in other regions of the world, the capacity of the sector to meet its potential critically depends on the growth of the agro-industry.

Agro-industrial development spurs growth in primary agricultural production because of the forward and backward linkages existing between these sectors (Hirschman 1958). Agro-processing in particular has several positive effects on agricultural production because it is a necessary part of the agricultural value chain. Thus, its absence retards the flow of value in an agricultural economy. Agro-industrial development also promotes job creation and inclusive development because of its potential to provide jobs for disadvantaged groups like women. Further, a growth in agro-processing reduces postharvest losses, thereby increasing incomes and helping people fulfill their economic aspirations. However, while agriculture-led growth has played an important role in reducing poverty and transforming the economies in many Asian countries, the strategy has not worked in Africa. For example, most African countries have failed to meet the requirements of a successful agricultural revolution. An obvious corollary to this is deep and prevalent poverty in the region as compared with the other regions in the world (Kharas 2007; Strawson et al. 2015; UNDP 2011).

Two mutually reinforcing problems are contributing to the high prevalence of poverty in the region: bad policies and low agricultural productivity. For instance, Fuglie and Rada (2013) point out that some of the lowest levels of agricultural land and labor productivity in the world are found in sub-Saharan Africa. Anderson and Masters (2009) say that farmers in many parts of Africa continue to face more discriminatory policies as compared with farmers in other global regions because farmers in the continent are confronted with policies that lower economic incentives to invest in agricultural production and modern inputs.

This situation stresses the need for strategies that stimulate more rapid agricultural growth in sub-Saharan Africa. However, increased exploitation of natural resources or a spike in commodity terms of trade may only spur limited growth in the long run. In contrast, policies anchored on key productivity determinants (Binswanger and Townsend 2000) can help maintain agricultural growth over the long run. In our paper, we pursue the question of how agro-industrial activities and exports of agricultural raw materials can be used to generate effective agricultural productivity growth in SSA. Our study differs from the literature on sources of total factor productivity (TFP) growth in agriculture in two aspects. First, we circumvent the simultaneity equation bias associated with TFP estimations from the panel data by using the hybrid Olley and Pakes (1996) and Levinsohn and Petrin (2003) procedure. Second, as against the deterministic forecasting approach in most studies, the simulation approach that we use acknowledges that uncertainties are associated with realization of values of some TFP determinants, and by extension, the random nature of TFP itself.

The rest of the paper is organized as follows. Section 14.2 presents the conceptual framework, while Sect. 14.3 gives details of the econometric model underlying the analysis. It also presents the estimated model and data sources. Section 14.4 discusses the results and gives a conclusion.

14.2 Agro-Industrial Development: A Conceptual Framework

14.2.1 Agro-Industrial Development and Productivity Growth

According to FAO (1997), agro-industry refers to a subset of manufacturing that processes raw materials and intermediate products derived from the agricultural sector. Agro-industry transforms products originating in agriculture, forestry, and fisheries and processes them into canned food, beverages, fruit juice, meat and dairy products, textile and clothing, leather wood and rubber products, and animal feed, among others.

Support for the development of agro-industry as a precursor to agricultural productivity growth is rooted in the "linkage hypothesis." The original version of the theory of unbalanced growth pioneered by Hans Singer, Alfred Hirschman, and Wait Rostow emphasized the need for investments in strategic sectors of the economy instead of all the sectors simultaneously. In Hirschman's (1958) view, the other sectors will automatically develop themselves through what are known as "linkage effects." The implicit assumption is that the best development path for developing countries with income scarcity lies in selecting those enterprises and industries where progress will induce further progress elsewhere. By implication, therefore, any industry that shows a high degree of dependency as measured by the proportion of output sold to or purchased from other industries, can provide a strong stimulus to economic growth. Thus, where a complementary backward relationship exists between industry A and industries B and C, growth of output of industry A may generate demand for products of B and C and may also reduce the marginal cost of production in these industries.

Correspondingly, through its backward and forward linkages, the agro-industry can play a substantial role in spurring agricultural growth, providing employment in rural areas, ensuring food security, and stimulating innovativeness among farmers. According to FAO (1997), the agro-industry could spur productivity growth in agricultural production through market expansion because establishing processing facilities is an essential first step toward stimulating both consumer demand for processed products and an adequate supply of the needed raw materials. Second, the provision of transport, power, and other infrastructural facilities required for agro-industries also benefits the agricultural production process and enhances productivity. Ramachandran (2009) further states that agro-based industries can spark innovativeness among farmers by encouraging them to resort to new production techniques because the agro-industry helps agriculture become more productive by enlarging the supply of inputs like fertilizers, pesticides, and improved farm implements and equipment. The development of an agricultural output-based industry automatically encourages farmers to produce the concerned crops. In the absence of agro-based industries, the farmer community develops a sort of frog-in-the-well attitude toward farming (Ramachandran 2009).

Another important effect of agro-processing is a substantial increase in employment that may result from setting up an industry using raw materials. For instance, considerable employment may be generated in agriculture by being the raw material base, even if the agro-industrial process is itself capital-intensive (FAO 1997). In particular, food processing in the early stages of development can be an important direct complement to agriculture as a source of employment for seasonal labor. The off-farm employment opportunities provided by food processing may thus represent the first instrument of time-smoothing in the labor market and as such is an important factor of capital accumulation in rural areas. Ramachandran (2009) further argues that by helping provide employment opportunities locally, agro-industries stop the dangerous consequences of mass exodus of farmers and rural dwellers associated with rural-urban migration.

The agro-industry's capacity to generate demand and employment in other industries is also important because of its role in activating sideways linkages, that is, linkages derived from the use of by-products or waste products of the main industrial activity (FAO 1997). For example, animal feed industries can utilize several agro-industrial by-products such as whey, oilseed press cakes and blood, carcass and bone meat. In addition, many industries using agricultural raw materials produce waste that can be used as fuel, paper pulp, or fertilizers. Smallholder producers in developing countries have been experiencing high postharvest losses threatening their food security and negatively affecting the financial sustainability of their operations. For instance, the Africa Post Harvest Loss Index (2014) estimates that losses for roots and tubers were at 10–40%, for fruits and vegetables at 15–44%, while fish and sea food at 10–40%. Developing the agro-processing potential, either through indigenous knowledge (drying, salting, crushing, pre-cooking) or modern technology-based methods (extraction, canning, bottling, concentration), has the capacity to reverse these losses. Therefore, agro-industrial activities also have the potential to contribute toward food security.

However, unplanned agro-industrial development may generate negative externalities and sustain primary agricultural production in a low level of equilibrium. For example, there may be significant risks in terms of equity, sustainability, and inclusiveness when value addition and capture are concentrated in the hands of a few value chain participants to the detriment of the others (da Silva and Baker, 2007). This will be the case in a situation of unbalanced market power in the agri-food chain. Moreover, sustainability of agro-industrial development depends on its competitiveness in terms of costs, prices, operational efficiencies, product offers, and other associated parameters. Establishing and maintaining competitiveness may constitute a particular challenge for small- and medium-scale agro-industrial enterprises and small-scale farmers.

The preconditions for developing agro-industries include necessary transportation, information, and communication technologies and access to reliable supplies of key utilities, notably electricity and water. Therefore, infrastructural constraints influence the cost and reliability of the physical movement of raw materials and end products, the efficiency of processing operations, and responsiveness to customer demands. The prevailing macroeconomic and business conditions and the level, quality, and reliability of infrastructure are also critical determinants of competitiveness in the export of processed agro-food products (Crammer 1999). In a situation of acute infrastructural constraints, the additional complexities of processing operations may outweigh the benefits of diversification in the exports of primary commodities toward value addition (Love 1983). Weak infrastructure may further put agro-processing enterprises at a competitive disadvantage vis-à-vis their industrialized competitors and distort the competitiveness of developing countries relative to one another. Unreliable and costly supplies of utilities may also prevent enterprises from operating at or near full capacity utilization. Overall, a weak infrastructural environment will lower the rate of transition of agro-industries from informal to formal operators and steer the structure of the sector toward a higher level of concentration.

14.2.2 Export of Agricultural Raw Materials and Productivity Growth

Arguments supporting commodities trade across international borders are rooted in the export-led growth hypothesis (see, Adams 1973; Crafts 1973; Edwards 1992, 1998). According to this model, export trade is a key determinant of economic growth. The key premise of this argument is that overall growth in a country can be generated not only by increasing the amount of labor and capital within the economy, but also by expanding exports. Accordingly, exports can serve as an "engine of growth." An offshoot of this idea is the assumption that developing countries have comparative advantages in agricultural production, thus only needing to forward their agricultural produce to international markets (Akande 2012). However, empirical analyses to confirm this proposition have shown mixed results. While positive for some countries (Krueger 1978; Lussier 1993), they were negative for others with more than half the empirical investigations published in the 1990s finding no long-run relationship between exports and economic growth, suggesting that correlations between these variables arise as a result of short-term fluctuations.

A critical factor that affects the chances of developing countries benefiting from export trade in agriculture is increasing consumer concerns about food safety. Specifically, food exports from the developing world are exposed to demanding food safety standards from organizations such as Codex Alimentarius and by unilateral requests from individual importers. Also, attitudes and standards in vogue in the developed world spill over to local markets (Pinstrup-Andersen 2000). A new form of protectionism often arises in which high quality and safety standards imposed by importing countries cannot be accommodated rapidly by local production technologies or guaranteed by local analytical capabilities. The latter may lead to increased levels of rejection at entry ports. Moreover, even if the problem regarding the safety of an imported food has been overcome, the credibility of the exporting country to produce safe food may be at stake, thus affecting the volume of its food exports. For this reason, developing countries that consider implementing or strengthening their food-borne disease controls and investigation and surveillance systems are unlikely to gain in the long run from food and agricultural export trade.

In summary, the review indicates that depending on the prevailing factors the correlation between agricultural productivity, agro-processing and raw material exports can be positive or negative and is also subject to random influence from market forces. Hence, the focus of this paper is establishing this correlation and how the equilibrium can be shifted in a way so as to achieve sustainable growth and inclusive development in SSA.

14.3 Econometric Framework and Data

The simulation approach examines the future evolution of TFP in SSA agricultural production under the assumption that uncertainties are associated with the evolution of certain TFP determinants (Davidson and MacKinnon 2004). First, we estimated the TFP data from the aggregate agricultural production function using the hybrid Olley and Pakes (1996) and Levinsohn and Petrin (2003) procedure. Second, the fixed coefficients in the TFP simulation model were estimated from a Tobit regression. Finally, the impact of varying scenarios of agro-processing activities and raw material exports on TFP's evolution under uncertainties were forecast using the Monte Carlo simulation. The random values of the uncertain variables in the simulation model were generated from their probability distribution functions (PDF).

Specifically, the simulated TFP (θ) model is:

$$\theta = E[f(X_{it})], X \sim \text{PDF}(X_{it}) \text{ or}$$
$$E(f(X_i)) = \acute{\theta}_N = \frac{1}{N}\sum_{i=1}^{N} f(X_{it}) \tag{14.1}$$

where X is a vector of TFP determinants.

By the law of large numbers, the approximation $\acute{\theta}_N$ converges to the true value as N increases to infinity. Therefore, the $\acute{\theta}_N$ estimate is unbiased if:

$$E(\acute{\theta}_N = \theta)$$

As a first step, agricultural TFP was estimated from the hybrid Olley and Pakes-Levinsohn and Petrin production function:

$$y_{it} = \beta_{oi} + \beta_k k_{it} + \beta_l l_{it} + \beta_{ld} ld_{it} + \omega(k_{it}, i_{it}) + u^q_{it}. \tag{14.2}$$

where lower case letters represent the log transform of the respective variable, y is gross domestic product measured in million purchasing power parity in dollars (PPP\$); k is the gross capital investment measured in million US dollars; l is agricultural labor measured in million people employed in agriculture; ld is agricultural land measured in square kilometers; i is gross agricultural investment measured in million US dollars; u is the error term $\sim N(0, \sigma^2)$.[1]

The fixed parameters in the TFP simulation model were estimated from the Tobit regression:

$$\begin{aligned} \text{tfp}^*_{it} &= \alpha_{oi} + \alpha_1 * \text{agvadd}_{it} + \alpha_2 * \text{agrmtexpt}_{it} + \alpha_3 * \text{agr\&d}_{it} \\ &+ \alpha_4 * \text{agfdi}_{it} + \alpha_5 * \text{agoda}_{it} \end{aligned} \tag{14.3}$$

where α_{0i} are fixed effects parameters on countries; $\alpha_{(j:j>0)}$ are parameters on the associated variables; agvadd is value addition to agricultural products through agro-processing measured in current market prices (USD); agrmtexpt is the value of agricultural raw materials exported measured in current US dollars; agr&d is the public expenditure on agricultural research and development measured in million constant 2011 US dollars; agfdi is the value of foreign direct investment in agriculture measured in current US dollars; agoda is the value of official development

[1]Annexure A gives a derivation of this model.

assistance to agriculture measured in constant 2012 US dollars; ε_{it} is the error term $\sim N(0, \sigma^2)$.

Finally, TFP was simulated from the stochastic model:

$$\begin{aligned} \text{tfp}^*_{it} = \alpha_{oi} + \alpha_1 * \left(\text{agvadd}_{it} + \eta_{1,it}\right) + \alpha_2 * \left(\text{agrmtexpt}_{it} + \eta_{2,it}\right) \\ + \alpha_3 * \text{agr\&d}_{it} + \alpha_4 * \text{agfdi}_{it} + \alpha_5 * \text{agoda}_{it} + \xi_{it} \end{aligned} \tag{14.4}$$

where $\eta_{1,it}$ and $\eta_{2,it}$ are uncertainties associated with measurements of agro-processing and agricultural raw material exports, respectively. They are expected to capture random events associated with these business and open economy variables. ξ_{it} is an exogenous white noise disturbance in the model.

Given the stochastic nature of this model, the behavior of TFP growth under various scenarios was investigated. The simulated scenarios consisted of concomitant yearly positive changes to the state of agro-processing activities and decreases in exports of agricultural raw materials by 1, 2.5, 5, 7.5, and 10% with 1981 as the starting point.

14.3.1 The Data

Data for the study is the longitudinal time series or panel data on 13 countries in sub-Saharan Africa. The data covered the period 1981–2005. Data was collected from the databases of the Food and Agriculture Organization (FAO) of the United Nations, Agricultural Science and Technology Indicators (ASTI) (www.asti.cgiar.org), and the World Bank (www.worldbank.org). Data on agricultural raw materials exported was derived by multiplying the proportion of agricultural raw materials in the total merchandize export by the total merchandize export. The value of agro-industrial value addition was proxied by the industrial value added. This was obtained by multiplying industrial value added as a proportion of GDP by the GDP. Values of official development assistance in agriculture (agoda) and foreign direct investment in agriculture (agfdi) were obtained by weighting the aggregate of these variables by the proportion of agriculture value added in GDP.

14.4 Results and Discussion

14.4.1 Results

Annexure B summarizes the data, while Table 14.1 and Table 14.2 give estimates from production function and the TFP model. The goodness of fit statistics of the hybrid Olley and Pakes-Levinsohn and Petrin production function indicates a good fit of the data to the model. The returns to scale statistics show that agricultural

Table 14.1 Parameter estimates of hybrid Olley and Pakes-Levpet and Petrin regression model of agricultural production in sub-Saharan Africa

Variable[a]	Coefficient	Std. error	Sig. level
Labor	0.72	0.36	0.05
Land	−0.16	0.46	0.74
Gross capital	1	0.42	0.02
Investment	0.001	0.10	0.99
Wald	0.43(0.43)		SS

Source Author's computation
[a]All variables are in logarithm form

Table 14.2 Parameter estimates of the Tobit regression model of TFP in SSA's agriculture

Variable	Mixed effects model	Random effects model
	Coefficient (std. error)	Coefficient (std. error)
agr&d	−0.15(0.05)**	−0.133(0.032)***
Agoda	0.04(0.02)**	0.027(0.021)
Agfdi	−0.004(0.001)*	−0.004(.002)**
Agvadd	0.09(0.02)**	0.034(0.024)
Agrmtexpt	−0.04(0.01)***	−0.032(0.013)**
Burkina Faso	−1.56(0.05)**	
Madagascar	−2.35(0.06)*	
Ghana	−0.37(0.07)*	
Mali	−1.42(0.06)*	
Togo	0.06(0.05)**	
Kenya	−1.47(0.09)*	
Nigeria	−1.20(0.14)	
Malawi	−0.80(0.07)*	
sigma_u	$2.68e^{-19}$(1.00)	0.79(0.206)***
Sigma_e	0.12(0.01)***	0.12(0.01)***
Rho	$4.81e^{-36}$($3.69e^{-19}$)	0.98(0.01)
Fit stat.:		
Log likelihood	90.23	63.96
AIC	−150.46	−113.92
BIC	−106.01	−93.18
Wald Chi-square	7163.81***	29.96***
Likelihood ratio (LR)	52.54***	

Source Author's computation
***(**)(*)—significant at 1, 5, 10%

production in SSA exhibits constant returns to scale. The coefficients on labor and gross capital were significantly different from zero, whereas those on land and investment were not significant. Specifically, the elasticity coefficient on labor indicates that a percentage increase in the variable increased aggregate agricultural production by 0.71%. A percentage increase in capital on the other hand increased the value of agricultural production by the same percentage. In other words, this implies that agricultural output changed at the same rate as gross capital. This result is consistent with the findings of Grilliches (1998) that if TFP is correctly estimated, the coefficient on capital should be roughly equal to unity. The negative but insignificant coefficient on the land variable points to the potential for productivity depletion arising from extensive land use practices without corresponding nutrient replenishment through the use of fertilizers and other soil additives. These results support Nkamelu's (2013) findings that the land extensification path in Africa is rapidly becoming unsustainable or impractical as land grows scarcer.

The estimated TFP Tobit model indicates a good fit of the model to the data. The likelihood ratio (LR) test showed a better fit of the mixed effects model relative to the random effects model (LR = 52.54; $P \leq 0.01$). Other fitness parameters of the model, including log likelihood, the Akaike information criteria (AIC) and the Swatch information criteria also selected the mixed effects Tobit model in preference to the random effects model.

The elasticity coefficients on agro-industrial value addition and on export of agricultural raw materials for the mixed effects Tobit model were statistically significant. Specifically, the coefficient on value addition through agro-processing was positive indicating that intensification of agro-processing activities improved agricultural production in SSA. In contrast, the negative coefficient on raw material exports points to the fact that increasing exports of agricultural raw products has a decreasing effect on productivity of the agricultural sector in the region. Moreover, the coefficients of the control variables including public investment in agricultural R&D, agricultural development assistance, and foreign direct investment in agriculture were statistically significant. However, while the coefficient of value of development assistance to agriculture was positive, those of R&D and foreign direct investment in agriculture were negative. These negative coefficients suggest that excess public investments in research and development crowd out private participation while the level of investments by foreign nationals in the agricultural sector is inconsistent with the growth of the agricultural economy in sub-Saharan Africa.

The simulation (Table 14.3 and Fig. 14.1) revealed that policies that yearly and concomitantly increase agro-industrial value addition and reduce agricultural raw material exports by 2.5%, assuming 1981 as the base year, will lead to acceptable progressive growth in TFP in agriculture in SSA.

14.4.2 Discussion

Evidence from the regression analysis points to the fact that increases in agro-processing activities and its corollary decrease in the export of raw agricultural materials increase agricultural production in SSA. However, the low elasticity coefficient on value addition (less than unity) implies that agricultural productivity in the region responds little to changes in value addition activities, which further

Table 14.3 Scenario analysis of the effect of increases in agro-industrial activities and decreases in export of agricultural raw materials on TFP in sub-Saharan Africa

Scenario (% increase in agro-processing plus corresponding % decrease in agric raw materials export)	Percentage of progressive growth in TFP over the baseline (total)	Percentage of progressive growth in TFP over the baseline (marginal)
Baseline	0	0
1	1.33	1.33
2.5	8	3.2
5	13.33	2.67
7.5	20	2.67
10	21.33	2.13

Source Author's calculation

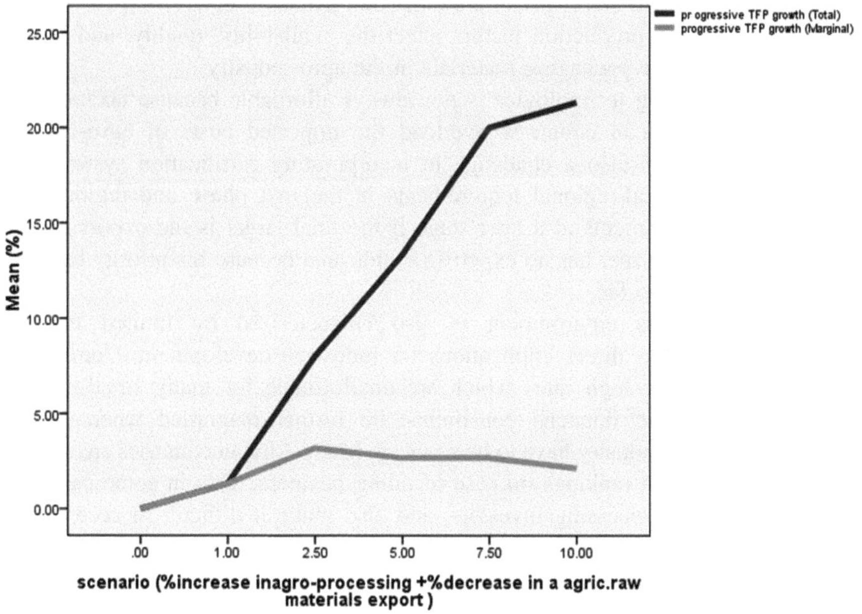

Fig. 14.1 Effect of improving agro-industrial activities and decreasing agricultural raw material exports on progressive growth of TFP in agriculture in SSA

suggests that the growth of agro-industry in SSA faces some challenges. AfDB (2008), the World Bank, and Information Development/Agribusiness (2013) identified the challenges including lack of infrastructure, storage, finance, competencies, adequate technologies, and a good policy environment which confront agro-industrial development in many parts of Africa. Specifically, these studies say that lack of storage capacity in conjunction with poor rural electrification and water access, insufficient road networks, and difficult access to communication tools (telephone, e-mail, etc.) affect the competitiveness of the final agro-processing products in terms of costs, quality, and supplies. Low and unstable agricultural productivity in Africa further constrains the success of the agro-industry.

Moreover, the level of capacity building in agro-processing in sub-Saharan Africa is low with the focus being on production extension. This partially explains the high percentage of postharvest losses apart from lack of appropriate logistics and storage capacity. Public R&D has also focused on production and prioritizing investments in agricultural research extension but not in postharvest and food technology. Most ongoing agricultural operations in Africa (especially at the small-medium farmer level) continue to be focused on production aspects with no forward linkages. And, in most cases, agro-processing at the rural level in Africa ranges from nonexistent to just very basic. This is linked to the fact that access to agro-processing technologies is very limited due to lack of expertise/know-how and affordable costs. Besides, due to poor infrastructure, production factors such as water, electricity, and diesel-petrol are either not available or very expensive. The high costs of these production factors affect the availability, quality, and cost of other key inputs like packaging materials in the agro-industry.

Further, accessing technologies is not always affordable because taxation systems in many African countries overload the imported costs of agro-industry equipment. There is also a challenge in incorporating certification systems that could fulfill the local-regional requirements in the first phase and regional and international requirements at a later stage if the final target is the export market. A typical African farmer has no expertise in this area because his priority has been simple production so far.

Africa's business environment is also characterized by limited financial resources, which has direct implications for industrial development. Commercial banks work at very high rates which are unaffordable for many small-medium entrepreneurs. These financial constraints are further magnified when start-up businesses in agro-industry have to be serviced. Many African countries are still at a very low position in rankings on ease of doing business. This in some cases can stop foreign agro-processing investors, and also make it difficult to access technologies and equipment. Licensing, business start-up costs, trade procedures, and time required are worse in sub-Saharan Africa as compared with other developing regions.

Overcoming these challenges for successful agro-industrialization requires carefully chosen policy strategies. The solution to this problem must start with the policy environment recognizing that appropriate infrastructure together with capacity building are the key pillars that can successfully decrease postharvest losses and serve as an initial trigger for attracting private sector investments. Road and market infrastructure is also important as they provide critical linkages for connections and transactions between value chain participants besides the other rural functions that they perform that indirectly support the development of the value chain. While roads are useful for value chains, they must connect agricultural areas with competitive advantage to strategic markets.

Similarly, more infrastructure for production (irrigation schemes, dams) is needed in SSA to increase production, making it more cost-effective and fulfilling the demands of volume and quality of the agro-industry. The needed policy strategy must consider strengthening market intelligence and market linkages and make them sustainable, especially in rural areas. An enabling environment must also be established for developing the value chain through policies, regulations, and supporting institutions. To facilitate increased private sector engagement, greater clarity is needed on the evolving and expected roles of the public and private sectors. Public–private partnerships can support the development of agriculture value chains, but require significant inputs to identify opportunities and implementation arrangements.

Extension support services also need to be closer to a business development model than the traditional agricultural extension model; they should also be able to bring the market and value addition needs to the farmer and the small-medium agro-processor level. Farmers' associations and cooperatives based on the scale economy could also overcome the gaps that individual farmers cannot. However, the challenge may be how to promote and support them in a sustainable way and how to equip them with a comprehensive tool package (finance and marketing services, technical and managerial skills, extension services) that could make them competitive enterprises.

Access to credit is a key requirement for all participants in a value chain just as access to timely market information such as on prices and is essential for a functioning value chain. This helps participants like producers in the chain to respond to changes in market prices and improves their negotiating powers with traders and processors. The creation of free trade areas at the regional level can help overcome problems when local equipment is required, but still the challenge is how to make international technology available and affordable without undermining the potential emergence of local technology providers.

14.4.3 Limitations and Suggestions for Further Studies

The limitation of our study is associated with the fact that the findings may be affected by the quality of the data used. Specifically, nonavailability of data on many variables and missing data reduced the number of countries used for the analysis. A more precise estimate may be obtained by a study that uses datasets with improved quality.

14.4.4 Conclusion and Recommendations

This paper investigated the question of how agro-processing and agricultural raw material exports can be effectively used to improve productivity of agriculture in

SSA. Our findings lead to the conclusion that while intensifying efforts in exporting raw agricultural materials lead to decreased productivity growth in agriculture, increasing agro-processing activities marginally lead to improved agricultural productivity growth, suggesting that agro-industrial activities are locked in a low level of equilibrium.

To overcome the challenges associated with agro-industrialization and improving the value of agricultural exports thereby improving agricultural productivity growth, there is a need for a policy, regulatory, and institutional framework across countries in the region that enables agro-industrial development to become stronger; creating opportunities for increased private sector engagement including through the formation of public–private partnerships for developing synergies; providing access to credit for participants along the agricultural value chain; providing rural infrastructure that reduces postharvest losses and transport costs and shortens transit time while increasing overall rural mobility; supporting innovations and technology for developing competitive value chains; providing access to value-responsive markets; providing access to timely information to improve bargaining powers; establishing organizations to reduce transaction costs; and including women, poor, and/or marginal groups into value chains. This strategy will have optimal results if it concomitantly and yearly increases agro-industrial activities and decreases agricultural raw material exports by 2.5% from their existing values.

Appendix 1: Model Derivation

In deriving TFP data as Solow's residuals, the aggregate agricultural production function was conceived as,

$$Y_{it} = A_i K_{it}^{\beta_k} L_{it}^{\beta_l} \tag{14.5}$$

where Y is the aggregate output, K is the vector of capital input, L is the labor input, A is the Hicksian neutral efficiency level.

While Y, K and L are all observed by an econometrician, A is not observed by a researcher. Taking the natural logarithm results of Eq. (14.5) yields:

$$y_{it} = \beta_{0i} + \beta_k k_{it} + \beta_l l_{it} + \varepsilon_{it} \tag{14.6}$$

where the lower case letters refer to the natural logarithm of respective variables and $\ln(A) = \beta_{0i} + \varepsilon_{it}$. Where β_{0i} measures productivity that varies over countries, and ε_{it} s, the time specific deviation from that mean. When ε_{it} is decomposed into a predictable and unpredictable component, Eq. (14.6) becomes:

$$y_{it} = \beta_{0i} + \beta_k k_{it} + \beta_l l_{it} + v_{it} + u_{it} \tag{14.7}$$

where $\omega_t = \beta_{0i} + v_{it}$ represents sector specific productivity and u_{it} is a iid error term, representing unexpected deviation from the mean due to measurement or other unexpected circumstances. The task is to estimate Eq. (14.7) and solve for ω_t. TFP can then be calculated by exponentiating (ω_t) and then expressing it as a function of its relevant determinants such as:

$$\text{TFP} = g(X), \tag{14.8}$$

where X is a vector of TFP determinants.

Estimation of Eq. (14.7) using the OLS technique on panel data from continuing firms or countries faces three particular difficulties: multi-collinearity, selection, and simultaneity bias. An endogeneity or simultaneous equation bias arises because investments in inputs are likely to be correlated with past productivity shocks. Specifically, endogeneity occurs because productivity is known to profit maximizing firms (but unknown to an econometrician) when they choose their input levels (Marschak and Andrews 1944). Production units will increase their use of inputs as a result of positive productivity shocks. Under this condition, any unobserved shock to productivity that raises output could indirectly raise investments on inputs, inducing a correlation between the explanatory variables and the error term in the productivity equation. Moreover, if no allowance is made for entry and exist owing to productivity shocks, a selection bias will emerge (Van Beveren 2012). The implication of this is that the production elasticities of the observed factors are not identified because the compound error v_t an u_t are not identically and independently distributed. Therefore, parameter estimates of the production function with OLS will be biased. Specifically, input coefficients will be biased upward if there is serial correlation in productivity shock, ω_t (Petrick and Closs 2013). This effect will be stronger, the easier to adjust input use in response to productivity shocks.

Several approaches have been proposed to overcome these problems. Arellano and Bond (1991) suggest the instrumental variable-based estimator. Within estimators have also been employed in studies on productivity of R&D investments. Olley and Pakes (1996) developed a semi-parametric estimation algorithm using investment and age as proxy for productivity. Levinsohn and Petrin (2003) contribution to Olley and Pakes' (1996) semi-parametric estimator by using material as an alternative to investment proxy. However, the shortcoming of the fixed effects estimator is that it overcomes the simultaneity problem only if we are willing to assume that the unobserved, firm specific productivity is time invariant (Yasar et al. 2008). Moreover, the within and difference estimator may remove too much variance from the data and render the estimation impracticable. The strength of Olley and Pakes' (1996) algorithm is that it explicitly takes both the selection and simultaneous problem into account by taking cognizance of the idiosyncratic productivity shocks and exit behavior of the production unit. In this model, a firm is assumed to maximize the expected discounted value of net cash flows (Van Beveren 2012). The investment exit decision will depend on the firm's perception about the distribution of the future market structure given the information currently available. To achieve consistency a number of assumptions have been further made. First, the productivity of the firm is assumed to be the only state variable, evolving through the first-order Markov process. Second, a monotonicity assumption is imposed on the investment variable to ensure stability of the investment demand function. Therefore, investment increases in productivity are conditional on the values of all the state variables. Consequently, only nonnegative values of investments can be used in the analysis. Moreover, if industry-wide prices are used to deflate the input and output measured in value terms to proxy their respective quantities, it is implicitly assumed that all firms in the industry face common prices (Ackerberg et al. 2007).

Overall, the investment decision will depend on capital and productivity as:

$$I_{it} = i_t(k_{it}, \omega_{it}) \tag{14.9}$$

where lower case letters represent the logarithmic transformation of variables. If we assume that investment is strictly increasing with respect to productivity, conditional on capital, the investment decision can be inverted to allow the expression of the unobserved productivity as a function of the observables such that:

$$\omega_{it} = i_t(k_{it}, i_{it}) \tag{14.10}$$

where $h_t(.) = I_t(.)$.

Given this understanding, Eq. (14.7) can be written as:

$$Y_t = \beta_0 + \beta_l l_{it} + \beta_k k_{kt} + h_t(i_{it}, k_{it}) + u_t^q \tag{14.11}$$

Next, if we define the investment function $\varphi_t(k_{it}, i_{it})$ as follows:

$$\varphi_t(k_{it,}, I_{it}) = \beta_0 + \beta_k k_{kt} + h_t(I_{it}, K_{it}) + u_t^q$$

Then, Eq. (14.11) can be rewritten as:

$$Y_t = \beta_l l_{it} + \varphi_t(i_{it}, k_{it}) + u_t^q \tag{14.12}$$

Estimation of Eq. (14.11) proceeds in two stages (Olley and Pakes 1996). In the first stage, output (value added) is regressed on log of labor and capital and a polynomial function of investment and capital (i and k) to obtain a consistent estimate of the labor elasticity parameter and $\varphi_t(k_{it}, I_{it})$, the combined effect of capital and efficiency or productivity level. By this action, the estimated labor coefficient and other included free variables are expected to be lower since this corrects for downward bias in capital (Hall and Mairesse 2007; Van Beveren 2012).

The second stage of the estimation process, which recovers the coefficient on capital variable, exploits the information on firm dynamics. Specifically, productivity is assumed to follow a first-order Markov process, that is, $\omega_{it+1} = E(\omega_{It+1}|\omega_{it} + \xi_{it+1})$.

where ξ_{it+1} represents the news component assumed to be uncorrelated with productivity and capital in period t + 0.1. Firms will continue to operate provided their productivity levels exceed the lower bounds.

$\chi_{it+1} = 1 \geq \omega_{it+1} \geq \underline{\omega}_{it+1}$ where χ_{it+1} is a survival indicator variable. Because the news component ξ_{it+1}, is correlated with freely variable inputs, in the analysis labor and other freely variable inputs are subtracted from the output. Therefore, the analysis considers the expectation of:

$$E\left[(y_{it+1} - \beta_l l_{it+1})|k_{it+1}, \chi_{it+1} = 1\right]$$
$$= \beta_0 + \beta_k k_{it} + E\left[\omega_{it+1|\omega_{it.}} \chi_{it+1} = 1\right]$$

The second stage of the estimation algorithm is then derived by using the law of motion.

In contrast to Olley and Pakes' (1996) decision to use investment as proxy for productivity, Levinsohn and Petrin (2003) relied on intermediate inputs as proxy. Second, their estimation does not correct for selection bias.

In our study, a hybrid Olley and Pakes (1996) and Levisohn and Pakes (2003) estimator was implemented. Specifically, the model is similar to the Olley and Pakes (1996) estimator in terms of employing investment as a proxy for productivity. It resembles Levinsohn and Petrin (2003) as it does not correct for selection bias. The latter is consistent with the aggregate nature of the data used.

Appendix 2: Data Summary Statistics

See Table 14.4.

Table 14.4 Summary statistics of the data

Country: Benin Rep.	Mean	Std. dev.	Min	Max
Agricultural GDP	2506.621	546.5719	1494.044	3162.646
Raw materials export	2.70e+08	1.08e+08	2,983,042	4.21e+08
TFP	1.008466	0.1942747	0.7939172	1.404898
Burkina Faso				
Agricultural GDP	3119.91	990.331	1435.468	4184.47
Raw materials export	1.68e+08	1.04e+08	2.53e+07	3.62e+08
TFP	0.9114271	0.2677091	7.18e−16	1.142234
Madagascar				
Agricultural GDP	3316.498	415.5445	2538.141	3980.411
Raw materials export	2.32e+07	1.34e+07	3231.464	5.87e+07

(continued)

Table 14.4 (continued)

Country: Benin Rep.	Mean	Std. dev.	Min	Max
TFP	0.988527	0.472788	0.8466374	1.074218
Ghana				
Agricultural GDP	6883.188	1316.675	4959.785	9789.318
Raw materials export	1.58e+08	7.88e+07	1.52e+07	2.48e+08
TFP	3.76258	9.772114	0.6393817	34.79007
Mali				
Agricultural GDP	2840.574	515.3017	1957.09	3426.025
Raw materials export	3.29e+08	1.81e+08	8.33e+07	5.24e+08
TFP	0.9706709	0.0782413	0.8783707	1.109699
Togo				
Agricultural GDP	1356.446	350.0368	819.9999	2016.686
Raw materials export	8.00e+07	4.97e+07	1.34e+07	1.76e+08
TFP	5.70297	20.34471	0.2488871	92.08675
Kenya				
Agricultural GDP	9471.444	1797.619	6628.193	11,837.5
Raw materials export	1.38e+08	9.73e+07	5.53e+07	4.25e+08
TFP	0.948233	0.20344	0.0231489	1.125005
Nigeria				
Agricultural GDP	42,000.04	9416.445	25,909.01	57,168.83
Raw materials export	3.49e+07	6.54e+07	1,108,543	2.60e+08
TFP	1.018321	0.1350183	0.695404	1.195999

References

Adams NA (1973) A note on trade as a handmaiden of growth. Econ J 83(329):210–212

AfDB (African Development Bank) (2008) Key challenges in agro-industrial development in Africa. Paper presented at Global Agribusiness Forum, New Delhi, April

Ackerberg D, Benkard CL, Berry S, Pakes A (2007) Econometric tools for analyzing market outcomes. In: Heckman JJ, Leamer EE (eds) Handbook of econometrics, vol 6A. Elsevier/North-Holland, Amsterdam, pp 4171–4176

Aghion P, Howitt P (1992) A model of growth through creative destruction. Econometrica 60 (2):323–351

Anderson K, Masters W (eds) (2009) Distortions to agricultural incentives in Africa. The World Bank, Washington, DC

Arellano M, Bond S (1991) Some tests of specification for panel data: Monte Carlo evidence and an application to employment equations. Rev Econ Stud 58(2):277–297

Agricultural Science and Technology Indicators (ASTI). Internationally comparable data on agricultural R&D investments and capacity for developing countries. International Food policy Research Institute, Washington, DC. Available at: http://www.asti.cgiar.org

Akande, O.R. (2012). "Do Domestic Food Producers in Food Deficit Countries Benefits from International Trade: Evidence from Five Rice Markets in West African Countries", Paper presented at the 86th Agricultural Economists Conference, Warwick UK, 16–18 April 2012. Available at: https://ideas.repec.org/p/ags/aesc12/134725.html

Binswanger H, Townsend R (2000) The growth performance of agriculture in sub-Saharan Africa. Am J Agr Econ 85:1075–1986
Crammer C (1999) Can Africa industrialize by processing primary commodities? The case of Mozambican cashew nuts. World Dev 27(7):1247–1266
Davidson R, MacKinnon JG (2004) Econometric theory and methods. Oxford University Press, New York
da Silva CA, Baker B (2007) Introduction. In: da Silva CA, Baker B, Shepherd AW, Jenane C, Miranda-Da-Cruz S (eds) Agro industries for development. Food and Agriculture Organization (FAO) and United Nations Industrial Development Organizations (UNIDO), Rome
Edwards S (1992) Trade orientation, distortions and growth in developing countries. J Dev Econ 39(1):31–57
Edwards S (1998) Openness, productivity and growth: what do we really know? Economic Journal 108(2):383–398
FAO (Food and Agriculture Organization) (1997) "The state of food and agriculture 1997", FAO agriculture series No 30. FAO, Rome
Fuglie KO, Rada NE (2013) Resources, policies, and agricultural productivity in Sub-Saharan Africa, ERR-145. US Department of Agriculture, Economic Research Service, February
Grilliches Z (1998) R&D and productivity: the econometric evidence. University of Chicago Press, Chicago
Grossman G, Helpman E (1991) Innovation and growth in the global economy. MIT Press, Cambridge, MA
Hall BH, Lotti F, Mairesse J (2007). Employment, Innovation, and Productivity: Evidence from Italian Microdata. NBER Working Paper No. 13296, August 2007
Hirschman AO (1958) The strategy of economic development. Yale University Press, New Haven
Kharas H (2007) Trend and issues in development Aid", Wolfensohn Center for development working paper 1. Brookings Global Economy and Development
Krueger AO (1978) Foreign trade regimes and economic development: liberalization attempts and consequences. Ballinger, Cambridge, MA
Levinsohn J, Petrin A (2003) Estimating production functions using inputs to control for unobservables. Rev Econ Stud 70(2):317–342
Love J (1983) Concentration, diversification and earnings instability: some evidence on developing countries' exports of manufactures and primary products. World Dev 11(9):787–793
Lussier M (1993) Impact of exports on economic performance: a comparative study. Journal of African Economics 2(1):106–127
Marschak J, Andrews WH (1944) Random simultaneous equations and the theory of production. Econometrica 12:143–205
Nkamelu GB (2013) Extensification versus intensification: revisiting the role of land in African agricultural growth. Proceedings of African economic conference, Johannesburg, South Africa, 28–30 October. Available at: http://www.afdb.org/en/aec-2011/papers/extensification-versus-intensification-revisiting-the-role-of-land-in-african-agricultural-growth/
Olley GS, Pakes A (1996) The dynamics of productivity in the telecommunications equipment industry. Econometrica 64(6):1263–1297
Petrick M, Kloss M (2013) Identifying factor productivity from micro-data: the case of EU agriculture. Factor markets working paper No. 34, January
Pinstrup-Andersen P (2000) Food policy research for developing countries: emerging issues and unfinished business. Food Policy 25:125–141
Ramachandran MK (2009) Economics of agro-based industries: a study of Kerala. Mittal Publications, New Delhi
Romer P (1990) Endogenous technological change. J Polit Econ 98:S71–S102
Strawson T, Beecher J, Hills R, Ifan G, Knox D, Lonsdale C, Osborne A, Tew R, Townsend I, Walton D (2015). Improving ODA allocation for a post-2015 world: targeting aid to benefit the poorest 20% of people in developing countries. United Nations Development Initiatives and UK Aid

UNDP (2011). Towards human resilience: sustaining MDG progress in an age of economic uncertainty. United Nations Development Programme Bureau for Development Policy, New York

Van Beveren I (2012) Total factor productivity estimation: a practical review. J Econ Surv 26(1):98–128

Yasar M, Raciborski R, Poi BP (2008) Production function estimation in Stata using the Olley and Pakes method. Stata J 8:221–231

Chapter 15
Determinants of Service Sector Firms' Growth in Rwanda

Eric Uwitonze and Almas Heshmati

Abstract The service sector is an avenue for economic transformation as not all countries have a competitive edge in manufacturing. Findings from a micro-level research on the service sector confirm that ICT integration, firm's age, the education of the owner, the boss' attitude, family business, networks, new processes, major improvements, market share, on the job training and know-how significantly, and positively increase the probability of a firm's growth. Even though the growth rate of services is currently impressive in the Rwandan economy, no investigations have been done on the determinants of the growth of the firms in the service sector. This paper studies the development of services over the years in Rwanda's economy in detail and empirically estimates its determinants by using an econometric methodology. The empirical results are based on micro-data collected by the Rwanda Enterprise Survey (2011) and the 2014 Establishment Census. The survey has data on 241 firms and establishments. Linear and limited dependent variable techniques are employed to investigate the factors behind the development of service firms. Models are specified and estimated to assess the factors contributing to sales growth, innovations, and turnovers of service firms. The results show that the key factors driving the development of service firms in Rwanda include access to credit, application of ICT, availability of skilled labor, employee development and acquisition of fixed assets. The results suggest that the government should uphold the use of ICT in all service firms, promote access to finance to new service firms and promote on-work training in service firms to speed up Rwanda's shift from a low income to a middle-income state.

E. Uwitonze
Ministry of Gender and Family Promotion (MIGEPROF), MIGEPROF,
Single Project Implementation Unit, Kigali, Rwanda
e-mail: uwitonzeric@gmail.com

A. Heshmati (✉)
Jönköping International Business School (JIBS),
Jönköping University, Jönköping, Sweden
e-mail: almas.heshmati@gmail.com

A. Heshmati (ed.), *Studies on Economic Development and Growth in Selected African Countries*, Frontiers in African Business Research,
DOI 10.1007/978-981-10-4451-9_15

Keywords Limited dependent variables · Services · Openness · Growth · East Africa · Rwanda

JEL Classification Codes C35 · F13 · G29 · O47 · O55

15.1 Introduction

15.1.1 Background

As per the 2014 Rwanda Services Policy Review, the service sector was the largest and most dynamic sector in the Rwandan economy. The Rwandan service sector is subdivided into two broad categories of trade and transport services. Trade and transport services include maintenance and repair of motor vehicles, wholesale and retail trade, transport services and other services such as hotels and restaurants; information and communication; financial services; real estate activities; professional, scientific and technical activities; administrative and support services; public administration and defense; compulsory social security; education services; human health; social work services; and cultural, domestic and other services.

The service sector spearheaded the strong economic growth journey as it accounted for a bigger share of GDP by 2015—47% GDP as compared to 33% by the primary sector (agriculture, forestry and fisheries) while the growth of services was impressive at around 9% by 2014 against 7% for industry and 4% for agriculture. Trade and transport services contributed to services' share in GDP at 159 billion RWF[1] in 1999 which increased to 784 billion RWF in 2014 of which wholesale and retail trade had 615 billion RWF in 2014 against 133 billion RWF in 1999. Other services including hotels and restaurants, information and communication and financial services increasingly contributed to GDP from 430 billion RWF in 1999 to 1505 billion RWF in 2014. The service sector's contribution grew to 2290 billion RWF in 2014 as compared to 563 billion RWF in 1999. Authorized loans by the central bank to the service sector increased from 1.5 billion RWF in 2010 to 12 billion RWF in 2014. All these statistics are at fixed 2011 prices and suggest increased attention and public support for the service sector's development.

The Doing Business in Sub-Saharan Africa Report (2013–2014) ranked Rwanda second after Mauritius and its service sector received a big share of foreign private investments. As a matter of fact, 41.4% of foreign private investments were allocated to ICT and tourism (12.8%), while others like mining received 13.8%, manufacturing (10.8%) and other sectors received a significant (21.7%) share of private investments. Meanwhile, as documented in the Rwandan Vision 2020 document, the service sector is believed to be the engine for Rwanda's economy with a growth rate of 13.5% and a contribution of 42% to GDP.

[1]USD 1 = 746 RWF on 9 March 2016.

15.1.1.1 The Rwandan Service Sector's Development and Growth

According to the Rwandan Integrated Household Living Condition Survey (EICV4), the indicator of an increase in private and business-oriented mixed establishments by industry in 2011–2014 went up to 24% in which the contribution of each service sub-sector showed a rise and fall in percentage change. An increase was found in wholesale and retail trade and repair of motor vehicles and motorcycles (21%); accommodation and food service activities (34%); transport and storage (7%); professional, scientific and technical activities (3.9%); administrative and support services (23.1%); health and social work activities (33.1); art, entertainment and recreation (31.0%); financial and insurance activities (18.4%); private form of education (0.6%); and other service activities (32.0%), whereas a fall was recorded in information and communication (−28.3%) and real estate activities (−76.5%).

Employment changes in private and business-oriented establishments by industry in 2011–2014 increased up to 34.5% within which in the service sub-sector a large increase was recorded in administrative and support activities (268.3%); financial and insurance activities (81.2%); transport and storage (54.9%); arts, entertainment and recreation (67.7%); health and social work activities (50.2%); accommodation and food service activities (37.7%); and wholesale and retail trade and repair of motor vehicles and motorcycles (28.7%).

By 2020, the contribution of services is projected to be 57% of GDP as compared to 24% of agriculture followed by 19% of industry. As per EICV4, the service sector was the biggest contributor to GDP growth with 2536 billion RWF in 2013 compared to 774 billion RWF for industry and 1785 billion RWF for agriculture in the same year. This reflects the transition of the Rwandan economy toward a service-based one. This is also evidenced by a change in the share of economic sectors in GDP from 1970 to 2010. In 1970, agriculture led other sectors as it had a 55.9% share in GDP compared to a 19% share of industry and 25.0% of services. Since 2000, the service sector is leading with a contribution of 45.6% to GDP, 49.7% in 2010 and 53.3% in 2013.

15.1.1.2 Developing Services by Economic Activity

The distribution of businesses by economic activity shows that the service sector achieved positive growth in both rural and urban areas. The main sub-sectors in the service sector that showed more than 30% growth include accommodation and food services; human health and social work activities; and art, entertainment and recreation activities. According to Singh and Kaur (2014) rapid urbanization is a key factor which contributes to the growth of services and leads us to analyze this growth of the service sector in urban and rural areas in 2011–2014. Accommodation and food service activities showed greater growth; they had 26,190 registered establishments in 2011 and 36,545 registered establishments in 2014 in rural areas showing a 40% increase whereas in urban areas 7095 establishments were registered in 2011 and 8076 in 2014 corresponding to a 13.8% increase. The average growth of the accommodation and food services sub-sector was 34% between 2011 and 2014 in private establishments and the business-oriented mixed sector by economic activity where 33,285 accommodation and food establishments were registered (out of 119,270) in 2011 and 44,621 establishments (out of 148,376) were registered in 2014. It is obvious that the accommodation and food services sub-sector is growing faster in rural areas than in urban areas and the growth of these sub-sectors contributed to the overall growth of the service sector (NISR 2014).

As stated by Latha and Shanmugam (2014), advancement of the service sector is correlated with the expansion of quality health services indicated by complete physical, mental and social well-being and not just the nonexistence of diseases and aliments. While analyzing the service sector's development in Rwanda, it was found that human health and social work activities demonstrated an interesting growth of 33.1%. In rural areas, 83 human health and social work establishments were registered in 2011 compared to 167 registered in 2014 showing a 101% increase over the period. In urban areas, 261 establishments in human health and social work activities were registered in 2011 as compared to 291 registered in 2014 or an 11.5% increase in human health and social work establishments in urban areas. The growth of establishments in human health and social work activities was eight times higher in rural areas as compared to urban areas from 2011 to 2014. Therefore, there is great conviction that the growth of the service sector is linked to high growth in its sub-sectors, particularly in rural areas.

Though wholesale and retail trade and repair of motor vehicles and motorcycles are not mentioned among the fastest growing service sub-sectors, it is worth analyzing them since they had a lion's share in the service sector. In wholesale and retail trade, there was an average increase of 7% by 2014 while the motor vehicles and motorcycle repair sub-sector had a 37% increase in rural areas as compared to a 7% increase in urban areas. This was a result of 30,708 establishments registered in 2011 going up to 42,101 establishments registered in 2014 in rural areas as compared to urban areas where 33,968 establishments were registered in 2011 and 36,352 in 2014. Generally, the rural areas spearhead economic activity in the service sector. Figure 15.1 shows the remarkable growth of the service sub-sectors accommodation and food activities and wholesale trade, repair of motor vehicles and motorcycles.

15.1.1.3 Employment Growth in the Service Sector

A growing body of literature supports employment to measure the growth of firms since they reflect both short-term and long-term changes (Isaga 2015). In keeping with this thinking, this section gives a descriptive analysis of employment in the service sector in Rwanda.

According to the Establishment Census (2014), the service sector employed 401,173 workers or 81.3% of the total workers. The biggest service sub-sectors in

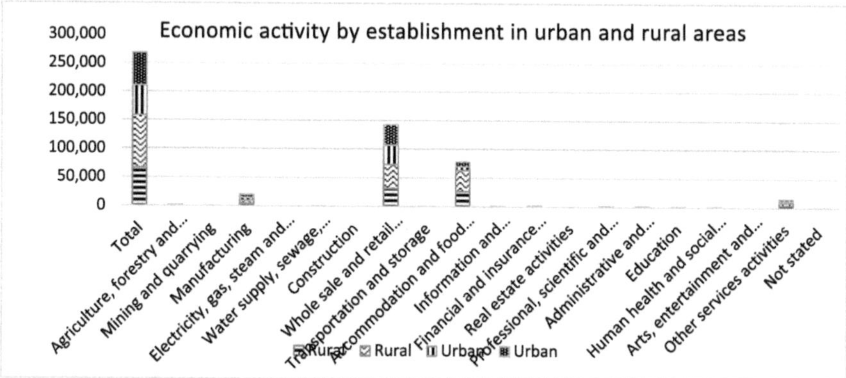

Fig. 15.1 Economic activities of private and business-oriented mixed establishments according to urban/rural areas (2011 and 2014) *Source* NISR's Establishment Census (2014)

terms of the number of people employed included wholesale and retail trade, repair of motorcycles and motor vehicles (with 120,482 employees equivalent to 24.4% of the total employment), followed by education employing 83,569 (16.9% of the total employment) and accommodation and food service activities having 82,213 employed people (16.7% of the total employment). These sub-sectors supported the growth of the service sector since they provided more jobs as compared to other economic sectors.

Men were predominant in almost all the service sub-sectors except human health and social work activities where they represented 47.7% of the total employed while female workers reached 52.3%. A general picture of the share of employment within the service sector shows that gender inequalities persist. Only 36.8% of the total employment in the service sector was with females as compared to male workers who had the lion's share of service sector employment at 63.2%. Considering women's share in the total population of Rwanda—53% as compared to 47% for men—there is hope that the service sector will continue to grow if there is full participation of women in its employment. Figure 15.2 illustrates the way employment is divided across economic activities.

15.1.1.4 GDP Share of Service Sector Growth

According to the National Institute of Statistics of Rwanda (2014), the service sector was the biggest contributor to GDP. The shift from an agriculture-based economy to a service-led economy has been effective since 2004 when the annual output in agriculture was 879 billion RWF compared to the service sector output at 882 billion RWF. Till 2016, the service sector spearheaded the contribution of the economic sector to GDP growth in Rwanda.

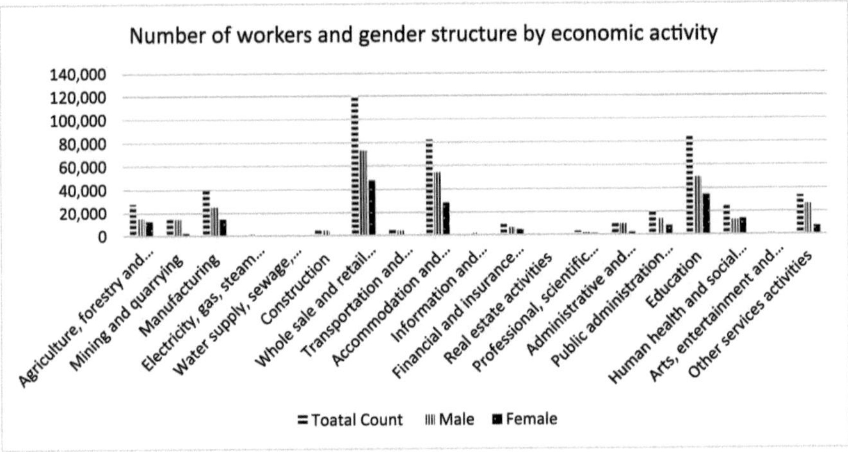

Fig. 15.2 Distribution of number of workers and gender structure by economic activity (2014). *Source* NISR's Establishment Census (2014)

The impressive growth of the service sector was documented around 9% by 2014 against 7% for industry and 4% for agriculture while the annual average GDP was 8% by 2014. The total output in the service sector increased up to four times from 1999 to 2014. The total output of the service sector in 1999 was 563 billion RWF which grew to 2290 billion RWF in 2014 (Fig. 15.3).

The service sub-sectors that contributed more include wholesale and retail trade with a contribution of 130 billion RWF in 1999 and 615 billion RWF in 2014. Though they did not show growth, real estate activities contributed more to the share of the service sector in GDP. In 1999, the total output in real estate activities was 283 billion RWF which did not grow much and amounted to 311 billion RWF

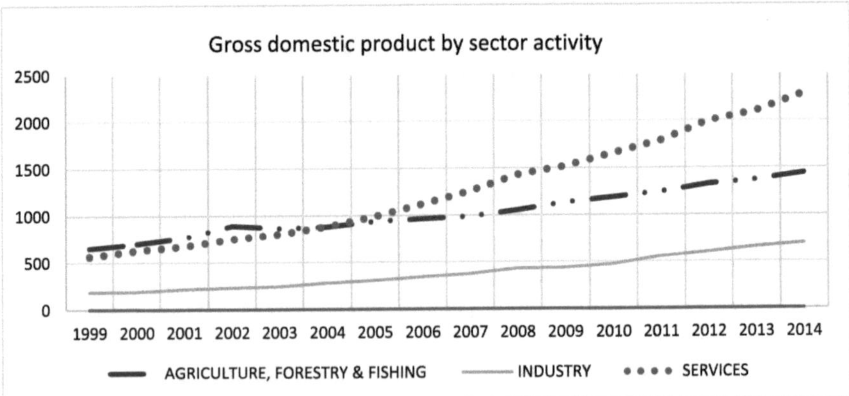

Fig. 15.3 GDP by sector activity at constant 2011 prices (in billion RWF). *Source* National Institute of Statistics of Rwanda (2014)

by 2014. Tremendous growth in hotels and restaurants (accommodation and food activities) was witnessed by the contribution of this sector to GDP. In 1999, hotels and restaurants contributed 19 billion RWF which grew to 113 billion RWF in 2014. In general, the contribution of the service sector to GDP shows that the sector has been growing since 1999. The effective transition of the economy happened in 2004, at a time when the service sector became the top sector. Though the contribution of the service sector is remarkable in the Rwandan economy, there are no studies which analyze service firms' growth or which specifically analyze the determinants of service firms' growth.

Our study analyzes the development of service firms and their contribution to economic growth in Rwanda. Thus, the prime purpose of our study is analyzing trends in the expansion of services in Rwanda and pointing out the contributing factors driving its development using survey data covering various parts of the service sector.

The general objective of our study is to investigate factors of development of service firms. Its specific objectives include (i) analyzing the contribution of service firms to economic growth in Rwanda and (ii) unveiling key factors contributing to the development of service firms in Rwanda.

The findings open up additional academic investigations in service firms' thus contributing to the body of knowledge about the role of the service sector in economic growth in developing countries of which Rwanda is classified as one. Further, it sheds light on Rwanda's ambitious target as listed in its Vision 2020 document for holistically understanding what to concentrate on in the service sector for the economic growth of the country.

This rest of the paper is organized as follows. The next section reviews literature on the service sector's development in the world, and in Rwanda in particular. Section 15.3 on methodology discusses data, the conceptual framework and empirical models. Section 15.4 focuses on understanding the empirical results and gives an analysis of the trends. The last section gives the conclusion, a summary of the findings and recommendations.

15.2 Literature Review

A literature review shows that a number of researchers and international organizations have supported the role of the service sector as a key driver in the growth of an economy in both developing and developed countries. Recently, the United Nations Economic Commission for Africa (UNECA) affirmed that the service sector was an avenue for economic transformation as not all countries had a competitive edge in the manufacturing sector (UNECA 2015). The service sector's development is also providing infrastructure that promotes productivity in manufacturing and agriculture.

15.2.1 Growth and Development of the Service Sector

The service sector's economic development is the only way of promoting economic structural adjustment and accelerating the transformation of economic growth (Zhou 2015). A declining share of agricultural employment is a key feature in economic development (Alverez-Cuadrado and Poschke 2011); structural transformation usually coincides with a growing role of industry and services in the economy (UNECA 2015). The growing size of the service sector and its impact on the other parts of the economy make it all the more important to promote efficiency in the provision of services thereby boosting economy-wide labor productivity as witnessed in OECD member countries. The slowdown in the service sector brought down labor productivity in the entire economy from more than 4% in 1976–1989 to less than 2% in 1999–2004 (Jones and Yoon 2008).

Acharya and Patel (2015) confirm that the service sector is the fastest growing sector in India, contributing significantly to GDP, economic growth, trade and foreign direct investment (FDI) inflows as the total share of this sector to India's GDP is around 65%.

Singh and Kaur (2014) state that the main reasons for the growth in services in India are rapid urbanization, expansion of the public sector and increased demand for intermediate and final consumer services. Domestic investments and openness also positively affect the share of the service sector in GDP, and the main service sectors attracting FDI in India are telecommunications, construction and hotels and restaurants. Lee and Malin (2013) says that the service sector has become the main contributor to GDP not only in developed economies such as the US, Japan and UK, but also in developing economies such as China, Indonesia, Pakistan and India. Concluding their study on the determinants of innovation capacity with empirical evidence from service firms, Madeira et al. (2014), affirms that the greater the financial investments in the acquisition of machinery, equipment and software; in internal research and development; in acquisition of external knowledge; and in marketing activities and other procedures, the greater the propensity of firms to innovate in terms of services.

According to Park and Shin (2012) general wisdom is that when a country industrializes, the shares of industry and service sectors in both GDP and employment increase whereas the share of agriculture falls and when a country de-industrializes and moves into the post-industrial phase, the share of services increases while the shares of both industry and agriculture fall. They found that when computing the contribution of agriculture, industry and services to GDP growth, in general the service sector made the biggest contribution. Further, the lower the per capita GDP, the greater the scope of labor productivity growth in the service sector, which implies that there is still a lot of room for growth in the productivity of services. Thus, Buera and Kaboski (2009) argue that as productivity grows, individuals consume new services. Eventually, labor productivity increases enough which makes the absolute cost advantage of market-production smaller and leads individuals to home produced customized versions of services which yield higher utility.

In the early 1980s, Fuchs (1980) argued that the decline in agriculture was attributable primarily to differences in income elasticity of demand while the shift from industry to services was attributable primarily to differential rates of growth of output per worker. Economic growth also contributes to an increase in service employment through an increase in female labor force participation because families with working wives tend to spend a higher proportion of their incomes on consuming services.

15.2.2 *Productivity of Service Sector Firms*

Sahu (2015) analyzed micro-data on service sector companies to test high growth in total factor productivity (TFP) assessing if better factor allocation led to TFP growth. He found that a reduction in the misallocation of resources in the service sector resulted in an accelerated pace of TFP growth. Therefore, the communication and community service industries registered the fastest growth in terms of moving toward efficient TFP levels. Acharya (2016) affirms what accounts for exceptional TFP growth performance in some ICT industries using industries where productivity gains in the production of ICT are given as an answer in the US and in the Organization of Economic Cooperation for Development (OECD) countries. Van der Marel and Shepherd (2013) confirm that ICT capital and legal institutions are particularly important determinants of a country's ability to successfully export services. Further, the tradability indices are strongly correlated with important factors such as country productivity and size, factor endowments, trade costs and regulatory measures.

Geishecker and Görg (2013) claim that measuring both service and material off-shoring is not straightforward and is greatly limited in available data when it comes to coherent and comparable information on such activities. Thus, trade economists usually revert to measuring trade in intermediaries as proxy. In addition, they assessed the impact of off-shoring activities on individual wages in an industry which are conceptualized as average hourly gross labor earnings including bonus, premium and other extra payments. The explanatory variables are demographic and human capital variables including age, age squared; dummies for the presence of children and being married; job tenure; tenure squared; a high education indicator; dummies for occupation; and dummies for firm size and regional dummies. Their results show that workers in industries with increasing levels of off-shoring services were likely to experience reduction in their wages. They conclude what would have been considered as a perfect case of spillovers from ICT using conventional methods—the impact of research and development and other intangible capital.

Madeira et al. (2014) investigated the main determinants of innovation in the service sector in the area of innovation activities. They found the use of the logit model to be appropriate for measuring direct and indirect effects of a selected set of explanatory variables of the innovation capacity of Portuguese service firms. They point out the existence of several factors that stimulate and limit the innovation capacities of firms such as investments in innovation activities, firm size and sub-sector services in the sector of the activity.

Many research findings show that the contribution of research and development activities is fundamental to the growth of the economic sector in any country. Jafaridehkord et al. (2015) argue that firms benefit immensely from spending on their human capital because this investment adds value to their companies. Heshmati and Kim (2011) discuss the fact that a decrease in research and development investments results in decreasing productivity growth. Schoonjans et al. (2013) claim that the effect of knowledge networking on firm growth is significantly larger for service firms than for manufacturing firms since it positively affects net asset and value-added growth of service firms.

According to Du and Temouri (2015), firms in both manufacturing and service sectors are likely to become high-growth firms (HGF) when they exhibit higher TFP. The TFP growth model shows that openness to foreign companies and the world economy, restructuring the economy through a shift of resources between sectors and the presence of foreign companies in Malaysia are major contributors to TFP growth (Jajri 2008).

15.2.3 Determinants of Productivity Growth in Service Firms

Capital, labor and knowledge-based capital are key inputs in the production of goods and services. Salehi-Isfahani (2006) claims that urban households are a source of growth in human capital in the Middle East and North of Africa (MENA) countries. But households in that region have to face the state playing a large role in the economy, which distorts the incentive to invest in education and the labor market and in social norms regarding gender. As a result, households invest in an inefficient portfolio of human capital with dire consequences for long-run growth.

Literature argues about the relevance of knowledge-based capital in a firm. Yli-Renko et al. (2001) found that knowledge acquisition was positively associated with knowledge exploitation for competitive advantages through new product development, technological distinctiveness and sale cost efficiency. Corporate entrepreneurship was positively associated with knowledge-based capital (Simsek and Heavy 2011) and business services can have an effect comparable to the traditional production factor only when it applies to the service sector (Drejer 2002).

A review of contemporary literature suggests that regulatory, policy and institutional environments, competition in the product market, spillovers and externalities and internalization and globalization are constituents of a business environment affecting a firm's performance.

Bouazza et al. (2015) confirm that the key factors of a business environment affecting Algerian firms are unfair competition from the informal sector; cumbersome and costly bureaucratic procedures; burdensome laws, policies and regulations; an inefficient tax system; lack of access to external financing; and low human resources capacity. The main internal factors responsible for unstable and limited growth include entrepreneurial characteristics, low managerial capacity, lack of market skills and low technological skills. Gale et al. (2015) confirm the existence of a negative relationship between the rate of firm formation and the top income tax rate by finding that a cut in top income tax automatically generates or necessitates growth.

The economic growth of a country in terms of GDP growth is determined by the real value-added growth of underlying firms. According to Pop et al. (2014), in an economic crisis it becomes clear that the smaller firms are often capable of responding faster, they are more targeted and flexible to fluctuations in the global economy and to withstanding the recessionary phase.

Khan (2011) tested the important determinants of a firm's growth. He highlights that a firm's age, the education of the owner, the boss' attitude, family business, networks, new processes, major improvements, market share, on the job training and know-how significantly and positively increased the probability of a firm's growth. The age of the owner, foreign trade regulations, taxes, other regulations, political instability, inflation and lack of skilled labor adversely reduced the probability of a firm's growth in terms of employment opportunities. Olivera and Fortunato (2008) and Lenaerts and Merlevede (2015) claim that a firm's growth is mainly explained by the firm's age and size.

Existing literature states that expenditure on ICT has a positive impact on exports of producer services (Guerrieri and Meliciani 2004) and sees ICT as the bedrock of improving business processes, customer relations and efficient delivery of goods and services to satisfy customer needs (Atom 2013). According to Bethapudi (2013), ICT integration provides a powerful tool that brings advantages to promoting and strengthening the tourism industry. Mihalic et al. (2015) mention that ICT is also becoming an important factor in business and competitiveness because of, as discussed by Borghoff (2011), its influence on the three sub-processes of globalization: internationalization, global network building and global evolutionary dynamics.

As for ICT applicability in the service sector, its role is crucial in facilitating trade (Gupta 2012). According to Liu and Nath (2013) the trade-enhancing effect of ICT is on its use. Internet subscriptions and Internet hosts have a significant positive effect on both exports and imports. ICT in transport services plays a decisive role in reducing energy consumption and CO_2 emissions in the road transport sector (Gupta 2012).

According to Agwu and Carter (2014) the use of mobile banking and automatic teller machines (ATMs) has made financial services easily accessible and has reduced costs for both customers and financial service providers in Nigeria. Information technology has enabled banks to understand and serve customers better than their competitors; they have developed and improved new products for customers and further improved processes and relationships with customers and business partners (Muro et al. 2013).

15.2.4 Employment and Productivity Growth in Services

Arnold et al. (2016) demonstrate the presence of a link between India's policy reforms in the service and productivity of manufacturing firms. They find that banking, telecommunications, insurance and transport reforms have all had significant effects on productivity in manufacturing firms; these effects tend to be stronger on foreign owned firms.

El-Said and Kattara (2013) researched the application of information technology versus human interaction services in an Egyptian hotel. They found that customers preferred to contact an employee rather than depending on technology-based self-services in a majority of service encounters. In Uganda, more than 80% of the households were employed in tourism services. Tourism employment can provide initial capital for supplementary activities.

Heshmati and Kim (2011) came to the conclusion that the competitiveness in Korea's service industry can be driven by an incentive system for skilled workers and investing more in research and development in order to increase labor productivity. In addition, the Korean government should implement an open market policy to liberalize labor movement and induce low paid labor to move to the production process to a large extent.

15.2.5 Summary of the Literature Review on Service Development

Departing from the macroeconomic point of view, the growing size of the service sector and its impact on the other parts of the economy makes it all the more important to promote efficiency in the provision of services thereby boosting economy-wide labor productivity (Jones and Yoon 2008). The main reasons for the growth in services are rapid urbanization, domestic investments, openness, expansion of the public sector and increased demand for intermediate and final consumer services (Singh and Kaur 2014). The lower the per capita GDP, the greater the scope for labor productivity growth in the service sector, which implies that there is still a lot of room for growth in the productivity of services (Park and Shin 2012).

Our microeconomic literature review supports that the development of service firms is mainly backed with knowledge acquisition (Yli-Renko et al. 2001), knowledge-based capital (Simsek and Heavy 2011), on the job training and know-how and skilled labor and ICT applicability (Gupta 2012). Firms benefit immensely from spending on their human capital because this investment adds value to their companies (Jafaridehkord et al. 2015). The effect of knowledge networking on firm growth is significantly larger for service firms than for manufacturing firms since it positively affects net asset and value-added growth of service firms (Schoonjans et al. 2013).

To conclude, throughout research it is claimed that the important determinants of a firm's growth include a firm's age, the education of the owner, the boss' attitude, family business, networks, new processes, major improvements, market share, on the job training and know-how which significantly and positively increase the probability of the firm's growth (Khan 2011).

15.3 Methodology

15.3.1 Understanding the Key Concepts

In our study, services are conceptualized as non-agricultural and non-manufacturing economic activities in firms operating in the Rwandan economy. National accounting of GDP complies with the International Standards Industrial Classification (ISIC) of all economic activities.[2]

Openness is conceived as an interaction with activities outside the Rwandan service sector in terms of import and export of services, foreign direct investment firms and acquisition of working capital externally. Yeboah et al. (2012) have argued that the trade effect on productivity is much greater in an outwardly oriented economy than in an inwardly oriented nation. The relationship between trade openness and economic growth is significantly positive in developing countries (Tahir and Azid 2015). The openness of a firm's founders and early preparations for growth determine both the extent of organizational learning and the speed at which it is developed and used (Hagen and Zucchella 2014).

Growth is conceptualized as the increase in the service sector measured as GDP. King and Levine (1993) claim that financial development is robustly correlated to the future rate of economic growth, accumulation of physical capital and improvements in economic efficiency. Growth in foreign sales contributes to a firm's growth if there is greater interaction among the management team's members

---

[2]ISIC classified services into sections from G to U as per individual categories in such a way to (U) include wholesale and retail trade, repair of motor vehicles and motorcycles, transport and storage, accommodation and food service activities, information and communication, financial and insurance activities, real estate activities, professional, scientific and technical activities, administrative and support service activities, public administration and defense, compulsory social security, education, human health and social work activities, arts, entertainment and recreation, other services' activities, activities of households as employers, undifferentiated goods and services producing activities for households for own use and activities of extra-territorial organizations and bodies (UN 2008).

and a higher degree of joint decision making among the owners and managers of small firms (Reuber and Fischer 2002). Sustaining economic growth and improving living standards requires shifting labor into both the manufacturing and service sectors (Eichengreen and Gupta 2011).

A firm's growth is conceived as an increase in the product or service as the main business, increase in sales, increase in the number of new employed persons and the size of the establishment in the service sector. Smith and Verner (2006) found that the proportion of women in top management jobs had a positive effect on a firm's performance and that the effect depended on the qualifications of female top managers in Denmark. Dawkins et al. (2007) argue that both large firms and those which are highly specialized, enjoy higher profit margins, whereas the more capital intensive the firm the lower its profitability.

15.3.2 Performance Models

In order to investigate the determinants of service sector development, we focus on the role of total annual sales and innovation and turnover in service firms as dependent variables. These are commonly used measures of performance throughout literature and are endogenous to firms in their decision making.

A number of hypotheses were formulated and tested. The first hypothesis was that the service sector's development can be investigated through total annual sales of a firm. In the Rwanda Enterprise Survey (2011), firms were asked what the establishment's total sales were in 2010 and what the establishment's total annual sales were in the three previous fiscal years since fiscal year 2008. Thus, total sales growth up to 2010 was used as the dependent variable. Variables that have an effect on total sales growth are employment cost, loan size, ICT and a firm's innovation characteristics. The null hypothesis is that these factors have no effect on total sales and growth rate, while the alternative hypothesis is that they have positive effects on total sales and growth rate.

Total annual sales were measured in terms of the amount of money a firm acquired by selling services domestically and through direct or indirect exports over three years starting 2008. Labor utility was included in the costs incurred for employment by a service firm. Working capital was estimated using the loan size approved to track the role of financial institutions as channels of access to financial service activities. ICT application was tracked by using e-mails to communicate with clients or suppliers and the use of cell phones for the operations of an establishment. A firm's innovation characteristics were defined as employee development, research and development activities, internal or external training, new methods, new practices, new marketing strategies and new logistics.

The model for investigating the determinants of total sales growth in service firms is constructed as:

$$\text{Total sales growth} = f\begin{pmatrix} \text{employment cost, working capital, ICT,} \\ \text{firm innovation criteria, acquisition of fixed asset} \end{pmatrix} \tag{15.1}$$

The second hypothesis is that the service sector's development is reflected in its innovations that are expressed in the introduction of new products or services. In the Rwanda Enterprise Survey (2011), firms were asked whether they had introduced new products or services in the last three year. The variable of the introduction of new products or services which is conceived as innovation is taken as the dependent variable. Independent variables include internal research and development (R&D) activities, external or internal acquisition of research and development (ext. R&D) as time given to employees in a service firm to develop or try out a new approach or a new idea about products or services, business process, firm management, marketing, training, access to finance as illustrated by the acquisition of fixed assets and a firm's characteristics in term of size. The null hypothesis suggests that these factors do not influence service innovation, while the alternative hypothesis suggests that they have a positive effect on service innovation of new products and services. The model to investigate the factors affecting service sales is structured as:

$$\text{Service innovation} = f\begin{pmatrix} \text{R\&D, ext.acquisition of R\&D, acquisition of training,} \\ \text{acquisition of fixed assets, other firms' criteria} \end{pmatrix} \tag{15.2}$$

The third hypothesis is that the turnover of a service firm is affected by a number of factors such as the capital used, openness conceived as buying and selling outside the country, the manager's gender, paying value-added tax, paying income tax and the service sub-sector. The turnover of a service firm is defined as the amount of money that is received in sales. In the Establishment Census (2014), the information collected on this variable is classified in categories where the first category includes all firms with turnovers less than 300,000 RWF, the second category includes all firms with turnovers ranging from 300,000 RWF to 12 million RWF, the third category has all firms with turnovers ranging from 12 million to 50 million RWF and the last category includes all firms with turnovers more than 50 million RWF. This is a category-dependent variable. Categorization of the turnover leads to information about losses within the category; it also sheds light on category differences in performance and the variations in their determinants.

The first dummy variable on openness contains information on whether a firm sells or buys goods or services abroad. The second dummy variable 'gender' defines whether the manager of a firm is female or male. The third dummy variable on value-added tax (VAT) contains information on whether or not the firm pays VAT. The fourth dummy variable has information on whether or not the firm pays income tax. There is also a factor variable on the service sub-sector where 7 stands for wholesale and retail trade and repair of motor vehicles and motorcycles, 8 stands for transportation and storage, 9 stands for accommodation and food service activities, 10 stands for information and communication, 11 stands for financial and insurance activities and 12 stands for real estate activities. The other factor variable 'capital' contains information classified in categories in such a way that the first category considers firms using less than 500,000 RWF as capital, the second using 500,000 to 15 million RWF, the third using 15 million to 75 million RWF and the last category using capital more than 75 million RWF. Thus, this is a categorical variable. Factors affecting change in turnover are constructed with the variables mentioned earlier and are expressed as:

$$\text{Turnover} = f(\text{capital used, openness, gender, taxes, service sub-sector}) \qquad (15.3)$$

15.3.2.1 Relationship Between Sales, Innovation and Turnover

As discussed earlier, sales are used as an indicator to measure a firm's growth and this growth as its turnover. In our study, sales and turnover are both used with different model specifications because the datasets used are different. Otherwise, they should have the same model specifications since they can be used interchangeably.

The model on the sales of service sector firms is constructed with the variables used in the collection of data during the 2011 Rwanda Enterprise Survey by the National Institute of Statistics of Rwanda in partnership with the World Bank. Because this database contained missing values, we constructed a model on turnover with the variable used to collect information in the Establishment Census (2014) by the National Institute of Statistics of Rwanda. This was done to track the main factors affecting sales or turnover.

For the innovation model, we used the same database as the sales model because the 2011 Enterprise Survey attached more interest to the innovation factor in the performance of firms. Only the predictors of the innovation model can appear in the sales model in order to prove the contribution of innovation in the growth of sales of service firms.

15.3.3 Description of the Data

Data about the performance of Rwanda's service sector used in this study was provided by the National Institute of Statistics of Rwanda. The data came from two important data collection channels—the 2010–2012 Enterprise Survey in Rwanda and the 2014 Establishment Census.

The Enterprise Survey focuses on the many factors which shape the business environment and is useful for both policymakers and researchers. The Enterprise

Survey is conducted by the World Bank and its partners across all geographic regions and covers small, medium and large companies. The sample is consistently defined in all countries and includes the entire manufacturing sector, the service sector and the transport and construction sector. The 2011 Rwanda Enterprise Survey covered 241 firms including 159 service firms and 82 manufacturing firms. The cleaned raw database contains 148 firm observations each with 247 variables describing various aspects of the firms and their activities (WB 2014).

The Rwanda Establishment Census (2014) consists of a complete count of all establishments practicing specific economic activities in Rwanda except not-for-sale government services. It covered themes such as economic activity, legal status, registration of establishment, taxation, capital employed, regular operation accounts, socioeconomic characteristics of an establishment's staff, payment status and sex of employees. The dataset contains 154,236 cases with 91 variables (NISR 2014).

The dependent variable is service firm growth which is measured by several attributes such as turnover/sales, employment, assets, market shares and profits. The Rwanda Enterprise Survey (2011) provides data on total sales for three years and the 2010 fiscal year and data on the introduction of new products or services which are a measure of innovation output in the previous three years. Factors affecting total sales, growth of employment and service innovation determine the development of the service sector. Literature highlights key measures of a firm's growth as sales, employment and innovation. Zhou and Wit (2009) and Isaga (2015) used sales and employment to measure the growth of a firm since they reflect both short-term and long-term changes in a firm.

In the model on service innovation, the dependent variable is a binary variable on the introduction of new products or services in three years from 2010. According to Neely and Hii (1998), innovation has a direct impact on the competitiveness of a firm. The values created by innovations are often manifested in new ways of doing things or new products and processes that contribute to wealth. In their studies, Arvanistis and Stucki (2012) and Madeira et al. (2014) used a firm's innovations for measuring growth because it is argued that innovation start-ups are important drivers of economic growth.

The model on turnover uses a categorical dependent variable where the turnover of a firm is classified into four categories as described earlier. An ordinary scale with many categories (5 or more), interval and ratio are usually analyzed using the traditional approaches of statistical tests (Newsom 2013).

Independent variables in new service development are classified into four categories—firm characteristics, innovation characteristics, managerial characteristics and business environment. In this study, a firm's characteristics consider the firm's size, gender composition and legal status. Considering firm size, Madeira et al. (2014) found a positive and increasing effect of firm size on firm innovation. Medium-sized firms showed greater propensity to innovate than small sized firms.

Innovation characteristics include market conditions, new management practices, new market methods, spending on research and development activities, a service firm's employees' development, a firm's access to finance expressed in the acquisition of fixed assets and degree of competition. Acs and Audretch (1988) and Prajogo and Sohal (2006) claim that there is a positive relationship between innovation and research and development activities of firms.

Managerial characteristics are pointed out with the top managers' levels of education and the years of their working experience in the service sector. Education is measured by level of education attained classified as: no education, primary school, secondary school, vocational training, some university training and graduate degree. Queiro (2016) found that firms which switch to more educated managers' experience sharp increases in growth relative to comparable firms managed by less experienced managers. More educated managers increase the use of incentive pay and are likely to report new products and services and incorporate new technologies. The correlation matrix of the dependent and independent variables is given in Appendix 1.

15.3.4 Estimation Methods: Linear and Logistic Regression Models

Madeira et al. (2014) have argued that a firm's capacity to innovate is a complex phenomenon influenced by a wide range of factors. Thus, the logistic regression (logit model) helps to study the statistical relationship of the dependent variable in relation to more than one determinant variable. Stock and Watson (2011) discuss a regression with a binary dependent variable and conclude that when dependent variable Y is binary, the population regression function is the probability that $Y = 1$, conditional on the regressors. The resulting predicted values are predicted probabilities and the estimated effect of a change in regressor X is the estimated change in the probability that $Y = 1$ arising from the change in X. The standard estimation in the maximum likelihood method and its estimates proceeds in the same way as it does in linear multiple regressions.

In our study, dependent variables for service innovation are conceived as the introduction of new products or services; they are binary variables where value of zero translates into the fact that a firm did not introduce a new product or service and 1 for firms that introduced new products or services. The same applies to independent variables.

According to Verbeek (2004), who discusses models with limited dependent variables, when the dependent variable is zero for a substantial part of the population but positive for the rest of the population with many different outcomes, the logistic regression model is particularly suited for these types of variables. Since a violation of distribution leads to inconsistent maximum likelihood estimators, testing for misspecifications is to be conducted and necessary measures undertaken.

To estimate the total sales growth in service firms, we used the multivariate regression analysis since growth is expected to be analyzed in the three years' total annual sales of a service firm. We need to track the factors that contributed to the change in total annual sales in service firms. In this case, using the linear regression model is helpful.

15.3.5 The Empirical Model and Its Specifications

Empirical models for an analysis of the service sector's development and its determinants in Rwanda are expressed on the basis of total annual sales, service sector innovativeness and service sector turnovers to track the factors influencing the dependent variables. Starting with the factors affecting sales in service firms (Model 1), we can construct the multivariate regression model as:

$$\begin{aligned}\text{Sales}\, i = {} & \beta_0 + \beta_1 x_1 + \beta_2 x_2 + \beta_3 x_3 + \beta_4 x_4 + \beta_5 x_5 + \beta_6 x_6 \\ & + \beta_7 x_7 + \beta_8 x_8 + \beta_9 x_9 + \beta_{10} x_{10} + \beta_{11} x_{11} + \beta_{12} x_{12} + \varepsilon_i.\end{aligned} \quad (15.4)$$

In this model, the dependent variable 'Sales' stands for the level of total sales given the values of X's that are independent or determinant variables. X_1 stands for the total annual cost of labor including wages, salaries, bonus and social security payments as the performance expression in service firms, X_2 stands for the size of the most recent loan or line of credit approved as a source of finance, X_3 stands for a dummy variable on the use of Internet expressed by e-mails to communicate with clients or suppliers as an ICT application, X_4 stands for a dummy variable of employees' development activities through new ideas or approaches about products or services, X_5 stands for a dummy variable on the spending on formal research and development activities to create new products or to find more efficient methods of production, X_6 stands for a dummy variable on innovation expressed as the introduction of products or services, X_7 stands for a dummy variable on engaging in internal or external training of personnel, X_8 stands for a dummy variable on the acquisition of fixed assets such as machinery, vehicles, equipment, land or buildings, X_9 stands for a dummy variable on the new or significantly improved methods of offering services, X_{10} stands for a dummy variable on the new or significantly logistical or business support processes, X_{11} stands for a dummy variable on introduced new or significant improved marketing methods, X_{12} stands for a dummy variable on the new or significantly improved organizational structure or management practices.

The coefficients are represented by the symbol β with subscripts from 0 to 12 according to the dependent variables. On the one hand is the null hypothesis H_0: $\beta_i = 0$, that is, $\beta_1, \beta_2, \ldots, \beta_n = 0$. In this case, no independent variable has any effect on the total annual sales of service firms, and on the other hand, is the alternative hypothesis, H_1: $\beta_i \neq 0$ meaning that in the independent variables the results change in total annual sales of service firms. A positive coefficient is interpreted as having a positive effect and a negative effect on sales. Thus, the main focus is on the properties of the effects namely the signs of the effects and their consistency with our expectations, the size of the effects and their statistical significance. The model can also be specified in the form of changes in sales between two years or labor productivity that is sales per employee.

The innovation model was also used to assess the determinants of service sector innovativeness which can influence firms' growth. The model for service innovation (Model 2) is specified as:

$$\begin{aligned}\text{Pr.}(Y = 1|z) = \varphi_0 + \varphi_1 z_1 + \varphi_2 z_2 + \varphi_3 z_3 + \varphi_4 z_4 + \varphi_5 z_5 + \varphi_6 z_6 + \varphi_7 z_7 \\ + \varphi_8 z_8 + \varphi_9 z_9 + \varphi_{10} z_{10} + \mu_t.\end{aligned} \tag{15.5}$$

The probability that the service firms introduced new products or services is portrayed with Y as the binary dependent variable. The symbol z with subscripts ranging from 0 to 10 stands for different independent variables or determinants of innovativeness that are thought to have an effect on the extent to which a firm innovates.

As conceived in Eq. (15.5), z_1 stands for new or significantly improved methods of offering services, z_2 stands for a dummy variable on the new or significantly logistical or business support processes, z_3 stands for a dummy variable on introduced new or significant improved marketing methods, z_5 stands for a dummy variable on spending on formal research and development activities to create new products or to find more efficient methods of production, z_6 stands for a dummy variable on employees' development activities through new ideas or approaches about products or services, z_7 stands for a dummy variable on engaging in internal or external training of personnel, z_8 stands for a dummy variable on the acquisition of fixed assets such as machinery, vehicles, equipment, land or buildings, z_9 stands for a dummy variable on having a line or a loan from a financial institution, z_{10} stands for a factor variable on the firm size defined as small (5–19 employees), medium (20–99 employees) and large (100 employees and above) and μ_t stands for the random error term.

For this model, the null hypothesis, H_0: $\varphi_i = 0$, implies that all the independent variables do not affect or generate the introduction of new products or services and the alternative hypothesis, H_1: $\varphi_i \neq 0$, suggests that the independent variables have an effect on the introduction of new products or services. Although maximum likelihood estimators have the property of being consistent, the likelihood function has to be correctly specified for this to hold. The most convenient framework for such a test is the Lagrange multiplier framework (Verbeek 2004).

Turnover as a measure of growth is used to assess the factor that influences it in the service sub-sectors. The model on the service firm turnover (Model 3) is constructed as:

$$\text{Turnover} = \theta_0 + \theta_1 X_1 + \theta_2 X_2 + \theta_3 X_3 + \theta_4 X_4 + \theta_5 X_5 + \theta_6 X_6 + \epsilon_i \tag{15.6}$$

The level of the turnover of service firms given the predictor X_i in this model is represented by G and the coefficients are symbolized by θ with subscripts 1–6. The independent variable X_1 stands for the gender of the manager, X_2 stands for openness in the service firm as selling and buying goods or services abroad, X_3 stands for tax on added value, X_4 stands for tax on income, X_5 stands for a categorical variable on the main service sub-sector, X_6 stands for a categorical variable on the capital used by the service firm and ϵ_i represents the error term. The null hypothesis, $H_0\colon \theta = 0$ implies that the independent variables have no effect on the level of turnovers in service firms. The alternative hypothesis, $H_1\colon \theta \neq 0$ implies that independent variables affect the level of turnover in service firms. The sign of the coefficient is checked to be consistent with expectations.

15.4 Estimation, Testing and Results

15.4.1 Linear Regression of Service Sales Model

The results of the multivariate linear regression of the service sales model (Model 1) are presented in Table 15.1. At a 5% confidence interval, the variable on employment coefficient, loan size, employees' development and Internet use are statistically significant with a positive effect on the growth in sales except employees' development. Therefore, we reject the null hypothesis. Other coefficients are statistically insignificant, thus we fail to reject the null hypothesis. Innovation, training, acquisition of fixed assets, new methods, new practices, new marketing and new logistics do not have any effect on total annual sales. The R^2 is 0.84, meaning that the independent variables explain variations in sales of service firms at 84%.

15.4.2 Logistic Regression of the Service Innovation Model

The results of the logistic regression of the service innovation model (Model 2) in output are given in Table 15.2. The results for the innovation model show that the independent variables on new or improved methods of offering services, engaging in internal or external training and acquisition of fixed assets are statistically significant at 5%, that is, they effect the service firms' innovation. Thus, we reject the null hypothesis. The other variables in the model are statistically insignificant as they have no effect on the innovativeness of the service sector.

Testing the fit of the model, we find that AIC is lower than BIC which implies that our model is well fit (see Table 15.3). The logistic model of innovation is correctly classified at 76.58%. The log likelihood ratio test is recommended with inference at −80.4422 with Chi2 (1) = 1.63 and Prob > Chi2 = 0.2015 at 5%, implying that the model is fully fitted (Appendix 2). According to Scott (1997), the LR test assesses constraints by comparing the likelihood of the unconstrained model to the log likelihood of the constrained model. If the constraint significantly

Table 15.1 Linear regression of service sales model (Model 1) and its determinants

Source	SS	df	MS	No of Obs = 48
Model	152.5216	12	12.7101	$F(12, 35) = 15.80$
Residual	28.1634	35	0.8046	Prob > F = 0.000
Total	180.6851	47	3.8443	R-squared = 0.8441
				Adj. R-squared = 0.7907
				Root MSE = 0.8970

Log total sales	Coef.	Std. Err.	t	$p > \|t\|$	[95% conf. interval]	
Log employ cost	0.7220	0.1079	6.689	0.0000	0.5029	0.9412
Log loan size	0.2361	0.0852	2.771	0.0089	0.0631	0.4090
Internet use	1.2684	0.5292	2.397	0.0220	0.1940	0.3428
Employe dvt	−1.0810	0.4163	−2.596	0.137	−1.9262	−0.2358
Research devpt	−0.9456	0.3223	−2.934	0.0059	−1.5999	−0.2914
innovation	0.1124	0.4208	0.267	0.7910	−0.7419	−0.9668
Trainings	−0.1875	0.4509	0.416	0.6801	−1.1028	0.7278
Fixed asset	−0.2912	0.3970	−0.733	0.4681	−1.1028	0.5147
New methods	−0.6576	0.4593	−1.432	0.1611	−1.5901	0.2749
New practices	0.1796	0.4846	0.371	0.7132	−0.8043	1.1634
New marketing	−0.6149	0.3739	−1.645	0.1697	−0.3740	0.1442
New logistics	0.7042	0.5023	1.402	0.1697	−0.3155	1.7239
_Cons	3.4132	1.5283	2.233	0.0320	0.3105	6.5159

Table 15.2 Logistic regression model of innovation performance (Model 2) and its determinants

Logistic regression	Number of obs = 158
	LR chi2 (12) = 46.28
	Prob > chi2 = 0.0000
Log Likelihood = −81.257932	Pseudo $R^2 = 0.2217$

Innovation	Coef.	Std. Err.	Z	$P > \|z\|$	[95% Conf. Interval]	
New methods	1.0971	0.4907	2.236	0.0254	0.1354	2.0587
New logistics	0.2143	0.5451	0.393	0.6943	−0.8542	1.2827
New practices	−0.1162	0.5654	−0.205	0.8372	−1.2243	0.9920
New marketing	−0.2969	0.4911	−0.605	0.5454	−1.2595	0.6656
Research dvpt	0.2238	0.4919	0.455	0.6491	−0.7402	1.1878
Employee dvpt	0.8771	0.4861	1.804	0.0712	−0.757	1.8399
Training	0.9657	0.4720	2.046	0.0408	0.0406	1.8909
Fixed asset	−1.1771	0.4449	−2.646	0.0082	2.0491	−0.3051
Loan	0.6215	0.4092	1.519	0.1288	−0.1805	1.4234

(continued)

Table 15.2 (continued)

Innovation	Coef.	Std. Err.	Z	$P > \|z\|$	[95% Conf. Interval]	
Firm size						
1	−0.4398	1.0077	−0.436	−0.6625	−2.4148	1.5352
2	0.0959	1.0425	0.092	0.9267	−1.9473	2.1391
3	1.0922	1.2691	0.861	0.3895	−1.3952	3.5797
_Cons	−0.8578	1.0347	−0.829	0.4071	−2.8858	1.1702

Table 15.3 Summary of post-estimation of Akaike's and Baysian information criteria (AIC, BIC)

Model	Obs	11(null)	11(model)	df	AIC	BIC
–	158		−80.44222	14	188.8844	231.7608

reduces the likelihood, then the null hypothesis is rejected. The results of an alternative skewed logistic regression of innovation are presented in Appendix 3.

15.4.3 *Ordered Logistic Regression of the Service Turnover Model*

In order to estimate the service turnover model, we used ordered logistic regression because turnover is a dependent variable defined as a categorical variable. If the primary interest is understanding how the explanatory variable affects the conceptual dimension represented by an ordinal variable, an ordinal variable is appropriate. The results of an ordinal logistic model are the same as those for a traditional logistic model with the exception that there is a cut point instead of a constant (Powers and Xie 1999).

The results presented in Table 15.4 indicate that the coefficients of gender, openness, value-added tax, income tax, capital used and service sub-sectors 8, 9 and 11 are statistically significant. Meaning that, they influence the level of turnover of a service firm. The others are statistically insignificant which implies that they have no effect on the change in the level of turnover.

15.4.4 *Analysis of the Empirical Results*

This section gives an interpretation and analysis of the results for the three models specified and estimated earlier. From this, we can gain advanced knowledge about the constituents of the service sector and the determinants contributing to the development of this sector. Service sector development is measured by considering key measures of a firm's performance and growth such as innovation, sales and

Table 15.4 Ordered logistic regression of service turnover model (Model 3) and its determinants

Logistic regression				Number of obs = 35575		
				LR chi2 (12) = 17,932.95		
				Prob > chi2 = 0.0000		
Log Likelihood = −21.21409.823				Pseudo R^2 = 0.2952		
Turnover	Coef.	Std. Err.	z	$p > \|z\|$	[95% conf. Interval]	
Gender manager	−0.0624	0.0280	−2.224	0.0262	−0.1174	−0.0074
Openness	0.7192	0.0891	8.075	0.0000	0.5447	0.8938
Value-added tax	1.8273	0.0816	22.380	0.0000	1.6672	1.9873
Income tax	0.2105	0.0479	4.394	0.0000	0.1166	0.3043
Ssubsectors						
8	0.7318	0.2213	3.306	0.0009	0.2980	1.1656
9	−0.3654	0.0277	−13.193	0.0000	−0.4197	−0.3111
10	−0.0246	0.2351	−0.105	0.9166	−0.4854	0.4361
11	1.9284	0.1207	15.983	0.0000	1.6920	2.1649
12	−0.4586	1.1115	−0.413	0.6399	−2.6371	1.7200
Capital						
2	2.7719	0.0334	82.892	0.0000	2.7063	2.8374
3	5.3948	0.1121	48.128	0.0000	5.1751	5.6145
4	6.4496	0.1464	44.058	0.0000	6.1626	6.7365

turnover, and these are taken to be dependent variables for forming and estimating the models. The growth in sales of service firms contributes to the growth of the service sector's share in Rwanda's GDP. Innovations bring in new products or services which in turn push the growth of the sector. The factors influencing growth in sales, service innovativeness and turnover are used to find the drivers of service sector development. These determinants are taken into consideration in shaping and sustaining the service-led economy path as it is a national strategy for economic growth.

15.4.4.1 Factors Affecting Total Sales Growth

Estimation results of the linear regression of the sales model indicate that employment costs, size of the approved loan and use of Internet positively affected the change in sales of service firms for the period 2008–2010. Growth in employment is a good indicator of a firm's performance whereby the cost of employment for three years is positively reflected in total sales. A 1% change in costs attributed to employment resulted in a 0.72% change in sales in service firms, other things holding constant.

UNECA (2015) reported that financial services are the oil of transactions and provide access to credit for investments for most other businesses. This is proven by the fact that in our model on sales, the size of the most recent loan or line of credit approved was positively correlated to the change in total sales of service firms. Other things holding constant, a 1% change in the size of the loan resulted in a 0.236% change in the total annual sales of a service firm.

Liu and Nath (2013) argue that the trade-enhancing effect of ICT infrastructure or ICT capability depends on its use. Internet subscriptions and Internet hosts have significant positive effects on both exports and imports. In our model on sales, the use of e-mails to communicate with clients or suppliers expressed as Internet use had a positive relationship to total sales as has also been found in previous studies. Holding other things constant, a 1% change in the use of Internet brought a 1.268% change in the sales of a service firm.

Both employees' development and research and development activities were negatively correlated with a change in the sales generated in service firms. Holding other things constant, a 1% decrease in employees' development resulted in a 0.108% decrease in total service sales. A 1% decrease in spending on research and development activities induced a 0.94% decrease in total sales, other things holding constant.

The change in total sales of service firms in Rwanda is attributed to financial services through access to credit, ICT applications in service provision principally via e-mail operationalization, employment growth expressed by the costs incurred by a service firm on employment, employees' development as a trial of a new approach or new idea about products or services, business process, firm management or marketing. Last but not least is the expenditure incurred on research and development activities. These variables are explained in the model at 84% as measured by R^2 and all are statistically significant as their t-statistic is greater than 1.96 with p-values less than 0.05.

15.4.4.2 Factors Contributing to Innovativeness

The logistic regression of the service innovation model (Model 2) finds the factors contributing to innovations in Rwanda's service firms. In the summary of results for Table 15.2, the number of observations shows that 158 firms were included in the estimation. The significance test of the likelihood ratio indicating whether the predictors in the model together accounted for significant variations in the dependent variable is 46.28 where the probability Chi-square test is 0.000. This implies that the independent variables influenced the dependent variable. Variables such as new methods, training and acquisition of fixed assets were statistically significant at the 95% confidence interval since their p-values are less than 0.05 and their z values in absolute terms are greater than 1.96. The approximate amount of variance is accounted for by independent variables in this model as expressed by Pseudo R^2 which is 0.22. The log likelihood is −81.2579.

A 1% increase in the use of new methods such as new or significantly improved technology, equipment and software for production, finishing, packaging or quality control resulted in a 1.097% increase in the innovativeness of a service firm, holding other things constant.

A 1% increase in the level of acquisition of internal or external training resulted in a 0.965% increase in the level of introducing new products or services in a firm, holding other things constant. This result is consistent with prior literature on the importance of training in the performance of a firm. In his study on the effect of training on employee performance with evidence from Uganda, Nassazi (2013) reported that training and development had an impact on employees' performance with regard to their jobs. Training develops skills, competencies and abilities and ultimately improves employee performance and organizational productivity (Amir and Amen 2013).

A 1% decrease in the acquisition of fixed assets such as machinery, vehicles, land and buildings resulted in a 1.17% decrease in the introduction of new products or services, holding other things constant. This indicates that the acquisition of fixed assets is a key factor for the innovation process in service firms. It is clear that a lack of fixed assets not only hampers service innovation, but also affects existing service provision which is bad for the country's economy. Silva found that the greater the financial investment in acquisition of machinery, equipment and software, the greater the propensity for firms to innovate in their services.

In conclusion, service firms' innovations in Rwanda are attributed to the new methods applied, acquisition of internal or external training and acquisition of fixed assets. These factors affect the service sector's performance and growth by enabling the introduction of new products or services.

15.4.4.3 Factor Determining Levels and Variations in Turnover

Turnovers of service firms are conceived as the amount of money taken by a business in a particular period. The estimation of the ordered logistic regression model on turnover in the service sector revealed that the gender of the manager, openness and taxes were statistically significant and influenced the turnover of service firms at a 95% confidence interval. This implies that the *p*-value of the independent variable was less than 0.05. The control variable on the level of capital used was positive and statistically significant at the 95% confidence interval due to the fact that the *p*-values were less than 0.05. The service sub-sectors of transport and storage (8), accommodation and food service activities (9) and financial and insurance activities (11) were statistically significant because their *p*-values were less than 0.05 at the 95% confidence interval. In accordance with our estimated model on turnover, these three service sub-sectors influenced variations in turnovers of service firms in Rwanda which impacted the service sector as a whole. The estimation results are presented in Table 15.3.

Table 15.3 shows that the gender of the manager was statistically significant and negatively correlated to the turnover of a service firm. In our study, being a male manager negatively influenced the turnover in a service firm at the 6% level. Meanwhile, Johnsen and McMahon (2005) report that consistent statistically significant differences in financial performance and business growth do not exist between female and male owned/managed concerns once appropriate demographic and other relevant controlling influences are taken into account. According to Watson (2003), female managers are just as effective (as males) in using resources. However, females (on average) invest fewer resources in their ventures and also seem to get involved in less risky enterprises. Their overall performance is likely to be the same as that of the males provided appropriate measures of performance are used such as sales or profits. Considering prior research findings, the negative relationship found in our study does not imply differences in female and male managers in terms of performance, rather it is possible to view this in terms of the risk associated with a business and this is a subject for subsequent studies for more clarifications.

Openness is conceived as an interaction outside the Rwandan service sector in terms of imports and exports of services. In our study, interaction was assessed through buying and selling services abroad and the estimation results show that there was a statistically significant and positive relationship between turnover and openness in service firms. A 1% change in the level of openness increased the level of turnover by 0.71%. Singh and Kaur (2014) claim that openness positively affects the share of the service sector in gross domestic product. According to Halpern et al. (2015) importing all inputs will increase a firm's revenue productivity by 0.22%, about one-half of which is due to imperfect substitution between foreign and domestic inputs. They argue that productivity gains from a tariff cut are larger when the economy has many importers and many foreign firms.

An assessment of the determinants of service sector development looked at the role of Rwanda's taxation system to boost the service sector. The estimation of ordered logistic regression of turnover to value-added tax and income tax showed that there was a statistically significant positive relationship at the 95% confidence level. This means that the tax system in Rwanda positively affects the development of the service sector. A 1% change in payment of the value-added tax resulted in a 1.82% change in the growth of turnover in services and a 1% change in the payment of income tax increased the turnover of the service sector up to 0.21%, holding other things constant. Stoilova and Patonov (2013) claim the existence of a clear and strongly expressed impact of direct taxes on economic growth. In addition, they argue that a tax structure based on direct taxes is more efficient in terms of supporting economic growth. Wu et al. (2012) argue that in China private firms with politically connected managers enjoy tax benefits. Chude et al. (2015) conclude that the positive and significant relation between profitability and taxation explanatory variables indicates that if policymakers expand tax revenue through more effective tax administration it will positively impact a company's profitability.

Capital is used as a control variable since the capital used by a service firm is categorized as its capability. Estimation results show that the capital used at all levels was significantly positive. Holding other things constant, for a service firm using capital ranging between 500,000 and 15 million RWF, a 1% change in the level of capital used resulted in an increase in turnover of up to 2.77%. For firms using capital between 15 million and 75 million RWF, a 1% increase in capital resulted in a 5.40% increase in turnover, holding other thing constant. For firms using more than 75 million RWF, the estimation results indicated that a 1% change in the capital used resulted in a 6.44% increase in turnover, holding other things constant. Briefly, the more the capital used, the more the turnover of a service firm. Thus, capital is another factor contributing to the service sector's development since any increase in the capital used results in an increase in the turnover of a service firm.

An ordered regression of the service sector's turnover as per different sub-sectors indicates that the transport and storage, accommodation and food services and financial and insurance sub-sectors had a significant positive effect on the turnover of a service firm. Holding other things constant, a 1% increase in transport and storage for a service firm resulted in a 0.76% increase in its turnover. A 1% decrease in the level in the accommodation and food services sub-sector resulted in a 0.36% decrease in turnover, holding other things constant. Lastly, a 1% increase in financial and insurance activities brought in a 1.94% increase in turnover, holding other things constant.

15.4.5 Usefulness of the Results

The ultimate goal of this study was to carry out an analysis of trends in the development of service firms in Rwanda and identifying contributing factors driving its performance using survey data covering various aspects of the service sector. Literature was reviewed to assess the similarities and dissimilarities in findings all over the world, a descriptive analysis of existing data and an empirical analysis of micro-data on service firms were used to understand the functioning of service firms in Rwanda and in other parts of the world. The results are interesting and are useful for academics and both the public and private sectors.

15.4.5.1 Adoption and Scaling-Up of Innovation Activities

The results of factors influencing innovation in service firms are very useful for the government because innovation is a key to economic growth and development. In public sector management, innovation is a priority for all nations because the current wealthy nations have got a wide range of innovations in various disciplines. In our study, innovation as a stand-alone variable did not influence any change in total sales; though some of the variables characterizing innovation were statistically significant, namely new methods and training. Therefore, the government could use these findings to scale-up innovation activities in service firms and shape capacity building strategies and policy with these empirical facts. Innovation is a prime contributor to sales growth and needs to be geared up to sustain service firms' development as a way for economic growth.

This study is an asset for academicians and for future studies by researchers and graduate students. Its findings on service innovation can form the basis for expanding research in economic growth since it is Rwanda's national policy in Vision 2020 of becoming a middle-income country. Thus, it is the responsibility of academia to support the government by providing facts to monitor the implementation of government policies for evidence-based interventions and decision making.

15.4.5.2 Diversification of Sources of Service Firms' Development

The results of the linear regression of the sales model are very useful in assessing the role of economic integration. One of the objectives of economic integration is to operate in a large market where nationals buy and sell their products and services. Having openness as a significant variable to change turnovers indicates that economic agents in service firms should take advantage of this information to increase the returns to their businesses. The private sector can use this information to exploit unused channels and do a study of regional markets to expand their businesses since it has been a while since the government signed the agreement to be a member of East African Countries (EAC) and other regional economic integration cooperation efforts.

Focus on ICT is found to be another source of better performance in service firms. Daily use of Internet as a communication channel must be looked at as a strategy to be widely adopted by competitive managers of service firms. This fits well with Rwanda's national commitment of becoming an ICT regional hub and an ICT connected country.

For academic research purposes, this information is crucial since it opens up the ground for further empirical studies to assess how the government is benefiting from regional economic integration in terms of economic growth and development. Further, it will be interesting to conduct an empirical study on ICT applicability and economic performance in Rwanda.

15.4.5.3 Providing Insights on Turnovers of Firms and Their Access to Finance

All firms aim to increase their turnovers as they are profit-based entities. The results from the model on service firms' turnovers gives information on interacting with the foreign market by either buying or selling products or services. The more the capital used, the more the turnover increases which could inform investors attracted by service related economic activities such as transport and storage and accommodation and food services. These service sub-sectors are found to be more profitable in the overall service sector. The spillover effects of taxes are marked in the turnovers of service companies. This could be used to back the importance of paying taxes by service sector taxpayers. Looking at the value-added tax, which is paid by consumers, helps us conclude that the service firms' development is demand elastic because the more the consumers pay VAT, the more the turnovers are generated. Income tax is normally paid depending on the income earned by a firm through the year. The correlation of income tax and growth in turnover implies good performance of service firms. Generally, taxes support the economy at large and it is important to know how taxes affect the service firms' development in particular.

Access to finance is one of the most needed inputs for the good performance of a service firm; this is provided by financial institutions like banks. Our investigation of the determinants of service sector development qualifies it to be more appropriate for service firms' performance as indicated by acquisition of fixed assets, loan size and capital used. The government should take note of this in steering monetary policy and encourage financial institutions to facilitate service firms' investors in accessing funds.

15.5 Conclusion and Recommendations

15.5.1 Conclusions

Our study on service firms' development and their performance in Rwandan economic growth provides useful details about service firms over years and empirically estimates the determinants of service firms' development by using the econometric methodology. The measures of firm growth used include innovation, sales and turnover. The estimation was enabled by using micro-data collected by the National Institute of Statistics of Rwanda namely the 2011 Rwanda Enterprise Survey and the 2014 Establishment Census.

The literature review on the service sector supports that services contribute more to economic growth. Zhou (2015) and William (1997) claim that services accelerate the transformation of economic growth, raise employment and boost economy-wide labor productivity. The key factors that contribute to the growth of the service sector include rapid urbanization, expansion of the public sector, increased demand for intermediate and final consumer services, domestic investments and openness, education skills, cultural adaptability, financial attractiveness, business environment, expansion of quality health services, application of information and technology, increase in consumption expenditure, incentive systems and investing more in research and development. In Rwanda, the services are dominated by wholesale and retail trade, motorcycle and motor vehicle repairs, accommodation and food services and human health and social work sub-sectors.

After estimating models on sales, innovation and turnovers in service firms, the results show that service firms' development in Rwanda is driven by access to finance, an increased labor force, training personnel, ICT applications, embryonic innovations and the tax system. Access to finance has enabled service firms to grow over the past few years in Rwanda. The size of the loans approved by financial institutions such as banks and cooperatives had a positive effect on three years' total annual sales, capital used by the service firms which also positively impacted turnovers of service firms and the acquisition of fixed assets which positively influenced service innovativeness. FinScope Rwanda (2016) has revealed that 89% of the adult population has access to finance.

Increased labor participation in services, employee development and training of personnel have boosted services in Rwanda. As it has been explored through literature, service firms' development can be attributed to employment. Our study shows that the cost allocated to employment in services is positively correlated with total sales generated over three years and a descriptive analysis confirms that the service sector is at the top in employment, even though there is gender inequality in the sector. Despite lack of innovations influencing changes in sales, some variables characterizing innovation are inducing service innovativeness such as internal and external training. Further, research and development and employee development were found to influence sales over the three years studied. This draws attention to future research to assess the innovation propensity in the service sector.

Openness and ICT applications have definitely contributed to the growth of service firms in Rwanda. Benefiting from accessing a wider market was a national aspiration when Rwanda signed the regional economic integration agreement. Our study indicates that it is on track whereby openness has had a positive effect on turnovers of service firms. In addition, we have seen the Government of Rwanda putting more effort in extending optic fiber across the country that has influenced service firms. Our study finds that communication via e-mails influenced sales generated over the three years studied.

Tax collection, typically VAT and income tax, impacted services' development in Rwanda. As previous findings have illustrated, there is a positive relationship between taxes and economic growth. Our study also reaffirmed this as it found that value-added tax and income tax had a positive effect on turnovers of service firms. It is suggested that data should be collected on the sub-sectors in the service sector to better understand why some service firms are growing faster than others in the same sector. Our study opens up a number of research avenues for the future on the contribution of regional economic integration to service sector development, an analysis of ICT applicability and contribution to old service firms and an empirical analysis of gender inequalities in the service sector's growth in Rwanda.

15.5.2 Recommendations

As the Government of Rwanda has opted for driving its economic growth through service development and aims to become a middle-income country, this study makes recommendations that can help it in speeding up the shift form a low income to a middle-income economy.

Our study shows that both employees' development and research and development activities are negatively correlated with a change in the sales generated in service firms. From literature's point of view, research and development has a great effect on the development of service firms (Madeira et al. 2014). Reducing expenses on research and development reduces the sales of service firms. From the results of our study, it is worthy to recommend that policymakers encourage research and development in service firms to increase and sustain their levels of performance in the Rwandan economy.

The use of ICT in service firms as expressed by use of improved technology, equipment and software for production and the use of Internet were relevant factors in the sales performance of service firms. A review of microeconomic literature on service firms reaffirmed ICT as a bedrock for improving business processes, customer relations and efficient delivery of goods and services to satisfy the needs of customers (Atom 2013). The study recommends that the government should advance and sustain the use of ICT in all service firms in Rwanda. In addition, the application of ICT in service firms can generate multiple effects on the performance of service firms which is correlated with the national aspiration of becoming an ICT regional hub to accelerate its target of economic growth.

Our study shows that the size of the loan approved and capital used by a service firm influence its sales. New service firms need to be supported to generate additional value on the performance of service firms in the economy. For this reason, the study suggests that the government promote access to finance to new service firms through, for instance, setting up an affordable collateral value and extending the time for paying back the loan approved by giving a sufficient grace period.

In our study, we found both employees' development and acquisition of internal or external training to have a great impact on the performance of service firms in Rwanda. Prior to this study, it was also found that training develops skills, competencies and abilities and ultimately improves employee performance and organizational productivity (Amir and Amen 2013). Hence, the government should promote on-work training in service firms to speed up Rwanda's shift from a low income to a middle-income state.

Due to the fact that the acquisition of fixed assets such as machinery, vehicles, equipment, land and buildings has multiple effects on innovation, the government should facilitate the import of necessary fixed assets to be used by service firms. This could be tax exemptions and incentives depending on the value of the imported fixed assets. Further, since the acquisition of fixed assets is a proxy indicator for accessing finance for firms, the government should regulate finance in a way that facilitates firms to have easy access to finance from financial institutions like working out the interest rate charged from a firm when it wants to purchase fixed assets.

The key recommendations from the analysis of service firms' development and economic growth in Rwanda can be summarized as:

- Advancing and sustaining the use of ICT in all service firms, specifically the use of the Internet;
- Promoting new service firms' access to finance in terms of loans to acquire fixed assets;
- Promoting on-work training in service firms to increase the level of firm performance;
- Putting in place a services innovation policy complementing existing employment with emphasis on employees' development and enhanced training strategies;
- Expanding ICT applications for service firms to become mobile based for targeting the countryside population; and
- Putting in place a foreign trade policy with emphasis on service exports in forms that benefit from existing economic integration.

Appendix 1: Correlation Matrix of Different Covariates, *n* = 158

	New methods	New logistics	New practices	New marketing	New research developments	Employee	Training	Fixed asset
New methods	0.2407							
New logistics	−0.0909	0.2972						
New practices	−0.0117	−0.0840	0.3197					
New marketing	−0.0513	−0.0224	−0.0104	0.2419				
New research developments	−0.0092	−0.0172	−0.0262	−0.0136	0.2419			
Employee	−0.0128	0.0054	−0.0699	−0.0381	0.0028	0.2363		
Training	−0.0039	−0.0356	−0.0186	0.0480	−0.0563	−0.0295	0.2228	
Fixed asset	0.0138	−0.0328	−0.0245	−0.0226	−0.0131	−0.0298	−0.0101	0.1980
Loan	−0.0066	−0.0255	−0.0073	0.0047	−0.0119	0.0210	0.0332	−0.0172
1. Firm size	0.0115	−0.0644	0.0660	−0.0040	0.0435	−0.0713	0.0018	−0.214
2. Firm size	−0.0148	−0.0355	0.630	0.282	0.0304	−0.0624	−0.0236	−0.0742
3. Firm size	0.0049	−0.0589	0.0078	0.0174	0.0028	−0.0327	0.0099	−0.0623
_Cons	−0.0485	0.0358	−0.1518	−0.0462	−0.0102	0.0072	−0.0161	0.0229

	Loan	1. Firm size	2. Firm size	3. Firm size	_Cons
Loan	0.1674				
1. Firm size	−0.0165	1.0154			
2. Firm size	−0.0221	0.9493	1.0868		
3. Firm size	−0.0684	0.9390	0.9593	0.6107	
_Cons	−0.0518	−0.9038	−0.8926	−0.8474	1.0707

Appendix 2: Logistic Model for Innovation

+	87	25	112
−	12	34	46
Total	99	59	158

Classified + if predicted pr (D) > = 0.5
True D defined as innovation! = 0

Sensitivity	Pr (+ | D)	87.88%
Specificity	Pr (− | ~D)	57.63%
Positive predictive value	Pr (D | +)	77.68%
Negative predicative value	Pr (~D | −)	73.91%
False + rate for true ~D	Pr (+ | ~D)	42.37%
False − rate for true D	Pr (− | D)	12.12%
False + rate for classified +	Pr (~D | +)	22.32%
False − rate for classification −	Pr (D | −)	26.09%
Correctly classified		76.58%

Appendix 3: Skewed Logistic Regression of Innovation

Skewed logistic regression	Number of Obs = 158
	Zero = 59
Log likelihood = −80.44222	Nonzero outcomes = 99

Innovation	Coef.	Std. Err.	z	$p > \|z\|$	[95% conf. Interval]	
New methods	0.7162	0.3399	2.107	0.0351	0.0499	1.3824

(continued)

(continued)

Innovation	Coef.	Std. Err.	z	$p > \|z\|$	[95% conf. Interval]	
New logistics	0.1210	0.3527	0.343	0.7316	−0.5703	0.8123
New practices	−0.0990	0.3551	−0.279	0.7804	−0.7950	0.5970
New marketing	−0.1649	0.3152	−0.523	0.6009	−0.7827	0.4529
Research dvpt	0.2385	0.2765	0.862	0.3885	−0.3035	0.7804
Employee dvpt	0.6093	0.3223	1.891	0.0587	−0.0224	1.2410
Training	0.5703	0.2875	1.984	0.0473	0.0068	1.1339
Fixed asset	−0.6896	0.2680	−2.573	0.0101	−1.2149	−0.1643
Loan	0.4360	0.2527	1.725	0.0845	−0.0593	0.9313
Firm size						
1	−0.3431	0.6728	−0.510	0.6101	−1.6617	0.9756
2	0.0838	0.6807	0.123	0.9021	−1.2504	1.4180
3	0.5803	0.7563	0.767	0.4429	−0.9020	2.0626
_Cons	−15.5998	1523.5291	−0.010	−0.9918	−3.00e +03	2970.4623
/lnalpha	14.5702	1523.5288	0.010	0.9924	−2.97e +03	3000.6318
alpha	2.13e+06	3.24e+09			0.0000	

References

Acharya R (2016) ICT use and total factor productivity growth: intangible capital or productive externalities? Oxf Econ J 68(1):16–39

Acharya R, Patel R (2015) Contribution of telecom sector to growth of indian service sector: an empirical study. Indian J Sci Technol 8(4):101–105

Acs ZJ, Audretsch DB (1988) Innovation in large and small firms: an empirical analysis. Am Econ Rev 78(4):678–690

Agwu EM, Carter AL (2014) Mobile phone banking in Nigeria: benefits, problems and prospects. Int J Bus Commer 3(6):50–70

Alvarez-Cuadrado F, Poschke M (2011) Structural change out of agriculture: labor push versus Labor pull. Am J Macroecon 3(3):127–158

Amir E, Amen I (2013) The effect of training on employee performance. Eur J Bus Manag 5 (4):137–147

Arnold JM, Jovorcik B, Lipsomb M, Mattoo A (2016) Services reform and manufacturing performance: evidence from India. Econ J 129(590):1–39

Arvanitis S, Stucki T (2012) What determines the innovation capability of firm founders? Ind Corp Change 24(4):1049–1084

Atom B (2013) The impact of information communication technology (ICT) on business. Asian J Bus Manage Sci 3(2):13–28

Bethapudi A (2013) The role of ICT in tourism Industry. J Appl Econ Bus 1(4):67–79
Borghoff T (2011) The role of ICT in the globalization of firms. J Mod Account Audit 7(10):1128–1149
Bouazza AB, Ardjouman D, Abada O (2015) Establishing the factors affecting the growth of small and medium-sized enterprises in Algeria. Am Int J Soc Sci 4(2):101–115
Buera FJ, Kaboski JK (2009) The rise of the service economy. Am Econ Rev 102(6):2540–2569
Chude DI, Nkuru P (2015) Impact of company income taxation on the profitability of companies in Nigeria: a study of Nigerian breweries. Eur J Account Audit Financ Res 3(8):1–11
Dawkins P, Feeny S, Harris MN (2007) Benchmarking firm performance. Benchmark Int J 14 (6):693–710
Drejer I (2002) Business services as a production factor. Econ Syst Res 14(4):389–405
Du J, Temouri Y (2015) High-growth firms and productivity: evidence from the United Kingdom. Small Bus Econ 44(1):123–143
Eichengreen B, Gupta P (2011) The service sector as India's road to economic growth. NBER working paper no. 1675
El-Said OA, Kattara HS (2013) Customers' preferences for new technology-based self-services versus human interaction services in hotels. Tour Hosp Res 13(2):67–82
Fuchs VR (1980) Economic growth and the rise of service employment. NBER working paper no. 486
Gale WG, Krupkin A, Rueben K (2015) The relationship between taxes and growth at the state level: new evidence. Nat Tax J 68(4):919–942
Geishecker I, Görg H (2013) Services offshoring and wages: evidence from micro data. Oxf Econ J 65(1):124–146
Guerrieri P, Meliciani V (2004) International competitiveness in producer services. Available at SSRN: https://ssrn.com/abstract=521445
Gupta R (2012) The role of ICTs in facilitating India's external trade. J Decis Making 12(1):11–15
Hagen B, Zucchella A (2014) Born global or born to run? The long-term growth of born global firms. Manage Int Rev 54(4):497–525
Halpern L, Koren M, Szeidl A (2015) Imported inputs and productivity. Am Econ Rev 105 (2):3660–3703
Heshmati A, Kim H (2011) The R&D and productivity relationship of Korean listed firms. J Prod Anal 36(2):125–142
Isaga N (2015) Owner-managers' demographic characteristics and the growth of Tanzanian small and medium enterprises. Int J Bus Manage 10(5):168–181
Jafaridehkordi H, Rahim RA, Jafaridehkordi P (2015) Intellectual capital and investment opportunity set in advanced technology companies. Int J Innov Appl Stud 10(3):1022–1027
Jajri I (2008) Determinants of total factor productivity growth in Malaysia. J Econ Coop 28(3):41–58
Johnsen GJ, McMahon RGP (2005) Owner-manager gender, financial performance and business growth amongst SMEs from Australia's business longitudinal survey. Int Small Bus J 23 (2):115–142
Jones RS, Yoon T (2008) Enhancing the globalisation of Korea. Economic department working papers no. 614. OECD
Khan KS (2011) Determinants of firm growth: an empirical examination of SMEs in Gujranwala, Gujarat and Sialkot districts. Interdisci J Contemp Res Bus 3(1):1389–1409
King RG, Levine R (1993) Finance and growth: Schumpeter might be right. Q J Econ 108(3):717–737
Latha CM, Shanmugam V (2014) Growth of service sector in India. IOSR J Humanit Soc Sci 19 (1):8–12
Lee S, Malin BA (2013) Education's role in China's structural transformation. J Dev Econ 101:148–166
Lenaerts K, Merlevede B (2015) Firm size and spillover effects from foreign direct investment: the case of Romania. Small Bus Econ 45(3):595–616

Liu L, Nath HK (2013) Information and communications technology and trade in emerging market economies. Emerg Markets Financ Trade 49(6):67–87

Madeira MJ, Jorge S, Sousa G, Moreira J, Mainardes EW (2014) Determinants of innovation capacity: empirical evidence from service firms. Innov Manage Policy Pract 16(3):404–416

Mihalic T, Praniceric DG, Arneric J (2015) The changing role of ICT competitiveness: the case of the Slovenian hotel sector. Econ Res Ekon Istraživanja 28(1):367–383

Muro MB, Magutu PO, Getembe KN (2013) The strategic benefits and challenges in the use of customer relationship management systems among commercial banks in Kenya. Eur Sci J 9 (13):327–349

Nassazi A (2013). Effect of training on employee performance with evidence from Uganda. Business Economics and Tourism, 1–57

Neely A, Hii J (1998) Innovation and business performance. University of Cambridge, London

Newsom J (2013) Levels of measurement and choosing the correct statistical test. USP 634 data analysis, Spring 2013, New York

NISR (2014) Establishment census. National Institute of Statistics of Rwanda, Kigali

Oliveira B, Fortunato A (2008) The dynamics of the growth of firms: evidence from the services sector. Empirica 35(3):293–312

Park D, Shin K (2012) The service sector in Asia: is it an engine of growth? ADB economics working paper series no. 322

Pop ZW, Stümpel HJ, Bordean ON (2014) From strategic decisions to corporate governance in the SME sector in Germany. Stud Univ Babeş-Bolyai Oecon 59(3):57–67

Powers AD, Xie Y (1999) Statistical methods for categorical data analysis. Academic Press Inc, Austin

Prajogo DI, Sohal AS (2006) The integration of TQM and technology/R&D management in determining quality and innovation performance. Omega 34(3):296–312

Queiro F (2016) The effect of managers education on firm growth. Q J Econ 118(4):1169–1208

RES (2011) Rwanda Enterprise Survey. Rwanda National Institute of Statistics. http://www.statistics.gov.rw/

RES (2016) Rwanda Enterprise Survey. Rwanda National Institute of Statistics. http://www.statistics.gov.rw/

Reuber AR, Fischer E (2002) Foreign sales and small firm growth: the moderating role of the management team. Entrep Theory Pract 27(1):29–45

Sahu S (2015) Source of service sector TFP growth in India: evidence from micro-data. South Asian J Macroeconom Pub Financ 4(1):62–90

Salehi-Isfahani D (2006) Microeconomics of growth in MENA: the role of households. Contrib Econ Anal 278:159–194

Schoonjans B, Van Cauwenberge P, Vander Bauwhede H (2013) Does Formal Business Networking contribute to SME Growth?—An empirical examination. Working Papers of Faculty of Economics and Business Administration, Ghent University, Belgium from Ghent University, Faculty of Economics and Business Administration, 2011/708

Schoonjans B, Van Cauwenberge P, Vander Bauwhede H (2013) Formal Business Networking and SME Growth. Small Business Economics 41(1):169–181

Scott L (1997) Advanced quantitative techniques in the social science. International Educational and Professional Publisher, New Delhi

Simsek Z, Heavey C (2011) The mediating role of knowledge-based capital for corporate entrepreneurship effects on performance: a study of small- to medium-sized firms. Strateg Entrepreneurship J 5(1):81–100

Singh M, Kaur K (2014) Indian's service sector and its determinants: an empirical investigation. J Econ Dev Stud 2(2):385–406

Smith N, Smith V, Verner M (2006) Do women in top management affect firm performance? A panel study of 2,500 Danish firms. Int J Prod Perform Manage 55(7):569–593

Stock JH, Watson MW (2011) Introduction to econometrics, 3rd edn. Pearson Education Inc, Boston

Stoilova D, Patonov N (2013) An empirical evidence for the impact of Taxation on economy growth in the European Union. In: Proceedings TMS international conference 2012: Financial management, accounting & taxation, vol 2, pp 1031–1039
Tahir M, Azid T (2015) The relationship between international trade openness and economic growth in the developing economies: Some new dimensions. J Chin Econ Foreign Trade Stud 8 (2):123–139
UN (2008) International standards industrial classification of all economic activities. Revision 4
UNECA (2015) Economic report on Africa 2015: industrializing through trade
Van der Marel E, Shepherd B (2013) International tradability indices for services: policy research working paper no. 6712
Verbeek M (2004) A guide to modern economitrics, 2nd edn. Wiley, Rotterdam
Watson J (2003) SME performance: does gender matter. A paper for the small enterprise association of Australia and New Zealand 16th Annual conference. Ballarat
WB (2014) Enterprise surveys: Rwanda country profile 2011. Enterprise surveys country profile. World Bank Group, Washington, DC
Williams CC (1997) Understanding the role of consumer services in local economic development: some evidence from the Fens. Environ Plann 28(3):555–571
Wu W, Wu C, Zhou C, Wu J (2012) Political connections, tax benefits and firm performance: evidence from China. Journal of accounting and public policy. J Account Public Policy 31 (3):277–300
Yeboah O, Naanwaab C, Saleem S, Akuffo A (2012) Effects of trade openness on economic growth: the case of African countries. Agribusiness, Applied Economics and Agriscience Education—NC A&T, Birmingham
Yli-Renko H, Autio E, Sapienza HJ (2001) Social capital, knowledge acquisition, and knowledge exploitation in young technology-based firms. Strateg Manag J 22(6–7):587–613
Zhou Z (2015) The development of service economy: a general trend of the changing economy. Development Research Center of Shanghai, Shanghai
Zhou H, de Wit G (2009) Determinants and dimensions of firm growth. SCALES EIM research reports (H200903). Groningen

Chapter 16
Labor-Use Efficiency in Kenyan Manufacturing and Service Industries

Masoomeh Rashidghalam

Abstract This study uses the labor-use requirement model to estimate labor-use efficiency of Kenyan manufacturing and service sectors. It also studies the determinants of labor-use efficiency. The data are obtained from the World Bank's Enterprise Survey (ES). The Cobb–Douglas functional form of labor-use frontier estimates shows that wages, sales, capital, fuel, and electricity affected the amount of labor used in Kenya. The determinants of labor-use efficiency were the manager's experience, female share, labor training, education, and obstacles. The results show that the estimated firm labor-use efficiency ranged from 0.14 to 0.87 with a mean labor-use efficiency value of 0.66. According to the results, most of the firms operated within the labor-use efficiency range of 0.70–0.80 suggesting that there is space for improvements in labor use of 20–30% as compared to the firms with best labor-use practices.

Keywords Firm · Kenya · Labor-use efficiency · Labor-use requirement frontier

JEL Classification Codes C23 · E24 · J23 · L60

16.1 Introduction

The World Bank's most recent Kenya Economic Update (KEU) (March 2016) projected a 5.9% growth in 2016, rising to 6% in 2017. The report attributes this positive outlook to low oil prices, good agricultural performance, a supportive monetary policy, and ongoing infrastructure investments. According to the latest Kenya National Bureau of Statistics' (KNBS) quarterly report, Kenya's economy expanded by 6.2% in the second quarter of 2016 as compared to 5.9% in the same period in 2015. This growth was mainly supported by agriculture, forestry, and fishing; transportation and storage; real estate; and wholesale and retail trade.

M. Rashidghalam (✉)
Department of Agricultural Economics, University of Tabriz, Tabriz, Iran
e-mail: maso.azar@gmail.com

A. Heshmati (ed.), *Studies on Economic Development and Growth in Selected African Countries*, Frontiers in African Business Research,
DOI 10.1007/978-981-10-4451-9_16

Manufacturing, construction, and the financial and insurance sectors slowed down during this quarter while accommodation and food services, mining and quarrying, electricity and water supply, and information and communication sectors recorded improvements.[1]

Although manufacturing companies in Kenya are small, they are the most sophisticated in East Africa. Industries in Kenya have been growing since the late 1990s and into the new century. These companies are also relatively diverse. The transformation of agricultural raw materials, particularly of coffee and tea, remains the principal industrial activity. Meat and fruit canning, wheat flour and cornmeal milling, and sugar refining are also important. Production of electronics, vehicle assembly, publishing, and soda ash processing are all significant. Assembly of computer components began in 1987. Kenya also manufactures chemicals, textiles, ceramics, shoes, beer and soft drinks, cigarettes, soap, machinery, metal products, batteries, plastics, cement, aluminum, steel, glass, rubber, wood, cork, furniture, and leather goods. It also produces a small number of trucks and automobiles. The most common manufacturing industries in Kenya include small-scale consumer goods (plastic, furniture, batteries, textiles, clothing, soaps, cigarettes, and flour), agricultural products, horticulture, oil refining, aluminum industries, steel industries, lead industries, cement industries, and commercial ship repairs.[2]

Kenya is also a leading sub-Saharan African (SSA) producer and exporter of services. According to the World Bank, Kenya has a comparative advantage in services production. It has the largest service economy in the East African Countries (EAC). It produced $19 billion of services in 2012; this amount represents almost half of the nation's GDP and accounted for an estimated 43% of the EAC's total services output (Serletis 2014). As East Africa's distribution hub, telecommunication axis, and financial center, Kenya has a broad array of well-developed service industries with an abundance of service suppliers. These factors make Kenya a promising source of increased exports of services. In addition, the Government of Kenya is aiming to spur economic growth by promoting exports of services, including professional services, which are critical for Kenya's economic development and also serve as key inputs for East Africa's growth. In most of the years, this sector accounts for the largest share of jobs in Kenya.

In 2006, Kenya's labor force was estimated to include about 12 million workers of which almost 75% worked in agriculture. About 6 million were employed outside small-scale agriculture and pastoralism. Approximately 15% of the labor force was officially classified as unemployed in 2004. As Kenya became increasingly urbanized, the labor force shifted from the countryside to cities (The World Bank 2015). The service sector absorbed a majority of the inflow of labor to urban areas. Labor force participation rates for both women and men were constant between 1997 and 2010. In 1997, 65% of the women were employed in some type of labor market activity, while the corresponding number for men was 76%

[1]http://www.worldbank.org/en/country/kenya/overview.

[2]https://softkenya.com/industry/.

(the World Bank 2015). Around 60% of the women and 70% of the men were in the labor force in 2005. Their shares increased in 2010, when 61% of the women and 72% of the men were a part of the labor force.

In this regard, studying labor-use efficiency in these two main economic sectors of Kenya is important. Therefore, our study investigates labor-use efficiency and its determinants in manufacturing and service sectors in Kenya. Labor efficiency is a measure of how efficiently a given workforce accomplishes a task when compared to the standard in that industry or setting. As labor efficiency goes up, costs go down. It may also be possible to increase production because more labor hours are available for producing goods and services. This will be even more important in periods of increased demand when a company needs more laborers to make more goods or offer more services. More efficiency can also translate into wider opportunities for research and development as a company has workers available to put to these tasks instead of having to focus on meeting the needs of the production line. One way of looking at labor efficiency is by comparing the number of hours actually required to produce a given product or service with those usually spent. If the workforce is producing products and services at below the usual rate, it is operating with high efficiency, cutting time off production. This can translate into significant savings as the company will spend less money on wages and overheads because it is turning out finished services and products at a more efficient rate.[3]

In particular, we address the following questions in our paper: What are the levels of labor-use efficiency in manufacturing and service sectors in Kenya and which factors determine the efficiency of labor in Kenya? The results of our study will provide researchers and employers with information about how labor and farm characteristics affect labor-use efficiency.

The rest of the paper is organized as follows. Section 2 includes a brief review of relevant literature. Section 3 outlines the relevant labor-use requirement model and determinants of efficiency. Data sources along with identification of inputs and outputs are reported in Sect. 4. Section 5 discusses the findings from the empirical analysis, and Sect. 6 gives a conclusion.

16.2 Literature Review

A number of studies in production, cost, and performance analysis literature analyze labor-use efficiency including those by Heshmati and Su (2014), LaFave and Thomas (2016), Nagler and Naudé (2014), Ogutu et al. (2014).

Abid and Drine (2011) studied the determinants of the inefficient functioning of the Tunisian labor market. They took advantage of recent developments in stochastic frontier techniques and estimated the matching function for Tunisia using disaggregated data. They included control variables as determinants of matching

[3]http://www.wisegeek.com/what-is-labor-efficiency.htm.

efficiency and regional disparities and confirmed that the persistently high rate of unemployment was the result of not only excess labor supply but was also related to a shortfall between supply and demand (sector, location, and qualification).

Anyiro et al. (2013) examined labor-use efficiency by smallholder yam farmers in Nigeria. The Cobb–Douglas functional form of labor-use frontier estimates showed that the quantity of harvested yam, size of the cleared farmland, and the quantity of fertilizers applied significantly affected the amount of labor used in yam. The socioeconomic determinants of labor-use efficiency were age, education, farm size, gender, labor wage, and household size; these were statistically significant. According to their results, labor-use efficiency ranged from 0.20 to 0.97 with a mean labor-use efficiency value of 0.76. Policies aimed at increasing yam farmers' scale of operations through improved access to production inputs such as fertilizers, agrochemicals, and capital are required for increasing labor-use efficiency in the area.

Das et al. (2009) used a data envelopment analysis to measure labor-use efficiency of individual branches of a large public sector bank in India. They introduced the concept of area or spatial efficiency for each region relative to the nation as a whole. Their findings suggest that the policies, procedures, and incentives handed down from the corporate level cannot fully neutralize the detrimental influence of the local work culture across different regions. Most of the potential reduction in labor cost appeared to come from possible downsizing in the clerical and subordinate staff.

16.3 Methods

The labor-use requirement frontier model determines the minimum amount of labor required to produce a given level of output. This model is expressed as (Akanni and Dada 2012; Anyiro et al. 2013; Martinez and Burns 1999; Masso and Heshmati 2004):

$$\text{Labor}_i = f(W_i, \text{Output}_i, Z_u : \beta) \tag{16.1}$$

where

Labor_i	labor-use requirement frontier model
W_i	real wage
Output_i	sale
Z_u	vector characterizing the production process
β	unknown parameters associated with determinants of optimal labor use

Our study estimated a Cobb–Douglas labor-use frontier as a function as:

$$\begin{aligned} \text{Ln Labour} = {} & \beta_0 + \beta_1 \text{Ln Wage} + \beta_2 \text{Ln Capital} + \beta_3 \text{ Ln sale} \\ & + \beta_4 \text{Ln Electricity} + \beta_5 \text{Ln Fuel} + \varepsilon \end{aligned} \quad (16.2)$$

where

Ln Labor	natural log of annual employment
Ln Wage	natural log of wage per employee in KES
Ln Capital	natural log of annual investment per employee
Ln Sale	natural log of total sales (in Kenyan shilling, KES)
Ln Electricity	natural log of annual cost of electric energy per labor
Ln Fuel	natural log of annual cost of all fuels per labor (fuel intensity) in KES

To study the determinants of labor-use efficiency (LE), the following model was formulated:

$$\text{LE} = \delta_0 + \delta_1 Z_1 + \delta_2 Z_2 + \cdots + \delta_8 Z_8 \quad (16.3)$$

where

LE	labor-use efficiency
Z_1	experience of manager (in years)
Z_2	female share of employees
Z_3	training programs for employees (yes = 1, No = 0)
Z_4	average number of years of education of a typical female production worker (years)
Z_5	percentage of full-time permanent workers who have completed secondary school (%)
Z_6	age of firm (years)
Z_7	does the firm face minor and moderate obstacles (Yes = 1, No = 0)
Z_8	does the firm face major and severe obstacles (Yes = 1, No = 0).

16.4 Data

The data used in this study are from the World Bank's Enterprise Survey (ES). As part of these surveys, the World Bank collects data from key manufacturing and service sectors in every region of the world. The surveys use standardized survey instruments and a uniform sampling methodology to minimize measurement errors and to yield data that is comparable across the world's economies and as such is suitable for comparative economic studies. The initial dataset consisted of 670 firm-level observations in Kenya's manufacturing and service firms in 2013. Data for estimating labor efficiency determinants comprised of dependent, independent, and characteristic variables. The dependent variable is labor (LABPRO) defined as the number of workers.

The independent and characteristic variables include two categories classified as main labor and firm-related variables. Main variables include capital intensity, electric intensity, fuel intensity, wages, and sales. The capital intensity (CAPINT) variable is measured as the sum of annual investments in machinery, vehicles, and equipment, and annual investments in land, buildings, and structures per labor. The electricity intensity (ELEINT) variable is the annual cost of electric energy per employee purchased from public or private utility companies or received from other establishments that belong to the same firm. The fuel intensity (FEUINT) variable is the annual cost of all fuels per labor which are consumed for heating, power, transportation, or the generation of electricity.

SALE is value of all annual sales counting manufactured goods and goods that an establishment has bought for trading per labor. For services, it refers to the value of all the services provided during the year per unit of labor. Finally, the wage (WAGE) variable is the average wage per employee in a given firm and is obtained by dividing total wages by the total yearly average number of workers. It includes wages, salaries, and benefits including food, transport, and social security.

The second category includes eight variables related to employment: experience of manager (EXPERI), female share of employees (SFEM), training programs for employees (TRAIN), average number of years of education of a typical female production worker (FEDUC), percentage of full-time permanent workers who have completed secondary school (PSEC), age of firm (AGE), does the firm face minor and moderate obstacles (MMOBS), and does the firm face major and severe obstacles (MSOBS). The variable training program for employees is a dummy variable where 1 indicates skill upgrading for a firm's labor force and zero no skill upgrading. A firm's age (AGE) is measured in years. The fourth category—infrastructure—includes eight variables that play a crucial role in the smooth operations of a firm. The other variables include the degree to which telecommunications are seen as an obstacle by a firm (TOBSTA).

16.5 Empirical Results

Tables 16.1 provide summary statistics of the data for the input and output variables and labor, firm, and market characteristics used in this study. Sales averaged at 1170 million Kenyan shilling (KES) with dispersion 6.54 times the mean. The average employment in a sample firm was 98 persons. It varied in intervals 1 and 8000, with a dispersion of 4.32 around the mean value. The ratio of the two variables, the amount of sales per employee, which measures labor productivity varied from 3000 to 1720 billion KES with mean and standard deviations of 14.4 and 90.2 million KES. The value of investment per employee indicates considerable variations in the dataset. Mean wage per employee was 1.05 million KES with

Table 16.1 Summary statistics of key variables and labor-use efficiency determinants in the Kenyan (2013) enterprise data ($N = 670$)

Variable	Variable definition	Mean	Std. dev.	Minimum	Maximum
A. Key variables					
Employment	Annual employment	98	424.80	1	8000
Sale	Total sales (in Kenyan shilling, KES)	1,170,000,000	7,650,000,000	90,000	120,000,000,000
LABOR	Sale per employee (labor productivity) in KES	14,400,000	90,200,000	3000	1,720,000,000
CAPINT	Annual investment per employee (capital intensity) in KES	7,806,039	35,000,000	0.16	484,000,000
EENINT	Annual cost of electric energy per labor (energy intensity) in KES	238,817	1,610,259	0.00	36,000,000
FENINT	Annual cost of all fuels per labor (fuel intensity) in KES	4,821,125	10,800,000	0.00	200,000,000
WAGE	Wage per employee in KES	1,049,785	7,095,087	1000	170,000,000
SALE	Total sales (in Kenyan shilling, KES)	1,170,000,000	7,650,000,000	90,000	120,000,000,000
B. Labor-use efficiency determinants					
expe	Manager's experience in years	18.79	10.77	2	57.00
femsh	Female share of employees	0.81	1.27	0	9.50
train	Training programs for employees (equals 1 if	0.45	0.50	0	1.00

(continued)

Table 16.1 (continued)

Variable		Variable definition	Mean	Std. dev.	Minimum	Maximum
		employees underwent a training program)				
feduc		Average number of years of education of a typical female production worker	11.66	2.95	0	25.00
psec		Percentage of full-time permanent workers who have completed secondary school	79.18	28.09	0	100.00
age		Enterprise age in years	24.63	18.14	2.00	108.00
tobst	To what degree are telecommunications an obstacle?					
	Tobst0	No obstacle = 0	0.41	0.49	0	1.00
	Tobst1	Minor and moderate obstacle = 1	0.39	0.48	0	1.00
	Tobst2	Major and severe obstacle = 2	0.19	0.39	0	1.00

Note US$1 = 99.7. Kenyan shilling on March 13, 2016

a large standard deviation of 7.1 million. It varied in the interval 1000 and 170 million KES. Energy and fuel intensity variables also showed large variations among firms.

The sample average capital intensity per employee was 7.8 million KES with standard deviation of 35 million KES. The highest in the sample—a capital-intensive technology firm—used 484 million KES in capital per employee. Variability in energy (electricity and fuel) use per employee also varied greatly. An average manager's experience was about 19 years in our dataset, which varied between 2 and 57 years. The average age of firms was 25 years with a standard deviation of 18 years. It varied in the interval 2 and 108. On average, the male labor share was 0.81, and, on average, firms' CEOs had about 12 years of education. Around 80% of the permanent workers had completed secondary schooling.

In order to check for collinearity among the explanatory variables, correlation coefficients among all the 14 variables are presented in Table 16.2. Labor use, as expected, was negatively correlated with wages and sales; it correlated positively with sales and electricity intensity. The remaining pairs were low correlated with each other and did not show any signs of serious multi-collinearity. The age of a firm, training for workers, secondary education of workers, and female education were positively correlated with labor.

The model in Eq. 16.2 is estimated by ordinary least squares. The labor requirement frontier is a function of wages, capital, sales, fuel, and electricity, and the results are presented in Table 16.3. The parameters are statistically significant at any conventional significant level. The elasticities with respect to wages, sales, and electricity were significantly negative. The signs of the average elasticities were as expected; wage was negative; and sale was positive.

Wage elasticity was negative (−0.261) and statistically significant at the less than 1% level. Consistent with theory and our expectations, a higher level of wages decreased labor demand.

Sales had the strongest effect on the level of labor use.

In this model, the effect of capital intensity on labor use was negative (−0.083), implying that labor and capital were competitive. A third significant factor with effects on labor use is sales, as expected, had a positive effect on labor use, implying that to increase sales we need to increase labor. Two other significant factors which effected labor use are electricity and fuel intensity that are significant in our model.

The determinants of labor-use efficiency in manufacturing and service sectors in Kenya are presented in Table 16.4. The table shows that experience, female share, training, age of the firm, and infrastructure obstacles were statistically significant.

Female share in employment showed a negative relationship (−0.025) with labor-use efficiency. This implies that increasing female share will lead to a decrease in labor-use efficiency.

The coefficient for labor training (0.022) was positive and had a significant (at 5% level) relationship with labor-use efficiency. This implies that an increase in the level of training led to an increase in labor-use efficiency. A firm's age also showed a positive effect on labor-use efficiency. (0.001). This result supports the argument that labor becomes more efficient in older firms.

As expected, minor and major telecommunication obstacles had negative coefficients (−0.019 and −0.023, respectively). This indicates that labor-use efficiency in yam production was gender sensitive. Further, it can be adduced from the results that males were more efficient in the use of labor.

Table 16.4 presents the distribution of labor-use efficiency in the manufacturing and service sectors in Kenya. According to Table 16.4, in 2013, the mean technical efficiency of labor in Kenya was 0.66 with a maximum of 0.87 and minimum of 0.14. Therefore, the gap between the most efficient and inefficient labor was about 0.34. However, the results show that about 40.14% of the firms operated within the labor-use efficiency range of 0.70–0.80. The estimates are skewed to the right, implying a high level of efficiency.

Table 16.2 Correlation matrix of the variables (N = 670)

	llabor	lwagei	lcapi	lsale	leleci	lfueli	expe	femsh	train	feduc	psec	age	obst1	obst2
llabor	1.00													
lwagei	−0.07	1.00												
lcapi	−0.28	0.08	1.00											
lsale	0.68	0.34	−0.13	1.00										
leleci	0.13	0.36	0.02	0.27	1.00									
lfueli	−0.28	0.18	0.12	−0.09	0.13	1.00								
expe	0.23	0.00	−0.06	0.20	0.08	−0.15	1.00							
femsh	−0.43	0.15	0.21	−0.25	−0.05	−0.16	−0.06	1.00						
train	0.28	−0.01	−0.14	0.26	0.03	−0.06	0.00	−0.09	1.00					
feduc	0.12	0.05	−0.10	0.11	0.08	0.09	−0.03	−0.12	−0.01	1.00				
psec	0.10	0.10	0.06	0.14	0.10	0.10	0.00	−0.16	0.00	0.25	1.00			
age	0.31	0.02	−0.08	0.28	0.06	−0.20	0.32	0.02	0.10	−0.01	−0.07	1.00		
obst1	0.06	0.02	−0.07	0.09	0.12	−0.12	0.10	0.06	0.02	0.05	0.05	0.09	1.00	
obst2	−0.01	0.03	0.00	0.04	−0.06	0.06	−0.07	−0.08	0.06	0.04	−0.02	0.01	−0.39	1.00

Table 16.3 Estimates of ordinary least squares parameter of frontier model and efficiency determinant ($N = 670$)

Variable	Coefficient	Std. err.	Variable	Coefficient	Std. err.
A. *Frontier model*			B. *Efficiency model*		
Intercept	−0.503	0.367	Intercept	−0.679[a]	0.025
WAGE	−0.261[a]	0.024	expe	0.001	0.000
CAPINT	−0.083[a]	0.014	femsh	−0.025[a]	0.004
SALE	0.440[a]	0.017	train	0.022[b]	0.010
ELEINT	0.031[b]	0.013	feduc	0.001	0.002
FEUINT	−0.042[a]	0.007	psec	−0.001	0.000
			age	0.001[a]	0.000
			Tobst1	−0.019[c]	0.011
			Tobst2	−0.023[c]	0.013
sigma_u	0.448[a]	0.086			
sigma_v	0.754[a]	0.047			
F-value					

Note Significant at less than 1% (a), 1–5% (b) and 5–10% (c) levels of significance

Table 16.4 Distribution of labor-use efficiency in Kenyan manufacturing and service sectors

Labor-use efficiency range	Frequency	Percentage
0.10–0.20	4	0.59
0.20–0.30	9	1.34
0.30–0.40	29	4.32
0.40–0.50	35	5.22
0.50–0.60	88	13.13
0.60–0.70	201	30.00
0.70–0.80	269	40.14
0.80–0.90	35	5.22
Total	670	100.00
Maximum labor-use efficiency	0.87	
Minimum labor-use efficiency	0.14	
Mean labor-use efficiency	0.65	

16.6 Summary and Conclusion

This paper analyzed labor-use efficiency at the firm level using data from 670 firms in the manufacturing and service sectors in Kenya. The data were sourced from the World Bank's Enterprise Survey (ES). It was concerned with two important issues. First, modeling labor-use requirements, and second, considering labor-use efficiency and its determinants. In estimating the labor-use requirement model, we studied the effects of wages, sales, capital, electricity, and fuel use in labor demand.

Then, to study labor-use efficiency, we considered the manager's experience, female share, employee training and education, age of the firm, and infrastructure obstacles.

The results imply that a firm's labor use decreased with an increase in wages and capital, and it increased with an increase in sales and electricity use. Mean technical efficiency of labor use was 0.66 with a maximum of 0.87 and minimum of 0.14. Most of the firms operated within the labor-use efficiency range of 0.70–0.80. The results suggest that firms, on average, can reduce labor use by 20–30% compared to firms with best practices in the use of labor. According to the results of labor-use efficiency, training programs for labor increased their ability and hence improved efficiency. The older a firm, the greater will be labor efficiency. Female education might be regarded as a factor for increased efficiency since it enhances their ability to read and adopt recommended practices. As the rate of female share in labor use increases, efficiency decreases. Finally, as expected, infrastructure obstacles decreased efficiency.

References

Abid AB, Drine I (2011) Efficiency frontier and matching process on the labor market: evidence from Tunisia. Econ Model 28:1131–1139

Akanni AK, Dada AO (2012) Analysis of labor-use patterns among small-holder Cocoa farmers in South Western Nigeria. J Agric Sci Technol 2:107–113

Anyiro CO, Emerole CO, Osondu CK, Udah SC, Ugorji SE (2013) Labor-use efficiency by smallholder yam farmers in Abia State Nigeria: a labor-use requirement frontier approach. Int J Food Agricul Econ 1(1):151–163

Das A, Subhash CR, Nag A (2009) Labor-use efficiency in Indian banking: a branch-level analysis. Int J Manag Sci 37:411–425

Heshmati A, Su B (2014) Development and sources of labor productivity in Chinese provinces. China Econ Policy Rev 2(2):1–30

LaFave D, Thomas D (2016) Height and cognition at work: labor market productivity in a low income setting. Available at doi:10.1016/j.ehb.2016.10.008

Martinez MG, Burns J (1999) Sources of technological development in the Spanish food and drink industry, a 'supplier dominated' industry. Agribusiness 15(4):4431–4448

Masso J, Heshmati A (2004) Optimality and overuse of labor in Estonian manufacturing enterprises. Econ Transit 12(4):683–720

Nagler P, Naudé W. (2014) Labor productivity in rural African enterprises: empirical evidence from the LSMS-ISA. IZA Discussion Paper No. 2014: 8524

Ogutu SO, Okello JJ, Otieno DJ (2014) Impact of information and communication technology-based market information services on smallholder farm input use and productivity: the case of Kenya. World Dev 64:311–321

Serletis G (2014) Kenya's services output and exports are among the highest in Sub-Saharan Africa. USITC Exec Brief Trade 202:205–3315

The World Bank (IBRD-IDA) (2015) Labor force participation rate, female (per cent of female population ages 15+) (modeled ILO estimate). Available at http://data.worldbank.org/indicator/SL.TLF.CACT.FE.ZS?

Author Index

A. Heshmati (ed.), *Studies on Economic Development and Growth in Selected African Countries*, Frontiers in African Business Research,
DOI 10.1007/978-981-10-4451-9

K

L

M

Subject Index

A. Heshmati (ed.), *Studies on Economic Development and Growth in Selected African Countries*, Frontiers in African Business Research,
DOI 10.1007/978-981-10-4451-9

MIX
Papier aus verantwortungsvollen Quellen
Paper from responsible sources
FSC® C105338

If you have any concerns about our products,
you can contact us on
ProductSafety@springernature.com

In case Publisher is established outside the EU,
the EU authorized representative is:
Springer Nature Customer Service Center GmbH
Europaplatz 3, 69115 Heidelberg, Germany

Printed by Libri Plureos GmbH
in Hamburg, Germany